I0187869

The Civil War Diaries of Cassie Fennell

The Civil War Diaries of
Cassie Fennell

A Young Confederate Woman in North Alabama, 1859–1865

EDITED BY Whitney A. Snow

Voices of the Civil War Michael P. Gray, SERIES EDITOR

Knoxville / The University of Tennessee Press

The Voices of the Civil War series makes available a variety of primary source materials that illuminate issues on the battlefield, the home front, and the western front, as well as other aspects of this historic era. The series contextualizes the personal accounts within the framework of the latest scholarship and expands established knowledge by offering new perspectives, new materials, and new voices.

First Edition.

Library of Congress Cataloging-in-Publication Data

Names: Fennell, Cassie, 1842–1884, author. | Snow, Whitney Adrienne, 1985- editor.
Title: The Civil War diaries of Cassie Fennell : a young Confederate woman in north Alabama, 1859–1865 / edited by Whitney A. Snow.
Other titles: Voices of the Civil War.
Description: Knoxville : The University of Tennessee Press, [2020]
Series: Voices of the Civil War | Includes bibliographical references and index.
Summary: "Born near Guntersville, Alabama, Catherine (Cassie) Fennell was nineteen when the Civil War began. Starting with her time at a female academy in Washington, DC, the diaries continue through the war's end and discuss civilian experiences in Alabama and the Tennessee Valley. Fennell was fairly well off and highly educated, moving easily in very elite social circles. Most of her relatives were staunch Confederates, and the war would take its toll, with multiple members of her family killed or captured. As she recounts the consequences of war—the downward spiral of the family fortune, the withering of hope at news from the battlefront, and the general uncertainty of civilian life in the South—Fennell's diaries constitute one of the few contemporaneous records of north Alabama, including the shelling and burning of Guntersville, which has been poorly documented in the historiography of the Civil War. Editor Whitney Snow's compilation adds to the now growing genre of women's Civil War diaries"— Provided by publisher.
Identifiers: LCCN 2020030518 (print) | LCCN 2020030519 (ebook) | ISBN 9781621906063 (hardcover) | ISBN 9781621906070 (pdf)
Subjects: LCSH: Fennell, Cassie, 1842–1884—Diaries. | Women, White—Alabama—19th century—Diaries. | Alabama—History—Civil War, 1861–1865—Personal narratives. | Guntersville (Ala.)—History—19th century. | LCGFT: Diaries.
Classification: LCC E487 .F46 2020 (print) | LCC E487 (ebook) | DDC 976.1/9405092—dc23
LC record available at https://lccn.loc.gov/2020030518
LC ebook record available at https://lccn.loc.gov/2020030519

Dedicated to my mother

Barbara Jean Snow

. . . the first seconds of fall always seem like soar.

William Faulkner, *Requiem for a Nun*

Contents

Illustrations

Following Page 140

Arthur C. Beard
Portrait of John Rayburn
Dr. John Allan Wyeth
Colonel James L. Sheffield
Portrait of Thomas Hubbard Hobbs
Samuel K. Rayburn
Evergreen Rayburn's Parasol

Acknowledgments

I would like to express my thanks to the people who made possible this project's completion. All of the dedicated volunteers at the Marshall County, Alabama, Archives are to be credited for the work they do in preserving local history. Suggestions were gleaned from Billy Alexander, Margene Black, Rosemary Darnell, Tyrus Dorman, Keith R. Finley, Neal Johnson, William E. "Sonny" Lewis, Danny Maltbie, Larry Smith, Barbara Snow, Dr. Julian "Pete" Sparks, Dale Strange, Betty Taylor, Macey Taylor, and Lynn Tipton. Keith deserves special commendation for connecting me with one of the diarist's direct descendants—her great-granddaughter Carmen Hurff. Carmen, who has an impressive collection of letters, court records, images, and other Fennell memorabilia, gave unwavering support for my ambition to annotate the diaries she has long cherished as family heirlooms. John P. Rankin, Madison County historian, has provided a wealth of knowledge on the diarist's Huntsville relatives. I am most appreciative of the efforts executed by Dr. Alyssa D. Warrick (Visitor Guide, US Capitol Building), one of my best friends from graduate school, who graciously agreed to find and copy the needed pages from the gunboat logbooks at the National Archives. Dr. Sean C. Halverson (Assistant Professor, Alabama A&M University) has furnished advice on my selection of illustrations. Several of my colleagues at Midwestern State University have generously provided their thoughts on the manuscript: Sarah Butler, Dr. Peter Fields, Dr. Yvonne Franke, Dr. Dittika Gupta, Dr. Claudia Montoya, and Dr. Beverly L. Stiles. For commenting on an earlier draft, much gratitude is also extended to the following: Dr. Sam Hyde (Professor, Southeastern Louisiana University), Dr. Connie L. Lester (Associate Professor, University of Central Florida), Dr. Erinn McComb (Associate Professor, Del Mar College), Dr. Christine E. Sears (Associate Professor, University of Alabama in Huntsville), and Dr. Deanne Stephens (Professor, University of Southern Mississippi).

Working with the University of Tennessee Press has been an exhilarating and edifying experience. Two reviewers, S. Kittrell Rushing and anonymous, contributed useful suggestions. Copyeditor Meg Olsen offered a much-needed set of fresh eyes. Editorial Assistant Jon Boggs gave wonderful assistance during the proofing stages. Scot Danforth (Director) and Michael P. Gray (Series Editor, Voices of the Civil War) delivered steadfast guidance. These six individuals helped me produce a better product and for that, I extend my heartfelt thanks.

Throughout the writing process, I often thought of sage advice once bestowed on me by Huntsville historian Nancy Rohr, whose diligent scholarship has served as an inspiration since my time as a master's student. Carol Codori, former president of the Tennessee Valley Civil War Roundtable, has also motivated me to learn all I could about nineteenth-century Alabama. I remain forever indebted to Dr. Johanna N. Shields (Professor Emerita, University of Alabama in Huntsville), the educator who first sparked my interest in the Civil War. Last but not least, I would like to recognize two individuals who greatly helped this Alabama girl adjust to living in a Texas world. Dr. Harry Hewitt (Professor Emeritus, Midwestern State University) and Kay Hardin (retired secretary, Midwestern State University) provided unfailing support and invaluable wisdom. I will always remember their kindness.

Editorial Decisions

I first came across the name Catherine "Cassie" Fennell while volunteering at the Marshall County Archives in Guntersville, Alabama, over three years ago. While sorting vertical files, I saw an undated, partial, typed copy of a Civil War–era diary and thought about writing a journal article on the diarist.[1] When I finally sat down to read the pages sometime later, I was absolutely captivated and inspired to attempt an annotation. Excited, I mentioned my aspiration to Betty Taylor, the director, who informed me that another volunteer, Keith R. Finley, had already transcribed the diary from the handwritten version owned by Cassie's great-granddaughter Carmen (Russell) Hurff. I approached Keith, who gave me a copy that was just that, a typed, spiral-bound transcription with no annotation. Aware that historians are often territorial, I asked Keith if he would mind if I annotated the diary. He said he had no intention of doing so and gave me his blessing.

My next step was to contact Carmen, a resident of Guntersville, who welcomed and encouraged my efforts. Carmen is the daughter of Carmen Matthew Russell and Phoebe Mae Esslinger, the granddaughter of Wade Hampton Esslinger and Ethel May Green, and the great-granddaughter of Andrew Jackson Esslinger and Cassie Fennell. She regaled me with stories of the Fennells and shared scores of letters and other family memorabilia, including the diary that turned out to be three diaries. Unfortunately, what Carmen possessed were scanned copies of the original handwritten diaries. I asked if she knew the whereabouts of the originals, and she said that, to her knowledge, her uncle Frank Esslinger had owned the diaries. True enough, in 1950 William Francis "Frank" Esslinger, Cassie's eldest child, self-published a book, *Two Hundred Years of the Esslinger Family*, in which he said, "This Catherine M. Fennell . . . was the mother of this writer, in whose care some of her wartime diaries are kept and treasured."[2] Presented with this clue, I soon tracked down one of Frank's grandchildren.

The daughter of Frank's son William Francis Esslinger Jr., Susan (Esslinger) Selig, lives in Eugene, Oregon. Using the phone book, I found her landline number and called, hoping that she either possessed the diaries or knew of their whereabouts. The conversation we had was pleasant but unexpected. Susan told me that, while she had never seen the diaries, she thought they might be in her father's vast papers, which were in storage. That said, she wished me luck on my endeavor to annotate the copies I had. Undeterred, I sought out another of Cassie's direct descendants.

Betty Hampton Esslinger, one of Cassie's great-granddaughters through the Wade Hampton Esslinger line, lives in Huntsville, Alabama. Using the white pages, I looked up her landline and made a call, fingers crossed. She did not have the original diaries either and suggested I contact her cousin Carmen Hurff. Frustrated but wanting desperately to locate these diaries, I resorted to looking in surrounding archives.

My search was unsuccessful. Though I found a vertical file on the Fennells in the Heritage Room at the Huntsville-Madison County Public Library, there were no diaries. I did find two copies of the diaries at the University of Alabama in Huntsville (UAH). Its Salmon Library has a typed, bound copy available for check-out on the third floor, and its archives house a copy of the cursive, handwritten diaries. While disappointed, my search at UAH solved one puzzle. Keith had long told me that he had heard the original diaries were in a safe-deposit box in Florence, Alabama. He could not, however, remember where he had learned this information. Under "Diary of Miss Catherine M. Fennell" in the UAH catalog listing, the notes portion reads, "Original diary is in bank vault in Florence, Alabama." When I called Salmon Library, a staff member told me the diary had been acquired decades ago, so she had no idea if that note remained accurate. I made further inquiries to various local, county, and university archives before contacting the state archives. Still no luck! The original diaries remain elusive, if they still exist at all. Fortunately, history has been preserved through the copies, and it is Carmen's on which I relied.

In the draft stage, a colleague who had kindly agreed to review the edited manuscript questioned my choice to refer to my diarist by her first name. She thought such practice lacked professional distance. This being my first attempt at editing, I mulled over my response. I had read several annotated diaries of Civil War–era women wherein the editors used their subjects' first names and assumed it the norm. I granted, however, that I had recently purchased Steven M. Stowe's *Keep the Days: Reading the Civil War Diaries of Southern Women* and observed that he had used the surnames of women diarists. In the end, I opted not to refer to my diarist by surname, not due to any kind of presumed familiarity, but because she had an exceptionally large family. I thought calling her Fennell would be terribly confusing to readers. At first, I referred to my diarist as Catherine, her given name, but ultimately decided upon Cassie, her nickname. Friends and family called her Cassie, never Catherine. She referred to herself as Cassie.

As emphasized by Stowe, editors are often far too focused on "readability" to the detriment of a diary.[3] In other words, things get lost in transcription. I have largely refrained from imposing textual modifications, with the exception of spelling corrections. Initially, I set about marking all misspelled words with [*sic*]. Pretty soon, these abounded, and I saw them as distractions to the content. To make a smoother read, I corrected myriad words. Cassie tended to capitalize or underline some words and sentences, so I made no alteration in those cases, because she evidently intended greater meaning by their inclusion. Items she underlined appear in italics. Because of its difficulty to replicate, I omitted her tendency to delineate death notices by drawing a dark mark above and below such entries.

I chose not to edit the diaries for punctuation issues. Cassie, like other diarists of her time, used unnecessary apostrophes like "work some sum's" instead of "work some sums." She also tended to add spaces. Examples are "some time," "up stairs," and "any how." These reflect typical nineteenth-century writing styles, so I saw no reason to replace them with contemporary spellings.

Dates appear as she wrote them. In most instances, Cassie provided the month and day. In others, she only gave the month. Where she failed to write a date, I have added an asterisk. At times, perhaps due to paper shortages during the war, Cassie scribbled entries on older pages. So, an entry from 1864 might have been written in between entries from 1861. Though the last entry in the diary is dated 1865, Cassie later jotted an 1872 entry in the section for 1859. This may indicate that she kept postwar diaries, but if so, they have never surfaced.

Cassie frequently used parentheses to clarify her entries. They appear to be afterthoughts, as if she wrote a sentence and then felt the need to better explain or elaborate. My comments, by contrast, are provided either in endnotes or in brackets [ ] in the text, so they are not mistaken for her words. There are several mentions of a "Mr. McJ____Jr." and "Mr. McJ____." The underlined segment is Cassie's doing, as she fancied this young man and, perhaps fearful that her younger sister/roommate might read the diary, never provided his full name, though I believe I have discovered his identity. Sometimes Cassie used large letters to write over old entries and/or marked lines through entries. In one instance, she attempted to do both. On June 13, 1860, she wrote an unremarkable entry and then did something atypical. Across this entry in large letters, she wrote, "Mrs. McJ, Jr." She later tried to erase this imagining by scribbling across the entry, but it remains legible. Whenever she made doodles or textual comments that were not in dated entries, I have mentioned them in the endnotes.

I considered how to cite the page numbers on the diaries, which Cassie intermittently referred to as books, volumes, and journals. For my purposes, I call them Diary One, Two, and Three. Diary One has two sets of page numbers. One set is on the diary pages, and another is on the surrounding edge and appears to have been written by someone else, perhaps Cassie's son Frank, to whom the diaries passed. Diaries Two and Three have no page numbers on the diary pages, but the same person who numbered Diary One wrote numbers in the top right corners of the copied pages. Whoever wrote the second set of numbers began each diary with "1." I found this pagination extremely helpful, and this individual's inserted page numbers are in my citations of Carmen's copies.

I made every effort to identify each individual mentioned in the diaries. I consulted census, marriage, death, and war records, as well as newspapers. When more information was needed, I resorted to family trees on Ancestry.com and Find a Grave. I am aware that these sites are not infallible but believe they can nevertheless be useful tools for historians. In cases where there were multiple candidates for a name, I provided information on all possibilities in the endnotes. In many instances, I managed to discover an individual's birth year, but not his or her death year. In such cases, the unknown year is designated with a dash.

It may rightly be asked why I chose to include four appendices. I always intended Appendix 1 to include mini-biographies of all the key figures in the diaries. It serves as an easy reference for readers by providing each individual's life story. From the start, I also thought the 1938 memoirs of Cassie's youngest brother Caius might interest readers. Provided in Appendix 4, they offer insight into family drama, a subject on which Cassie remained largely mum. I began with only these two appendices but then found two more primary sources that I thought complemented Cassie's diaries in a variety of complex ways.

The diaries give us Cassie's voice and view of the world. But to whom does she speak? As previously mentioned, Cassie wrote not one but three diaries. She started Diary One to record her school days, but it was exceptionally common for southern and northern women to keep diaries during the nineteenth century. Doing so was cathartic, and Cassie used hers to do a great deal of venting. Diary One, written during her time at a Washington, DC, girls' school, began on September 12, 1859. Containing her thoughts on boys and frustrations about teachers, it ended on February 4, 1860. She commenced writing Diary Two on March 19, 1860, while still at school. Upon graduating, she traveled home to Alabama, where she stated that henceforth, she planned to write of politics. Seen in most Civil War-era diaries, this shift reflected an insatiable desire to analyze and understand the political climate. Likely, wartime entries were a means of expressing power in a world over which Cassie, much like other women, had little if any control. As explained by historian Kimberly Harrison, author of *The Rhetoric of Rebel Women: Civil War Diaries and Confederate Persuasion*, keeping a diary exhibited agency while shaping both Confederate nationalism and identity.[4] Cassie closed this diary on July 10, 1862. As the war went on, paper became scarce, and her writing became very tiny. She gave no reason for the transition when she started Diary Three on July 12, 1862. She continued writing until June 23, 1865, ceasing abruptly. I believe she intended Diary One, with its private matters, for her eyes only. She never imagined it might be read by others, except perhaps her little sister (without her permission), and that explains her secrecy about "Mr. McJ____." Diaries Two and Three, however, I believe she wrote for posterity, because they largely regurgitated information she read in newspapers. Cassie crammed the pages with entries on war and said surprisingly little about day-to-day family matters. This blatant omission left me wanting to know more about her relatives, and I set out to fill in the gaps.

Appendix 2 contains a May 29, 1861, letter written to Cassie by her seventeen-year-old double-first cousin Katie Fennell, who lived in Bellefonte, Alabama. Katie, the daughter of Francis Marion Fennell and Isabella Allison, received occasional mention in Cassie's diaries. In fact, with a touch of resentment, Cassie described Katie as the favorite niece of their Aunt Catherine (Allison) Cobb. The two cousins were nevertheless friends, but I think the value of this letter lies not in their relationship, but in Katie's inclusion of a speech she wrote to send the men of Bellefonte off to battle. She composed it herself, and her words emanate the passion many north Alabama women had for the Confederate cause.

Though my focus has ever been on Cassie, her brothers Willie and Wattie filled many of the pages of her diaries. She devoted entry after entry to their exploits and plights, but these are her words, not theirs. Appendix 3 is my attempt to remedy that absence. While serving in the Confederate armed forces, one of the two brothers penned a short diary. I located a typed, transcribed copy at the Marshall County Archives. Labeled the diary of Wattie, it is a Confederate soldier's experiences in Virginia. In 1953, the *Journal of Southern History* reported that a copy of this same diary had been acquired by the Southern Historical Collection at the University of North Carolina. The *JSH* described it as "a short Confederate Army diary of Isham Watkins Fennell, surgeon, 55th Alabama Infantry."[5] I conclude that cannot be the case, as Wattie never served in Virginia. If the diary belonged to one of the Fennell brothers, it must have been Willie's. A surgeon's assistant, Willie served in the 9th Alabama Infantry and was in Virginia at the time the diary was written. Since Willie died unmarried and childless in 1878, his diary likely passed to Wattie, his closest sibling. One may ask what gave me confidence to even assert that a Fennell authored the diary. First, the diarist spoke of an "Uncle Frank," and both Willie and Wattie had an uncle named Francis "Frank" Marion Fennell. Second, the diarist mentioned that somebody named Sam had become a colonel. Charity, the elder sister of Willie and Wattie, had married Sam Henry of the 9th Alabama Infantry, and he had achieved the rank of colonel. Third, the diarist regretted his brother "W" being captured at Fort Donelson. Wattie was captured at Fort Donelson. Using these three connections, I maintain that this diary was written by Willie Fennell.

As to my overall treatment of the appendices, the only changes I made were to the punctuation in Willie's diary. Whoever transcribed the original tended to end sentences with either commas or semicolons. This made it rather difficult to surmise where one sentence ended and another began. To make the diary easier to read, I replaced several semicolons and commas with periods. Where parts of various letters proved indecipherable, the unreadable portions are marked with ______.

When reading histories, I like to be able to put a face with a name. Being able to study a person's face somehow makes them more real, at least for me. I managed to discover images of most of Cassie's family members in either the Marshall County Archives or Carmen's private collection. Although I made every effort to locate images of Charity (Fennell) Henry, Sam Henry, Frank Fennell, Catherine (Allison) Cobb, and Charity (Allison) Cooper

Lea, none were found. I can only suggest possible explanations for their absence. In his later life, Sam Henry, by that time widowed, became the target of an arsonist, who burned his house. This may have destroyed what images he possessed. Frank Fennell, Cassie's younger brother, died at sixteen and may never have sat for a daguerreotype or an ambrotype. Catherine (Allison) Cobb, the wife of US congressman Williamson Robert Winfield "W. R. W." Cobb, died childless during the Civil War. After her death, her widowed husband's home in Bellefonte, Alabama, was burned by Union troops. Though several images of her famous husband remain, I have not been able to find any of Catherine. Though the twice-married Charity (Allison) Cooper Lea remains fodder for gossip by today's local historians, many of whom bill her as an eccentric, the only images I have seen in relation to her are of her house, which still stands today, although it has been moved from its original location. In different ways, these five individuals greatly impacted Cassie's life, and though we have no idea what they looked like, they still live on her pages. As to non-relatives, I was successful in locating images of Albert Gallatin "A. G." Henry, Sam's cousin and business partner, and Arthur C. Beard, one of Cassie's neighbors. I included famed New York surgeon Dr. John Allan Wyeth, who, when a teenager, witnessed the shelling of Guntersville. I also added one of Colonel James L. Sheffield (48th Alabama Infantry), a prominent local officer whose daughter married Cassie's brother Johnnie. While I found several images of Samuel Rayburn, I was unable to find any of his wife Evergreen, one of two casualties from the shelling of Guntersville. I have, however, included an image of Samuel, one of his son John, and one of Evergreen's parasol, which remains on display at the Guntersville Historical Society's Gilbreath House.

Introduction

On September 12, 1859, seventeen-year-old Cassie Fennell began a diary to record her school days. At the time, she resided at the Young Ladies' Institute in Washington, DC. She kept this diary, which she referred to as a book, until February 4, 1860, when she ceased writing for the simple reason that she had filled its pages. She soon purchased a new diary, one she called a journal, and kept it from March 19, 1860, through July 10, 1862. Content-wise, this second diary differed little until July 4, 1861, when Cassie announced that she would henceforth record information on "my country and politics." This sudden drive to become a scribe of history derived from her recent graduation and return home to Deposit Ferry in Marshall County, Alabama, where she became caught up in secessionist fervor. From that time onward, she wrote her observations on political, economic, and military affairs, began a third diary on July 12, 1862, and continued writing until June 23, 1865. Written for entirely different purposes, the second and third diaries are vastly dissimilar from the first.

Diary One is a hodgepodge of shopping, gossip, and angst, pretty much what one might expect from a teenage girl of her era. It contained Cassie's private thoughts and emotions about boys, coursework, classmates, and teachers, as well as church and entertainment. And yet, in these pages, she also wrote of visits to Congress, as well as the Smithsonian and White House; her acquaintance with several important politicians whom she met through her uncle, US congressman W. R. W. Cobb (D-AL); and political happenings. Thanks largely to the *Evening Star*, I was able to fact check the vast majority of her entries and identify the senators and congressmen she referenced. Though Diary One contains an array of subjects, the personal nature of many entries leads me to conclude that Cassie wrote it for herself, not with the intent that it be read by others.

Cassie differentiated Diary Two, on the other hand, by declaring soon into its pages that she planned to write mainly on political matters. Cassie's foci became narrow once she had made up her mind to shift gears. An ardent rebel, she embraced the Confederate cause with ferocity and knew she was witnessing history in the making. She wrote of secession, loyalty, Lincoln's election, and later, battle. Entries on officers and soldiers filled her pages in Diaries Two and Three. Aside from her three brothers who served in the Confederate forces, Cassie spoke little of her family. She never talked about cooking, cleaning, helping her mother, or taking care of her younger siblings. She did not mention socializing with girlfriends or her musings about potential suitors. The war consumed her mind and her pages. In fact, Cassie may have been too zealous in her attempt to record history.

Eager for every scrap of news, especially when Union forces occupied nearby Huntsville, Cassie devoured any newspaper she could find, no matter how old and regardless of origin.[1] Initially, she appeared to believe much of what historians might now refer to as scuttlebutt. Wiser as the war progressed, she soon began correcting herself by marking through and over past entries or prefacing new ones with doubt about the accuracy of her source. In this way, Cassie is similar to other Civil War diarists like Catherine Ann Devereux Edmondston and Emma Holmes, southern women who depended heavily on newspapers for their wartime information.

As I uncovered more about Cassie, I kept asking myself what she brought to the table about Civil War life. In other words, what made her experience unique? Every time I thought I had found an answer, I soon corrected myself. Many teenage girls and women kept diaries before, during, and after the war, so her young age is nothing special. Many southern parents sent their daughters to boarding school. Many diarists came from wealth, and Cassie, as the daughter of a planter/physician who owned almost thirty slaves, is no different. At one point, I thought I had found her niche in the form of her avoidance of the words slavery and slave, but research revealed that the vast majority of mistresses and would-be mistresses acted similarly. I wondered if perhaps her uncle by marriage, W. R. W. Cobb, might be her significance but then thought she needed no famous male link to give her words relevance. Moreover, several southern diarists like Floride Clemson, the granddaughter of John C. Calhoun, had political connections. Ultimately, I concluded that Cassie Fennell is extraordinarily typical. Her contribution to the historical record, however, lies primarily with her location—north Alabama.

In the course of my annotating process, I read many diaries written by women in various southern states like Virginia, South Carolina, North Carolina, Tennessee, Georgia, Kentucky, Mississippi, and Alabama.[2] I found only a few written by women in north Alabama and no others from Marshall County, where Cassie did the bulk of her writing. Though Cassie resided in Marshall County, diarists Mary Jane Chadick and Sarah Lowe Davis lived thirty-seven miles away in Huntsville, Madison County, which was occupied for much of the Civil War. *Incidents of the War: The Civil War Journal of Mary Jane Chadick*, edited and annotated by Nancy Rohr, speaks volumes about civilian life during the intermittent occupations. Davis's diaries, located at the Alabama Department of Archives and History, were written in 1861 and 1862 while she attended Huntsville Female College, and they include commentary on the occupation's impact on the school.[3] Virginia (Tunstall) Clay-Clopton wrote her memoirs, *Mrs. Clay, of Alabama*. Prior to the war, Virginia, the aristocratic wife of US senator Clement C. Clay Jr., split her time between Washington, DC, and Huntsville, and utterly despised Cassie's uncle W. R. W. Cobb, whom she deemed a classless, uneducated buffoon who had somehow managed to defeat her husband in a congressional election.[4] Many other diaries/memoirs I found from the north Alabama area were written not by women but men: *The Journals of Thomas Hubbard Hobbs: A Contemporary Record of an Aristocrat from Athens, Alabama written between 1840, when the diarist was fourteen years old and 1862, when he died serving in the Confederate Army*, edited by Faye Acton Axford; and *From Huntsville to Appomattox: R. T. Cole's History of 4th Regiment, Alabama Volunteer Infantry, C.S.A., Army of Northern Virginia*, edited by Jeffrey D. Stocker.[5] Note that Hobbs was Cassie's cousin.[6] Cassie's diaries, with their entries on Huntsville, contribute to a small but growing historiography on Union occupation in north Alabama. Perhaps more important are Cassie's entries on Guntersville, which was shelled and later burned by Union forces. Because of this destruction, only a handful of prewar Guntersville newspapers remain, issues of the *Marshall Eagle*, and none are from the wartime era. Aside from court documents, whatever archival records the city possessed went up in smoke. As such, historians have been forced to rely on mentions of Guntersville in newspapers and archives in other locations in and outside of Alabama. Cassie's diaries are invaluable to the historical record, especially as it concerns Marshall and Madison Counties.

Cassie lived five miles from Guntersville, a bustling town that sat on a bend in the Tennessee River. Guntersville began as Gunter's Landing, a ferry and trading post operated by Scottish immigrant John Gunter in the late eighteenth and early nineteenth centuries. After the passage of the Indian Removal Act in 1830, settlement soared, and the landing flourished. In 1847, Gunter's Landing was incorporated and changed its name to Guntersville. The following year, Guntersville became the seat of Marshall County. Nearby towns were Claysville, Honeycomb, Paint Rock, and Boshart. Villages included Beard's Bluff, Manchester, and Warrenton. By the time of the Civil War, Guntersville still had no track but was not far from the Memphis & Charleston Railroad in Scottsboro, some twenty-eight miles away. In addition to Gunter's Landing, Guntersville boasted nearby ferries at Columbus City, Fearn's Landing, and Deposit Ferry by war's dawn.[7] These ferries made it a target.

According to Union general John W. Geary, his orders included the destruction of ferries between Law's Landing and Whitesburg, an area that included Guntersville.[8] The man who ordered the actual shelling of Guntersville was Union major James W. Paramore of the 3rd Ohio Cavalry, who, on that day, commanded the 15th Kentucky Infantry, part of Loomis's Battery, and the 3rd Battalion of the 3rd Ohio Cavalry. On July 27, 1862, Paramore and his men marched from Woodville with the express intent of destroying Guntersville's ferries to prevent their use by Confederates. The following day, Paramore began shelling from a nearby bluff because Confederate cavalry were present in the town.

Since war's end, local historians in Guntersville and Marshall County have repeatedly denied that Confederate forces were present when the city was shelled in 1862. Many of their local histories disclaim the official reports written by Geary and Paramore.[9] Instead, they often resort to Civil War–era newspaper articles and accounts that condemn the attack as a vicious, heartless assault on a city full of women, children, and a home guard of boys and old men. According to noted surgeon Dr. John Allan Wyeth, who witnessed the shelling at age fifteen, no Confederate troops were in town, only the local militia and a few soldiers home on furlough. Cassie's brother Caius later wrote that there had been a "handful of cavalry."[10] Newspapers across the Confederacy condemned the shelling as a brutal act of savagery against women and children.[11] In response to the Guntersville shelling, the *Tuscaloosa Observer* warned, "Such acts of unmitigated villainy and vandalism upon defenseless women and children, show clearly what we may expect from the detested Yankees, in the future conduct of the war. An avenging God will not suffer such wanton inhumanity to pass unpunished."[12] On the shelling, the *Charlotte Democrat* titled its article "Town Shelled—Ladies Killed."[13] A more contemporary account of the shelling appeared in a September 19, 1981, issue of the *Advertiser-Gleam*, Guntersville's newspaper: "Since the local men were away in the Confederate Army, the only ones left to defend Guntersville were women and 12 or 14-year old boys. Some of the boys fired at the Yankees, and in retaliation the Yankees shelled and burned the north end of the town."[14] While this is the version that has filled the pages of local newspapers and books in Marshall County for over 150 years, Confederate forces moved often throughout north Alabama and were very much in Guntersville the day it was shelled.[15]

In his report, Paramore described Guntersville as "strongly garrisoned by Forrest's cavalry and some independent companies of guerrillas and bushwhackers raised in the vicinity, with a heavy picket guard down at the landing guarding their boats and a warehouse filled with forage and commissary stores."[16] Paramore justified his actions by saying that the "enemy" fired on his men and that his shelling from a nearby bluff was intended to destroy their camp. Finding Confederate evidence to substantiate the Union reports was easier said than done. Perhaps the most convincing source I came across was a letter in an 1898 issue of *Confederate Veteran Magazine*. Written by John F. Fore, a veteran of the Forty-Second Alabama Infantry, the letter described his wartime experiences, including his time in Guntersville. In his words:

> We were then ordered to Guntersville, Ala. During the summer the Federals came up on the opposite side of the Tennessee River and opened fire on Guntersville, across the river, with their artillery. I was ordered to take a posse of men out to a cross-roads south of town (now known as Wyeth City), to keep the enemy from coming into town on that side. The citizens had to leave town during the fight. A lady was brought through my lines who had been struck with a cannon-ball. It was a horrible sight. Our men got on an island in the river with their small guns and drove the enemy back and held the town.[17]

While Fore expressed pride in driving the enemy off, in actuality, Union forces left because they had accomplished their objective. In his report, Paramore wrote that he ceased fire at roughly 6:00 p.m. He explained, "When, having completed the destruction of their boats, and having no sufficient means of crossing my command to pursue the enemy further, I withdrew all the command except one company of cavalry and one of infantry (which I left to hold and watch the movements of the enemy)."[18] Though Cassie lived roughly five miles from Guntersville, her riverside home meant she no doubt heard the cannonade.

Cassie's comments on the shelling of Guntersville are succinct but sympathetic, especially regarding one of the two civilian deaths. Evergreen Findley

Rayburn, the woman mentioned by Fore, was decapitated when Union forces shelled Guntersville.[19] The widowed Evergreen (Rainey) Findley had only recently remarried, becoming the second wife of former Alabama militia general Samuel Rayburn and stepmother to Confederate captain John Rayburn. With her marriage to Samuel, Evergreen stepped into the role of proprietress of a hotel owned by her new husband. The building, located on the banks of the Tennessee River, served the Rayburns as both home and business. When the shelling began, many Guntersville residents like Evergreen attempted to take shelter or evacuate the city, and while they survived, she did not.[20] According to the *Nashville Dispatch*, as she and two guests tried to flee out the back door, "a shell passed through the house and cutting a peach tree in two, exploded," killing her instantly.[21] Yet another version of events came from Sonny Lewis, one of Evergreen's great-great grandsons. In a 2015 newspaper article, Lewis explained, "She [Evergreen] had gotten everything loaded up [in a wagon] and was starting down Hill Avenue when she realized she had forgotten her good silver. She went back to get it and got to the front porch when a bomb hit a peach tree in the yard and the shrapnel cut off her head."[22] Even now, the whereabouts of her grave remain unknown, but Lewis donated her parasol to the Guntersville Historical Society's Gilbreath House. In the aftermath of the shelling, Evergreen's death became a rallying cry for vengeance among Guntersville natives.

It should be noted that Paramore claimed he wanted nothing more or less than the destruction of the ferries, until his men were fired upon. His report made it sound like his men kept their distance from Guntersville's civilians while perched on a nearby bluff across the river. However, in a letter to his wife, Union private George Kryder (3rd Regiment Ohio Cavalry) mentioned his comrades encountering at least one rebel woman. In his words, "They said there was one woman came out of a house and showed her backside to the men and then went into the house. After she shut the door the Artillery threw a shell which exploded in the house and in an instant the whole house was in flame and nothing more was seen of the woman."[23] Given that only two civilian deaths were reported, that of Evergreen and a Nashville man named Henry Clay McNairy, this defiant woman who mooned Union forces must have survived. Though Cassie said little about what befell Guntersville, her remarks, however brief, showed the fear and bewilderment so prevalent in war-torn north Alabama. Guntersville remained a target for Union forces for the duration of the war. Perhaps foreshadowing the flames to come, Paramore wrote, "I think that nest of treason and rendezvous of guerillas and bushwhackers should be entirely destroyed and purified by fire, for as long as it is permitted to remain, their facilities for reconstructing their boats and its proximity to the railroad will make it a dangerous place for our trains and railroad bridges and require it to be closely watched."[24] Years later, on January 15, 1865, Union marines from the USS *General Thomas* and the USS *General Grant*, both part of the 11th District of the Mississippi Squadron, burned Guntersville almost to the ground.[25]

Local historians have long debated just why the gunboats chose to burn Guntersville. One argument, suggested by Dr. John Allan Wyeth, had to do with the killing of a popular Union sergeant. On January 14, Confederate general Hylan B. Lyon, while moving south from Kentucky, stopped at Guntersville with some three hundred troops. From the top of Beard's Bluff, he used two twelve-pound guns to harass Union gunboats. As he marched to Blount County near Red Hill, Lyon selected a campsite near the home of Thomas Noble but failed to post sentinels. While the Confederates slept, the 15th Pennsylvania Cavalry surprised them and took roughly one hundred men as prisoners. The Union forces apprehended Lyon in the Noble home. At one point, an underwear-clad Lyon asked to put on his uniform. The request was granted, and while dressing, he managed to procure a gun, which he used to shoot Union sergeant Arthur Lyon point blank in the head, killing him, before escaping.[26] Wyeth suggested that the death of Lyon motivated Union gunboats to burn Guntersville the following day. It may have been one factor or irrelevant, as none of the gunboat logbooks mentioned the killing of Lyon. They did, however, record shots being fired at them from Guntersville in days past, and perhaps those from General Lyon's forces had been the last straw.

In addition to the USS *General Thomas* and USS *General Grant*, other Union vessels patrolling the Tennessee River included the USS *General Sherman*, USS *General Burnside*, and steamer *Stone River*. Each of these boats frequented both Deposit Ferry and Guntersville. In the logbook of the USS *General Grant*, on January 11, a "battery" had been fired on them at Guntersville, and in retaliation, they had opened fire between 12:00 and 1:40 p.m. On January 13, the logbook of the USS *General Sherman* mentioned being fired upon at Guntersville. On January 15, the USS *General Thomas*'s logbook relayed that, after burning several Beard's Bluff homes, including that of Cassie's neighbor Arthur C. Beard at 10:00 a.m., the gunboat sailed to Guntersville and, between 12:00 and 3:30 p.m., burned the town. The entry's author gave no reason. While this logbook mentioned ferrying members of the 15th Pennsylvania Cavalry the previous morning, that would have been before Lyon's death, so his demise could not have been the motivation. Based on the logbooks of the four gunboats, the commanders frequently met on each other's vessels, and no doubt discussed their encounters with enemy forces; several entries in the various logbooks mentioned being fired at by both gun and shellfire in and around Guntersville within a week of the burning.[27] Local historians have argued over just how many of the gunboats participated in the burning of Guntersville.

Most contemporary local historians blamed the USS *General Grant*, some credited the USS *General Thomas*, and one argued that all four of the gunboats had done the deed. In reality, the logbooks left little doubt. On January 15, a USS *General Grant* logbook entry read, "steamed up the creek at Guntersville, fired three (3) shell and sent party of fifty (50) men ashore." Later that day, an entry read, "2:35 our men and the USS *General Thomas*'s returned having destroyed Guntersville." As to the remaining vessels, the USS *General Burnside* had been at Bridgeport on January 15, so its logbook made no mention of Guntersville that day. The USS *General Sherman*, on the other hand, did. One entry explained that at 2:00 p.m., the USS *General Sherman* landed at Guntersville to find the USS *General Grant*, USS *General Thomas*, and *Stone River* already there. The entry provided no clue as to whether its men helped with the burning, but explained that the USS *General Sherman*, USS *General Grant*, USS *General Thomas*, and *Stone River* all headed to Deposit Ferry, which the logbooks sometimes called Port Deposit, shortly thereafter and landed at 4:20 p.m.[28] Several of the logbooks mentioned a tendency to ferry Union troops and take aboard both enemy prisoners and deserters. While it may well have been feasible for someone to have informed one or more of the gunboats about Lyon's death on the morning of January 15, the motive behind the burning was probably the repeated gun and shellfire that had peppered the gunboats over the previous days.

In the aftermath of the burning, Cassie observed that Guntersville had become desolate. She no doubt counted her blessings because, while the homes and plantations of neighbors like Beard had gone up in flames, her mother's house had been spared, largely because various Union officers had been using it as resting spot. As for Guntersville, historians Katherine Duncan and Larry Smith maintained that only seven buildings were left standing: the Guntersville Hotel; the courthouse; the jail; a school; the Masonic hall; and two homes.[29] Though newspapers like Raleigh's *Daily Confederate* had once praised Guntersville as a "spunky little town" for having endured all it had during the war, this almost complete destruction further demoralized area natives and intensified Cassie's mounting anxiety.[30]

Cassie often expressed her fear that her home would be burned by the gunboats that frequented Deposit Ferry. On May 14, 1864, Cassie mentioned her brother Frank finding a "note sticking on the breastworks which said, 'If the gunboat General Sherman is fired upon, I will burn Dr. Fennell's place.'"[31] Whether the gunboat commander Joseph Morehead believed the Fennell family was apt to fire is unknown, but odds are that the threat had more to do with guerillas. Each gunboat that passed by Deposit Ferry had experienced gunfire from the shore. Oftentimes, Union forces, angered by the actions of guerillas, burned civilian homes in response.[32] In any event, the threatening, unsigned note scared the family to the extent that Cassie's mother sent her to another daughter's house eight miles from the river. This precaution did little good, as both homes were visited by several groups of Union troops who raided and demanded cooked food.

Throughout Diaries Two and Three, Cassie referred to Union soldiers as the "enemy," "Northern invaders," "Northern vandals," or "Yankees." Although it should be stated that she attributed negative qualities to "yankees" in general, she granted some were "gentlemen." Evidently, she found it easier to judge a group rather than individuals. In addition, she saw herself as a lady, and expected chivalry in all men, regardless of origin.[33] Her statements are often contradictory, even within the same entry. On September 1, 1862, for example, she wrote, "The Yankees are in a bad fix. Oh, I do hope they will be all taken or killed."[34] In another aside, she explained, "Both sides speak of hoisting the black flag (that is, to take no more prisoners but to kill all) but I hope they will not have to do that."[35] Perhaps this revealed the inner struggle countless southern women endured attempting to balance faith and Christian charity with Confederate patriotism and a zealous thirst for revenge. In this way, Cassie's encounters with Union forces, while by no means unique, contribute to the historical record.

Though, in the words of historian James Oakes, "protecting slavery was the reason *d'etre* of the Confederate States of America" and the "Confederate nation was conceived in slavery and dedicated to the proposition that it would last forever," Cassie opined that secession was motivated by an earnest southern desire to achieve independence, rather than by a quest to preserve and expand slavery.[36] This attitude predominated in diaries written by many rebel women who justified the war as a battle for states' rights, honor, and duty, rather than slavery.[37] Southern and northern concepts of duty differed. Whereas northern duty was synonymous with "patriotism, loyalty to the Constitution, law and order, defense of the Union, and later the advancement of human freedom," southern duty meant "self-sacrifice to family, community, race, and region against outside forces of evil and ruin."[38]

As noted by historian Steven M. Stowe, women slave owners and those who benefitted from their parents' ownership of slaves "are not sympathetic figures," but historians need to attempt to empathize with them "in order to understand."[39] On the subject of slaves, Cassie exhibited overwhelming dismissiveness and indifference. In his book *Keep the Days: Reading the Civil War Diaries of Southern Women*, Stowe explained that for some women, slavery served as a backdrop, the given of their existence, "natural, like the weather."[40] It was such for Cassie, who largely avoided the issue of slavery. She rarely spoke of slaves and never referred to those in her parents' possession by that name, choosing instead to use the words negroes, servants, or "black men." This very deliberate attempt to avoid using the word slave is telling. As Stowe phrased it, "Slaves was too rough, too public, a man's term, or an abolitionist's, and saying it let disturbing things inside."[41] Moreover, lumping slaves together as a "faceless mass" made it easier to deny their humanity.[42]

Only twice did Cassie refer to slaves by name. Prior to the war, she wrote that her nurse Queen had died.[43] This is the only instance in any of her three diaries where Cassie showed affection toward a slave. Even so, it is nevertheless a self-absorbed comment. Her mother Matilda told Cassie that, prior to death, Queen had expressed the wish to see them again in heaven one day. This gave Cassie comfort, but she remained focused on how Queen's death affected her, not Queen's family. Queen is an example of a "loyal" slave who, in the words of Stowe, was seen not as an individual "so much as part of the diarist's personal landscape of home and things cherished."[44] The second time Cassie named a slave took place during the war, when she suspected Isham, a runaway, of revealing the layout of the family home to Union troops.[45] Her deliberate use of Queen and Isham in these two cases indicated that she was well aware of the slaves' names, but, for the most part, chose not to use them.[46]

Cassie never wrote about slaves' personalities, families, or assigned roles. She never mentioned any discussions or interactions with slaves. Again, this intentional omission suggested dominance. As Stowe argued, silence was "one style of mastery."[47] Cassie, unlike her youngest brother Caius, never wrote of playing with similar-aged slave children. This is likely due to the fact that Cassie had readymade playmates in the form of nine siblings, several of whom were close in age. Caius, on the other hand, was much younger than his brothers and sought the company of similar-aged slave boys. Had

Cassie been an only child or been one of fewer children, she may well have had a different relationship with younger slaves. At first glance, it appears that she had little interaction with slaves, but, with her older brothers away at war and her older sister married, Cassie, as the eldest remaining child, probably shouldered a great deal of responsibility when it came to the slaves. Indeed, the household mistress, in this case her mother Matilda, may have delegated responsibility when it came to tending to the slaves in the form of supervising the making of clothing and distributing food and medicine.[48] Perhaps this undesirable work irked Cassie, because when she did mention slavery, it was often in a scornful manner. She repeatedly maintained that the Confederacy would be better off without slaves.

Cassie longed for an end to slavery. Abolitionists may have had humanitarian or fiscal/labor motivations, but Cassie's reasoning stemmed from neither. Rather than freeing slaves of masters, she wanted to free masters of slaves. She saw slaves as both bothersome and burdensome. In 1862, when Union troops confiscated an uncle's slaves, Cassie snidely commented, "I am sure I don't know what they want with them."[49] In another entry, when roughly 600 hundred slaves were taken by Union forces in Huntsville, she remarked, "No one was sorry but glad to get rid of them."[50] Using what historian Kimberly Harrison referred to as "rhetorics of denial," Cassie professed that she neither cared if her family's slaves left nor worried about what might happen to them if they did. As elucidated by historian Catherine Clinton, "Southern women, like men, explicitly and openly viewed slaves as chattel and commonly associated blacks with their dollar value . . . even young children knew the cash value."[51] That said, Cassie could not have been ignorant of the slaves' importance to her family's estate. In fact, her parents only had 178 acres, a comparatively moderate plantation; much of their wealth was tied up in slaves. While Clinton emphasized that it was often new brides or experienced matrons, women managing "plantation affairs," who complained most about slaves, Cassie is representative of unmarried women who were equally vociferous about slaves as a cross to bear. Like brides and matrons, Cassie "groaned over the evils of slaves rather than the curse of slavery."[52]

So, in age, class, education, and thoughts on slavery, Cassie is common as southern diarists go, but I argue that her words fill gaps about civilian wartime experience in Guntersville; Marshall County; Madison County; north Alabama; and the Tennessee Valley. While annotating, I struggled with something Stowe wrote in *Keep the Days*. He stated that a diary should mean more than the bits and pieces historians remove to quote in their monographs. I suppose I erred in assuming a Civil War–era diary automatically warranted attention because of the time in which it was written. And yet, I confess I have been unable to shake my belief that historians will find much to harvest not merely from Cassie's diaries but from her life.

Cassie's ancestors, the Fennelles, were French Protestants who immigrated to New York before moving to Virginia, where they dropped the "e" from their last name. In time, the family decided to uproot and settle in Alabama. They located in Madison County, but Cassie's father James Fennell (1810–1864) eventually migrated to Marshall County, not long after the passage of the Indian Removal Act of 1830. He built a home at Deposit Ferry, which was south of the Tennessee River and roughly five miles west of Guntersville.[53] James acquired 81 acres in 1834, 40 in 1845, and 57 in 1853, for a total of 178 acres.[54] He and his wife Matilda (1815–1893) produced five sons and five daughters, who were raised in affluence. Their children, in order of birth, were Charity Elizabeth; James William "Willie"; Isham Watkins "Wattie"; Catherine Margaret "Cassie"; Mary Jane; John Houston "Johnnie"; David Francis "Frank"; Isabella "Belle"; Caius Grattan; and Martha Matilda "Mattie."[55] Both parents wanted each child to have the best possible education.

While son Willie attended Columbian College in pursuit of a medical degree, his siblings were another story. The eldest child, Charity, had married and was already out of the household, so James and Matilda turned their attention to the two eldest remaining daughters, whom they sent to the Young Ladies' Institute in Washington, DC.[56] After Cassie and Mary Jane graduated on June 28, 1860, they returned home and arrived on July 2. Once back in Alabama, Cassie wrote in her diary of the upcoming presidential election.

While she preferred John Breckinridge, the bulk of her family supported Stephen Douglas. Both were Democrats, although the former was far more popular throughout the South. It was a moot point, however, for she believed that Republican Abraham Lincoln would win. As she explained, "The great question of the time is 'What Shall We Do If He Does Succeed?' Some say 'Secede from the Union!,' others say, 'Try him a while and then if we do not like him: secede."[57] Lincoln's name did not even show up on southern ballots because many in the South feared he would end slavery, or at least halt its spread west. They deemed this unthinkable, because it would strike a devastating blow to the southern economy and southern honor by bringing about equality with blacks, a prospect they found abhorrent and terrifying.[58] Though Cassie seemed to dislike the idea of Lincoln as president, she did not initially express her opinion on secession. When she heard that Lincoln won, she wrote, "I hardly know what we will do about it."[59] Though Lincoln had made no threat to end slavery where it currently existed, historian Daniel W. Croft explained that "by simply electing a Republican president, northerners had insulted and dishonored the South."[60]

The South had voted overwhelmingly for Breckinridge, and the same held true for Alabama, though the results were a trifle more complicated. In Alabama, Douglas won 15 percent of the vote to Breckinridge's 54 percent. The port city of Mobile voted for Douglas, as did four northern counties, including Marshall and Madison. Whereas southern Alabama, especially the rich Black Belt, had a tremendous drive for secession, mountainous northern Alabama was populated by a large number of poor farmers who ranged from cooperationists to Unionists. They wanted no part of secession and may have believed that they "were being dragooned into conflict to protect somebody else's slaves."[61] Though Douglas had long advocated popular sovereignty, his staunch loyalty to the Union appealed to many north Alabama residents, even slave owners like Cassie's father.

According to the memoirs of Cassie's youngest brother Caius, who was only seven when the war began, "My father opposed secession. Others twitted my father on his loyalty to the state, to which he replied: 'Tis better to endure the evils that we have, than to rush into others we know not of.'"[62] Though Cassie mentioned her family's support for Douglas, she never quoted her father's positions. There may have been any number of reasons for James's stance. He may have expected political instability and economic uncertainty. As a slave owner, he may have predicted that secession would lead to war, which would almost certainly bring an end to slavery.[63] Or, given his disdain for "manworship," he may have feared that secession might pave a path for demagoguery.[64] Cassie, however, had no reservations. Rather than mention the centrality of slavery to secession or what might befall the rebel states when it came to economic and infrastructural challenges, she instead wrote of a quest for freedom. When Alabama seceded on January 11, 1861, Cassie wrote, "We are now free."[65]

Cassie's oldest brothers gave serious thought to which side to take during the war. Willie came to his decision more quickly than Wattie, so much so that several family members wondered if the latter would "take service with the enemy."[66] Ultimately, three of Cassie's five brothers served in the Confederate forces. Each was captured one or more times during the war. Each spent time in a prisoner-of-war camp. All survived the war.

As for Cassie, her passion for the Confederate cause never wavered. During these years, she lost a father, grandmother, aunt, nephew, and several cousins. Her relationship with her uncle W. R. W. Cobb, someone to whom she had been close, became fractious, if not severed, due to his unionism. When the war finally ended, Cassie responded with a mixture of self-pity and resignation.

Cassie and the rest of the family waited impatiently for Willie and Wattie to be freed. The raids had ceased, and Captain Joseph Morehead, commander of the USS *General Sherman*, the same gunboat that had threatened to burn her mother's home, offered the family a ride. Cassie expressed annoyance by the conciliatory behavior exhibited by the remaining Union troops. She said the Yankees were "trying to gain the friendship of the South while the poor 'Rebs' can hardly bear the sight of a Yankee . . . some of our most noted 'Bushwhackers' have given up and been treated with the greatest kindness."[67] Cassie mentioned having been advised to write her brothers Willie and Wattie and beg them to take the oath of allegiance, but penned, "I am not 'Unionized' enough for that yet."[68] Eventually, family loyalty trumped that to the Confederacy, and on May 25, 1865, she reluctantly wrote her brothers, asking both to take the oath if only to come home. She found it difficult to swallow her pride, but this decision may have been fueled by events in Guntersville, as well.

Earlier that month, Cassie fumed that the US flag had been raised in Guntersville. She wrote, "They hoisted the old Stars and Stripes, the symbol of oppression, amid the cheers of several hundred of our citizens. Yes—they cheered the old flag when their hearts were almost breaking and they felt like tearing it down and trampling it into the dust."[69] Several meetings had taken place in the town, and on May 16, former Confederate officers made speeches. Two had been reluctant rebels who had voted no to secession at the 1861 convention in Montgomery. Major Arthur C. Beard said, "We have met to bury the tomahawk—to smoke the calumet of peace. All of us ought to reverence the government which we could not destroy, and to which we have been compelled to submit. I shall do it cheerfully."[70] Then Colonel James L. Sheffield, formerly of the 48th Alabama Infantry, stood up and announced, "I have done all I could to establish the Southern Confederacy. I carried a musket for three years. I am whipped. I have been whipped for twelve months. The Southern Confederacy does not exist. I stand today like an erring child who has been whipped by his father."[71] These men accepted defeat, while Cassie continued to hope the Confederacy might revive.

Distraught more over the capture of Jefferson Davis than over the assassination of Lincoln, she expressed a desire to "try to be a good unionist."[72] Plagued with doubt, she wondered if she had the capacity to do so and questioned if death might be preferable.[73] In this venting, Cassie, who rarely spoke of slaves and slavery, did just that. In her words, "I believe we could have given up slavery at the beginning and it would have been still better if we had abolished slavery and stayed in the Union but it is too late now and we should do the same if it were to be done over again."[74] This statement is rather profound as it is the first instance in which she conceded that slavery had been intrinsic to the war. As previously mentioned, Cassie had never been a defender of slavery, because she thought it imposed an onerous responsibility on owners. Even so, she never attempted to hazard a guess as to what form of labor might take slavery's place or what fate lay in store for freedmen. On the question of whether the South should maintain an agricultural focus or pursue industrial development, she gave no comment. Like so many other southerners, Cassie had fallen into a deep melancholy fueled less by the end of slavery than by the shame, dishonor, and helplessness she felt over losing the war.

When the Civil War ended, Cassie's family tried to regain some semblance of normalcy and struggled financially. Much of their wealth had been tied up not in land but in slaves, so with emancipation they suffered a significant economic blow. Most of their livestock and crops had been confiscated by Union troops.[75] Matilda and her children attempted, to no avail, to regain some of the cotton that had been seized by the Union. Cassie's younger sister Belle later filed a lawsuit against the US government. She claimed the following losses: 131 bales of cotton, 5,000 pounds of meat, 43 hogs, 150 bushels of corn, 2 mules, 1 horse, 3 oxen, 1 cow, 1 steer, 1 heifer, poultry, and barrels of lard, molasses, honey, and preserves. Belle valued the foodstuff at $4,002.50 and the cotton at $12,400. Ultimately, the US government granted the Fennells $1,330.[76] Matilda leased land to settlers, and according to Cassie's letters and Caius's memoirs, she had some difficulty with her tenants, but neither child specified the problem.

Perhaps more daunting were lawsuits brought against the Fennell estate by Sam Henry, the husband of Cassie's elder sister Charity. The first lawsuit had to do with Charity's inheritance. In 1859, James had given Charity five slaves as a dowry. In the court records, Willie argued that the slaves were intended to have been the entirety of Charity's share of the estate. Sam, however, insisted that the slaves had been nothing more than an advance on her share of her father's estate. In his memoirs, Caius maintained: "He

[James] then gave her [Charity] two families of negroes and they were well content with their share. But after the war negroes were no property and the Colonel sued my mother for $2,000, an amount he figured to be one tenth of the estate. He got judgement and the Supreme Court sustained him with one Judge (Stone) dissenting. Meeting that judgement and costs were as devastating as the war. We were only recovering from the war when this disaster occurred. We met it but it took all our savings."[77] Caius failed to mention that Matilda had made Willie administrator of the Fennell estate on October 9, 1865, and it was he who paid the settlement to Sam on September 20, 1869.[78] This lawsuit placed a permanent wedge between the Fennells and the Henrys, so much so that things were never the same, and Sam would no longer visit Matilda's home. Just what role Charity played is unclear. According to historian Catherine Clinton, "Socialized from birth to devote herself wholly to her blood relatives, a woman experienced no small dilemma when she married and was required to shift her loyalties to her husband and an inherited family."[79] Though she did write affidavits about her version of James's intent, it is unknown if Charity was voluntarily complicit in the lawsuit or if she opposed, silently or otherwise, her husband's actions against her mother and siblings.

Sam brought another lawsuit that caused great consternation for Matilda. When her son Frank died unexpectedly in 1867, he was only sixteen, unmarried and childless. Years later, on December 6, 1878, Sam asked to become administrator of the estate of the late Frank. Matilda wanted Frank's share to be divvied among his siblings, but Sam insisted that it remain separate and, moreover, that he should oversee it. In fact, Sam demanded an itemized listing of everything owned by the late Dr. James Fennell. Sam even challenged Thomas Street, the sitting probate judge, because he was the half-brother of Johnnie's wife, and accused him of prejudice. As a result, former militia general Samuel Rayburn, then Marshall County's registrar in chancery, acted as special probate judge to avoid what was seen as Street's conflict of interest. On May 30, 1879, Sam agreed to have James McDonald serve as administrator of Frank's estate. McDonald held this position briefly and resigned sometime before June 13, the day of his death. On June 23, 1879, Andrew J. McDonald, the son of the aforementioned James, was named administrator of Frank's estate. In July 1879, the court ordered that Frank's estate, worth $10,000, be distributed among all of his siblings. Though resolved equitably, this ordeal caused immense vexation among various family members.[80]

Resentment may have remained, but Matilda made peace with the lawsuits and with Sam, perhaps for Charity's sake.[81] Though Matilda may not have been as financially comfortable as before the war, her late husband's estate was estimated at $100,000, a fortune in 1873.[82] Matilda's postwar struggle may have had more to do with her uneasy adjustment from plantation mistress to landlord than with money troubles.[83]

As to Cassie, her postwar life contained marriage, motherhood, and illness worsened by multiple pregnancies. Throughout the war, Cassie had collected the names and regiments of Confederate troops who passed by her mother's home and her sister Charity's.[84] Though the war had interrupted her aspirations for matrimony by taking away, through distance or death, local eligible men, marriage remained ever present in her mind, if her decorative collage of men's names is any indication.[85] On a page in Diary Three, Cassie wrote a series of derivations of her future name as Mrs. A. J. Esslinger, C. M. Esslinger, and Cassie Esslinger. She also scribbled, "Rare as is true Love, true friendship is *still rarer*. Friendship often ends in Love but Love in friendship—*never.*—Colton."[86] Sure enough, on December 27, 1866, she married Andrew Jackson "A. J." Esslinger.[87] They may have met either when his regiment visited Matilda's home or on one of Cassie's trips to visit relatives in Madison County, where his parents resided. As Cassie's son later reflected, his flame-haired mother had been absolutely smitten with his handsome, brunette father.[88] Though she would have been twenty-four years old, almost an old maid by the standards of the day, the war had caused thousands of women to marry late or not at all. A passionate woman, Cassie most certainly wed for love, if the letters written to her husband are any indication.

After their marriage, the newlyweds moved in with Charity (Allison) Cooper Lea, Cassie's aunt who lived in Whitesburg, Madison County. While there, Cassie went through three pregnancies and gave birth to three children, Frank, James, and Earnest, at her mother's home at Deposit Ferry. While at Matilda's house, she wrote numerous letters to A. J., and he responded in kind. A. J.'s family was quite poor compared to the Fennells; in 1860, his father William had real estate valued at $800, a personal wealth of $550, and no slaves.[89] A. J. had received little schooling, so his letters written to his parents during the war are rather childlike in their composition. When it came to spelling, punctuation, and structure, however, he showed marked improvement after his marriage, perhaps due to Cassie's tutelage.

After a few years with Aunt Charity, A. J. and Cassie rented land from her Aunt Nancy (Cobb) Allison before purchasing a homestead close to Berkley, Alabama. Though her first three pregnancies greatly weakened her constitution, Cassie had four more children: Wade, Andrew, Arthur, and Martha. In poor health, Cassie did her best to attend to household duties. Being the daughter and sister of physicians, Cassie knew medicine, and according to her son Frank, "She dosed out quinine and calomel, just like a physician, for all the family and farm hands, as well as their families."[90] In late September 1884, then forty-two-year-old Cassie once more put these skills to work by tending to her ill daughter, sister-in-law, and a neighboring family. In a letter, one of her sons reported, "So Ma had to wait on the sick very often not sleep an hour in the night nor a minute the next day 'twas cook, cook sew, sew and give medicine."[91] He continued, "She was taken with a severe ague which lasted seven hours. I never saw anybody shake so."[92] The end came swiftly, and Cassie died a little over a week later. Her obituary in the *Huntsville Independent* read as follows: "Mrs. C. M. Esslinger beloved wife of Mr. A. J. Esslinger, near Berkley, Madison Co., Ala., and daughter of the late Dr. J. W. Fennell of Marshall Co., Ala., departed this life the 9th of October 1884. Deceased was ill with pneumonia but a little over two weeks: was lovingly tended by her mother and other relatives. She leaves a husband and several little ones to mourn her loss besides innumerable friends. She lived a consistent member of the M.E. church nearly 30 years and testified to her reliance and perfect trust in the merits of the Good Lord who had always cared for her."[93] At the time of her death, Cassie's youngest child was two and her eldest just sixteen. Cassie was buried at the Beason-Esslinger cemetery, close to Berkley. Her tombstone inscription read: "She was a kind and affectionate wife, a fond mother and a friend to all."[94]

To quote historian Elliott Ashkenazi, "Southern diaries are permeated with a sense of tragedy in which forces more powerful than the individual shape the lives of all concerned."[95] Without a doubt, Cassie possessed significant flaws, especially in regard to her opinions about slavery. And yet, these shortcomings fail to negate the contributions her second and third diaries make to the historical record by providing a glimpse of wartime life in north Alabama, a region from which remarkably few Civil War–era diaries have surfaced. Though Cassie never spied like Belle Boyd or served in the Confederate forces like Loreta Janeta Velazquez, she believed that by keeping a diary, she made a small contribution to the war effort and history itself.[96]

ONE

When the Sun Shone Brightly: Schoolgirl Days in Washington, DC, September 12, 1859–February 4, 1860

Cassie Fennell's Journal—1859 [written before the first entry]

Sep. 12th

I have come to the conclusion this day to keep a journal of all that takes place in the ten months that I will go to school here.[1] School commenced today had 21 scholars, but expect more in a few days. Mr. Norton seems to be in a very bad humor; I don't know what is the matter unless he is mad because a young gentleman went to church with me (Mr. McJ___).[2] I feel very badly some times I almost persuaded myself that I am home-sick.

Sep. 13th

I said my lessons very well this morning and feel better satisfied than I did yesterday. Blanche Naylor and Hattie Lindsley were here this afternoon. It is very windy but I went to prayer meeting with Belle Naylor, it was led by Dr. Hill a Baptist-minister.[3] It was a very interesting meeting. Received a letter from home, all very well. No news of importance.[4]

Sep. 14th

I feel very badly this evening. I think Mr. Norton is angry at us for going to church with a lady and gentleman. Mrs. Tayman called for us and Mr. Zimmerman was with her.[5] We heard a very good exhortation from Rev. Mr. Ball, two persons made profession of religion, there was nine that went up to be prayed for.[6] Mr. Rawlings came home with me. I did not want him to come much because I was afraid Mr. Norton would not like it,—but hated to tell him not to come. I went to prayer meeting this afternoon. It was conducted by the Rev. Mr. Slidell, a Methodist-E [Episcopal] minister. The orphans were there, sung a song very prettily, there was about 45 of them, some boys and some girls.

I begin to think I should like to board with Aunt Cobb in the winter.[7]

Sep. 15th

I said my lessons very well today but Mr. Norton has not commenced marking us yet. He does not look angry today. I believe I only imagined he was angry yesterday. Miss Town came to live here today. We all like her very much. She teaches in mathematics. She is suffering much with her eyes.[8] It is very cold today.

Sister Mary and myself went to see Mrs. Tayman this afternoon, Mollie was in the parlor, we talked about our school and Miss Polk (who is dying) while we were there, the firemen marched by, they were dressed beautifully.[9] From there we went to see Belle and Blanche Naylor, they were not at home but Miss Lizzie was. She entertained us until the young ladies came in. Miss Hattie Lindsley was with them. Our conversation was about Mr. Rawlings' prayer meetings and journals. I came home just in time for tea.

Sep. 16th

It commenced raining about 12 o'clock last night and has rained incessantly ever since, but that did not prevent many of the girls attending school; I said my lessons very well this morning.

One of my acquaintances died last night (Miss Sallie Polk) rejoicing in the Lord; her funeral will take place tomorrow afternoon at 4 o'clock.[10]

As today is Friday we sat in the parlor after tea, with Mr. & Mrs. Norton.[11] Our conversation was about Ala. [Alabama] and traveling. Mr. Norton is expecting his sister today or tomorrow from New Orleans. I anticipate a great-deal of pleasure when she arrives. I have heard so much of her I think I will like her very much.

I wrote home today. Every time I write I feel like going home. Oh! How I do want to see home folks; just to think ten months before I can see them. My heart almost fails within me when I think of it. Sister has retired and it is time that I should.

Sep. 17th

It continues to rain. It has not stopped one minute today, nor does it look like it will stop soon.

I received a letter from home this morning. All were well. Ma said that they had received Cousin Ben Allison's weddings cards.[12] I should like to be at his wedding very much, but I am denied that pleasure.

I spent most of the morning sewing and writing. Cousin Web was in this evening to see us, he said he was going home soon.[13] I gave him one of Ma's letters to read. After tea I sat in the parlor but sister had a book to read so she came up to our room, Mr. Norton attempted to teach me how to play chess but I made slow progress. Just before I came up I took up this evening's paper to read. It was lying on the other side of the table not knowing that Mrs. Norton was reading it—I felt so badly about it. I did not know what to do. I begged pardon and came off as quick as possible. She tried to make me take the paper but I would not. I shall be more cautious hereafter. I have concluded not to write Sundays.

Sep. 19th

I will write today for yesterday (Sunday). I did not go to Sabbath school yesterday morning because I was there last Sunday and none of my scholars were there, but I went to church. I heard one of the best sermons I ever did hear. Mr. Marshall of Miss. [Mississippi] preached from these words "For me to live is Christ and to die is gain". Mr. Granberry [Reverend J. C. Granberry] our pastor looks very badly.[14] Mr. Marshall preached for him last Sunday also. At 5 o'clock in the afternoon we went to prayer meeting at rooms of the Young Men's Christian Association. It was led by Mr. Gurley.[15]

At night we went to the E St. Baptist Church, heard a very good sermon by Rev. Mr. Kennard of Philadelphia from 10th chap of Mark from the 17th to 22nd verses.[16] We wanted to go to the Wesley Chapel, but Mrs. Norton wanted us to go with her. Cousin Web came home with us. Belle and Blanche Naylor were with us. Saw one of the handsomest gentlemen I ever saw.

Monday Sep. 19th

I felt very low spirited this morning when I first arose. I thought I would not know my lessons and Mr. Norton commenced marking us today but I studied very hard and did not miss any in my lessons. I did not practice an hour today as I went to the prayer meeting at a Presbyterian Church on the Island. I did not learn the name of the minister that conducted it. It was a very good meeting. I lost a handkerchief in the church. Mr. Norton's sister from New Orleans arrived today about 3 o'clock. All were very glad to see her. I hope I will like her. She sings and plays beautifully. I expect she wants to give music and singing lessons.[17]

There was a great deal of music and parades in the streets today and yesterday. Belle Naylor and myself went to see Mr. Anderson. We talked about home & etc.

Cousin Web Parker was here this evening. He gave $90. I wish he would come again. It is very warm today and the sun shone beautifully.

Sep. 20th 1859

It was pouring down rain when I awoke this morning and has been raining ever since.

I said good lessons today but had to get up very early this morning to study them. Mr. Huggans was here to see me today about money, he said that Mrs. Huggans had gone to Ala., the first I had heard of it.

I sat down after dinner to do some mending thinking as it was raining I would have no company but I had hardly taken my seat when Belle Naylor was announced. She staid until after time and then Mr., Mrs. & Lou Whorton came in and staid until nearly ten; and I do not know my lessons; but intend to study tonight and get up soon in the morning.[18]

This evening Miss Lottie Norton brought in the parlor some green oranges that she had gathered from the trees in La. [Louisiana]. I never saw any (green) before.

Sep. 21st 1859

It has rained all day and is still raining. I wish it would clear up. I want to go out to pay some calls that I ought to have paid several weeks ago. I got up about 5 o'clock this morning so I could get my lessons; said them very well.

We went out this afternoon to take our music lessons, it was raining but very little when we started but it poured down before we got to Miss de Boyer's. Mr. Norton walked part the way with us. I was disappointed when I got there; she said she would have a new piece for me; but it rained so hard that she could not get out to get it.

Sat in the parlor a short time after tea, to hear Miss Lottie play and sing.

I have got my lessons for tomorrow. Got a letter from Cousin Maggie Fennell, no news.[19] I understand that Cousin Ben Allison is to be married today to Miss Mollie Gardener. I wish them a happy life.

Sep. 22, 1859

Oh! How disappointed I was this morning when I awoke to find it raining. I want to go out to do some shopping. It rained all day excepting about two hours at 12 o'clock.

We got our report books today and sister and myself have not a single *bad mark*. I said my lessons perfect today and intend to try to have them perfect all the time. Miss Lottie is sick today. She thinks her sickness was caused by traveling in the cars so long and getting so little rest.

I have been thinking about home a great deal today.

Miss Lottie sent in to borrow No. 27 of the newspaper Ledger from me a few minutes ago but I did not have it. I found I had sent it home. She concluded she could get it from some of the girls as nearly all of them take it. I must get my lessons.

Sep. 23

It was rather cloudy this morning but cleared off before 12 o'clock. It was a very pleasant day. I said my lessons as well as usual.

After dinner I went down to Mrs. Tayman's to get a Ledger I had loaned her intending to come back in a few minutes but when I got down there I found that Miss Sarah Smith had got back home and that Mollie Spates had just gotten in from the country. I sent her word that I would stay there for tea and for her to come over.

Miss Mollie said that her son Junkin said he was coming to see her so she had to go to her Aunts (she was staying there) and made us a promise that we would come over after tea and that Cousin Web would come home with us. We went and had a very pleasant time. Got home about 10 o'clock. Mr. Ayers and Mr. Zimmerman went with us. Because I looked a little solemn they said that I was in love but—Oh! How mistaken they are. I had a dream last night that troubles me a great deal.

Sep. 24th

It was sprinkling rain this morning when I got up but cleared off about 9 o'clock. Mollie Spates, Sarah Smith, Mrs. Hoyle and myself went to market this morning. I got some beautiful flowers, gave Mollie Spates and Mrs. Dalton a bouquet. Sister had to leave before we did to take her music lesson. After I came back from market Belle Naylor came for me to go to the Capitol. We went through a good many rooms; saw some new statuary and then we went into the Library and got some books with engraving in them to look at. We got back about two o'clock. After dinner Belle came for me to go to the prayer meeting at the same church we went to last Monday. It was led by Mr. Samson, a Baptist minister. I found my handkerchief that I lost last Monday. It is very warm and cloudy. I think it will rain before morning. I wrote home today.

Sep. 26th for Sep 25th

Yesterday morning we went to Sabbath school, four of my scholars were there. We remained for preaching. Mr. Granberry preached his last sermon. He is going to be chaplain of a University in Virginia. I saw three or four in tears near the close of his farewell. He preached from Luke 16th chapter 31st verse.

I intended to go to the prayer meeting at the Young Men's Christian Association rooms, but I went to sleep (I ought to be ashamed) and when I woke up I thought it too late. Mr. Norton and his mother went.[20]

At night Mrs. Norton, sister and myself went to hear Dr. Butler, an Episcopal minister. He preached from the 10 chap of Rev. He has commenced a series of sermons on the Rev. I was perfectly delighted with his sermon. I intend to attend more of them.

Sep. 26th 1859

This morning I got up by 5 o'clock and studied hard until breakfast and then I had to get Miss Town to show me how to work some sum's. All went on as usual in school today excepting a new scholar came. I have not found out what her name is yet.

After dinner I went and had my fall bonnet trimmed anew. I do not like it much. I think it has too much ribbon on one side. I think I will have it changed. I also got me a pair of kid gloves. As I came on back I stopped to see Mary Todd a few minutes.[21] As soon as I got back home I put on my new bonnet and went to see Miss Smith but she was not at home. I had not been home but a very short time when Maggie and Rose Moore came to see us. They had hardly gone when I saw Belle Naylor coming up the street. I ran down and had a short chat with her. After Belle left I went in to see Miss Town, sat with her until tea time. After tea sat in the parlor a short time to hear Miss Lottie play and now I am up in my room writing this. I must get my lessons.

Sep. 27th

I got up earlier this morning than I did yesterday. I got up as soon as I could see how to read.

Every thing went on as usual until after dinner; I went to prayer meeting this afternoon. It was led by Mr. Rogges, a Methodist minister. It was one of the most interesting meetings that I have attended. There were a great many there. Sister and Belle Naylor went with me.

Miss Sarah Smith was here this morning. She gave us tickets to a festival that is going to be at Mrs. Tayman's. We have permission from Mrs. Norton to attend but I don't know yet whether we shall go or not. After tea we went to the Wesley Chapel to a revival that is going on there. Mr. Ball preached from [illegible]. There were two ladies that went up to be prayed for. We got home about half after 9 o'clock.

Sep 28th

I awoke very early this morning and got my lessons perfect.

After dinner we had to go to take our music lessons. On the way we stopped to get Sister's bonnet trimmed and myself a headdress. I took a new piece today. After I got through my music lesson I thought I would go down to see Miss Sarah Smith as Mollie Tayman had told me this morning that she wished to see me about a festival that they are going to have there. Mrs. Norton has given us permission to go but I don't know what to wear. Cousin Web is going. I wrote to Mollie Spates today telling her when the festival was going to be. I hope she will come.

I got home from Mrs. Tayman's just in time to get ready for tea. Miss Lottie Norton went out (for the first time since she came here) today.

Sep 29th

Oh! I feel so badly tonight because I did not get perfect marks today but intend to have them (my lessons) perfect tomorrow to make up for it. Mr. Norton spoke of putting me in geometry. I think I will study it. I want to learn all I can while I stay here. After dinner was over I came up in my room to sit all the afternoon but it was not long before Belle Naylor was announced. I was glad to see her and made her spend the afternoon with us. She wanted us to go with her to prayer meeting but we could not go as we were expecting our Mantua-maker. Cousin Web came in while Belle Naylor was here. We talked about churches, ministers, beaux, etc. We walked with

Belle up to the corner of C St. I have concluded that I will wear my brocade silk to the festival but don't know for certain. I told Belle that if she would go home with me that I expected I could get her married off in less than a year; says she thinks she will go.

Sep 30th

It has looked very much like rain all day. I was afraid this morning that it would rain so that we could not go to the festival. All went along in school as usual, two of the girls are going to leave for a short time. We went down to Mrs. Tayman's directly after dinner as she wanted us to assist her in fixing the tables (I did not know until I got there what they were raising money for. They are raising it for a Sabbath school down in the country). When we got there they had got through fixing the table so I helped carry chairs up stairs. As soon as we got through in the parlor, we went up stairs to dress. I wore a light silk, black and purple shawl head-dress. We staid until half-after 12 o'clock. We heard today that Miss Tucker (Sister's SC, teacher) was married to Mr. Smith of Baltimore.

I lost a handkerchief coming from the festival.

October 1st

Oh! How tired I have felt all day. I staid up so late last night. Directly after breakfast I went down to Mrs. Tayman's to get some things that I left there last night. As soon as I came back I had to get ready to go to take my music lessons. When I got back home I got some sewing, thinking I would stay in the house all day but there I was mistaken for it was not long until Mollie Spates came and wanted me to go with her to the post office and several other places. I went home with her as she had a letter she wanted to read to me and then she wanted me to come and go with her to the Capitol but as Miss Perkins, Miss Hanson and young Mr. Perkins came in after dinner we could not go. It has been raining ever since sunset.

Sister Mary is 15 years old today; 5 ft 5 inches high; two inches taller than me. We had to write compositions today. My subject was "Mind your own business" Sisters "Order."

Oct 3rd for the 2nd as it was Sunday

It was so cloudy that we carried umbrellas to church. Heard a very good sermon from Mr. Proctor.[22] He preached from the 12th chap of Hebrews, 3rd verse. "For consider him that endured such contradictions of sinners against himself, lest ye be wearied and faint in your minds". After preaching the Sacrament was administered. I felt so unworthy that I hardly knew whether I ought to partake or not but I prayed that I might be worthy and went forward with the rest.

Dr. Sunderland had just got home and Mrs. Norton wanted me to go out in the afternoon to hear him but I wanted to read, so I did not go. At night we went to the E St. Baptist Church [and] heard Dr. Sunderland preach from the same chapter and same verse that Mr. Proctor preached from in the morning.[23] I liked his sermon very much. In time of church an old blind gentleman went to sleep just before me, he snored so loud that every body could hear him. Almost all the ladies had their fans before their faces. Mr. Norton waked him up twice but he would go to sleep again.

Oct 3rd Monday

I had all my lessons perfect this morning. Something uncommon for Monday. We nearly always miss more on that day than any other. After dinner I thought I would go out and get Sister and myself a shawl but I concluded I could not go alone, so I thought I would wait until Thursday. Miss Sarah Smith said she would go with us then. So we went up to see Mrs. Dalton. She got me to work some on a bookmark she was working. I told her that we wanted shawls and she said for us to come tomorrow afternoon and she would go with us to look at some. So Thursday we will look at dresses instead of shawls. I received a letter from Katie Fennell today.[24] Speaks of coming on in the winter. After tea I came up stairs right straight and wrote home. I could not Saturday as Sister did not get through writing until late. I feel very sleepy but have to get my lessons before I retire.

Oct 4th

I got up this morning as soon as I could see to read. Said my lessons perfect. Florence Clark, one of the school-girls came here to board today. Her room door opens into ours. She is about 11 or 12 years old. In the afternoon I went to see Mrs. Dalton to get her to go out with me to get Sister and myself a shawl apiece. I got back a little while before tea, put on my new shawl and went into Mrs. Norton's room to show it to her and Miss Lottie. They liked them very much.

After tea Mr. Zimmerman came to go with us to a singing school that is at our church.[25] We expected cousin Web but as he did not come we went without him but he came up to the church and came back home with us. It was about 9 o'clock when we got back. I wrote to Maggie Fennell today and carried it to the post office myself.

Oct 5th

The forenoon passed off today just like it did yesterday. In the afternoon we went to take our music lessons and from there I went down to see Miss Mollie Spates but she had gone out—the servant said she was going home (in the country) tomorrow. I wish she would stay here awhile. Well, I thought if Mollie was not at home I would go to see somebody any how; so I went up to see Belle Naylor and two young ladies that are staying there from the country. I do not remember their names. They were not in when I first got there but came in after awhile, had been out riding. I got home in time to comb my head before supper and lo! And behold! When I got down to the table there sat a pretty stranger, Miss Lou Norton, no relation of this family of Norton's. She intends to leave tomorrow.

Oct 6th

Every thing went on as usual before dinner today excepting one of the school girls (Daisy McDonald) came this morning to tell us all goodbye. She was going to Va. to stay four or five weeks.

After dinner we went out to look for some dress goods. Sister got a very pretty dress. I did not get any things as I did not carry enough money with me. I will have to get some from Cousin Web. Miss Sarah Smith went out with us. When she came to go with us Miss Lida Hanson was here so we had to wait until she went in to see Miss Town. I saw four gentlemen and one lady when I was out that I was acquainted with; Mr. Cooksy, McKee, Latimer and Sullivan were the gentlemen and Mrs. Latham was the lady. After tea Cousin Web came to go with us to a singing school at our church. There is four or five dozen in the singing class. I expect to go next Tuesday if Mrs. Norton does not object. She said last night she was afraid we went out too much at night.

It is very cold for this season of the year. Had to wear a shawl when I went out today.

Oct 7th

It is very cold today. It was so very cold that I had to wear a shawl this afternoon. Sister and myself wanted to go to church tonight, but we had no one to go with us. Belle and Blanche Naylor wanted to go. I went up there in the afternoon to find out whether they were going or not. Belle had been sick all day and her mother would not let her go so we all had to stay at home. Belle says she will go with us to the singing school Tuesday night if she is well enough. I told her that Mr. Knight was there the night before. I think that one reason she wanted to go. We sat in the parlor a short time after tea to hear Miss Lottie play and sing. Florence Clark has left and I am very glad of it. She was so inquisitive and besides that she said that she saw Mr. Norton kiss me which was a story. I don't like her any how.

We got a letter from Brother William today. He is going to college in Florence, Ala.[26]

Oct 8th

Directly after breakfast I went up to Miss deBoyer's to take my music lesson. The last lesson I expect to take from her. From there I went on up G St. to get myself a dress. I got a very pretty muslin. I heard today that the tight sleeve was going to be worn this winter. I hope it is a mistake. I do not like them. I wrote home today and also to Brother William. I spent nearly all the afternoon reading. Old Mrs. Norton has a good many books. She loans them to me. I did a little sewing but not much. We do not have much sewing to do. I got almost, if not quite, mad at Sister this evening. She said she had something to tell me if I would answer her correctly. I told her I would, I did not care what it was, I would tell her. Then after all that she would not tell me, it's too bad.

It commenced raining about 3 o'clock and has rained ever since.

Oct 10th for Sunday the 9th

I thought it only a little cloudy when I got up as I prepared to go to church but it was not long before I found out I was mistaken. It commenced raining before breakfast and rained all day long without stopping a single time. I do believe I thought if we could not go to church in the morning we certainly could go in the afternoon to hear Dr. Sunderland preach as it was only about two squares from here but no! It rained harder and harder so we had to give it up for the afternoon and also for the night. After tea we sat in the parlor. Miss Lottie played and we all joined in and sang. I did not like the playing part. I was never use to hearing the piano on Sunday at home and would not play myself.[27] We have been from home exactly a year yesterday (Sunday).

Oct 10th Monday

Oh it is so cold. It feels almost like winter. The girls wanted to know why Mr. Norton did not have fires in the school rooms. I think he is going to have a fire tomorrow. I sit right by the door and get all the benefit of the cold wind.

While we were at dinner we heard some one come in and go up stairs. Mr. Norton's mother was very much frightened. She thought it was robbers but we soon found out that it was our dress maker come to cut out our dresses for us. As soon as I got through with dinner I went out to find how to have my dress made. Belted bodies are going to be worn this autumn. By the time she fitted our dresses it was dark and as it was a good while before tea I thought I would go and sit with Miss Town. I had a very pleasant time and always do. We talked about painting. Mr. Huggans was here this morning to see if we could take some of Uncle Cobb's things in our rooms. He was going home. He heard that Katie was very sick.[28] We took Uncle's things.

Oct 11th

I believe nothing happened this morning uncommon excepting I saw a show pass by. There was an elephant [with] two or three men on him. It is going to stay here only one night. We are not going.[29]

While we were at dinner Belle Naylor came for us to go with her to prayer meeting but as I had to go and get some things I nor Sister could not. Mr. and Miss Norton went with her. She made me promise to go to see her tomorrow afternoon as she is going away the day after. After they left I went out to the post office and one or two stores. From there I went down to see Mrs. Tayman & Miss Smith. While I was there Mrs. Hoyle came to see me.[30] I met her on the street as I came back. After tea Cousin Web came to go with us to the singing school. We staid until 9 o'clock. It is very cold, had fire in school room.

We received a letter from home today. All were well excepting Mattie had the chills.[31]

Oct 12th

It was cold this morning but turned warm by 2 o'clock. Mr. Norton looks peevish today. Some days he gives us good marks for lessons, and perhaps if we would say them the same way he would give us bad marks but he does not do it as much as Miss Town. I wanted to go out directly after dinner to get some fringe for our new dresses but had to wait until late for Cousin Web to come. He promised to bring us money this afternoon but he did not come until after tea. I borrowed a dollar from Miss Town and went out. As I came on back I stopped to see Belle Naylor but she had gone out. I don't know what to think of her, she knew I was going to see her this afternoon.

I feel more at ease today than I have felt for a long time. I am going to try to be good so I will have nothing to feel bad about.

Oct 13th

It is some warmer today than it has been this week. Mr. Norton is as cross today as he can be. The girls penned papers on each other and Mr. Norton would not let them off. He said they must go home that way. The girls begged him to let them take them off and he would not. Nearly all the girls dislike him and I dislike him more and more every day. In the afternoon we went over on the island to see our dress maker. She was not at home so I left the things I carried over to her with a woman that is staying with her. From there I went up to see Miss deBoyer to pay her for our music lessons but she was not at home either. I thought as it was yet soon I would call on Mrs. Merchant but she had gone out too. Mr. Merchant came in the parlor.

I have a very bad cold today.

Oct 14th

Every thing went on as usual this morning excepting it commenced to rain a little while before dinner and rained until dark. I am still suffering with my cold, I feel worse than I did yesterday. It has turned into the croup and I am afraid that I will not get much rest tonight.

I intended to have gone to pay some calls this afternoon but it rained and even if it had not rained I felt so bad I could not have gone.

I wrote to Uncle John Allison and Aunt Nancy today for the first time since I came here and I have been here a year yesterday.[32] I have not sent the letter off yet as I do not know where to direct it. I will have to wait until Cousin Web comes to tell their address.

Oct 18th

Ever since the 14th I have been confined to my bed. Saturday I suffered a great deal. It was with great difficulty I could breathe. After tea Saturday Miss Town came up to see me. She saw I was suffering so much [and] proposed sending for a doctor. Mr. Norton went to get Dr. Smoot but he was sick so he went and got Dr. Garnett.[33] He said my left lung was affected and that in a short time I would have had the pneumonia. I slept very little that night but felt better next morning. Sunday was a beautiful day but Sister did not go to church as I was sick.[34] The Dr. came to see me three times while I was in bed; gave me 8 pills, half a cup full of some kind of emetic. Had my side rubbed with mustard and turpentine. It hurt me very bad but did a great deal of good. I had to drink flax-seed tea but I didn't like it.

Monday morning I felt almost well and wanted to get up but Mrs. Norton would not allow it so I had to stay in bed until dinner time. Lizzie Bradley came up in my room after school was over. It rained all day Monday. Mrs. Granberry died Monday. She was the wife of the pastor of our church and was much beloved by every one.[35]

Today (Tuesday) I got up and dressed. I expected to go down tomorrow if Mrs. Norton will let me.

It is a beautiful day and warmer than it has been for some time.

Sunday night an insurrection among the negroes commenced at Harper's Ferry.[36] There is a great deal of excitement here and the surrounding country. The soldiers were parading the streets all Monday night as it was thought that they might come on here but did not.

Oct 19th

I feel almost well today, went down to the parlor this afternoon and staid there until about 9 o'clock. Mollie Tayman came this morning to give us an invitation to a party at her mother's but of course we will not go as I am not well and Sister would not go unless I could.

I read the whole account of the insurrection from beginning to end. There was 17 killed and 5 or 6 taken prisoners. Troops were sent on from Va. to stop it. It was thought that white men had more to do with it than the negroes.[37] Some of the people here were very uneasy for fear they would come on here as they intended to do. It is right cold today. The wind is blowing.

Exactly a year today since I commenced going to school here. Expect to stay until the last of June.

Oct 20th

I went down to dinner today. Feel quite well. I expect to go to school tomorrow. It has been very cold all day feels like December, the wind is blowing very hard.

As there was no fire in my room I went down in the parlor where it was warm. Lou Whorton came in while I was there to practice on the piano. She seemed very glad to see me.

After dinner Sister & I came up in my room to write some letters but it was so cold we had to go in the school room. We sat there until tea. After tea we sat in the parlor. Miss Lottie sang and played five or six times for us. I am almost frozen. It is so cold. Time I was going to bed. I got a letter from home this afternoon.

Oct 21st

I have heard a good many persons say that this is the coldest day that they ever experienced this season of the year, old people that ought to know. I know for certain that it is the coldest that I ever saw for this time of the year. There was ice this morning but I have not seen any.

I went in school today. The girls seem glad to see me after so long an absence.

Cousin Web was here this evening. He asked Miss Lottie to play for him. She played four or five times but has such a cold that she could not sing much, she sings beautifully.

I wrote to Pa, Ma, and Aunt Charity Lea today.[38]

I wanted to walk out this afternoon but it was so very windy I could not go.

Oct 22nd

When I awoke this morning it was pouring down snow and snowed until about 12 o'clock but it all melted as soon as it touched the ground. Snow is very uncommon this time of the year. It continues to be cold but not as cold as it was yesterday.

I have been very busy all day making up some flannel and fixing up some winter dresses. I wrote a composition this morning on "The folly of trying to please every one". Mr. Norton gave all the large girls the same subject. I wrote two pages and a half but fear I shall get a very low mark for it. Sister has not finished hers yet.

We paid Miss deBoyer today for our music lessons. Mr. Norton sent in our tuition bill today but I have not the money but will have to wait until the first of new month when I will get my money. I feel very bad about it.

Oct 24th

Yesterday was one of the most beautiful and pleasant days we have had in a long time. We went to the Sabbath School in the morning. Mr. Smithson (the Superintendent) spoke very touchingly of the death of Mrs. Granberry and delivered her message to her class. Nearly every one in the room was in tears. We staid for church very unexpectedly Mr. Granberry preached. When he first commenced speaking his voice trembled with emotion. He preached from the 25 & 26 verses of 2nd chapter of 2nd Timothy. Near the last of his sermon when he spoke of leaving the church in which he had preached two years he wept and the congregation wept with him. He looked very bad. Mrs. Granberry had been dead only a week exactly. They had been married one year. At night we went to the E St. Baptist Church. Dr. Sunderland (Presbyterian minister) preached from the same words that Mr. Granberry did. Mr. Norton would hardly let me go, he was afraid I would take another cold but I wrapped up warm and went.

Monday Oct 24th

It was rather cold this morning. A light frost was lying on the ground but [melted] because [it was] very warm about the middle of the day. I had all my lessons perfect and as I got through all my lessons by two o'clock I asked Mr. Norton to let me go out. He said I might. So I came up here and got ready and went down to see Mrs. Tayman and Sarah Smith. When I asked the servant for them she did not understand me and went and told another lady I want to see her. She came down and asked me if it was her I wanted to see. I told her and she left the room in a hurry. I got back a little while before dinner. After dinner I thought I would go out but it was so late I concluded to stay and practice. I feel so bad today about various things. One is I think a gentleman is displeased at something I said about a month ago. I did not have time to explain it to him so he gave it a wrong meaning. I have been feeling bad about it ever since I said it.

Oct 25th

It has been cloudy all day and hailed a little this afternoon. It is very pleasant. After dinner I went out to walk. Sister did not feel like going so I had to go by myself. I first went and got a paper and walked up Penn. Avenue as far as 7 St. and went up as far as D St. and there I met Angy Anderson. (I didn't know that she was in the city. She has been in Paris for four or five months.)[39] She made me go back with her to purchase some things [and] after she got through we came back to 4 ½ St. and went in the Presbyterian Church to see how the workmen were getting along with it. They are enlarging it. We received a letter from home today and answered it immediately. Ma said that it was reported that Cousin Web was going to be married today to Miss Lizzie Gardener but he is in this city same as ever and not thinking about being married today.[40]

Oct 26th

It was very pleasant all this morning but toward noon it began to get cloudy. It became very cold and looked very much like snow and did snow after dark. After dinner Mrs. Norton Sr., Miss Lottie and myself went out shopping. I did not get any thing but Miss Lottie did. After they got through trading Miss Lottie and myself went to the post office. I got a letter from Maggie Pickett.[41] She had the sore eyes. We got letters for Miss Town and for Mr. Norton. Mr. Norton is sick with a cold today. Sent for a doctor but could not get him. This morning Mrs. Hoyle came to see us and invited us to a party at her house tomorrow night. We do not know yet whether we shall go or not. I should like to go very much.

Oct 27th

I think that today is the coldest day we have had this fall. The wind is blowing very hard. Just before school was out Mollie Tayman came to see me. She said that Miss Sarah Smith wanted me to come to see her as soon I could get out of school. As soon as I got through my lessons I asked Mr. Norton to let me go. It was about 2 o'clock. I went to see Miss Smith right straight. She wanted to know whether we were going to the party or not and if we were not going she wanted to borrow some things. Mr. Myers and Mrs. Tayman were in the parlor when I first got there. We did not find out whether we were going or not until after tea. Mrs. Norton said we might go if we would dress warm. Cousin Web came for us. We enjoyed ourselves very much. Got acquainted with [a] good many ladies and gentlemen. Got home ten minutes before twelve o'clock. I am in trouble about many matters.

Oct 28th

It still continues to be cold. It was so cold that the girls had to sit near the fire all the morning.

Mr. Norton is not well yet but is well enough to teach.

Going out last night did not hurt me as Mrs. Norton expected it would. I had all my lessons perfect this week and intend to study hard and be perfect all the time.

I felt rather sleepy after dinner as I did not go out this afternoon. I came up stairs got a book and lay down to read myself to sleep but it was a long time before I could sleep. I awoke about dark. I thought it was late in the night and went down to see if tea was over. After tea I sat in the parlor. Sister was in our room asleep.

Oct 29th

It is right cold and the wind is blowing today but it was not cold enough to keep me in the house all day. Sister and myself went up on the Capitol Hill to see Miss Lida Hanson. We staid there until half after twelve (their dinner hour). We thought it so early we would go to see Miss Adams but when we got near the Capitol the wind blew so hard we concluded not to go. We stopped as we came back to get some candy for my cough.

I wrote home today. Spent all the afternoon in fixing up for Sunday and reading.

Oct 31st for Oct 30th

We started off yesterday morning as soon as we got through our breakfast to the Sunday school. An Englishman spoke to the school and took so much time we did not have lessons. Only one of my scholars was there.

We remained for preaching. I did not find out the name of the preacher. He preached about 20 minutes. I thought of going to hear Dr. Sunderland preach in the afternoon but I felt tired so staid at home. Miss Wilcox was here at tea. Mrs. Norton, Sr., Miss Norton, Sister and myself went to Trinity Church to hear Dr. Butler, an Episcopal minister. He preached from the 16 Chap of Rev, pouring out of the 5th vial, one of the most interesting sermons I have heard in a long time. I intend to go there often.

Oct 31st Monday

I hardly know how I feel today. I know for certain I feel very bad about something but what it is, is hard to tell. There are so many things that I feel bad about I would give almost anything to [be] perfectly contented for one week but that cannot be until I leave this city.

I had my lessons perfect today. After school I practiced until after the dinner bell rang. After dinner I came up here and studied and read the remainder of the afternoon. After tea we sat in the parlor until nearly nine. Miss Lottie played some beautiful songs.

We received a letter from Ma. & Johnnie today.[42] Oh! How I wish I could see them all. It seems as if I cannot wait until next June.

November 1st 1859

There was a heavy frost this morning. The first of any consequence that we have had this year. The sun shone all day beautifully. Some think we will have the Indian summer yet. I hope we will. I am tired all ready of cold weather.

I have been suffering all day with the headache and I fear I am going to be sick again. We got a letter from home today and I got one from Maggie Fennell. I was very glad indeed to hear from my Ala. friends.

After tea I sat in the parlor and read the New York Ledger. Miss Lottie did not play as she has a bad cold.

Nov 2nd

There was frost again this morning but became very warm by noon. I am still suffering with the headache; went to see Dr. Garnett today but he was not in but after tea Mrs. Norton gave me some medicine which I hope will do me some good.

After dinner I went down to see Cousin Web about getting money (it was directly after dinner and the parlor was crowded with gentlemen). I felt abashed and staid but a short time. He said that he would come to see me this evening. He came after tea and gave me $45. From there I went to see Mrs. Dalton and she went with me to see Mrs. Crawford who lives in the same house and then we (Mrs. D and I) went to see the Doctor but he was not at home.

I forgot to bring the ink up from the school room. I can hardly write with this. I read today that [John] Brown, the captain of the insurrection, is condemned to be hung the 12th of next month. I was afraid he would get loose. There has been great excitement about Brown's trial.[43]

I know if Ma knew I was sick she would be very uneasy, therefore I never write I am sick.

Nov 3rd

As I have the good ink I will try to write better than I did yesterday. I was so provoked to find out last night after I got through writing to find out that Sister had brought the ink up stairs and I was trying to write all that time with the other. Oh, it has been a lovely day. There was frost this morning but became very warm by the time school was out. My head felt quite well this morning until after I went into school. It began to ache again but does not ache now. After dinner Sister and myself went up to see Miss deBoyer and to pay a little debt that we owed her. I stood at the door until Sister went in to see her. From there we intended to go to see Miss Moore but it was so late we thought we would stop to see Angy Anderson. When we got there she was not in so went down 7th St. and got some paper and then it was time we were coming home. We got in company with Miss Town coming back.

Nov 4th

This has been a beautiful day. I think we have our Indian Summer at last. A while before school was out Mrs. Dalton & Mrs. Merchant came to see me. They said they were afraid that I was sick as I had not been to see Mrs. Dalton yesterday to get her to go with me to see Dr. Garrett.

After dinner Sister and I went up to see the Miss Moore's. When we got there we found out that they had moved. We could not find out where to. A little boy came to the door that use to come to see Uncle last winter. I have forgotten his name. I believe it was Willie Dunn. We went from there down on Penn Av. to do some shopping. Mrs. Blackwell (Mrs. Norton's sister) arrived here from New York this evening. She is very pleasant and reminds me of Aunt Mary Parker.[44] I wrote home this afternoon.

Nov 5th

Directly after breakfast we dressed to go to see Miss Perkins who lives a long way from here but it was so early I concluded to write some letters before we started. I wrote to Cousin Maggie Fennell & put up a paper to send to Pa. I told Maggie what the fashions were and drew some patterns. We started to Miss Perkins about 11 o'clock. When we got there we found that she was not at home so we came on back by Mrs. Townsend's to see Henrietta. While we were there her brother (about 13 or 14 years old) came in and shook hands with us. We had never seen him before nor had an introduction. We could not keep from laughing.[45] From there we went to see Mrs. Massie about rooms for Uncle as we got a letter from him this morning requesting us to do so. We went up to see Mrs. Dalton while there. We did not go out after dinner but staid in and fixed up our things for next week.

November 7th for the 6th

Yesterday was rather colder than Saturday. The wind blew all the fore noon but calmed off toward dark. We went to Sabbath School in the morning and

I received a new scholar into my class. After school we went up in to the church and heard a very good sermon by Mr. Cross (the Presiding Elder). His subject was Christian's Hope. After preaching had the communion. About 60 or 70 persons communed. Had love-feast in the afternoon but we did not go as it was so far. Miss Lottie was very anxious to go [as] she *had never* been to one but her mother thought it best for her to stay.

We went to hear Dr. Butler (Trinity Church) at night. He preached a very interesting sermon from the 16 chapter of Rev. the pouring out of the sixth vial. Mr. Cooksey came home with me and Mr. Zimmerman came with Sister. I don't know what Mrs. Norton & Miss Lottie thought but they did not say anything about it. I hope Mr. & Mrs. Norton did not hear of it.

Nov 7th

This has been one of the most beautiful days that we have had since fall set in. One of the young ladies (Miss Ellis) who has not been to school for some time and who has been sick came to school today. We were all very glad to see her. Another is very ill (Miss Whorton). As soon as dinner was over I went over to see how she was getting along but no one came to the door. I rang the bell three times.

Sister braided my hair which took up the remainder of the afternoon. She braids my hair about once every week. She says she wants to learn how to braid well enough for me to wear it to parties in the winter.

I am in want of dresses but have to wait until Aunt Cobb comes. It looks like every body has more clothes than we have and can dress with much more taste.

Nov 9th

It has been very cloudy all day. I was almost sure that it would rain or snow but it has not done either. It is very pleasant. We have not had any fire today.

I had all my lessons perfect today. At recess I got Blanche Naylor (as she was going out) to get me the New York Ledger. We get it one week and Mrs. Norton gets it the next. It is very interesting.

I did not go out in the afternoon but I think I ought to take a walk every day.

I begin to look forward to the time when Aunt Cobb will come not quite a month now. Oh! I shall be so glad to see her and I expect too that Cousin Katie Fennell will come with her.

Nov 9th

It was cloudy again today and very pleasant. Everybody nearly was talking about the pleasant Indian Summer. Lou Whorton (who I visited was sick) came in school at recess and she was coming to school tomorrow. Mrs. Norton is sick; the Doctor has been here all afternoon.

After dinner I went to see Mrs. Hoyle and Campbell. When I went in the parlor Mrs. Lindsley was playing on the piano but stopped as soon as she saw me. I had not been there very long until a young lady called on Mrs. Hoyle and Lindsley. I had an introduction to her but did not understand her name. From there I went to see Mrs. Naylor. She and Blanche were both in the parlor. Lizzie Bradley said she was coming here tonight but did not come. Mrs. Naylor and Miss Lizzie Naylor came but as Mrs. Norton was sick they went back home without going in the parlor. After I came up stairs, I enjoyed myself trying my fortune by a book that Lizzie Bradley had here.

Nov 10th

It has been very pleasant today although it rained this morning a little. The fog was as thick this morning that I could hardly see across the street.

Mrs. Norton became the mother of a fine son last night.[46] I went in to see him directly after school. He is a large, fat baby, got black hair and dark blue eyes. Mrs. Norton is very well or as well as could be expected.

Bettie Tobbits's sister (Mrs. Grimes) died yesterday, therefore Bettie was not at school yesterday nor today. She died very suddenly. Her baby died a short time after she did.

We went to see Mrs. and Angy Anderson today. Angy was out but Mrs. Anderson we saw. She was not well. Most of our conversation was about slavery.

After tea Cousin Webb came to go with us to see the Panopticon of the War in India. We saw two or three battles fought and the cities of Calcutta & Delhi. Delhi is one of the most beautiful cities I ever saw. The king's palace was beautiful, made of pure white marble. The soldiers moved rather slow but it looked right well. The last scene was a storm at sea. We could see the ships rock up and down. Sometimes they would almost sink then again be thrown up on the top of some large billow.[47]

[Editors' note: Along the outer edge of this page is written: "Nov. 10th 1872. Sunday. Three children house keeping at Uncle John Allison's old home."]

Nov 11th

Oh! I have been so busy all day. I had sewing to do after school which took until dark to finish. Mrs. and Miss Norton, Sister and myself thought we would like to go to hear a celebrated Irish minister speak about the great revival in Ireland. He was very eloquent. He spoke of the United States as "this Great Country". He has only been in the country two or three weeks. I saw a good many of my acquaintances there but did not speak to any of them excepting Miss Hanson & Miss Anderson. The house was crowded to overflowing.[48]

After we came back we went in to get supper. After we four had sat down Mr. Norton came in and took his place. We all commenced turning our plates up and Mrs. Norton had poured out a cup of coffee and I was just about to hand Sister the bread when Mrs. Norton said "Stop! Cassie, Stop!" I did not know what was the matter but Mr. Norton bowed his head and commenced asking the blessing. I was convulsed with laughter and Miss Lottie was too but we had to look as solemn as we could. I felt ashamed to laugh but could not help it. I will be sure hereafter to wait for the blessing.

Nov 12th

I intended to have gone to the prayer meeting this morning but I did not finish some letters that I intended to before breakfast. Mrs. Norton Sr. and Mr. Norton went.

After I had finished my letters (one home and the other to Maggie Pickett) I carried them to the post office and stopped at one store as I came back. Saw no one that I was acquainted with except Mrs. Todd. I commenced sewing as soon as I got back and sewed until nearly dark. After supper I intended to have gone in the parlor but as Mrs. Norton is sick they never have music after tea now. I came up into our room and read until near time for bed and then wrote this. I must get ready for bed.

Nov 14th for 13th

Although it looked very much like raining yesterday morning we went to the Sabbath School. We were not there long before it commenced to pour down rain. There were a great many there for the day. A strange minister spoke to the school. He also preached from 7 verse of the 12 chap of Eccl. "Remember now thy creator in the days of thy youth while the evil come not & c". He came down from the pulpit and stood in front of it. He said he did it because he was going to preach to the children. His sermon was very interesting. Mr. McJ____Jr. came home with me. He has been a long time offended at me (so I think) but yesterday I explained every thing to him in a satisfactory manner. I told him about two months ago that he had not better come to see me while I was boarding here but he did not exactly understand me and thought that I had commanded him not to come any more. Oh! The wind did blow so hard, it almost blew us away coming from church.

We went to hear Dr. Butler preach at night. He preached a very interesting sermon from the 16, 17 & 18 chapters of the Rev. I thought that I would go through all the forms with them (they are Episcopalians) but when it came to praying aloud I could not do that. It seemed to me that I could not raise my voice above a whisper. I saw several of the school girls and two gentlemen that I am acquainted with. In the afternoon I went into Miss Town's room to read for her as her eyes are so sore that she cannot read for herself. I think I shall go in and read to her every Sabbath.

Nov 14th Monday

This has been a beautiful but very cold day. It feels like winter and I think if it is much colder than this in winter we cannot stand it.

One of the girls (Daisy McDonald) that has been absent a long time returned to school today. Bettie Tobbits came also but dressed in black for her sister. As soon as school was over I went in to see Mrs. Norton and the baby, but he was asleep so I could not see his eyes. It looks like he always goes to sleep when he thinks it is time I was coming. After dinner Miss Lottie and myself went to the prayer meeting at the Lutheran Church corner of 11 & H Sts. Mrs. & Miss Anderson came back part of the way with us.

When I went down to the tea table and turned up my plate I found a letter there from home dated Nov. 2nd. It has been 12 days coming. Ma wanted to know if we would like to come home when Cousin Web goes but as he is not going until January I think we can stay until we graduate.

Cousin Web has been here and brought us another letter from Ma. He told us of the death of Kate Huggans. Her father got there in time to see her before her death.

Nov 15th

After I had got through writing last night Mrs. Tayman and Mr. Cooksey came to see Sister and I. I did not have room on the other page.

We have had a lovely day, rather cool but still the sun shone out all day very bright. After recess a little while Miss Sarah Smith came to see us and as I had no more lessons Mr. Norton let me out of school. She staid until the dinner bell rang. She invited me to go down and take dinner with her tomorrow but I guess I will not go.

After dinner I went out to see one of my Sunday School scholars, Annie Till, but could not find her home. I then went over on 7 St. to make some purchases and down on the Avenue met Mr. Patterson and passed by Mrs. Matthews but she did not see me. I saw Mr. Cooksey in one of the stores.

Nov 16th

It looked very much like rain this morning but the sun came out about 12 o'clock and was very pleasant the reminder of the day.

I wanted to call on some ladies that I have not been to see in a long time but could not go as I had to go and hunt up some of my Sabbath School scholars. I found where two of them live on I St. They said that they were going to start to the Baptist Sabbath School next Sunday. Their mother was a very nice looking woman and said that she would send her little girl to school next Sunday. From there we went to 7 St. to do some shopping.

I was very tired when I got home but cut out some work (a skirt) and have finished it. After tea Miss Lottie came in our room and sat awhile. I begin to feel sleepy and think it time to retire.

I feel happier today than I have felt in a long time.

Nov 17th

It looked cloudy again today and I was almost certain that it would rain but was mistaken for it cleared off and was very pleasant.

I hardly knew whether to go out after dinner or not but at length concluded to go to see Mrs. Tayman and Miss Smith. Mr. Upperman was standing in the door when I got there but turned around as soon as he saw me and ran up stairs. I found Mrs. Tayman sick in bed and Miss Smith had gone out but I was not there long before she came in. Mrs. Tayman said she had a chill and that her brother had one too that morning.

I found two letters under my plate when I went down to tea. One was from Aunt Cobb & Katie Fennell. The other from Sister Charity.[49] I hardly know how to answer Aunt's letter.

Oh! How I wish I could write every thought on this paper but am afraid some body will see it some day. I don't feel so much at ease as I did yesterday.

Nov 18th

It has been raining nearly all day but nearly all the girls were here. I think the rain has done a great deal of good. It was so very dusty before. After school I went into Miss Town's rooms to see about a mark she gave me in one of my lessons. She said that she would not make out the average until just before I leave for home.

I wrote home today. Wrote six pages and could have written more but was afraid that the letter would be too heavy.

We had an invitation from Blanche Naylor to go to her house tonight. They were going to have some tableaux. But we are not going it rains so hard.

There is great excitement here about the insurrection at Harper's Ferry. There have been new outbreaks.

Nov 19th

The sun shone out very pleasant but the wind blew right strong. I intended to have gone to the Capitol with Miss Lottie but the wind blew so hard and as Mr. Norton was going I thought I would not go.

I wrote to Sister Charity today. I had so much to write that I hardly knew where to begin. If she was here I would have so much to tell her that I cannot write. Somehow I cannot tell Sister Mary everything like I could Sister C. [Charity] or Ma.

In the afternoon Sister went with Mrs. Norton Sr. to the prayer meeting. I staid and went in to see Lou Whorton who has not been to school for several days. She has had a very bad cold and now is suffering with her throat. Mr. & Mrs. Whorton both were in the room when I went in but left soon after. Mr. Whorton kissed Lou very affectionately when he went out.

Miss Brewster came here to board this morning but I have not seen her yet. We went to the Young Men's Christian Association rooms to hear Dr. Sampson lecture on the Old Testament.[50] Cousin came home with us as Mr. Norton had to stay to a prayer meeting.

Nov 21st for 20th

Yesterday morning, when we went down to breakfast Miss Brewster was at the table and what was my surprise to find that she is a lady that I became acquainted with last winter but I thought her name was Steel and did not speak as if I had ever seen her before but after breakfast when we started to the Sabbath School she was going a short distance on the same street she asked me if we were not the persons she saw last winter. Then I explained to her why I did not recognize her.

After I had got through with my class Mr. McJ___ came and took a seat by me. [He] wanted to know why I did not go to the Capitol Saturday. (I had told him that I was going).

Rev. Mr. Bates preached for us from the 1st & 2nd verses of the 63rd Psalm. He is the pastor of the Protestant Methodist Church. Nearly all of his congregation were there, therefore the house was filled to overflowing and the choir sang beautifully. Mr. Zimmerman came home with us. He told us that *500 troops* had passed through the city that very morning (Sunday). We saw some of them. They were on their way to Harper's Ferry as there had been a fresh outbreak. Burning houses and shooting people is very common there. Here in the afternoon 500 troops more came over from Va. but did not start for Harper's Ferry until this morning. I believe some of them are going to Charleston as Old Brown is confined there. He is to be hung on the 2nd of Dec.[51]

We went to hear Dr. Butler at night. He preached from the 19, 20, & 21st chapters of the Revelation. Mrs. & Miss Norton, Sister and myself went together but had not been there long before Mr. Norton and Mrs. Blackwell came in. We did not know that they were going.

Nov 21st

The sun shone very brightly this morning until about 11 o'clock and then it became very cloudy, commenced raining about 3 o'clock and has been raining ever since. I wanted to take a walk this afternoon but it rained so hard that I could not go.

After dinner I sat in the school room and read until I could not see the letters and then came up stairs lay down and slept until the tea bell rang. Sister did not go down. She very seldom eats any supper.

The fire bell has just been ringing. I think the fire is on the Capitol Hill. I can see the light of the fire but cannot tell exactly where it is. Yesterday there was a large fire on 7th Street, five houses were burnt to the ground.

I started with one of the girls to the door when school was out when one of them called out "come here Cassie, come quick". I ran to the door to see what was the matter and behold when I got there it was nothing but a young gentleman of my acquaintance (Mr. Myers) whom they often try to plague me about. I wonder what he thought to see me running to the door in such a hurry.

Nov 22nd

Oh! We have had a lovely day. It looked a little like raining in the morning but soon cleared off. Miss Lottie and Mrs. Blackwell intended to have gone to Mount Vernon but just as they were going to start Mr. Norton came in and said that the boat was not going down today. They were very much disappointed.

After dinner I wanted to go see Mrs. Dalton & Crawford but just as I got on my bonnet Miss Lottie came and said some one wanted to see me. I went down in the parlor but no one was there. I thought maybe that some one was standing at the door but no one was there. I asked the servant, she said that Miss Hanson was in Miss Town's room. She staid till late so I could not go to see any one. I promised her that I would meet her at the Capitol tomorrow.

I received a letter from home and from Bro. Willie.[52] Cousin Web came after ten and staid late. We told Mrs. Blackwell goodbye before we came up as she is going away tomorrow.

Nov 23rd

I was in great trouble this morning about my lessons. I thought that I did not know them but I said them all perfect.

At recess I asked Mr. Norton to let Sister and I out of school as soon as we had said all of our lessons. He let us go as soon as we had finished our lessons and we went right straight to the Capitol to meet Lida Hanson. We went in the Rotunda first as she said she would be there but she had not come so we went into the East-Capitol grounds to wait for her. We waited about a half an hour and ____ came had three ladies with her. I have forgotten, we went down in the basement to get weighed but the workman had gone so went back and got a gentleman that we were acquainted with and went on top of the dome. We were about 200 feet above the ground. We were on our way home when Mr. Norton said he expected we could get weighed at another place so we went there. Sister weighed 112 pounds, Miss Hanson 105 and I 120, more than any.

Thanksgiving Day, Nov 24th

It looks like a day of Thanksgiving. The sun has shone as brightly all day and it has been so warm and pleasant for this season of the year.

We went to our own church to hear Mr. Bates (Protestant Methodist minister) preach. He preached a very good sermon from the 8th & 9th verses of the 66 Psalms. I did not like it quite as well as the sermon he preached last Sunday. There was not as many there as there is on the Sabbath. I wish I knew who our pastor is going to be next year. I think we will get him in about two weeks.

All the afternoon I spent in reading a book that Miss Lottie loaned me.

I feel sleepy but have to get my lessons for tomorrow.

Too bad!

Nov 25th

The girls all wanted Mr. Norton to give holiday today as well as yesterday (as some of the schools had) but he would not. He said he never had given the day after thanksgiving and never intended to.

It has looked very cloudy all day and commenced raining about 3 o'clock. I promised Blanche Naylor that I would carry her the Ledger and was getting ready to go when Angy Anderson called. She had not been to see us since she came home from Philadelphia. She did not stay very long. I walked as far as the Avenue with her and there concluded that I would go to see Miss Smith and Mrs. Tayman. When I went in the parlor Mr. Myers and Mollie Tayman were in there. Miss Smith was in but Mrs. Tayman not, but came in before I left. We sat in the parlor after tea. Miss Lottie played and sang some very pretty songs. I do not like her singing but she plays very well.

Nov 26th

Oh! It has been so warm and sunny today. I could not resist the temptation to go out. So about 11 or 12 o'clock I started out. Sister could not go as she had to be examined on her chemistry. I first went up on the Avenue and bought some things and then went up to see Mrs. Dalton & Crawford by the way of the Post Office. They (Mrs. D. & C.) were busy preparing for the orphans' fair that is going to take place in December.

We expect Aunt Cobb a week from today. After tea we went with Mr. Norton & Miss Lottie to hear Dr. Sampson lecture at the Young Men's Christian Association rooms on the first chapter of the Old Testament. There was a good many there. Cousin Web came home with us. He told me that he had seen Mr. Huggans since he came from Ala. and that Mrs. H. came with him. I did not know that they had got back.

I wrote home today. I think I write worse today than I ever did before. Not quite as bad as I have seen you [herself] write before.

Nov 28th for 27th

We went as usual to the Sabbath School but as there was to be no preaching we went with Miss Williams (Sister's teacher) to the Wesley Chapel to hear Mr. Morgan preach.[53] I do not like him, he jumps about so much and he speaks so low when he gives out the hymns that I could not understand him nor his text but his subject was "God's Love". I saw a good many of my acquaintances. The house was crowded. We staid at home all the afternoon and read and slept a good part of the time. I went to sleep and forgot to go into Miss Town's room to read to her. In the evening we went to the Trinity church. Dr. Butler preached on the Millennial. A very long and interesting sermon. Mr. Norton went with us there but did not stay but as there [were] four of us (Mrs. & Miss Norton, Sister and myself) we thought we would not be afraid to come back alone and after church Miss Brewster joined us making five in all. About nine o'clock a good many soldiers marched by. I did not learn who they were.

Nov 28th

I felt bad all this morning because I thought I did not know my lessons and sure enough I did not get perfect marks in two lessons. I think Mr. Norton gave me a bad mark when he ought not to because one girl missed the same and he gave her a perfect mark.

Directly after recess three ladies called on us. They were Mrs. & Miss Clare and Mrs. Claget. They did not stay long and I was glad of it. My hair was so rough Sister did not go into the parlor. In the afternoon I went up to see Mrs. Huggans who looks very bad and cried nearly all the time I was there. She did not say anything about Kate. I felt so sorry for her. I stopped at the Post Office and Mrs. Dalton's as I went on there. I gave Mrs. Dalton some ribbon for the fair. Got one letter for Mrs. Norton, Sr. As I was coming home I met Mr. & Miss Norton going to the office but they turned back with me when they found that I had been there. After tea Cousin Web came in to see us. He said he was going home next week. Before he left Miss L. Naylor & Mrs. Smith came in to see Mrs. Norton. Lou Whorton was in there this afternoon and says that she thinks she will come to school tomorrow. She is nearly well. The girls say that Mr. Myers was married today at 12 o'clock to Miss Smith. [A] good many went to see him married.

Nov 29th

The morning passed off as usual in school excepting that the girls said when they got to the church yesterday that no one was there and that Mr. Myers was not going to be married. We laughed a good deal at them for going without an invitation.

After dinner I went to see Mrs. Tayman to see Sarah. There was about a dozen in the parlor when I was there but did not know them all. Sarah said that Mr. Myers was not married nor thinking of such a thing.

It has been very rainy all day.

I do not know my lessons but will study before I retire.

Angy Anderson was to see us today. She is very well since she came home.

Nov 30th

It has been cloudy all day and rained a little after dinner.

Mr. Huggans was [in] to see me this morning. He wanted to see if there were any boarding houses near here that had rooms that would suit Uncle. I hardly knew where to go but as there are as many boarding houses here I could hardly miss if I wanted to go to almost any of them. Miss Lottie said she would go with me if [I] wanted company. I was very glad for I dislike very much to go by myself. We first went to Miss Polk's. Miss Lottie is acquainted with her and introduced her to me. We thought we would take a walk up the Avenue. I met a good many persons of my acquaintance. We stopped at Mrs. Holmead's to look at some of her rooms.[54]

After tea Cousin Web Parker came to go with us to hear the Swiss Bell Ringers. Oh! I was perfectly delighted. I can not imagine how they play tunes on bells. They sang too but I like the playing on the bells best. They also played on the harp and several other instruments. There was a very large crowd there.[55]

December 1st

It has been very warm all day. It was so warm in the school room that it gave me the headache. I would have put on a thin dress this evening but was afraid I would take [a] cold.

After dinner I thought I would go and look at some more rooms for Uncle but first went up to see Miss Andrews and Mrs. Huggans but both were out. We saw Miss Andrews come down the steps just before we got there with another lady.

Mrs. Dalton was at Mrs. Huggan's boarding house. [I] had just gone there and found she was out. We walked back to Mrs. Dalton's door with her and came on back by the Post Office but Mr. Norton had been there.

I stopped at Mrs. Ervin's to see some of her rooms. She carried me into a room where two ladies were but I suppose they are going to leave soon or she would not have that room to let.[56]

Dec 2nd

It has been a warm and clear day. The warmest day we have had in two months (I think).

The streets begin to look crowded like they do in winter. People are pouring in from all directions for Congress opens on Monday.

We have been expecting Uncle Cobb today or tomorrow. I hardly think he will come tonight.

Mr. Norton is also expecting Mr. & Mrs. Doolittle every day. They are going to board here this winter. He is a member of Congress. I do not know which state he is from.[57]

Mr. Norton's mother and Miss Town had a little dispute this morning. Miss Town said it made her so nervous to hear us all talk about a dissolving of the Union that she could hardly hold her knife and a great deal more that was enough to make Mrs. Norton angry. We were talking about the abolitionists and about the execution of Brown which took place today. I believe it was pretense, [she] made out as if she had finer feelings than any of us. She said I was so deeply grieved that I did not like to hear it talked about (nonsense!). I can't blame her much for it is enough to make anyone feel badly to think of disunion.[58]

Dec 3rd

It has been cloudy and rainy all day but I have enjoyed myself very well in the house as we had company all day.

This morning I was cleaning up by the time Aunt and cousins would get here and had just given the finishing touch when the servant came up and said that they were in the parlor. I was in such a hurry that I almost fell down the steps. They were not here long when Uncle came. Aunt and Uncle Cobb soon left to look for a boarding house but Kate & Sarah staid with us. I had so much to ask them about that I did not know where to begin and am so nervous now that I can hardly write. We do not know yet where we will board. I had rather go with Aunt. Kate & Sarah will board at the same place with us.[59] I have had the headache all day. It is very cold. Trees [are] covered with ice.

Mr. and Mrs. Doolittle arrived here today. He is a Senator from Wisconsin.

Dec 5th for 4th

Yesterday it rained all day so that we could not go to church in the morning nor evening.

Kate & Sarah were very uneasy about Uncle and Aunt Cobb. They did not know what had become of them. Uncle promised he would be here Saturday evening but he did not.

In the afternoon we all went down into the parlor to hear Miss Lottie sing and play.

I am seventeen today and I will soon appear in the world as a grown lady but I know I will always feel like a child.

Dec 5th

It has been raining incessantly ever since Saturday morning and does not look like stopping soon. Mr. Norton let us out at 11 o'clock so that those who wish to could go up to the Capitol to see Congress open. We did not go but Mr. Norton and his mother did. They said that there was a large crowd there. I intended to have gone but the rain prevented me. Uncle & Aunt Cobb were here about half past eleven o'clock. They concluded to let Kate and Sarah board here and they board next door.[60] We all had rather have gone with them but we are very well satisfied.

We have changed our dining hour. We have breakfast at 8 o'clock, dinner at 5 o'clock (dark) have only two meals excepting lunch at 12 o'clock.

Cousin Web and Aunt came in after supper. Cousin is going home soon.

Dec 7th

It has been raining all day but just at dark commenced hailing and snowing. The ground looks quite white [and] it is turning very cold.

We all went over to see Aunt after school and she and Uncle came to see us after tea. Uncle wanted to see about some boxes that we have been keeping for him this summer.

I wrote to Maggie Fennell this evening and to Charity Henry too.[61]

Some times since Kate and Sarah came I have felt more home sick than I have since I came here.

I think we are better satisfied to stay here than we were at first. We have a very pleasant time.

December 8th

Oh! It is so cold I believe it is cold as it ever gets to be in Ala. The girls said this morning that the pavements were so slippery from the sleet and ice that they could hardly walk. I think some of the small ones fell down.

Directly after school we went over to see Aunt. Mrs. and Miss Clare were there when we went in but soon left and then we started out to look at some bonnets. We got some beautiful ones. Mine and Sarah's were blue and Sister's and Kate's were pink. We carried them into Mrs. Norton's room to let her see them. She liked them very much.

We went over to Aunt's after tea but did not stay very long. Cousin Web was here to see us this evening. He is going home Saturday.

Dec 12th

I have been so busy that I have not had time to write since last Thursday. Mr. Norton has given us every day a piece of poetry to get so that it takes up all my spare moments that I used to devote to writing. It still continues cold but not as cold as it was last week.

Friday I did not go any where excepting to do some shopping and over to see aunt. Saturday morning I went out with Aunt (Cousins & Sister went to market with Cousin Web). I got a new dress. We went in to look at some pianos as we came back but did not rent one yet.

In the afternoon Sister and I went and had our Ambrotypes taken to send home by Cousin Web who started home Saturday evening.[62] I was sorry to see him go.

Sunday we went as usual to Sabbath School and church. Our new pastor was there but did not preach. I have forgotten the preacher's name. He preached an excellent sermon from the 24 verse of the 15th chapter of Job. We did not go out in the afternoon excepting to see Aunt. At night we went to the Wesley Chapel or at least Mrs. & Miss Norton, Kate & myself went. Sister had a bad cold so she could not go. Mr. Ball preached a very good sermon on friendship. I could not understand the text. Mr. Cooksey came home with me. I saw Mr. and Mrs. Crawford and spoke to them. Every thing passed off as usual today excepting the dress-maker came here this afternoon to fit some dresses on us all. After dinner went to see Aunt. Kate & Sarah have retired and I think it time that I should go too.

Dec 13th

It has been quite pleasant today but looks very much like snow this evening.

After school Kate and I went over to see Aunt about getting some trimmings for our new dresses. We met Belle Naylor at the door. I was very glad to see her as she has been from home. She was coming to see Mrs. Norton and the baby.

We went up between 10 and 11 Sts. to get our trimming. We stopped a few minutes at Mrs. Naylor's. Belle and Blanche were in the parlor. When we got back home our dress maker was here waiting for us. The dinner bell had rung so we had to hurry through trying on our dresses. We received a letter from home this evening. Ma was uneasy about my health but I think I am as well as I ever was.[63]

Dec 18th

It seems as if [I] cannot find time to write every night like I did before Kate and Sarah came.

The snow has been laying on the ground ever since Wednesday morning but it has been raining today. I staid in the house all day Wednesday and Thursday excepting going in to see Aunt. Friday, Sarah and myself went to see Mrs. Merchant but as she was at dinner we did not go in but left our cards. From there we went to see Mrs. Dalton and Miss Anderson. We went up to Mrs. Dalton's room. Mr. Dalton came in while we were there. The rest of Brown's companions were hung today, Friday.[64]

We have got a piano in our room to practice on. But do not practice much.

Dec 24th

It seems as if I can not find time to write of late. My studies take up so much of my time.

This week has passed away so swiftly that I can hardly believe it is Saturday again.

I have not been any where this week excepting out shopping and Thursday we (Kate & I) went to see Mrs. Powell, and Angy & Mrs. Anderson who were just starting to the prayer meeting so we did not stay long. At night Miss Lottie and I went to see Mrs. Naylor's family. They were all at home and we had a very pleasant time. Friday we rode around with Aunt to leave our cards at the Secretaries and President's. We went into the President's house.

Today (Saturday) we went up to the House of Representatives to hear them debate. It is very cold, coldest weather I ever saw.

Tomorrow is Christmas and Aunt has given us some very nice presents. We have bought Mr. & Mrs. Norton a very pretty one.

We have holiday until Tuesday after next.

Dec 26th for 25th (Christmas)

Yesterday it was very cold but it turned warm before night and we all thought it would rain but we were mistaken. We started for the Sabbath School as soon as we got our breakfast and we got there late. We staid over to church. Mr. Proctor, our pastor, preached a very interesting and appropriate sermon. We went over to see Aunt as soon as we got home and asked her to go with us to the Catholic Church. We started as soon as we got our dinner. The ceremonies were very interesting but I did not understand them. At night we went to the Wesley Chapel. Mr. Ball preached but I do not like him much. He is so slow and his words are hard to understand.

Dec 26th

Today has been a lovely day. It has been very warm for the season. I would like to have this kind of weather all the winter but of course we will not. Today was celebrated as Christmas here by firing cannons, fire-crackers and making all kinds of noises.

In the morning we went up to the Smithsonian but it was closed so we could not go through. There were several other ladies just behind us that were very much disappointed as they were strangers here. As we came back we stopped at several stores to get some little things among which there was a head-dress for Miss Town. I carried it to her room as I came up. She seemed very glad to get it and was very thankful.

After tea Miss Lottie and I went up to Mrs. Naylor's to get some rice for Mr. Norton as the stores were closed. Miss Town gave us all some almonds, raisins, and apples. Lou Whorton staid here a good while after tea. We enjoyed ourselves very much.

Dec 27th

Today was another warm day just cold enough to be pleasant.

In the morning Aunt, Miss Lottie, Lizzie Bradley, Kate, Sarah, Sister and myself went up to the Capitol. We intended to have gone all through the Capitol before we went to the House of Representatives but we did not meet the boy that was to show us the way through. We thought we would secure seats in the House. We sat there some time before we saw any one that we were acquainted with. At last we saw Mr. McJ___. I bowed to him as he came up where I was and staid until it was time for the House to open. Then he had to go. We sat there until we were tired and thought we would go some where else. We went into all the principle rooms including the Senate.

Sarah & I went up to the Post Office when we got back. I think I shall not go to the Capitol again soon.

Dec 28th

The first thing that greeted any eye this morning was the snow which was about an inch deep. It continued snowing all day and is snowing yet. Every thing looks beautiful. I saw two or three sleighs pass today. They were the first I ever saw. I think I should like to take a sleigh ride so much.

I did not go out excepting to see Aunt.

I can think of nothing to write so I will have to close my remarks. Hoping I will have something new for tomorrow.

Dec 29th

Nothing new to write today. It has been snowing all day. Went over to see Aunt and as Uncle wanted to sleep we went down in the parlor. Lou and Mr. Whorton and several others were in there but I have forgotten their names.

Dec 30th

Oh! The sun has been shining so brightly all day. The snow was five inches deep this morning. I got up from the breakfast table and measured it with a knife. Mrs. Doolittle said it was but 2 ½ inches and I did that to prove that it was deeper. There has been a great deal of sleighing today. I think I should like to take a ride very much if it was not so cold. Aunt was over here this morning [but] did not stay very long. Went in to see Lou Whorton this evening. Several persons were in the parlor.

Dec 31st

Today is the last day of this eventful year and I do think it is the shortest year I ever saw but I have heard persons say that "the older they grow the swifter time passes away". If that is the case I cannot imagine how next year will appear.

We went out shopping this morning with Aunt. The ground was frozen so hard it was difficult to walk. Kate and myself went to see Mrs. Dalton before we came back.

It is very cold and I think is getting colder. How I pity the poor! [Those] who cannot get wood and coal to make fires.

Jan 2nd 1860 for Jan 1st

Yesterday it was bitter cold but never the less we went to Sabbath School in the morning. We could hardly stand the cold until we got there. Sarah and I went in the church to get warm before we went into school. None of my scholars were there. As we were coming out Mr. McJ___ stopped and talked some time with me. He said "New Years gift". I told him I [had] nothing to give him but he insinuated that I had and he would tell me what it is the next opportunity he has. I hope it will be soon as I want to know what he meant.

Mr. Proctor preached a very interesting sermon but I did not hear the text but it was about "life passing away".

It was so cold that we did not go out in the evening excepting to see Aunt and Uncle. A gentleman came in while we were there. He is a Senator. His name was Salsberry or something that sounded like that.[65]

January 2nd

Today has been kept as New Year's day. Most of the stores are closed and every body has holiday. Sister, Kate and Sarah went up to the church as the teachers gave all the scholars a treat. I staid in my room alone all the time they were gone excepting I went into Mrs. Norton's room once and she and Miss Lottie came into see me. Aunt, Uncle, Lou Whorton and Kate Irvin came in after tea but did not stay long and Mrs. & Miss Norton and all [of] us went over to see them a little time after they went home.

It has been the coldest day that we have had. I cannot find out where the thermometer is standing but I know it must be below zero.

Jan 3rd

I have not done much today. It has been so very cold that we could hardly stand to walk.

Sarah and I went shopping this morning and to the mantua-makers to have our new silk dresses made. We had them made long points before and behind.

I spent the remainder of the day in the house as it was too cold to go any where.

Jan 4th

We all concluded to go to the Capitol this morning. Miss Lottie was going with us but did not feel very well and staid at home. We started about 11 o'clock and staid until 2 or 3 o'clock. Uncle came up into the gallery to see us. I saw Mr. McJ___ down in the house and bowed to him. Kate laughed at me a great deal for watching him every where he went but I was watching the speaker. Mr. Reagan from Texas spoke for some time on fugitive-slave law and several spoke about the manner of treating slaves down South.[66] Uncle made a short speech. Their discussions were very interesting. We were very much surprised when one came out to find that there had been a heavy fall of snow while we were in the Capitol. The snow had been lying on the ground one week.

Jan 5th

We all went up to Aunt's this morning to find out how we were to spend the day. We all concluded that as we had not been to the Smithsonian Institute to go there today. We started about half-past ten. I thought it was not very cold but Lou Whorton said it was and that I must dress warm and sure enough when I got up to the Smithsonian grounds it was bitter cold. We went all through the Institute and saw a great many strange animals and a great many things from foreign countries, idols, cloth made by the savages, their money, mummies from Egypt & etc. The most beautiful room was the Picture Gallery. Most of the pictures were of Indians, their dances, battles, & etc. From there Sister and I went to the Mantua-makers with some trimmings for Sarah's and my dresses. We stopped at the Post Office and to see Belle Naylor and Miss Coldtart (a young lady staying with her from Pittsburg).[67] Miss Coldtart is very pretty and lively and I think I will like her very much when I get better acquainted with her. Sister came home and I went to see Ella McCray. She had been very sick and looked very badly. I staid to see if Aunt was in. As I came out of the door I met Belle Naylor and Miss Coldtart going to the Capitol. They said that they had been to Mrs. Anderson's and that she wanted us to go there to spend the evening. Uncle, aunt and all of us (excepting Sarah) went by for Belle and her friend. We met Angy and Cousin at the door going somewhere but went in when they saw us. We all were introduced to Angie's cousin, Miss Anderson, Mr. Bradley, and another gentleman whose name I have forgotten.[68] Miss Washington came in while we were there. I never enjoyed myself more, played on the piano, sang and played several games such as "puss I want your answer", Criticism, Kitchen furniture & etc. Mrs. Anderson asked us in the dining room to take some refreshments. We got home at 12 o'clock neither tired nor sleepy. Mr. Bradley and another gentleman came home with us.

Jan 6th

At the table Mr. Norton asked us all who wanted to go to the Capitol. I said that I should like to go. [I] did not think he was in earnest but he asked me about it again after breakfast and when I went over to see Aunt I said I wanted to go very much. She said we all might go if we want to. So we came back and got ready to start. Mr. Norton went in the Omnibus as he was too weak to walk. We were walking on alone when I heard some one say "good morning Miss Cassie". I turned and saw Mr. McJ___. He walked with us to the Capitol. He said that he would have come up into the gallery and spoke to me the other day but he was busy and could not. We had to wait some time in the Rotunda for Mr. Norton. We staid up there until half after 5 o'clock making about six hours that we sat up there. There was a very interesting discussion going on between the Democrats, Americans, and Republicans. We met Mr. Bradley up there. He said that he would like to see us home but he had to go some where else. That other gentleman was with him. I can't think of his name.

I heard that the thermometer was five degrees below zero this morning.

Jan 7th

It has been looking cloudy all day and I fear it will rain so that we cannot go to church tomorrow. The snow is melting very fast and the streets are about as muddy as they can be.

Sarah and I intended to have gone to the dress-makers today to get our new dresses but as it has been raining we thought we would wait until Monday.

I went no where today excepting to see Aunt.

I do not feel very much like getting my lessons for Monday we have had holiday so long that we have almost forgotten where our lessons are.

Jan 9th for the 8th

Yesterday was one of the most disagreeable days that we have had this winter. The sun did not shine a single time (I believe) but, not-withstanding all that, we started for Sabbath School as soon as we got our breakfast. We remained for Church. I did not find out the gentleman's name that preached. Someone said that he was from Georgetown. I liked his sermon very much. They had communion after church but I did not remain as I did not feel very well and besides I felt that I was not worthy to partake of that holy supper. It seemed to me as if I could not get my thoughts fixed on holy things during the sermon. We did not go out at night as it was so wet. The fog was so thick that we could hardly see across the street. Belle Naylor sent word for us to stop for her as we were going to church.

Jan 9th

Although I did not expect to say good lessons this morning I had all perfect but a great many of the girls did not as they had forgotten where their [lessons] were.

After school we (Sarah, Miss Lottie & myself) went up to the prayer meeting at the Lutheran church. It was awful walking. We did not stay until the meeting was over but started home as we had to stop at the dress-makers. We did not stay there very long as it was getting late. They had got almost through dinner when we got back.

Went over to see Aunt after tea but did not stay long.

I like to [have] forgot to say that Mr. Norton has a new stove in the school room and parlor. I believe most of the girls like it wonderfully.

This week has been set apart for prayer for the spreading of the Gospel in all countries.

Jan 10th

Every thing went along in school as usual today. Although the walking is so bad, nearly all of the scholars were here.

I did not go out this afternoon but went to a prayer meeting at Trinity Church this evening. The fog was so thick that it felt like fine rain but there was a good many there considering the wet night. I saw a good many there that I am acquainted with but did not have an opportunity of speaking to them.

Jan 11th

As nothing of importance happened this morning I will skip over that to the afternoon. Well, in the afternoon Sarah and I went to see Mrs. Tayman and Sarah Smith. It had been a long time since I had been there. Mrs.

Tayman's brother had died since I saw her. She was in mourning for him. Mr. Myers, Mr. Zimmerman and another gentleman was in the parlor when we went in. The dinner bell rang and Mrs. Tayman went down before we came away. We had not been home long until Belle Naylor, Miss Coldtart, and Mrs. Bradley came to see us. Mrs. Norton and Miss Lottie came in before they left.

We went to a prayer meeting at the Wesley Chapel at night. The prayer meeting was for the young of different nations on the globe.

It looks very much like rain.

Jan 12th

It rained sure enough last night and has looked like raining all day and I hope it will rain tonight and be clear tomorrow. I am getting so tired of the wet weather. We can never go out unless we put on over shoes and I dislike them very much. It has been very warm for two or three days.

There was great excitement in the House of Representatives this morning. A man was speaking when he dropped a pistol. Some supposed that he drew it and intending to shoot the member he was speaking against. They had quite a quarrel but nothing serious happened.[69] They have not elected a Speaker yet and I think will not soon.

Jan 13th

Today has been more pleasant over head than usual but it was dreadful walking I heard the school girls say. I did not go out excepting to see Aunt. After dinner we all and Miss Lottie went over to see her (Aunt). I believe Sarah, Kate and Miss Lottie wanted Uncle to go with them to a prayer meeting on 13th St. but he had another engagement and could not go and it was very well as it commenced raining soon after. I went into see Lou Whorton as she is going to start to Philadelphia to stay two weeks.

There is a great deal of excitement here about a large cotton mill falling in Lawrence, Mass. It killed a great many and caught on fire directly after it fell burning many to death that were not hurt but were fastened in the lumbers so that they could not get their way [out]. There was 715 killed & missing. [There were] 165 wounded. Some will not get well. Oh! It was horrible.[70]

Jan 14th

It was pouring down rain when I got up this morning and has rained all day without stopping. I was very sorry it rained as I wanted to go out very much.

We all went over to Aunt's this morning. Lou Whorton called me into the parlor as I was going up. She said that her mother wished to see me. Mrs. Whorton said that she wanted me (if I had no objections) to stay with her tonight as she was afraid to stay in a room by herself. Mr. Whorton and Lou both started to Philadelphia today. (I staid).

I think we can not go to church tomorrow if it continues to rain this way.

Jan 16th & 15th

I was perfect as usual this morning in school.

The sun shines very bright but it is very sloppy.

We did not go to our own church yesterday but went to the Wesley Chapel. Heard a very good sermon from Mr. Ball. There was not a great many there as it was such very bad walking. All excepting myself went to a singing at our church in the afternoon [and] did not get back until very late.

Nothing remarkable happened today I believe.

We have invitations to Secretary Cass's tomorrow but I expect we will not go.[71] I don't care about it.

Bad writing today.

I staid all night with Mrs. Whorton last night and [will] stay again tonight.

Jan 17th

Aunt concluded that some of us had better go to Cass's tonight. She thought that Sarah and I had better go but I did not care about it so then she said Kate must go. Kate did not want to go either but we persuaded her that she had better go. I did not go because I wanted to go when Sister did and she did not want to go unless I did.

The girls looked very well when dressed. We went with them to Aunt's to see them off. Mrs. Salsberry and Mrs. Irven were in there while we were there.[72] Miss Lottie came while we were there to bring something they had forgotten.

Jan 18th

I did nothing today but sat in the house and nurse one of my teeth that aches very badly and has been aching all day.

I like to [have] forgot that Kate [and I visited] Mrs. Kesley, the latter was not at home. We saw her daughter.[73]

Jan 19th

My tooth aches worse and worse. I never suffered so much in one day in my life as I have today. I believe I had to leave the school room I was suffering so much. I went no where today excepting to Aunt's and she came here.

I have burnt my mouth very badly by putting creosote in my tooth, not only inside but out on the side of my face. It is quite sore.

Jan 20th

I awoke about 1 or 2 o'clock last night. My tooth was aching so badly that I could not lay in bed but had to get up and walk up and down the floor. It got a little better and I lay down on the sofa. I did not sleep much.

It ached so badly that I could not stay in the school room but went over to get Aunt to go with me to have it taken out but she was not in so I went out and got the oil of cloves and opium. That cured it directly.

We spent this evening at Mrs. Naylor's. We enjoyed ourselves very much [and] came home about half after ten o'clock.

Jan 28th

It looked like I could not find time this week to write one word in this book. I intend to do better in the future. I will commence where I left off and try to tell what I did each day. Saturday we girls and Aunt went over to Georgetown. We walked through the cemetery but it was so muddy that we did not stay long.

Sunday we went to our church as usual and heard a very good sermon by Mr. Proctor. We went back in the afternoon to a singing at the church.

Monday we intended to have gone to the Capitol & in the afternoon call on Annie Sturgis, as I had promised Sunday, but had to go out shopping and could not go.

Tuesday I was out shopping all the afternoon and we all went to the President's house at night. Mr. Vannerson went with me. I was not acquainted with the gentlemen that went with the other girls. We had a very pleasant time.

Wednesday afternoon we all went to the Capitol. I did not know the names of the gentlemen that spoke. I saw Uncle in the House and Mr. McJ___ but they did not see me.

Thursday I did nothing but sit in the house all day. [I] was in school of course in the morning.

Friday afternoon Kate and I went to see the mantua-maker. At night Belle and Blanche Naylor and Addie Coldtart came down. We had a very nice time.

Saturday (today) Kate and I went and made ten calls with Aunt, one of the ladies we called on was Mrs. Douglas, wife of Senator Douglas. She is one of the most beautiful ladies I ever saw.[74] We intended to go to our church tomorrow if it does not rain. I have written two letters today.

Jan 30th for 29th

Yesterday we went as usual to the Sunday School after lessons were over and they all commenced singing. Mr. McJ___ came and sat down by me and talked until School was dismissed.

We went up after school in the church and heard a very good sermon from Mr. Proctor. Mr. McJ___ came home with me. After we had taken off our things we went to see Aunt and staid there until dinner time. At 4 o'clock we went to a singing at our church. Mr. Zimmerman came home with me. We went to the Wesley Chapel at night [and] heard a very dry sermon from Mr. Ball. It was a delightful day and the moon shone beautifully at night.

Jan 30th

We got an excuse from Uncle to go up to the Capitol today instead of going to school as it was expected they would elect a Speaker. We started as soon as we got our breakfast and we got there at ten o'clock and then like to not got a seat. Congress did not open until 12 o'clock and the galleries were crowded by 11 o'clock. I never saw such a crowd. The number was estimated to be from 12 to 15,000 persons. Some ladies fainted but not a great many as they were anxious to see all that was going on. I saw a good many gentlemen that I knew on the floor. I asked one of them (Mr. McJ___) for a list of the members names as I saw gentlemen give this to the ladies. He threw three up to us. It was about half after four when we came out. We had hard work to get out. It was crowded, so Uncle Cobb came home with us.

I wrote to Cousin Web tonight.

February 4th

I have the same excuse that I always have for not writing. I have been so busy that I have not had time. Tuesday we did not go out as it rained all day. Wednesday we went up to the Capitol after school as every one said that the speaker would be elected. We sent our card out. Uncle, as he said he would, got us a seat if he could. He took us to one of the doors of the House of Representatives, as there was no other place to stand or sit when he (Pennington) was elected.[75] We stood inside of the hall and saw him conducted to the Speaker's chair. Two or three of the members that we were acquainted with came and talked to us. Mr. Ashmore, Mr. McRae was two of them.[76] The others I do not remember. Mr. Myers and Mr. McJ___ came and talked with me for some time. The Speaker is a Republican.

Wednesday night we went to a party at Secretary Cass's. There we got acquainted with a great many but would not know them now if I were to see them. I got acquainted with one gentleman (Mr. Kennedy) from Florence, Ala. he said he knew some Fennells about there. I guess they are some kin to me. Thursday I did not go out in the day but went over to the Smithsonian to the anniversary of the Young Men's Christian Association. [I] heard some very good speeches.

Friday went no where excepting to the Panorama of the Russian War. I was perfectly delighted.[77] Friday the thermometer stood 2 degrees below zero. Snow six inches deep. Today it is not quite so cold but very sloppy in the street. Sarah and I went out shopping this afternoon and found it very wet.

THE END OF THIS BOOK. I HOPE THE NEXT I WRITE WILL BE WRITTEN BETTER THAN THIS
Finis

August 30th 1864

I have just been reading over my old journal and have been comparing 1859 and 1860 with the present year (1864). Then we had peace & now war desolates the land from the Ohio to the Gulf.

Shall we ever see such days again?

I fear not for many of our (friends) have fallen in this mighty struggle for Independence and we shall miss them.[78]

Cassie Fennell
No. 30 4 ½ St.
Washington, D.C.

Cassie Fennell
Alabama U.S.
1859

C.M.F.

Washington City, 1860

A visit to the Capitol in 1860[79]
By Cassie Fennell

Friday being a clear sunshiny day and having some very hard lessons which we did not know we begged to be excused from school so that we could go with some friends to the Capitol.

Oh! How happy and free we felt when we got out in the pure morning air from the close school room and how we pitied the girls that we left there.

The Capitol is situated on a hill over looking the city surrounded by very extensive grounds shaded by large forest trees which have just begun to bud.

There are also a great many flowers which are now in full bloom and Oh! How I wanted to gather a bouquet but they do not allow that as I had to be satisfied with looking at them there.

We now approached a long flight of steps which leads to the door. About half way up there is a pool of water in which is erected a white marble monument to the memory of several great men whose names I am ashamed to say I have forgotten.

We continued our way up and soon reached the Rotunda which is the center of the Capitol and has passages leading from it to every room in the building. The wall is covered with large paintings most of them taken from important incidents in the history of this country. There are also busts and portraits of the Presidents and other great and good men.

Leaving the Rotunda we passed through the old House of Representatives which contains a great many beautiful statues to the New House and as the House was not in session we had the privilege of entering. Long benches are arranged regularly around in the center leaving considerable space between them and the wall. The Speaker's chair is elevated a few feet above the others. It is made of walnut with a red cushion and looks very comfortable.

The frescoing here is beautiful and the ceiling surpasses any thing I ever saw of that kind. There is a large gallery extending all around the room for spectators when the House is in session.

We now crossed a small hall into the Speaker's room. Of course it was not so splendid as the hall of Rep. but every thing was very rich and beautiful. The photographs of all the speakers were hanging around the room.

We next went to the Senate. It is very much like the house excepting yellow predominates here while red is the principal color of the House. The Senators have desks instead of benches. I like them much better.

We passed on to the President's and Vice President's apartments.

The wall of the Vice President's room is of white marble and has white marble pillars through the center of the room. There are three large mirrors set in the wall but are too high for me to see myself in them.

The President's room is not finished yet but there is some very fine frescoing on the wall and ceiling and I think will equal the V.P. when finished.

We thought as it was nearly time for us to return home we would go through the Library which is situated at the West front. This room is different from any that we had passed through but quite as splendid. We went out on the balcony and from there had a splendid view of the city and the country for several miles around. The books are arranged on galleries one above another nearly to the ceiling. We did not examine any of the books as we did not have time to read them there nor could we bring them with us.

TWO

Discord and Distance: Making the Most of Circumstances, March 19, 1860–July 4, 1860

March 19, 1860

It has been a long time since I took up my pen to record my actions and feelings. The reason is because I had no book. I finished the other one and neglected getting another until last Saturday. I can not remember all that has taken place since I wrote last. I have been out a great deal and got acquainted with a great many persons. I have been happy the greater part of the time but then again I have been at times low spirited. I have also been sick but was well nearly all the time.

I have concluded to turn over a new leaf; that is, to study harder, keep in a happier mood and then I think I will be happy. I have not been happy today. The first thing that made me feel bad was; Sarah lost our report cards and I had to spend nearly an hour hunting for them when I should have been in school getting my lessons and I thought I would get a bad mark but I didn't; the next thing was that Kate and Sarah got mad because I wanted to practice. They say I practice all the time when in fact they practice more than I do. Thirdly, and lastly, Kate said that Miss Murray said for Sarah and I to take music lessons together when sister [and] I want to take together.[1] Mr. Sarsley (a student) spent the evening here. He has been sick and looks very badly. Aunt and Uncle came over and sat a little while this evening. I wrote home and directly after I received a letter from home. It has been raining all day but not hard.

March 20th

It looked very much like rain this morning but by nine o'clock the sun came out in all his glory, and it has been perfectly delightful ever since.

I had to leave school about 12 o'clock to take my music lesson, got back about half after one o'clock. I said all my lessons perfectly today, and intend to do the same the remainder of this session. I went next door to see Aunt as soon as I got out of school but she was not in so I concluded to go to the union prayer meeting with Mrs. and Miss Norton. It was a very interesting meeting, the subject being "What is meant by being born again or in the change of heart?" I saw and spoke to Angy Anderson and Belle Naylor. I came back home, got my dinner and went up to see Mrs. Salsberry and her cousin, Miss MacCaslin, next door.[2] After, I went up to Aunt's room, was introduced to a gentleman from Alabama but I have forgotten his name.

March 21st

When I awoke this morning the sun was shining brightly through the window but the wind was blowing very hard outdoors. Kate and sister went to take their music lessons this morning at six o'clock and got back in time to get their breakfasts. Sister had the toothache so bad she could not stay in school. I went over to see Aunt at recess and she said we could get Mr. Norton to excuse us at one o'clock if we should like to go to see the paintings at the Art Association. We went and were perfectly delighted. There were paintings from all the best artists in this country and all kinds. Aunt wants to get one.[3] After dinner we all went into Mrs. Norton's room to sew for a fair that takes place Friday and we dressed several dolls. Aunt came over at night to see us.

March 22nd

It has been a beautiful day and would have been very pleasant had not the wind blown so hard. It is rather cooler than yesterday. A little while after school Annie Sturges came up to our room and stayed with us until dinner. It is the first time she has ever been to see us; she is very pleasant.[4] After dinner we went to see Aunt and met Mr. and Mrs. Fitzpatrick (Senator from Alabama).[5] They said they were going to see Aunt too. I invited them into the parlor and went up to tell Aunt that they were there. Uncle went down and asked them up to his room. Mrs. Salsberry was in Aunt's room as they came to see her too. I like Mrs. Fitzpatrick (I expect the name is spelt wrong very much). After I came from there I went with Mr. Norton and Belle Naylor to hear a lecture on Phrenology.[6] I saw several persons that I know there, among them Mr. Sorsby and Mr. Harmon.[7] Mr. Sorsby talked to me for some time; he sent his love to all the girls but told me not to go give it all away. I saw some ladies that I know but did not get to talk to them.

March 23rd

I awoke this morning with a bad cold which I took last night; caused by going out of a very warm room into the night air. It was very cloudy this morning and we all thought it would rain but it cleared off about 12 o'clock. Aunt came over to see us at recess. She said if we should like to go up to the Capitol this afternoon she would be there but as I wanted to practice I could not go. We went to a festival at the First Presbyterian Church this evening; saw a good many of the school girls that I am acquainted with. We had a very nice time and got back at half past ten o'clock. We stopped at Aunt's as we came back. Miss Phillips was here to see us this afternoon. Lizzie Bradley came while we were at dinner.[8]

March 24th

My cold, I believe, is worse instead of better today. Sarah and I went to take our music lessons at six o'clock this morning. I wanted to go over to Georgetown to see Minnie May but I felt so badly that I concluded to stay in the house for one day.[9] I had hardly come to this conclusion when in stepped Minnie herself. I was glad to see her as I had not since she moved to Georgetown. She stayed about an hour and a half and then went to see Aunt. We all went over to see Aunt after dinner. Uncle was not very well, he talked a great deal about his nephew who said he wanted a wife and wanted Uncle to choose one for him. Uncle asked us to pick out one for him but I believe we did not know of anyone that we thought would do.

Monday, March 26th for Sunday, March 25th

Yesterday it was colder than the day before and windy, but we did not stay at home for that but went to Sabbath School. They have moved the school back into the Church and have a new Melodeon. Young Mr. King played it for us. There were a great many at Church, a good many strangers. As we came home we stopped to see Aunt and sang several hymns for Uncle. As soon as we got our dinners we went back to Church to a Sabbath School meeting. There was a great deal of debating about an exhibition in June but they concluded to have it on the first day of June. We went to the Baptist Church at night with Mr. Norton. Rev. Kennard preached. We received invitations from some of the Columbian College students to go to the Smithsonian to hear an oration to be delivered on the 12th of April.[10]

March 26th

We all got along as well as usual in school this morning. I was afraid I would not know my lessons but I studied hard in school and had them perfect. Adlade, a servant, came into school about one o'clock and said someone wanted to see me; I went to the door and Mollie Tayman was there. She wanted to get some things to wear to a party. I told her I would carry them down after school, which I did. I asked for Miss Tayman but Miss Smith, Mr. Myers and several others were in the parlor. Mr. Myers had talked a good while with me when Mr. Brown came for him to go somewhere. While I was there Mr. Cooksey got home from the country; they were glad to see him. From there I went to see Alice Adams.[11] She looked very well, I had not seen her since her brother's death.

March 27th

It was right cold this morning but the sun shone out beautifully and made it look like spring. I thought it did not feel much like it, I had to leave school at 12 o'clock to take my music lessons. I took a new piece called "Bessie Polken"; I think it very pretty. In the afternoon we went to see Aunt and took a drawing lesson, after that I came home and put on my things and went to see Lizzie Bradley and her cousin but only Lizzie was in. Angy Anderson was there. We came away together and walked some distance up the Avenue (Pennsylvania). We met Mr. Anderson and he walked part of the way back with us. I got home about dark, got my dinner and went over to Aunt's but did not stay long. I am still suffering very much from my bad cold.

March 28th

Oh! The sun shone out beautifully and I felt as if it were a shame that we school girls were kept cooped up in the school room. I feel much better than I did yesterday and hope I shall soon feel quite well. I went over to see Aunt directly after school, to a drawing lesson and came home as I wanted to practice but had not been here long when Mrs. Doolittle sent for one of us. I went down and she asked me if we would not stop playing for this afternoon as she had a very bad headache. I told her "certainly" and got some papers and went up to my room and stayed until dinner. After dinner we went to see Aunt and were not there long when the servant came and said that Mr. Sorsby and Mr. Harmon wanted to see us. They stayed until about half past nine. Miss Lottie and I went over to see Aunt after they had left.

Uncle got Miss Lottie to play several times for him. Mr. Pearce came into the parlor while we were there.[12] Sarah was so sick that she had to leave the parlor before the gentlemen left.

March 29th

Another lovely day has come and gone and it looked so pleasant out of doors this afternoon that I could not stay in all the afternoon. Miss Lottie and I went over to Georgetown to see Minnie May but she was not at home so we walked home. It was about three miles. We met Minnie on the Avenue as we came back but had hardly time to speak as the Omnibus came up just then. Uncle came over here to ask us to go the observatory; he also asked old Mr. and Mrs. Norton and Miss Norton. We started about seven o'clock and stopped at the circle to wait for some ladies from Georgetown. We waited for half an hour before they came; there were 15 of us. I almost forgot that Mrs. Salsberry and her cousins were along. We saw the moon and Saturn and were perfectly delighted but I cannot begin to describe them. The moon was very ragged around the edges. We could see one ring around Saturn very plainly; it was about the size of a plate. We got home at 10 o'clock. Sarah was too sick to go so I expect we shall go again before we go home.

March 30th

We have enjoyed another beautiful day. Oh! How I wanted to go out but could not as I have to be examined tomorrow and stayed in to study for examination. We went to see Aunt after school but did not stay long.

March 31st

Kate and I went out about six o'clock this morning to take our music lessons. I took a new song called "Memory's Spells". I think it very pretty. We stayed in our room until four o'clock, the time for us to be examined. Susie Ingle came up to our room just a few minutes before the time.[13] We did not miss a single question. We employed ourselves after being examined in preparing for Sunday. Sarah is quite well today. Uncle came over and invited us all to go and hear Pattie, the celebrated songstress sing. We went and were perfectly delighted; she sings like a bird. There were three gentlemen that sang but I do not remember their names. Oh, if I could sing like them I would be satisfied; I will be ashamed to sing soon. Sarah is confined yet to her bed.

April 2nd for April 1st

Yesterday morning I thought we were going to have another fine day but what was my surprise to find it raining when we came out of Church; it did not rain very hard but the wind nearly blew us off our feet. We went to Sabbath School in the morning and remained for preaching. After preaching they had communion. When I went into Church I hardly knew Mr. Proctor, he had been shaved and he did not look like the same man. We did not go to Church at night; I felt so badly I almost thought that I was sick and sister had the toothache. We went to see Aunt after tea. Mrs. Norton and Miss Lottie came while we were there. I returned very early.

April 2nd

We all thought that it would rain last night and be very wet today but we were mistaken for this has been a splendid day, just cool enough to be pleasant. In the afternoon Kate and I intended to have gone to see Miss Perkins and we were going to call for Lizzie Bradley but Aunt came and wanted us to go out with her so I went and told Lizzie that I could not go. Aunt and Kate were to meet me at Shuster's store but they were not there when I stopped and then I went to Ellis's Music store to see if they had arrived but they had not been there so I went back and met them a short distance down the street.[14] Miss Lottie and her mother went into Ellis's with us to look at some pianos but did not get one to suit. As yesterday was Sunday, we have observed today as the first day of April. I put some salt in Miss Lottie's glass before she came to the table but did not know that she had company—well, when she came down the gentleman got her glass of water—he could not imagine what was the matter! We had gone to see Aunt at the time but they told us about it. He says he will repay me for it yet.

April 3, 1860

It was very cloudy this morning and we all thought it would rain before 12 o'clock but we were mistaken. All went along as usual this morning in school. Aunt came for some of us to go with her to look at some pianos and also some cloth for our riding habits. We did not get a piano but all of us got riding dresses. Kate's is brown, Sarah's is green, and Sister's and mine are blue. It commenced to rain right hard before we got back, we had no umbrellas to protect our bonnets but they were not injured much. We went to see Aunt after tea and then came back and sat in the parlor.

Uncle and Aunt came over after a little while and sat with us. There are two gentlemen here on a visit to Mrs. Norton and one of them keeps us laughing all the time.

April 4th

It has been raining nearly all day so we had to stay indoors. Mr. Norton was not very well this morning so we girls wrote a petition for him to give us a holiday. All the girls in school signed it but he said he felt as well as he had felt in a week; he did not know but that we wanted a holiday anyhow and only wanted that for an excuse to ask him. I went to see Aunt after school and had started home, Uncle (who was sitting in the parlor) called me and said it was raining very hard and that he would get an umbrella but I told him I did not care, it was such a short distance, but he would get one. I stopped in the parlor and talked to Mrs. Salsberry and cousin while he was upstairs. Miss McCollar was making a pink net, they are very fashionable.[15] It cleared up about dark and Uncle asked me to go to hear a lecture on phrenology. We went and as we came back we stopped at an ice-cream saloon and got some ice-cream and cake. Mr. and Mrs. Norton were with us. Oh! The moon did shine so bright! It is about 12 o'clock so I must go to bed. I forgot to mention that we got a piano today.

April 5th

Oh! This has been such a splendid day, it is really spring. How I would like to be in the country where I could get as many flowers as I want. The girls begged Mr. Norton to give us a holiday after 12 o'clock but he would not. A great many of the schools of this city did have a holiday. We all expect to go to the Catholic Church tomorrow as none of us have been there on Good Friday. Kate, Lizzie Bradley and myself went up to see Mary Perkins but she was not in. We saw Mrs. Perkins. Kate and Lizzie went up further in the city and I started walking home slowly; I thought that they would catch up with me. I saw them coming alright and right behind them were four or five students trying to catch up with them. I pretended not to see them and turned with the girls when I heard someone say "Good morning, Miss Cassie". It turned out to be Mr. Sorsby and Mr. Harmon. I pretended I was surprised it was them. They walked along with us until we came to their boarding house. After we came back Kate and I went to see Miss Brewster up on 73rd street.

April 6th

We had intended to have gone to the Catholic Church this morning but being such a beautiful day, Aunt and several others thought we had better go out to the Old Soldiers' Home. There were eight of us: Aunt, Mrs. Salsberry, Miss McColla, Miss Lottie Norton, Kate, Sister Mary, Sarah and myself. We got along very well until we got to Glenwood Cemetery, about three miles from the city, and then Mrs. Salsberry, Miss McColla and Miss Lottie Norton turned back.[16] They said they could walk no further. We thought as it was only a mile and a half further we would go on. We reached there just at 12 o'clock and saw the old soldiers go into dinner. We then got a negro boy to show us the way up the tower where we had a splendid view of the country for miles around. We came back a nearer way but we walked at least eight miles, the negro boy said it was six miles the way we came out there but I think he was mistaken for my feet are so sore that I can hardly walk. Kate's feet are sore too, we both had on new shoes and therefore suffered more than any of the others. Mrs. Salsberry called on us with her cousins after tea, as they are going home Monday. As today was Good-Friday we had a holiday.

April 7th

My feet were so sore that I thought that I would have to stay in the house all day, but we girls concluded to go over to Georgetown to see Minnie May as we could ride in the Omnibus. Minnie was home and seemed very glad to see us. She took us up to her room and after a while Mrs. Harrover came in with her niece, the sweetest little girl I ever saw.[17] We sat there some time when Mrs. Harrover asked us if we would like to look at her school rooms and we gladly consented. She showed us through twenty or thirty rooms, it is a beautiful place and I think it would be nice to go to school there. They have very large yards and shade trees. Minnie said she did not know the way through the house yet and Mrs. Harrover said she had not been in all the rooms yet although she has been living there over a year. After we got through looking at rooms we went to Oak Hill Cemetery. It is the most beautiful spot I have ever seen, monuments of all sizes and descriptions. When we got back Mrs. Harrover had a nice lunch prepared for us. One of the school girls was in the room and we were introduced to her as Miss Hopkins from Virginia. We stayed there about an hour when we concluded it was about time to come home. As we were going to our rooms we met Aunt who was just starting over to see Minnie. Miss Lottie and Mrs. Norton were going with her. Mr. Sorsby and Mr. Hatcher were here for tea; although we knew whom they came to see, we could not go into the parlor as Mrs. Norton seemed so afraid we would fall in love with some of them.[18] They told me afterward that they came to see us and asked for all the young ladies and why we did not come down. I told them that our teachers were opposed to our seeing gentlemen.

April 9th for 8th

Yesterday morning it looked so much like rain that we did not go to the Sabbath School nor did Kate and I go to our Church but Sarah and Sister went to hear Mr. Granberry preach as he was our old pastor and we liked him very much. I went to the Capitol with Mrs. Norton and Miss Lottie to hear Mr. Stockton preach. He is a very old man and his hair is as white as cotton. He is the Chaplain of the House of Representatives.[19] Everyone likes him very much, he has such an impressive manner. There were a great many there. I went to the Fourth Street Presbyterian Church at night and sat in Mrs. Norton's pew where the gas lights would not hurt my eyes. I always suffer so much in Aunt's pew with my eyes. Dr. Sunderland preached a very good sermon.

April 9th

It has rained all day, I believe, without stopping a minute. We could not go out at all. We had just started to go to see Aunt when Uncle came in and said that Aunt had gone to Philadelphia with Senator Salsberry and Lady to look at some pianos; she will be back in a few days. We will miss her very much. We went over to see Uncle after tea; he said he was very lonely since Aunt left. We have a holiday today as it is Easter Monday but can not go anywhere as it rains so hard. I wrote home today; every time I write I feel like I wish I was at home talking instead of writing. I have practiced a good deal today; hope I will have a good music lesson tomorrow.

April 10th

It still rains; I had hoped that the girls would not come to school in the rain and there would be no school today, but the rain did not stop them and when I went down to breakfast I found several of them already here. Senator and Lady Doolittle left here today.[20] Senator Doolittle is going to board on Capitol Hill. It is cooler there in the summer and Mrs. Doolittle is going back home in Wisconsin as soon as she sees that Mr. Doolittle is fixed comfortably. I went out to take my music lesson at 12 o'clock; it did not rain very hard going but coming back it poured down and I got very wet. We all went next door to see a young lady from Nebraska. She is one of Uncle's friend's daughter. I like her very much and she plays beautifully on the piano. Mrs. Irving and Mrs. Pearce were in the parlor when we went in.

April 11th

Rain, Rain! Nothing but wind and rain from morn' till night; Oh! I like to have forgotten that the sun shone out for a short time this afternoon. We have commenced having dinner at 3 o'clock since Mr. Doolittle left and tea at half past six. We went over to see Uncle after tea and were surprised to find Aunt back again. We were very glad to see her, we missed her so much. Sister and Sarah left before Kate and I. As we left we stopped in the parlor to see Miss Kenney as she was alone and invited her to come over with us as she had expressed her desire to hear Miss Lottie sing again. Miss Lottie sang a great many times and then we asked her to play; Oh! She plays beautifully.

April 12th

I was somewhat surprised to find the sun shining this morning. It had been raining so long I looked for nothing but rain. The rain makes everything look so fresh and the air is so cool and pleasant. We went to see Aunt before school this morning. I went over again after dinner and took a drawing lesson and expect to paint soon. We all went to the Smithsonian at night to hear a poem and oration by Dr. Sunderland and Mr. Curry of Alabama. The house was crowded to overflowing. I saw a great many there that I am acquainted with. Two of the students sat just before me and they did all in their power to make me laugh. I think they did not pay much attention to the poem or oration. I forgot to say that they were delivered by the request of the Columbian students and of course a great many of them were there. Mr. and Mrs. Naylor went with us, Mr. Bradley walked home with Belle and myself.

April 13th

We all did not know our lessons this morning and Miss Kenney wanted someone to go with her to the Capitol, we begged Aunt to excuse us from school. We went up to the Supreme Court. It is a very different place from the House or Senate; all of the judges look awfully solemn and dignified.

I felt almost afraid to move for fear that I would make a disturbance. We sat there until we were tired and then went to the "House" but did not stay long as Miss Kenney was not very well. Uncle and Mr. Ashmore came up into the gallery and sat there sometime with us. We got home just as school turned out. We went to see Aunt after tea but stayed a very short time as we promised Mr. Norton to go with him to the Smithsonian to hear a lecture on "Explorations in the West" (Territories). It was not interesting and there were very few there.[21] Mr. Davis went with Sister and Kate. They did not want him to go with them but could not prevent it as he is Mrs. Norton's cousin.

April 14th

Sarah and I arose early this morning to take our music lessons. We came back by market and bought a very pretty plant for Mrs. Norton. We stayed in the house nearly all day to practice and study but just before sundown we commenced to get ready to go out when Ella McRea called to see us. She had not been here in so long a time that I had nearly forgotten her.[22] We went with Sister to the Dentist to have her tooth plugged and then went to various stores shopping. We looked at the new fashioned hoop skirts (made with a long trail) and some silks. I think Aunt will get us all a set of hoops apiece, although I have not had these that I wear long. After tea we went to see Aunt. She was in the parlor with Mrs. Taylor and two misses Taylors, to whom she introduced us. We had not been there long when a gentleman came in and was introduced as Mr. Pleasants. He is a great wit and kept us laughing nearly all the time.

April 25th

Well really, I began to think that I never would find time to write in this book again. I have been so very busy shopping, studying, practicing, etc., that I have not had time to go to see my friends that I have not seen in a long time. Besides that I have been sick and now have a very bad cold. I have quite forgotten all about the little incidents that have occurred since I last wrote. Some things that I remember are that we all got silk dresses and new hats. I received a letter from home a few days ago saying that one of our negro women (Queen) was dead. It made me feel quite sad as she was my nurse. Ma said she told her to tell us that she would meet us in Heaven. I wrote home today. Last Saturday was so warm we put on summer clothing but it is very cold now.

April 26th

It has been very cold today for the season but was very pleasant out in the air. Kate, Sarah, Sister and myself went to see the dressmaker in the afternoon to have our dresses made. We hardly know how to have them made, there are so many fashions. We concluded we would have them made with plain waist, low neck with a little bertha, a high neck cape and long wide sleeves. Kate and I came back before the others. We met Mr. Sorsby and he walked with us a while and gave us an invitation to go to the Smithsonian next week to hear the students speak. We called on Miss Phillips and Belle Naylor before we came back. A young gentleman was at Belle's; they were sitting on the sofa and looked as if they were not expecting company. We went to see Aunt as usual after tea and she asked us if we would not like to see a show that is in the city now. Of course we were willing. Mr. and Mrs. Kenney went with us; I was very much pleased. I saw a rhinoceros for the first time, it was very tame; I also saw many other animals.[23]

April 27th

It has been so cold today but the sun shone out very brightly, which made it pleasant. Kate, Aunt and myself went up to look at some bonnets directly after 12 o'clock. We went into nearly every store in the city and at last we all got bonnets large enough. They are wearing them very large now. All are white straws trimmed with white ribbon and flowers of different colors. We had quite a row or quarrel with the Norton family this evening. As we had our dinner very late we did not want any supper and so when the bell rang we did not go down—we also had to practice. A second bell rang and we made no movements excepting I asked Sister to go down to prayers as I was too tired and did not feel well. She was just getting up to go when the servant came in and said that Mr. Norton said that he had rang the bell three times and that we must come down to prayers. I told her that I did not feel like it and the other girls said they did not want to go but at last Sister and Kate went down and Sarah and myself commenced to comb our hair so that we could go too when another servant came up and said that Mr. and Mrs. Norton said for us to come down as they would not have prayers without us and if we did not come down they would turn us *out of their house* (which would gratify me very much as I am anxious to leave anyhow). I came very near not going after she told me what old Mrs. Norton said about me and the others. I believe I was as angry as I could be and of course did not feel like kneeling down pretending to pray; but I went down and as I entered the room I said "I reckon now you will have prayers." Mr. Norton said he was surprised and several other things among which was that I had used insulting language to him lately, which I knew nothing about and was perfectly surprised to hear it and therefore after prayers I asked him when I had used insulting language? He said it was when I spoke about some marks he gave me the other day for being late in the school room when there was a young lady who was late every day and he always gave her good marks and he said she had an excuse, while she said she did not have one. I told him she said she did not have any, when he became very angry and thought I had insulted him. We all went to see Aunt directly and told her all about it and tried to get her to ask Uncle to take us from this house, but I believe she did not think much about it. We had not been there long when Mr. and Mrs. Norton were announced; Aunt went down and after a while sent for us. We went down. I looked as angry as I could and did not notice them at all until they spoke to me. Mrs. Norton wanted to know why I was angry. I told them it was because Mr. Norton was going to compel me to do what I did not want to do and that no one ever threatened to drive me out of their house before. They said they did not threaten to do any such thing, but I know they did because Sister was there and heard them. Mr. Ganvier came in just then and put a stop to it until Aunt invited us up to her room and then it was renewed. They (the Nortons) pretended like they were very sorry and hoped that it would soon pass over but it is not as I do not intend to speak to any of them excepting young Miss Norton and Miss Town; I almost hate old Mrs. Norton and Miss Lottie and so do all the girls.

April 28th

I went to see Aunt as soon as I got my breakfast; she said last night that she would go out with me this morning but she did not feel very well and therefore she could not go. Sarah and I went out to see about our bonnets, paid for them and told the Milliners where to send them when finished. We then went up to a green house on 5th Street to see about some flowers that we wanted to give to the students that were going to speak Monday night.

I have not spoken to the Nortons this day. Aunt has been trying to persuade me but I can not act deceitfully, as they do. They pretended like they love Kate so much just because she is Aunt's pet and they want to keep on the good side of her.

April 30th for 29th

Yesterday we went in the morning to our Church. Mr. Proctor preached. He has not been here for several Sundays for he has been down to New Orleans to some kind of convention. I nor Kate went out in the evening as we both felt very badly. I went into Miss Town's room for a while to read to her. We went to see Aunt after tea. Miss Kenney was in her room but left after a short while to go to Church. Kate had the jaw-ache very badly all this evening. Mrs. Norton and Miss Lottie both came into our room to pet her, but I did not speak a word to them for which Aunt gave me a good scolding. I know it is wrong to dislike anyone but I cannot help it, they are so deceitful.

April 30th

Everything passed off as usual in school excepting I did not feel in so good a humor with Mr. Norton. After school Sarah and I went to see Lizzie Bradley to get her to go to the greenhouse with us to get bouquets. She did not get one but we got three; one for Sister, one for Sarah and one for myself. We did not know how we would get to the Smithsonian, the girls asked Mr. Norton at dinner and he said he was not going; then they asked Mrs. and Miss Norton and they said because the students did not send them invitations as well as us they were not going, so Lizzie Bradley said her brother would go with us. We got there very late and could hardly get seats. Belle Naylor and Mr. Folia came in first after us. Mr. Folia got Belle a seat then came and stood behind our seat for he could not get out; he begged me for my bouquet but I would not give it to him. I liked the speaking very much. I sent my flowers to Mr. Sorsby, Sister and Sarah to Mr. Harmon; Mr. Sorsby's speech was very amusing but Mr. Harmon's was the best.[24]

May 1st

It was very rainy today. We were all invited to a great wedding; Miss Parker and Mr. Boleany. Miss Parker is a resident of the city, very wealthy but not pretty. The gentleman is from Louisiana (member of Congress). He is not wealthy, not handsome and is very dissipated looking. I heard someone say that he was drunk yesterday.[25]

I went to take my music lesson at 12 o'clock; I saw a great many fine ladies going to the wedding. It rained all the time. I stopped at Aunt's as I came back and Miss Kenney was there; she thought she would start for home today but her Pa did not come back in time. I began to feel sorry that I did not go to the wedding when it was too late to get ready. I expect we would have gone if Aunt would have cared anything about going.

May 7th

Another busy or lazy week has passed away when I could not find time to write in this book. No one feels like writing in hot weather and I'm sure we have had it for the last few days. I believe nothing of importance has happened since I wrote last excepting Friday night we went to the Negro Minstrels. We were very much pleased with their singing.[26] Saturday we went to the Capitol to hear the music and I saw a good many there that I knew.[27] A Mr. Perkins walked once around with me, he is not handsome a bit. It is very warm today, the thermometer standing at 94 degrees. Uncle's nephew arrived in the city this morning, I have never seen him before. Yesterday we went to our Church but our Minister did not preach. A Baptist Minister preached in his place. We went there again at night and another Baptist Minister preached. A lady was baptized by Mr. Proctor; she was sprinkled. Mr. Linn came home with us.

May 8th

Another very warm day has passed but the night is so warm here that one does not feel much relieved. I have suffered all day with a very bad headache. I went out at 12 o'clock to take my music lesson, it was so hot that I could hardly stand it until I got there but Miss Murray's house was so shaded that it did not take me long to get cool. Coming back it was not so warm as I came home on the shaded side of the street. I heard some one say that they thought it would turn cold again which I am afraid of as I always take such colds.

May 9th

I have had a very bad headache again today. I did not feel like going to school but got through my lessons perfectly. We thought of going to the President's to the music this afternoon but it rained so hard we could not go. We went as usual to see Aunt. There is great excitement about the Japanese Embassy who are expected here next week. I am afraid we will not get to see them; I believe there are seventy-five of them.[28]

May 10th

My head ached so badly this morning that I did not go into school but went out shopping with Aunt. I bought me one of those long suits that are worn so much now. It was not so warm today as it has been. Aunt and I stopped at an ice-cream saloon as we came back; Mrs. Tayman walked part of the way with us.

May 11th

We all were glad to see the sun shining this morning but it commenced raining very hard about sunset. This is the way it has been doing for some time. I got through my lessons perfectly as usual. I went to see Aunt after school and sewed with her for a while; it had been so long since I attempted to sew that my fingers were very tired when I finished.

We were surprised this morning by the arrival of cousin Alex Penland from Alabama.[29] We were very glad to see him; he is not going to be here very long as he is on his way to New York.

May 12th

It was very cloudy this morning but cleared off before sunset. We had been thinking for some time of going to the theatre to see the performance of Heller (or "Polima") the magician.[30] I did not like all of it but some I could not account for; the "Cornucopia" was the best thing. How he kept it full I can not imagine. The "Second Sight" was also very good. The house was not crowded. We carried umbrellas for fear it would rain but it did not.

May 14th for 13th

I was not well enough to go to Church yesterday so I had to remain at home. I had nearly all day and stayed with Aunt part of the time. Mrs. Norton came into my room to see if I needed anything before she went to Church. The girls went to Sabbath School early in the morning; I asked Kate to take my class. In the afternoon, Aunt, Uncle, Miss and Mrs. Norton came in our room and sung several hymns but somehow we did not feel like singing much. It rained very hard towards night so that none of us could go to Church. The girls intended to have gone to our Church but were disappointed. Cousin William Cobb was going with them.

May 14th

We did not go to school this morning, in fact all the girls had a holiday, so that they could go to see the Japanese Embassy enter the city. Kate and I went to the dressmakers before it was time to watch for them. We first went to Miss Polk's on the Avenue and then went across the street to Mrs. Tayman's as there was so many at Miss Polk's. We stood there about an hour before they arrived. It was a grand sight; all the Washington Military were out to escort them to their hotel and there were about 20,000 persons following the procession. They are almost as black as negroes, very ugly and dressed elegantly in embroidered satin trousers, no hats, hair in a little knot on the top of their heads.[31] There were several ladies at Mrs. Tayman's besides us. I was introduced to them; Mr. Zimmerman came in while we were there. Kate and I went to Mrs. Anderson's after tea, cousin William went too. We also went to Mrs. Munson's; her three daughters were there, they are very pleasant.[32]

May 15th

I did not feel like going into school this morning but never-the-less had to. I said all my lessons perfectly. At 12 o'clock I went to take my music lesson; Miss Murray was not in when I first got there so I practiced until she came. She said I was improving very rapidly. I went to see the dressmaker again today, Sister and Sarah went too. We had our dresses made long, Basque to reach nearly to the ground, trimmed with buttons up the front and the skirts to trail behind. Sister and I went up to the Avenue to look for a breast pin for me but did not see any suitable. We met Minnie May and Mrs Harrover; we talked with them a while. Kate and I went with Aunt to see Mrs. Powell but she was not in so we went to see Mrs. Burr; her son came to the door, he is very handsome and very pleasant, Miss Burr was not in, we stayed for about an hour. Mr. Burr came home with us. We stayed with Aunt for a little while and then came home and are now ready to retire—Good-Night!

May 16th

Oh! This has been a delightful day, just warm enough and just cold enough. The sun shone brightly all day but not too warmly. There is great excitement here about the Japanese; it was reported that they would be at the President's this afternoon to hear the music but they were not there. A great many were disappointed; we all went but we knew before we started that they would not be there; we saw a great many of our acquaintances there, very few ladies but a great many men. I never saw such a crowd up there before. Miss Murray went up with us.

May 17th

This has been another delightful day; it clouded up towards dark and rained a little, we thought it would be quite a storm but was not. Sarah and I went out shopping this afternoon; I bought a large trunk for Sister and myself. We were in a great hurry to get back as we thought it would rain any minute. We looked in several stores for a breast pin for me but did not get one. Aunt bought Kate a watch while we were out, after tea she went to see Aunt. She was examining some dress goods that she bought today. I can hardly find anything to write about of late.

May 18th

It was very cloudy this morning but cleared off about 12 o'clock. We went to see Aunt before school. Kate and I went to see our dressmaker (Miss Payne) after dinner. We called in to see Mrs. Dalton on our way up. Kate got her dress but mine was not finished quite to suit me so I had to leave it until tomorrow morning. We stopped to see Mary Todd as we came back, her brother was in the parlor and her mother came in before we left. I spent the remainder of the day at Aunt's and reading. At night I went to a concert at a Baptist Church but saw very few of my acquaintances. Mrs. Powell spoke to me and Mr. Harmon and Mr. Coyle sat very near us and kept us laughing all the time.[33] Some of the singing was very good. We rode up there in an Omnibus but walked back.

May 19th

I was very busy all this morning sewing and preparing to go to the President's to [hear] music as the Japanese are going to be there. We thought we would go early to get a good place from which we could see them. We started about 4 o'clock and stood there until nearly 8 o'clock. The music commenced at six and the Japanese came out in about half an hour. They sat in the Portico of the President's house; we could see them very plainly. They were dressed elegantly but more like women than men. The President, Miss Lane and several others came out where they were. I never saw such a crowd in my life, the whole place was as full as could be. They were so thick it was difficult to get through the crowd. I got lost once. I could not see a single person that I knew but soon caught up with my company.[34]

May 21st for 20th

Yesterday we went up to Sabbath School as usual. We were not there long when Mr. Sorsby and Mr. Harmon came in. Mr. Sorsby came around to where we were sitting and asked if we would not like to go to the 13th Baptist Church with them; as I had never been there, I told him to come back in time for us and we would go. Dr. Hill preached but I did not like him much. Mr. Sorsby walked with Kate and I and Mr. Harmon with Sister and Sarah. Mr. Sorsby is angry at Mr. Norton's family about something so he asked me if he could not see me at Aunt's sometime as it is only next door. I did not know what to say but I thought as I had such a short time to stay here I told him we would see him. He admired Kate's and my new dresses very much; he said they were the prettiest he had seen. I don't know whether I ought to have consented for him to come to see us but I can not help it now. I went with Aunt to Church at night, heard a stranger preach a very good sermon. The others did not go, excepting Kate.

May 21st

We had a holiday today as it was the anniversary of the Sabbath Schools. 5000 children marched in procession through the streets. They all wanted me to go with them but I did not feel able to walk so far so the other girls went. I went with Aunt over to the Smithsonian to watch them form the procession. It was very warm. I pitied the little ones very much but they did not seem to mind it at all.[35] We went to Press Henry's house and got acquainted with his three daughters. From the Smithsonian we went to the Wesley Chapel and heard the children sing and several addresses by the Ministers. I saw a good many of my acquaintances. In the afternoon we went out shopping with Aunt. Mr. Latterman was in one of the stores; he said he was very tired as he had walked with the children this morning. That was all he could talk about. I feel very tired myself although I did not walk nearly so far as they.

May 22nd

Everything passed as usual in school this morning excepting the girls asked Mr. and Mrs. Norton to permit them to have a party on the last day of school or sometime before then. They did not give a very satisfactory answer although we all believe they will consent. I wanted to go to two places tonight; the Smithsonian and to Mrs. Burr's to a little party. I concluded to go to the latter place; the others went to the Smithsonian. I would have enjoyed myself a great deal more if I had been acquainted with more of the company, but I soon got acquainted with them enough to talk. We came away at half past ten, rather early but Uncle was in a hurry. The girls did not get in until some time after I did. They say they had a fine time. It has been very warm again today; it looked like rain but did not. We had strawberries for dinner today for the first time this year. Mollie Spates called here this evening. I had not seen her for a long time.

May 23rd

Sarah and I went out at five o'clock this morning to take our music lessons. It looked very much like rain but did not. We went to school as usual. (I suppose it is hardly worth while to write that but let it be known that this is *my* journal). I was very sleepy all day, I hardly know what is the matter with me. Kate and I went down to Mrs. Hoyle's this afternoon to see Mollie Spates but she had gone on a picnic party so we did not see her. We went from there to see Lida Hanson, it was a long walk and I was very tired when we got home again. We went to see "Italia" at night. It was the most beautiful panorama I have ever seen. We "went" into St. Peter's at Rome and "climbed" Mount Vesuvius; it is splendid when pouring forth fire and lava. We also saw a terrible storm at sea, heard the wind and thunder and saw the lightning.[36]

June 4th

It has been a long time since I have written but it was not because I had nothing to write but rather because I have been quite ill, so ill that I had to have a doctor (Dr. Garnett) three or four times. I suffered a great deal and had very high fevers. The doctor said it was caused by taking a very violent cold. The ladies had a strawberry festival for the Young Men's Christian Association this week but I could not attend but once and that was on the day that I got up.[37] I was well enough to go to a May party at Miss Harrover's school at Georgetown Thursday but was sick next day to pay for it. I enjoyed myself very much. A member of Congress went with me, he is Mr. Mollery of Arkansas (I think that is it).[38] I got acquainted with so many that I can not remember all their names. It is very cloudy today and we had a hard hail storm this afternoon. Hail as large as a small cracker.

There were a great many fights and riots today as it was [the] election of Mayor. I heard that several persons were shot; the whole sky was red tonight from the lights of the bonfires.[39]

June 5th

Kate and I arose at 5 o'clock this morning to go take our music lessons. I went in Sister's place as she had not got well enough to go out so early.

I heard a great deal today about the riot last night. Some of the school girls said that both Mr. Bradley and Mr. Magruder were both nearly killed in the mob. It seems rather strange as they are both Superintendents of Sabbath Schools. They did nothing but said a few words that were overheard by the mob. Mrs. Naylor and Blanche came to see Aunt while we were there. Mrs. Naylor said she was frightened nearly to death last night, she said she saw five pistols shot off before her door. Oh! It was awful. They were beating and shooting everyone that did not vote for their man.[40] The "Plug Uglies" from Baltimore are here; they are the ones who make the noise.[41] I have been afraid to go out today for fear of meeting a crowd.

June 6th

The sun shone very brightly all day and it has been very warm. Nothing of importance occurred today. I am so busy all the time now that I hardly have time to do anything but study.

June 13th

It has been a long time since I wrote in this book; I have been so busy that I have not had time. I do not remember all the little incidents that have taken place since I wrote last but do remember some of the important ones. Saturday Kate, Sarah, Aunt, Uncle and myself went to the Capitol for music. My Uncle introduced us to two very nice young men, one from Alabama, the other from Tennessee. Mr. McCraw, from Alabama, walked with me and Mr. Johnson, from Tennessee, with Kate and Sarah. We walked up to the Capitol to look at the statuary in the old hall of Representatives but the door was locked and we could not get in.

Sunday

We went to Church as usual.

Monday

We went to school and did nothing but study until tea time, went to see Aunt and sat in the parlor.

Tuesday

We all went to Mount Vernon (including Miss Lottie, although we did not want her to go at all). We started a little after six in the morning and when we got to the Omnibus we found that the boat did not start for Mount Vernon until ten o'clock so we concluded to go to Alexandria and see what was to be seen. We got there half an hour after leaving Washington (seven miles) and remained there until half past ten. While we were there we went to see the Church that Washington used to attend. We got some ivy leaves that were growing over the walls, saw old tomb stones that were placed there in 1771 (89 years ago), I think that was the oldest date we saw. Aunt and Kate took a sketch of the Church. We could not get in so we climbed up to one of the windows and looked in. The pulpit is very high and that was all that I saw different from other Episcopal churches. I forgot; they had the Commandments, The Lord's Prayer and The Creed on each side of the pulpit. We hurried from the Church for fear we would be left. When we got down to the wharf we found that the boat would not be there for an hour so we had to wait in a store for it and when it did come it was crowded. When we arrived at Mount Vernon there was a general rush to see who would get to the tomb first. I had a very hard time getting up the hill; my dress was long and got caught on everything.

The first thing we met of interest is the tomb; it is built of brick, has iron grates through which we could see the Sarcophagus of Washington and Mrs. Washington which are made of white marble. I got some pebbles from the inside of the tomb. We are not allowed to touch a single plant or weed of any kind. There are four marble monuments near the tomb erected to the memory of various relations of Washington. We next went to the old tomb. I could hardly tell what it had been; I think it was of brick and made so that the coffins would be underground. Next we went to the house. We passed by an old summer house which had nearly fallen to pieces. We first entered by a long piazza facing the east and about midway entered a hall that ran through to the back yard. In the hall was the key of the bastille hanging in a glass box. Everything looked like I expected it would excepting it had gone to decay more than I had expected to find it; but the ladies, I hope, will soon make it look beautiful again. The gardens were beautiful but we were not permitted to go in. I wanted to go into his parlor and upstairs so much but they would not let me. We had a splendid view of the Potomac for miles. Coming home it was very warm. We stopped at Fort Washington and saw a great many cannon etc. We went to a concert at our own Church tonight; the singing was splendid. The best singers in the city were there.

Saturday, June 16th

A few hot days have passed in which time I could find no opportunity to write. We are just as busy as we can be with our studies, stayed in all day Thursday until tea. We went to see Aunt and went into the parlor and were not there long when Mr. McCraw came in. He played several games of checquers [*sic*] with Kate and I and then proposed going to the Capitol as they have night sessions now. We consented and went up to the House but Congress had adjourned so we went to the Senate and stayed there until 11 o'clock. Friday we were very busy all day with our studies preparing for an examination and today we stood a perfect examination on Physiology.

The sun shone very brightly this morning but it is now pouring down rain but I think it will clear off soon. Mr. Norton has consented for the school girls to give a party the 22nd of this month. The girls will pay for everything.

June 28, 1860 On the Cars in Virginia

We left Washington yesterday at six o'clock in the afternoon. We had an exhibition in the morning; we all received our diplomas, Kate, Sister, Sallie and me and also premiums, they were handsome books.[42] A great many of the girls cried when we left, several came to see us off. I felt very badly on leaving my friends but also glad to go home to see my dearest relatives. I see that I cannot write very well in the cars so I will stop until some other time. (Later) As the cars have stopped I will write while I have time. I thought I wanted to leave Washington very badly and that I would not care a bit but when the time came I could hardly keep from crying. A great many of the girls promised to write to me. Mr. Smithson came to see us just as we were going to start. I had not spoken to old Mrs. Norton for some time until the day I started home; I managed to kiss her and tell her good-bye. None of us spoke to Miss Lottie, Sarah did not even speak to old Mrs. Norton. We had a "falling out" some time ago about the party we had at Mr. Norton's.[43]

June 29th

Our cars are in East Tennessee. (Later) Our cars are in Union, Tennessee at half past five o'clock in the afternoon. We are getting near home. We are getting very tired of the cars; it is so warm we can hardly stand it.

June 30th

We passed Chattanooga, East Tennessee this morning. I think it a poor looking city or maybe I could not see the city from where we were. We did not go out of the depot. We also passed around the Lookout Mountains. There is only room enough for the cars to pass between a solid wall of rock on one side and the Tennessee River on the other. We could see the tops of trees below us and I felt as if we were rushing to certain destruction but nothing happened to prevent us crossing safely.

(Later) We reached Bellefonte today; all of Uncle Frank's family seemed very glad to see us.[44] Pa arrived here this evening, he expects to start home Monday with us with him. At Stevenson Mr. T. Street and John Rayburn got on the cars.[45] We were right glad to see them as they were the first persons we met in Alabama with whom we were acquainted. I can hardly realize that I am in Alabama and will soon see Ma, brothers and sisters. I understand that Sister Charity has been quite sick and that she lost her baby.[46]

July 2nd

We got home this evening about 9 o'clock. I cannot tell how glad I was to get home nor how glad all were to see us. All look like they used to excepting Mattie, she has grown a great deal. She was but a babe when we went to Washington.[47]

July 4th

I am at home once more and my school days are over. I shall now try to write something of my country and politics. This is a fit day to begin being the day on which our forefathers declared our independence. All apprehend danger for our country and at present there is great excitement about the UNION.

THREE

Home in Marshall County, Alabama: Lincoln's Election and the Dawn of War, July 1860–December 1861

July 1860

GREAT EXCITEMENT PRE-VAILING THROUGHOUT THE WHOLE COUNTRY! There are four candidates for the presidential chair; Breckinridge of Kentucky, Douglas of Illinois, Bell of Tennessee and last, Lincoln of Illinois. The two first claim to be Democrats, the second a Whig and the fourth a Republican.[1] I am for Breckinridge but most of our family are for Douglas.[2] Every day we hear of some political speaking or barbecue. Nearly everyone thinks that Lincoln will be elected and the great question of the time is, "What Shall We Do if He Does Succeed?" Some say, "Secede from the Union!", others say, "Try him a while and then if we do not like him: secede."

August 1860

The political excitement is still running high. Some hold on to the hope that Breckinridge will be elected. Some of the most eminent lawyers have left their offices and are making stump speeches throughout the country. There is also excitement in the north concerning the Prince of Wales's visit to this country. Grand preparations are being made in the cities to welcome him with due respect. I think he does not intend to come very far south.[3] I always find fault with our Republic (men and women) for running almost crazy if a "Crowned Head" happens to visit this free country. All from President down seem to worship at the shrine of royalty.[4]

September 1860

One of my brothers (Watkins) has gone to Washington to attend medical lectures. He intends to remain there until next spring if the political troubles do not rise too high for him to remain. Politics is all the talk yet, even the ladies take a great interest in it. The contents of every paper are greedily devoured by all. All watch with anxiety the approach of the election and for the result. Wattie arrived at Washington a few days after the Prince of Wales left. He says that Breckinridge is more popular there than any of the [other] candidates.

October 1860

As the election approaches the excitement increases. We went to a Douglas barbecue on the 15th of this month; had two Douglas speeches and one Bell. There is great excitement in Huntsville, Ala.—Douglas is to be there soon and they are making preparations for a grand reception for him.

(Later) October 1860

Douglas arrived in Huntsville on the day appointed and thousands turned out to see him. Brother William went to hear him speak and he was perfectly delighted with his speech; very few were not pleased.[5]

November 1, 1860

Willie, Sister Mary, Ellen Parker, Tilley Parker and myself went up to Bellefonte to see our relations.[6] It rained and was very disagreeable; had a party the night after we got there. Cousin and Willie did not stay long after they got there as they wanted to come home to vote at the election which comes off on the sixth of this month.[7]

November 6, 1860 (At Bellefonte)

The excitement here was not as great as I expected it would be. Breckinridge got the majority but the Douglasites said they did not care as they got Huntsville. Douglas got but one state, Missouri.[8]

November 7, 1860

Hear today that Lincoln is elected, I hardly know what we will do about it.

November 15th

Saw several gentlemen with "secession" cockades on today.[9] One said that if Alabama did not secede he would leave the state; he did not say where he would go.

December 5, 1860

I am eighteen (18) years old today. I feel very singular and cannot realize that I am so old.

December 1860

Since it is known that Lincoln is elected the sole subject of conversations is about secession. Some in the northern part of the State are very strong Unionists but in the South they are just as strong for secession.[10] We left Bellefonte a few days ago; our cousins came home with us.

December 21, 1860

I heard today that South Carolina had seceded, but the U.S. troops still hold *Fort Sumter* near Charleston. It is commanded by Major Anderson of Kentucky.[11] South Carolina seceded the 20th of December; I expect several states will follow.

December 30, 1860

All of us started to Carrie Arnold's wedding today.[12] The snow is six inches deep but has begun to melt a little. We stayed at Mr. Parker's in Warrenton overnight.

January 1, 1861

We arrived safely at Mr. Parker's but were very tired. Carrie was married tonight to Mr. Watkins of Kentucky.[13] She had six bridesmaids; five were Fennells, Kate, Maggie, Mary, Sarah and myself. Jane Arnold was her other waiter.[14]

All are strong secessionists up here. I sang a Union song but very few would listen but when I sang a secession song nearly all were pleased.[15]

January 2nd

We would have gone home today but it rained so we could not go. The secession cockades are quite numerous. A great many blame Mr. Yancey for the secession movement in Alabama, while others think him the greatest person that ever trod this free soil. I think he is next to Breckinridge.[16]

January 11th

Alabama seceded from the Union today. Some are not pleased because they did not refer it to the people but the greater part are satisfied. They (the

Alabama Convention) have called a convention of all the seceding States to meet at Montgomery, Alabama, the fourth of February. WE ARE NOW FREE!

January 14th

Heard that Georgia and Florida seceded the tenth of this month, one day before Alabama.[17] This will be a memorable month in the history of our country; gaining ground every day, we will soon have all the Southern States.

> "Harrah for the South!"
> The Glorious South
> The land of song and story.
> Ye men of Alabama
> Awake! Arise! Awake!
> And rend the coils asunder
> Of this Abolition snake."

January 30th

Heard of the secession of Mississippi and Louisiana today. Mississippi seceded the 10th of January and Louisiana the 26th.[18] There is great rejoicing through the Country.

February 4th

This is the day for the convention of the seceding states to meet at Montgomery and the peace conference at Washington.[19] Davis of Mississippi was inaugurated the 18th of this month for our president.[20]

March 6th

One more state has joined us. Texas seceded the 4th of March, the same day that Lincoln was inaugurated. All were glad to hear of it. There were only six or seven in the convention that opposed secession.[21] We gain a large state by her seceding. It is reported that Lincoln has sent orders for Fort Sumter to evacuate but orders for Fort Pickens to be reinforced.[22] All are dissatisfied with Lincoln's inaugural address. Secession feeling is increasing. Stephens of Georgia is our Vice-President.[23]

April 1st

Nearly everyone thinks that there will soon be fighting at Fort Sumter. Lincoln did not send orders for its evacuation. A company of soldiers has formed at Huntsville and expects to leave soon for Fort Morgan.[24]

April 16th

It is reported that Fort Sumter has been taken by the Confederate troops. Have not learned the number of slain.[25]

April 18th

Frank and I went up to see Sister Charity.[26] Mr. Henry told us it was true that Fort Sumter was taken after an engagement of 35 hours and that not a single man was hurt. The Fort was taken April 13th, 1861, a glorious but bloodless engagement.[27] WAR HAS REALLY BEGUN! The papers state that Fort Pickens has been reinforced and that it will take a severe fight to take that stronghold. General Beauregard was the Commander of the southern army at the taking of Fort Sumter.[28]

April 19th

Glorious news! *Virginia* seceded the 16th of April.[29] We have no doubt that the other border states will join us. We also heard that they attacked Fort Pickens on the 16th; they had been fighting five hours when we received the news.[30] I can hardly realize that war is really going on in this once peaceful country but it is and we will have to bear it with fortitude. I have acquaintances at Fort Pickens.

April 20th

The people of this county met in Guntersville today to organize a company as the Governor of this State has called for three thousand troops.[31] Nearly all of the gentlemen of my acquaintance joined, among them was my brother William and my brother-in-law Sam Henry.

April 22nd

No news as yet from Fort Pickens. Cousin Joseph Fennell went with Willie to Guntersville this morning to join the Company there.[32] (Evening): Understand the report was false that Fort Pickens was attacked but we are not sure. Heard that General Scott had offered his services to Virginia.[33]

April 26th

There was quite a battle fought at Baltimore, Maryland the 19th of this month. The Massachusetts (abolition) troops tried to pass through to Washington but the citizens of Baltimore did not want them to go so they had to fight; one paper said that a hundred and thirty (130) were slain.[34] We also heard that there were thirty or forty killed at the taking of Fort Sumter.[35] The Governor has accepted the company formed in this county last week. They expect to leave soon. One of my cousins (John Allison) leaves in one of the Huntsville companies Monday; several of my acquaintances are going at the same time.[36] Sister and I wish to make a flag for the "Marshall Boys" (That is the name of the company).[37] We told brother William to find out if there were suitable materials in Guntersville. Everyone expects that a battle will be fought in Washington soon, the South will no doubt try to take the city. I received a letter from a friend (Mrs. Murray) stating that the city was filled with troops and that all business had stopped.[38] I hear today that the North is going to try Anderson and Scott for treason but do not know that it is true.[39]

April 29th[40]

Congress meets today in Montgomery, Alabama. It is reported the president will resign (Davis) and the vice-president (Stephens) will take his place; Davis will put himself at the head of the Southern army.[41] Understand today that the Baltimoreans have torn the railway bridges down to prevent troops from passing to Washington, and now have men stationed to prevent them rebuilding them.[42] Heard yesterday (Sunday) that the Confederate Army had taken Fort Pickens, had 1700 men killed but did not hear what day the battle was fought or how many were killed in the Fort. It is awful to think about it; I hope there were not so many killed as reported.[43]

May 3rd

The report about Scott offering his services to Virginia was false for he is still on Lincoln's side.[44] There has been another battle in Maryland, near Annapolis; over a hundred were killed.[45] We have been expecting Wattie home for some time and are now very uneasy about him as we do not know where he is nor what he is doing. We have not heard from him since the 16th of April. Fort Pickens has not been taken but we expect them to attack it soon. We hardly know what to believe, we hear so many reports. The report about the Baltimoreans taking so many Northern troops and arms was false but they did fight and made them run, killed 8 or 9 on both sides.[46]

May 4th

We attended a barbecue at Warrenton today given to the Volunteers. A great many were there; had six or seven speeches from various Volunteers. We are still very uneasy about brother Wattie; a great many were asking about him and expressed a great deal of uneasiness on his account. My brother-in-law Sam Henry is Captain of the company, "The Marshall Boys."[47]

"The love that for the Union,
Once in our bosoms beat;
From insult and from injury,
Has turned to scorn and hate.
And the banner of Secession
Today we lift on high,
Resolved beneath that glorious flag,
To conquer or to die."[48]

May 5th

We received a letter from brother Wattie. He is now at Emory and Henry College, waiting for Pa to send him some money; he said he left Washington in a hurry.[49] The city is full of Republican troops. All southern sympathizers were ordered to leave Washington twenty days before Wattie left.[50] He slipped out at night with some other Southerners.

May 7th

Wattie arrived home today very unexpectedly; we did not look for him until Friday. He says that there were about 15,000 troops (Republican) in Washington when he left, which was nearly two weeks ago, and they have been pouring in ever since. He also said that the people in Virginia are stronger for secession than they are here and are more excited. General Lee is the Commander in Chief of the Virginians.[51]

May 8th

Some say that they don't want peace but wish to fight. We hear a great many rumors about Fort Pickens being taken, "Battle of Cairo," etc., but give little attention to them as we have heard so many false reports.[52] I think I will write no more reports until I know they are true. I think there is no hope for *peace* now.

May 9th

We heard today that *Arkansas* passed the secession ordinance the 6th of this month. We have been expecting it for some time and all rejoice over the news. We now have nine stars in our glorious flag. I wish we had seceded twelve years ago for we have in fact had no union since General Jackson's presidential term. I think maybe if we had seceded then we would have gone out peaceably. We have no idea how long the war will last, some say four years or until Lincoln is put out of office while some think six months or a year will settle the question.

May 10th

We hear of a great many little skirmishes between the southerners and the northerners. We are expecting every day to hear of battles, hardly know where to expect they will fight first. We are anxious to hear the news from Europe as we wish to know whether the different powers will recognize our new government. We can only hope for the best; some think they will be obliged to recognize us as they cannot do without *cotton*.[53]

May 25th

North Carolina has passed the Ordinance of Secession, I did not hear what day of the month. Tennessee seceded some time ago, I could not find out what day but she seceded before North Carolina. That is the tenth star in our flag.[54]

The "Marshall Boys" received their orders to march today. They will leave Wednesday. There is an Irish company going to leave sometime. Their Captain is Mr. J. Williams.[55]

May 28th

Heard of three battles today. One at Harpers Ferry, Culpepper and Hampton, all in Virginia.[56] The report says the South was quite victorious every time. *If God is with us, who can be against us?*

May 29th

We all went to Guntersville today to see the two volunteer companies leave on the boat. I have never witnessed such a scene before. There were several thousand persons there and all were bathed in tears while some of the ladies' shrieks rent the air at intervals as they bid farewell to their husbands, brothers and sons for they knew that it was a last farewell. The ladies were not alone in shedding tears for I believe there was not a man present who did not weep. I had a brother, brother-in-law and cousin in the company.[57] The ladies of Guntersville presented them with a flag, Miss Hennie Walpole delivered a very neat speech.[58] Mr. Eubanks received the flag.[59]

The city of Alexandria, Virginia was taken possession of by about 5,000 Federal troops in the morning of the 24th of May. Our troops, about 600 in number, made no resistance but retired in good order to Fairfax, a station ten miles from Alexandria. In the fight at Hampton, 600 of the Lincolnites were killed and wounded; 50 of our men were killed or wounded.[60]

The Southern Congress adjourned (at Montgomery, Alabama) May 22nd to meet at Richmond, Va. on July 20th.[61] It is reported that smallpox has broken out among the soldiers quartered in Washington, D.C.

There has been quite a fight at St. Louis, Missouri. The Federal troops took Camp Jackson and a great many prisoners.[62]

June 19th

There has been no battle at Harpers Ferry, Culpepper and Hampton but they have been fighting in Virginia. The Confederate troops were surprised recently at Philippa by three thousand Federals and for the moment were thrown into confusion and retreated but being reinforced they marched on the town and surrounded the enemy. A fierce fire ensued in which the Confederates killed and wounded over a hundred Federal troops while only six were killed on our side. The Confederate troops are now in possession of Philippa.[63]

There has also been a battle at "Bethel Church". It seems that the enemy while marching before day were encountered at Bethel Church by 1500 Confederates; the Federals being 4500 in number. After a spirited combat of short duration, the enemy was defeated and pursued some miles by our victorious troops who were commanded by Magruder. Our loss is reported one killed; the enemy 300. Only 600 of our troops were engaged, the rest being held back as a reserve. Our forces took several prisoners.[64] We expect to hear almost every day of battle. We have heard several times from our volunteers since they arrived at Richmond. All are doing well.

June 29th

There is scarcely a day but what we hear of a skirmish or battle. We expect to hear of great things soon as the Lincolnite Congress meets the 4th of July.[65] I expect there will be fighting—hard fighting. It is supposed that there are 220,000 in the Northern army and 150,000 in the Southern army.[66] These are the names of some of the places where they have been skirmishing; Vienna, Va., June 18th, 10 Federalists killed but none of the Confederates were hurt.[67] In St. Louis, June 18th, on the accidental discharge of a gun, the Federal troops commenced an indiscriminate fire without order. Seven of the citizens were slain besides a great many wounded.[68]

On June 20th the town of Romney was taken possession of by the Confederates. No loss to the Confederates but several of the Federalists were killed and 300 prisoners were taken by 4,000 secessionists.[69] They have been skirmishing near Manassas Junction and Yorktown with few troops and trifling results. THE FIRST BAYONET CHARGE OF THE WAR WAS AT THE BATTLE OF GREAT BETHEL.[70]

The account from Missouri says that the Missourians are rallying over the state and with McCullough's aid will, I hope, meet and whip out the Northern invaders.[71] The Southerners have evacuated Harpers Ferry, they did it to meet the enemy.[72]

July 4th

We usually have great rejoicing on this day but this year—how different! I have hardly heard anyone say a word about it and if they did speak of this being the 4th of July, they only spoke of it as being the day on which the Lincolnite Congress is to meet. They seem to think that we have no right to celebrate the day as formerly but I can see no reason why we should not; it was on the 4th of July that we declared (some of the Southern States, I mean) our independence of the English as well as the North. Later—I understand that there were two picnics near here to celebrate the 4th.

July 7th

I understand that the 4th was celebrated all over the South.[73]

July 13th

We received Lincoln's message today. He has called for four hundred thousand men and four hundred millions of dollars![74] Davis has also called for more troops, 5,000 from each state, I think.[75] The war has really begun and nobody knows when it will stop. We continue to hear of skirmishing everyday. We received letters from Brother Willie and Sam Henry a few days since. Capt. Henry has been appointed Lt. Colonel of the 9th Alabama regiment; we have heard since that they have been ordered to Winchester to join General Johnston.[76]

Gen. McCullough, with the help of the Missouri troops killed 900 of the Federalists and took 1,700 prisoners.[77] I expect that Missouri will pass the Ordinance of Secession soon.

Johnston and Jackson have been skirmishing with the Lincolnites near Martinsburg, Va.[78]

July 16th

There was a battle fought near Beverly, Virginia on the 13th of this month in which Gen. Garnett (Confederate) was killed and nearly all of his men were taken prisoner. The Federalists were commanded by Gen. McClellan; his army was twice as large as Garnett's. It is called the Battle of Laurel Hill.[79]

July 19th

Victory perches upon our banners! The Confederate army under General Beauregard gave battle to the enemy on the 18th at Bull Run, Virginia. It is supposed that about *five hundred* of the enemy were killed and a large number of them taken prisoner. On our side the casualties were few. The enemy numbered 7,000 or 8,000 while we did not have over 2,000.[80]

July 25th

I have the inexpressible satisfaction of announcing today another victory of our arms. A decisive victory after the most hotly contested and most important battle every fought on the American continent. The Confederate army under Generals J. E. Johnston and Beauregard were met at *Manassas*, Virginia by the Federalists under Generals Patterson and McDowell on Sunday, July 21st.[81] They commenced fighting early in the morning and fought until late in the afternoon. Our men took all of their famous batteries, among them was the great "Sherman Battery."[82] They left upon the field nearly every piece of their artillery, a large portion of their arms, equipments, baggage, etc., and almost every one of their wounded and dead which amounted together with the prisoners to nearly 15,000 to 20,000. There were about 300 of ours killed and several thousand wounded.[83] Among the things left on the field by the Northerners were *boxes* containing 32,000 handcuffs; I suppose they expected them.[84] It was a complete victory. The invaders were driven disgracefully from the field and made to fly in disorderly route back to their entrenchments, a distance of over thirty miles. President Davis arrived at the field of battle just as the enemy had turned to fly. He, with 1500 troops, pursued for some distance.[85] The Northern army was nearly three times as large as ours, I do not know the exact numbers.[86] The 4th Alabama regiment was among the bravest on the field and suffered more than any other excepting a Georgia regiment.[87] I had a great many acquaintances in that regiment, only one was killed; he was William Arnold of Blount County.[88] Willie writes that he was there and saw the whole battle but the Quartermaster would not let him fight as his regiment (the 9th Alabama) was not there. He had gone through with the horses and got there ahead of his company. He was very much disappointed.[89]

August 30th

There has been another great battle in Missouri near Springfield. The Southerners whipped the Lincolnites and killed one of their great generals (Gen. Lyons). There were about 400 killed on the North's side and about 200 Southerners. Ben McCullough and Hardee were our Generals.[90]

September 4th

Three companies left this county today. The Captains were: Capt. Henry, Capt. Ames and Capt. Ledbetter.[91] Brother Watkins and Cousin Hub Fennell went in Capt. Ike Henry's company.[92] The ladies of the neighborhood presented Capt. Henry with a beautiful silk flag. I presented it in the name of the ladies; Lieut. Carter received it.[93] He made a very nice speech but the boat was in such a hurry to go that he did not get through. It was presented at Deposit Ferry.

October 15th

There is great trouble apprehended from Kentucky. She did not secede and about half of her citizens are for the North and other half for the South, so we do not know how they will settle it. The Lincolnites came down to settle the rebellion (as they call it) and the Southerners went up to drive them out as they (the Northerners) spread desolation everywhere they go. Capt. Ike Henry's company returned home from Decatur (as the brigade they expected to join broke up) and have left again for Tennessee expecting to fight in Kentucky. I have heard lately that most of the Kentuckians are friendly with the South.[94]

November 1st

Missouri passed the Secession Ordinance Oct. 28th. The Confederate Congress received her as a Confederate State before she passed the ordinance.[95] They are fighting nearly all the time along the border.

One of the greatest battles that has been fought since the beginning of the war was fought at Leesburg, Virginia. The Confederates took over 700 prisoners, 4 cannons and 1000 stands of arms. The Federalists acknowledge the loss of 1,200. Their force was superior to ours, that is in number. When the Federalists were retreating the Confederates pushed them so hard that a great many jumped into the Potomac River and drowned. This battle was one of the several on record and was fought, I think, on Oct. 20–21; 106 were killed on our side. Col. Baker, the Federal commander, was killed.[96]

Nov 16th

1,200 Southerners were attacked by 5,000 Lincolnites in boats opposite Columbus, Ky. The Southerners were driven back with great loss and the Northerners were on the point of gaining a complete victory when Gen. Cheatham came up with reinforcements which turned the tide of battle, the Southerners rallied and drove them back to their boats, killing great numbers and taking many prisoners. They also sunk some of the boats.[97]

Port Royal, South Carolina was attacked the same day by a fleet of Lincoln's ships. There were only a few troops stationed at Port Royal and they had but little ammunition and few guns; the ones they had were far inferior to the Federal guns therefore they (the Southern guns) were soon dismounted and ammunition having given out, the Southerners had to evacuate, but men are rushing from all parts of South Carolina and Georgia to retake the place.[98]

Yesterday, Friday, November 15th was observed as a day of fasting, humiliation and prayer throughout the Confederate States.[99] I think this is a good time for fasting and prayer for there is a dark cloud hanging over our Country which God alone can lift. We should also thank Him for His protecting care and for the many victories He has given us. Since the bombardment of Fort

Sumter on the 12th of April (which was itself a brilliant achievement) no less than nine fields have been won by the Confederate arms. The Battles of Big Bethel Church, Bull Run, Manassas, Springfield, Carnifex, Leesburg and last but not least, Columbus.[100] All terminated in the rout of the Yankees, with an aggregate of at least 6,000 killed, double that number wounded and eight or ten thousand prisoners; summing up, altogether not less than 20,000 of the enemy put "hors de combat" in the nine battles. If we were to count the numerous skirmishes in which we have been victorious, the number would be increased by at least 5,000 more.[101] We lost the battle of Rich Mountain, W.Va. nominally and accidentally, for the Federal troops were badly beaten and only succeeded by the treachery of a Virginia Tory who showed a secret path to the rear of our troops.[102] We lost Fort Hatteras, North Carolina by the overwhelming force of the Federals and the superior range of their guns.[103] In these two engagements about 1,000 of our men were captured and probably 100 killed and wounded.[104] Neither of these affairs exceed in importance some of the skirmish victories of the Confederates. The nine grand triumphs which we achieved will form splendid chapters in the history of the young Republic; never was there a brighter record. The South has proved herself worthy of an honorable membership in the family of nations. Jeff Davis and Stephens have been elected our President and Vice-President for the next six years, without opposition.[105]

Nov 19th

Gen. Scott has resigned and McClellan takes his place and Gen. Halleck takes McClellan's.[106] I am glad that Scott has resigned for I think the South had more to fear from him than any other Northern General.[107] Some time ago some of the Southern soldiers took a notion of breaking up an abolition camp on Santa Rosa Island and they succeeded finely, put the enemy to flight. Some say they could have taken Fort Pickens if they had pushed on. Our loss: 20 killed, 42 wounded and 29 prisoners.[108]

(Later) Cousin Tom Fennell came in very unexpectedly this evening from Texas where he has been for the last six years.[109] Ma spoke to him and called him "Tommy"; I could not imagine who he was. He was changed so much that his brother Joe did not know him.[110]

*We heard a short time ago of the death of cousin William B. Allison in Virginia. He had not been there long.[111]

Dec 2nd

There has been quite a battle fought on the 23rd or 24th of November between our forces at Pensacola and the Northern at Fort Pickens. The bombardment lasted nearly two days. Sixteen men were "killed on our side and the report says sixty on the enemy's"; they expect another engagement soon.[112]

We received a letter from brother Willie a few days ago stating that our brother-in-law, Lieut. Col. Henry had been promoted to Colonel of the 9th Alabama regiment.[113] They think there will be another fight in Virginia soon.

The Southern men in Tennessee have had a great deal of trouble with the Union men in the East part of the state. They (Union men) have burnt several very costly bridges on the railroad to prevent troops passing. Several have been caught and hung, others are waiting for trials.[114]

Dec 5th

(My nineteenth birthday) Mason and Slidell (The Southern ministers to Europe) were stopped on their passage to England and taken prisoners. They were on a British ship and a great many think that it will cause a quarrel between the English and the North. I hope it will.[115]

Dec 20th

Received news from England today. The seizure of Mason and Slidell caused a great excitement. They say the act is a flagrant violation of the laws of nations and a direct and international insult to England. Naval volunteers were offering to protect the British flag. The people declare that all persons aboard a British ship under a British flag are protected as if on the soil of Great Britain. France communicated with England and decided upon a mutual policy. The British are bitter and hostile to the Federals and demand the unconditional surrender of Mason and Slidell and Eustis and McFarland (their secretaries) and that the Federals humbly salute the British flag.[116]

We received intelligence today of a skirmish near Green River (about six miles from Bowling Green) in Kentucky. It appears that about 200 Texas Rangers under Col. Terry while out scouting came upon the enemy's pickets and drove them in about a mile this side of Green River. The Rangers were attacked by about 600 of an Indiana regiment. Col. Terry was killed while leading his men on a charge; when the Rangers saw that their gallant Colonel had been killed they became perfectly desperate and finally drove the enemy from their position. Six were killed on our side and the loss of the enemy was heavy, one of the Rangers counted sixty-six dead men on the field.[117]

There has been a fight in the Allegheny Valley near Cheat Mountain in western Virginia. Our losses were estimated at 20 killed and 97 wounded; the Federal loss was fully 500. General Milroy commanded the Federals and it is supposed that he was killed from reports made by prisoners. Col. Johnson commanded the Confederates.[118]

Dec 23rd

Heard today that the North refused to give up Mason, Slidell and their secretaries. I think war is inevitable between England, France and the United States. We must wait and see the end.[119]

Dec 25th

It was a false report about the North refusing to give up Mason and Slidell but it is now believed that they will comply with the demands of England. Today does not look like Christmas, it is so dull.[120]

FOUR

"Yonder Come the Yankees": Burned Cotton and Profound Sorrow, 1862

Jan 1, 1862

Cassie M. Fennell at Fort Deposit, Alabama.

Is it possible that another year has dawned upon us and to find our beloved Country distracted by war? I had hoped otherwise but all we hear now is war and rumors of war. May the first of next year find our Country enveloped in the Mantle of *Peace*.

Jan 10th

There has been a fight in Virginia recently in which our forces were driven back, the enemy outnumbered us. The battle was fought at Dranesville, Va. On December 23rd the 10th Alabama regiment was in the engagement and suffered more than any other. Lieut. Col. Martin of Alabama was killed.[1]

Jan 11th

This is a day long to be remembered by Alabamians; the day Alabama threw off the yoke and declared herself an independent state.

Jan 12th

Mason and Slidell have been given up; they embarked for England on the first day of January 1862.[2]

A great many think the war will end by April; I hope it will for what good will it do for either the North or us? England and France will soon recognize us, there is but little doubt. They say the blockade is ineffective.[3]

Jan 20th

What a mild winter we have had! No snow and very little ice, today looks like May. Flowers are budding and some blooming in the garden. I am glad it is not cold for I think of how much the poor soldiers have to suffer. I saw in a paper that it had been very cold in Virginia. I also saw a soldier from Mobile yesterday. He says when he was there he could hardly believe that it was winter it was so warm. He said he saw plenty of flowers there.

Jan 23rd

Heard of another skirmish in Kentucky. Twenty of our men killed; the number of the enemy I have forgotten.[4]

Jan 24th

Cousin John Henry was here today direct from the Army in Virginia on a *furlough*, his health being bad.[5] He says that 15,000 men have died in the Army in Virginia and more are dying every day. He also told us of the death of Mr. Washington May of Guntersville, who died in Kentucky.[6] He was in the same company as brother Watkins. He is the sixth young gentleman of my acquaintance who has died or been killed since the war began; here are their names: William Arnold, killed in the battle of Manassas; Albert Russell, died of the fever in Pensacola; Cousin William B. Allison, died with the fever in Virginia; William Richards, died in the Missouri Army and John Gardner, died at his father's in Madison County.[7] He was taken sick in camp and sent home. We cannot help being uneasy about our brothers when so many are falling around them but we hope a kind Providence will bring them safely back.

Jan 25th

We received information today of a battle being fought near Prestonsburg, Ky., on the 10th instant, between the Confederate forces under a Gen. Moore. Gen. Marshall's forces engaged did not exceed 1,300 (Col. Trigg's regiment being held in reserve) while that of the enemy is reported at six to ten thousand. Our forces repulsed the enemy *three* times with reported loss on their side of *400* killed; our loss, some *15 or 20* killed and wounded.[8]

Jan 28th

Heard of another battle in Kentucky in which the Confederates were defeated. The enemy were lying in ambush near Fishing Creek and fired on Gen. Crittenden's forces. The engagement lasted nearly all day. Gen. Zollicoffer was killed early in the battle. The enemy was repulsed three times but received large reinforcements and rallied in consequence. The Confederates fell back, abandoning tents and equipage. Two or three hundred of our men were killed. Crittenden's force numbered about 5,000, the enemy's 14,000. Gen. Crittenden has rallied his forces and made a stand at Monticello, Kentucky about nine miles from the battlefield and is now ready to oppose the enemy, having received reinforcements. The defeat did not amount to a disaster. Expect there will be another fight soon. The battle was fought on the 19th of January. The Federals were commanded by General Thomas. The loss of Zollicoffer excited a profound sorrow throughout the South.[9]

(Later) General Jackson has driven the Federalists from Romney, Virginia. They heard he was advancing upon them and did not wait for him to make his appearance but left as quick as possible, leaving many valuable stores which fell into Jackson's hands. We understand that Jackson, hearing that they (the Federals) could not cross the Potomac, pushed on after them and took the whole army which amounted to 6,000 under Gen. Lander. I do not know the strength of the Confederate forces.[10]

Jan 30th

Ex-president Tyler died in Richmond, the 18th of January. A universal feeling of profound sorrow was awakened throughout the Country by the announcement of his death.[11]

Prince Albert of England died in December. The country (England) is in deep mourning for him. It has not been long since the Queen's mother died and now her husband is taken.[12]

Feb 6th

The cause of the South appears gloomier than it ever has before. England, it seems has turned against us, or that is, she seems more inclined toward the North than before. We heard once that both England and France had recognized our independence but it was a false report. All we can do is to put our trust in *Providence* and all will turn out right. God alone knows how long this war will last, there appears no sign of PEACE now.

Feb 14th

The Federals are getting very bold. The waters have been so high that they have come up the Tennessee River in their gunboats as far as Tuscumbia and Florence, Alabama. They took Fort Henry as they passed. We since heard that the Confederates had retaken it but are not sure that it is true. They did not remain long in Tuscumbia or Florence but took 160 bales of cotton, turned and went off. It created great excitement in all this part of the state; those places are about 80 miles from here. The Federals have Fort Henry yet.[13]

Feb 22nd

Jeff Davis of Mississippi was inaugurated at Richmond today, President of the *Southern* Confederacy.[14]

March 3rd

A battle commenced at Fort Donelson, Wednesday, 12th of February and lasted until Sunday, the 16th. Our men drove them back every time and our victory would have been complete had not the enemy received reinforcements, and our men being so worn out. General Pillow and General Floyd retreated from the Fort leaving General Buckner to make the surrender with 12,000 brave Confederate soldiers. General Hindman was also in the Fort at the surrender.[15] There was one company from this county (Marshall), the one that I presented with a flag, in the fight, all of whom were taken prisoners, excepting thirty. Among the prisoners was one of my brothers (Watkins) and a good many of my acquaintances. There was also a cavalry company from this county but they all escaped except one that was killed; they were under Capt. Milner.[16]

The Southern Army evacuated Nashville, Tennessee a few days ago and it is now occupied by the Northern Vandals. Our army is retreating to Tuscumbia and Huntsville, Alabama and Chattanooga, Tennessee and intends to make southern Tennessee and northern Alabama the battle ground. The people are very much dissatisfied with the movement of our army. I have seen several that participated in the fight at Donelson and they say it was a harder fought battle than Manassas. There were about 1,600 killed and wounded on our side and the enemy lost from 6,000 to 7,000.[17] The whole country is in great excitement and prospects are gloomy but we trust in Providence.

Roanoke Island, on the coast of North Carolina, was taken by about 15,000 Yankees on February 8th. There were about 3,000 southerners nearly all of which were taken prisoners. There were about 300 Confederates killed and near 1000 Federals.[18] They intend to get the whole coast in their hands and I expect they will for we have not the boats to fight them on the water.

March 15th

Victory again perches on our banner. Our forces have gained two naval victories and one on land. Two of our vessels sunk two Federal vessels and ran two aground in Hampton Roads on the coast of Virginia. The other naval fight was somewhere on the Potomac, I have not got the particulars.[19]

The battle was fought in Arkansas under Price, McCullough and others. The Northerners hoisted the black flag. We hear that 11,000 were killed on their side and 2,000 on our side; we also understand that all their generals were killed as well as three or four of ours. It was the most terrible battle that has been fought.[20]

March 20th

General McCullough and several of our officers were killed in the fight in Arkansas (Pea Ridge or Elkton).[21]

March 29th

Understand that Gen. Robert Lee of Virginia is appointed Commander of our army, next in command to President Davis.[22]

Our army in Virginia has retreated some few miles as they had been in one place so long that they had about eaten the place out. Some say we had just as well give it up for they have so many more men than we, but I say not to give up as long as there is a man or woman in the South able to carry gun, pike or sword. The people in Tennessee, when they heard they (Northern Army) were coming, *burnt* cotton and everything they thought would be of any use to them and the people of *Alabama* will do it too, if they invade our *homes.*

March 30th

General Lee was appointed commander of our army but the President vetoed the bill, so he still commands on the coasts of South Carolina and Georgia.[23]

April 10th

There were three gentlemen to take tea here this afternoon who were direct from Huntsville, Alabama and they say that the Northern army took possession of that city early this morning.[24] We also hear of a great battle near Corinth, Mississippi. The enemy has lost so far 8,000 killed and 6,000 to 12,000 prisoners. Our losses in killed 2,000. I do not know anything about the number of prisoners they have taken. General Albert Sidney Johnston was killed. Forrest and a great many more of our brave men were wounded. I hope soon to hear the particulars. We could hear the cannonading very plainly last Sunday and Monday. Corinth is about 130 miles from here. We understand that the fight is still progressing, in fact, the negroes say they have heard cannon today. It is called the battle of *Shiloh*. General Beauregard commanded our forces.[25]

April 18th

It has been a week since Huntsville was taken and in that time scores of refugees from Madison County and from that city itself and Kentucky and Tennessee have passed here and a greater part of them stopped as they said they felt safe on this side of the Tennessee River. Huntsville is about 30 miles from here. One of my uncles was taken prisoner there but they finally let him loose.[26] As the train came down they fired into it and after stopping it took all who were in it prisoners. There is a sick soldier here now, a Mr. Ogden of Kentucky. He belongs to Forrest's regiment.[27] We understand a few days ago that there had been a great battle in Virginia in which we took 12,000 prisoners.[28] I have not the particulars as the mails have stopped since Huntsville was taken. I don't know that it is true.

In the latter part of the last or the first part of this month, Fort Craig, New Mexico was taken by our Texan troops. We took 5,000 prisoners.[29] A great many say that we must stop taking prisoners but kill all; but I do not think that is right.

The Yankees treat the negroes very badly in Huntsville. The negroes go to them for their free papers and they whip them and send them home. They have at last passed a law to shoot all who come to them as they are tired of them. They have shot several.[30]

There has been a fight at Cumberland Gap in which the Northern invaders were driven back with great loss; no one killed on our side, I think it was about the 25th of March.[31] I have a cousin there. (John Fennell of Mississippi).[32]

April 24th

We were all somewhat excited this afternoon as we heard that the Yankees were at Guntersville and Warrenton (about 5 miles from here) and that they were taking up all the refugees and all soldiers who were at home and as there were two soldiers here (Cousin Tom Fennell of Texas and Mr. Ogden of Kentucky) we felt a little uneasy. The people are almost afraid to offer resistance for fear they will destroy all their property. Cousin Tom and Mr. Ogden tried to get up a company to drive them away but there are not enough men left in this county to make a company.

April 25th

We understand this morning that the Yankees have left Guntersville and Warrenton. They did very little harm; stole a few horses and corn and took some army clothing at Guntersville, not much though. Last night they scattered about in Warrenton and went to private houses and ordered their supper. There were only 46 of them but they were well armed. The negroes were badly frightened as they have been treating them very badly over in Madison and Limestone counties. They have killed six or seven over there. I do not know why they do it.[33]

May 6th

So many reports reach us of battles, etc., that we do not know what to believe. I heard a gentleman say the other day that he could not believe anything that he heard and but half of what he saw himself. The latest we have from New Orleans is that they have been fighting for sometime and were expecting the enemy to bombard the city. Heard once that the city was burned but don't know that it is true.[34] We understood today that the enemy had all or nearly all of South Carolina and had taken Atlanta, Georgia.[35]

There has been another fight at Corinth (at least that is the report) in which our army was victorious. Some say the Yankees lost in killed and prisoners 26,000. I believe the battle was fought on the 28th of April 1862.[36] They have been fighting all along the railroad from Corinth to Bridgeport.[37] Our forces drove the Yankees from Decatur and would have captured all of them had they not burned the bridge at Florence. Some say our men burned it but I don't know.[38]

Had a little fight the other night about twenty miles from here, near Camden, Madison County. I saw a soldier today who was in the fight. About 18 of the enemy killed, not one of our men hurt. It was not a part of the army that was fighting but only about 100 of the citizens that were tired of the low Dutch "lording" over them. Most of the northern army at Huntsville are *Dutch*.[39]

There has been another little fight at Bridgeport, we did not hear the particulars but as part of a bridge floated by here, we suppose someone (we can't tell which side) had burned it.[40] There has been another fight at Cumberland Gap, April 28th, I think. We were victorious.[41] We can hear distinctly this morning (May 6th) the report of cannon. The Southern army under Price and the Northern army under Mitchel are now engaged in deadly conflict at *Huntsville*.[42] At every report I start and think of the immortal souls that are now hurried into eternity, maybe unprepared.

A few days ago the Yankees went to Uncle David Allison's (The same one who was taken prisoner at Huntsville) house and did all the mischief they could; breaking up the furniture, boxes, trunks, tearing up clothes and dashing them into the yard. Stealing money and letters to the amount of $1,700. They tried to tear down the house, etc., etc. Uncle and Sallie happened to be away from home. They are treating a good many of the Madisonites very badly.

(Continued) I feel that all is lost and that it is useless to try any longer to keep them back and then again I feel that God is on the side of Right and He will take care of us for I believe we are right.[43]

We will hear from the battle at Huntsville in a day or two, then I will write the particulars.

May 10th

The report that they were fighting at Huntsville was false, they (the Yankees) were firing off their cannon for the victory gained at New Orleans and Mobile. We cannot learn the truth, we do not know whether they have taken New Orleans or not, the Yankees tell so many lies, nobody knows when to believe them.[44]

There has been another fight near Paint Rock River, I think, in this County; our men fired on them and they ran. Could not tell whether they killed any or not as it was night time but someone was hurt as they traced them some distance by the blood. Just before our party attacked them, they had taken six men near Mr. Haden's about seven or eight miles from here. I was acquainted with all that were taken except one and with a good many who were in the skirmish.[45] Cousin Hub Fennell arrived here day before yesterday.[46] He came down the river in a canoe from Bellefonte where he has been ever since the battle of Donelson. He has been very sick. The Yankees came out to Uncle Frank's where he was staying and asked him to take the oath of allegiance to the United States but he would not and as he was not able to ride they had to leave and it was not long before he left. Had a little fight near Whitesburg; we were victorious. The County is full of troops.[47]

(April 24th

The Yankees are now in Guntersville, have been at Warrenton and are coming back this evening.)[48]

May 13th

We understand there has been a battle on the coast of North Carolina in which we were victorious; did not learn where the battle was fought or any of the particulars.[49]

Those six men who were taken prisoner near Paint Rock River were released yesterday. One of them (Mr. Scott) was here this morning.[50] He says there is a complete reign of terror in and near Huntsville. Nearly every man there has been arrested on mere suspicion.[51] He says one of Pa's cousins (Mr. Isham Fennell) is in prison. He (cousin Isham) did not know why he was arrested nor what they were going to do with him.[52] The yoke is galling but they must wear it for a while.

I forgot to mention before that Island No. 10 has been given up to the Federals. I heard once that they had taken 3,000 prisoners but heard another time that we lost nothing but evacuated.[53]

May 21st

There has been several battles [since] I wrote last. One at or near Corinth, Mississippi on the 9th of May, in which we took 800 prisoners, five cannons, etc. Five thousand Confederates run fifty thousand Federals.[54] Another was fought at Williamsburg, Virginia, in which our loss in killed and wounded was 500; the enemy's loss is supposed to be between two to three thousand. Gen. Longstreet commanded our forces.[55]

Another, near Staunton, Virginia, I neither know the loss of the Confederates nor the Federals but know the Confederates were victorious. General Stonewall Jackson commanded the Confederates.[56] Colonel John Morgan is gaining himself a great name by his bravery and great success by penetrating so far north of the enemy's lines. He is, or was the last we heard from him, in Bowling Green, Kentucky. The Yankees came very near taking him and all his men at Lebanon, Tennessee. They had been completely surrounded and he had to cut his way out, it would fill a book to tell of all his daring acts.[57]

Yorktown has been evacuated by the Confederates as they thought they could not well hold it.[58] All are expecting a great battle near there, or Richmond, soon. The Federals have New Orleans, but I believe I wrote of that before. We hear of skirmishing every day and very often hear cannon.

I believe I have never written anything about money matters. Well, nearly all the money we get now is Confederate bonds and they will hardly pass now. Some will not take it at all, they would rather take anyone's note. Gold and silver are very scarce.[59]

Fort Pulaski, near Savannah, Ga., was taken by the Federals some time ago but I forgot to write about it.[60]

June 3rd

Sister Charity received a letter from Col. Henry a few days ago. He said his regiment was in the fight at Williamsburg, Virginia and that we did not have more than 65 killed.[61] All of our wounded, dead and sick fell into the enemy's hands as the Confederate forces were retreating and could not take them. He says the Yankees were badly whipped.[62] Although I am glad to hear of another victory, I can scarcely refrain from weeping whenever I think of the battle for my oldest brother William was taken prisoner there. He was assistant surgeon and remained behind with the wounded. The law requires that he should be released but I fear that the Yankees will keep him to be exchanged. Both of my brothers that were in the army are now prisoners, we may never see them again, that thought makes me shudder, I try to drive it from my mind and look on the bright side.[63]

Last Thursday there was another fight at Whitesburg; killed a few, took a few prisoners and burned 160 bales of cotton that the Yankees were going to take across the river, I saw one of the men that was in the fight.

Homespun is now all the fashion as we can buy nothing else.[64] Calico (what little there is of it) is selling at $1.50 per yard. Shoes, we will have to do without, I reckon, as there are none for sale.[65]

Three hundred Confederate cavalry were in Guntersville last Saturday, crossed the river Saturday night; we do not know where they are going or what they are going to do. Four guarded the Deposit Ferry Friday night but crossed the river Saturday morning. Those that were here were Texas Rangers.

June 5th

Last night we were awakened about 11 o'clock by three of Pa's black men (who had been at the river fishing) running to the house and saying that the Yankees were at Deposit (about a half a mile from here). They came up the river in a house boat which they turned into a steamboat. There were about 300 of our cavalry at or near Warrenton. Pa would have sent them word but was not sure that it was a Yankee boat. They got word early in the morning and 100 of them were coming down when they met a runner who said the boat had started, so they turned back and went up on Beard's Bluff and looked at it through a spy-glass.[66] Some were very anxious to fire but their officers would not let them. I expect they will let it go on up the river until they get ready to attack it. I hope they get every one of them; I will write further particulars when I get them.

Our forces under "Stonewall" Jackson gained a glorious victory at Front Royal, Virginia on the 25th of May.[67] They took regiments at Front Royal and two more thousand at Winchester. The Confederate killed and wounded amounted to 100. The Confederates are still in pursuit. Banks commanded the Federals. I hope they will soon have him and all his army.[68]

June 9th

Yesterday afternoon Captain Taylor and his wife arrived here. He has been in the army and as he could not go home (he lives at Huntsville) he brought his wife here. I do not know how long they will stay but expect that they will leave soon as we don't know how soon the Federals will come over here.[69] Cousin John Fennell of Mississippi also came in the evening.[70] I had never seen him before but was truly glad to see him as I had heard a great deal about him. He left this morning expecting to go to his regiment but came in very unexpectedly this evening, bringing with him another soldier (Major Hollerwell).[71] A great many troops are passing through this country going to Chattanooga. All expect a fight there soon; I do hope the Confederates will be victorious.

June 11th

Heard today that the Federals had burned Bellefonte, Larkinsville, Stephenson and Woodville, in Jackson County.[72] I do not know that it is true, but it is known that Gen. Mitchel has sent a force to burn those places. It is awful the way the Federals are doing in New Orleans. Ladies are scarcely allowed to speak and if they do speak but do not speak to suit old Gen. Butler, they are insulted by the law of soldiers and in some cases have been imprisoned. One lady was thrown into prison for wearing a small Confederate flag in her bonnet; some are arrested for wearing red, white and blue ribbons. Oh! It makes my blood boil to think of it.[73] I have two cousins in Madison County, Alabama. Isham Fennell and Hubbard Hobbs, who the Yankees have ruined. They have taken all their meat and corn, torn up their beds, broken up their furniture and stolen their money; they even went so far as to examine cousin Hubbard's wife and daughter's persons to see if they could find anything.[74]

June 19th

That Yankee boat I spoke of before passed down the river this morning. The day after they passed up our men fired into them and killed a good many of them but could not take the boat as the Yankees had cannon. It did not stop, although we understand they intended to have paid us a visit. John Fennell came near to being taken this morning as they went up to the house where he was with two or three more soldiers, but a little negro boy saved them by giving them warning to leave.

Our forces under Gen. Beauregard have evacuated Corinth, Miss. The Yankees can't imagine where he has gone. They censure Gen. Halleck greatly for letting Gen. Beauregard slip out of his hands. General Beauregard wanted to fight them at Corinth but they would not fight so he had to leave as that place was so sickly.[75]

June 12th

Capt. Taylor, wife and cousin John Fennell left this morning. We are looking for the Yankees.

June 13th

This morning just as the bell rang for breakfast, someone saw a body of armed men coming up the road from the river and ran in shouting, "*Yonder Come the Yankees*" and so it proved to be, but we were not surprised as we had been looking for them for so long. None of them came into the house and about a dozen came around through the orchard at the back of the house, I suppose to catch any soldiers that might run out but there were none here and I was very glad for they asked for Confederate soldiers the first thing. They took two guns from Pa and got some milk from Ma and then left in a hurry. I think they were afraid Confederate Cavalry would come down and kill or capture all of them. They broke Pa's guns and threw them into the river. The negroes were badly frightened. They took a great many things from Mr. Scott, just across the river; broke up his boat and skiffs. They also broke up two of brother John's canoes. We were glad they did no more damage and we hope they will never return. After they left here they went to Guntersville, fired at the houses on the bank, stole a few horses and burnt all the boats and left there for some other place where they can get more spoil.[76]

We heard today they were fighting at Chattanooga, Tennessee.[77]

There has been a great battle near Richmond, Va. in which our forces were victorious.[78] Col. Henry's (my brother-in-law) regiment was in the fight and took several pieces of artillery. It is said the Alabamians beat them all fighting there. I hope to hear the result soon.

The Federals now have Memphis, Tennessee.[79] It is nothing more than we all expected, but we never will give up as long as there is a mile left unoccupied.

June 14th

Heard today that our troops crossed the river at Chattanooga and that the enemy were retreating.

General "Stonewall" Jackson has been fighting up in Virginia. He has whipped both Shields and Banks.[80] Oh! That we had more generals like him!

June 19th

Our victory at *Chattanooga is complete*! Have not heard the particulars yet. I am very thankful for the victory for I know the Yankees would have over run this whole country if they had gained the day. Night before last we understood they were crossing the river and would be here very soon. There was one soldier here and he flew for his life for they said they would hang him if they caught him; but it proved to be a false report and he is here again this evening. I am sorry to say that Col. Ashby of the Virginia Cavalry was killed in the battle near Richmond, Va. He was one of our bravest soldiers and a true patriot. The Confederacy feels his loss greatly.[81] General Joseph E. Johnston was wounded, I hope not badly.[82]

June 22nd

Nothing of interest has occurred since I last wrote except that we have heard that our cavalry are burning all the cotton on the other side of the river as the Federals are taking all that they can find. They pay for some of it and others they just go and take it without leave or license.

June 23rd

The Federals in Huntsville are deserting in great numbers. One was here today. He was from Kentucky, and said he was fighting for the Union and not against slavery. He said *since the Federal Congress had* passed *the* law *freeing all the slaves*, several regiments said they would not fight against the South.[83] I wish they would all be of the same mind. Cotton still burning over the river.

June 24th

We understood today that the Southern soldiers had burned Aunt Charity Lea's cotton which she had sold to the Yankees and that they (the Yanks) had taken her prisoner for it, as if an old lady sixty years old could keep a body of troops from burning it if they wanted to. But that is like them, they make war on women and children as well as men.[84] I heard several days ago that they had made several ladies take the Oath of Allegiance to the North. I do hope and pray that they may never come on this side of the river again. That Tennessee River has been a great blessing to us. I used to almost wish it were not there, but now I am glad of it as it keeps the Federals away from us. Pa wrote to Wattie yesterday and sent the letter by a friend to Huntsville to have it mailed. I hope we will hear from him.

June 28th

In the fight at Richmond, our losses amounted to *six thousand* killed, wounded and prisoners. The enemy's *loss* amounted to ten thousand *killed*, wounded and prisoners. Both sides claimed victory.[85]

It is reported that France has or will soon recognize the independence of the Southern Confederacy. It is thought that if that be true, the war will soon end.[86] The French and Mexico are now at war, they fought a battle not long ago in which the French were defeated.[87]

There was a battle fought on James Island on the coast of North Carolina, June 16th. The Confederates were victorious.[88] Burning cotton is bringing England and France to their senses.

We are expecting a great battle at or near Richmond every day. General Lee, Johnston and President Davis are all there and I do pray and hope that we will gain the victory.

A great many negroes are running to the Yankees, expecting to be freed by them but they put them to work and most of them want to come home but it is hard to get away.

The Yankees have all the Mississippi River excepting Vicksburg City, Miss., and they have been fighting there. We did hear that the Confederates had evacuated that city but do not know that it is true. (Later—not true).[89]

July 3rd

This evening we received the glad news of brother William's exchange or release from prison. We also received a letter from him. He says in his letter that he was taken to Washington with the sick and wounded prisoners, was on board a vessel for three weeks and did not have a change of clothing. They kept him confined closely until General Jackson released all the Federal surgeons and then let him out on parole but he would not leave until they released him unconditionally. One of his old acquaintances (Mrs. Clare) took him to her house and her *son-in-law* (Mr. Clegett) and several other gentlemen gave him clothing. He says there are a great many friends of the South there but they dare not speak their sentiments. He also found a great many in Baltimore. He stayed four or five days in Fortress Monroe. We also heard this evening that they were fighting in Richmond, so he just got back to the army in time to be in the great fight.[90]

July 7th

A few days ago a company of our cavalry went scouting across the river, had taken a few prisoners, who, to make our men think that they were only Federals about, gave themselves up very willingly. It was not long after they came dashing up and had almost surrounded them before they knew it. Our men fired one volley and most of them jumped on their horses and made their escape but unfortunately one of them could not get to his horse before he was completely surrounded. He was determined he would not be taken alive for they had said they would hang or shoot all *"Bushwhackers."*[91] He fought bravely before he was shot down to arise no more. He was Mr. J. Cornwell of Guntersville and one of our best citizens. He was the only Confederate killed; nine of the Feds were made to bite the dust. It is said before Mr. Conwell was killed, he killed four or five himself.[92] Heard today that General Buell (Federal) was at Huntsville with 75,000. I suppose it means all the troops on that side of the river. Buell is going to try to make all that have been in the army or had any office under the Confederate Government take the Oath of Allegiance to the United States and if they will not take the Oath he will have them arrested and put into prison. The people say he is more of a gentleman than Mitchel and if he is not he ought to be hung for Mitchel should be hung to the highest tree in Alabama. Everybody hates him, even his own men.[93]

July 10th

GLORIOUS NEWS! The Confederates have won a complete victory at Richmond, Virginia. They commenced fighting the 27th of June and the last we heard from there was the 4th of July and the battle was not over. The General that the Yankees make so much over commanded the Federals; he is General McClellan. The Confederates captured 50 or 60 thousand prisoners, besides clothing in abundance, money, arms and ammunition.[94] Have not received the account of the loss on either side. An armistice of two days, it is reported was asked by McClellan to bury the dead, etc., but General Lee, it is said, replied, "There is not time now to think of the dead. The only proposition I can receive from General McClellan is unconditional *surrender*." I know not if this be true. By mutual agreement, surgeons are not considered prisoners of war, hence at the close of the late battle, many Federal surgeons remained on the field to take care of the wounded. I see from the papers that the Brigade, Wilcox's, that the 9th Alabama regiment was in fought very bravely.[95] Brother William and my brother-in-law are in the 9th Alabama. Wilcox's Brigade is in Longstreet's Division. The Alabamians again gained laurels by their bravery. The Federals burned great quantities of army stores to prevent it falling into the hands of the Confederates.

July 12th

Every sweet has its bitter. While we rejoice over our late victory, news came last night that causes us a great deal of uneasiness. Hop Beard came down after supper bringing a paper having the names of the killed and wounded in the 9th Alabama Regiment.[96] Among the wounded was brother William's name. He had been released from prison just in time to be in the late battle. We all set up nearly all last night preparing Pa to start for Virginia. He left this morning. Oh, I do hope Willie is not hurt much, and that he will come home with Pa. We all are so uneasy we do not know what to do. Several from this county were killed and a great many wounded.

There has been a little fight near Holly Springs, Mississippi on July 2nd. Four thousand Federals were attacked by Jackson's and Renson's Cavalry, fifteen hundred strong. After a short contest they (The Feds) were routed and driven back. Our loss, four; Federal, seven.[97] They are still fighting at Vicksburg.

July 15th

Heard today that Brother William was shot through both legs above the knee.

July 20th

Received a letter from Pa today; he said that Willie was getting better although he had been very low; bled almost to death before any assistance could be given him. They fought six or seven days at Richmond. Confederate loss: 15,000 killed, wounded and prisoners. The Federal loss is hardly known, it is thought 40,000 would cover their loss. They say their loss is some over 20,000. We captured several generals, among them Major General McCall.[98]

August 9th

Pa came in very unexpected today and said that Willie and John Allison were behind in a wagon and as they were coming very slowly, he sent the carriage back after them.[99] They got here about eight o'clock. I can't tell how glad we were to see Willie, it had been nearly fifteen months since he went away. Cousin John looks very badly. He has a discharge. Willie can walk on crutches, his wounds are healing very rapidly. Cousin Tom Hobbs, captain of a company from Athens, Alabama died from wounds received in the late battle before Richmond a few days before Pa left Richmond.[100] Pa found cousin Isham Fennell almost dead in one of the hospitals. He belongs to the 4th Texas Regiment. Pa thought he would get well if well attended, his thigh was broken.[101]

Our forces have penetrated away up into Kentucky and few have crossed into Indiana. The North is in great excitement. Morgan and Forrest commanded our forces. Morgan said in his dispatch that he had taken 19 cities and towns. He left with a small force and returned with nearly twice as many as the people joined him all along. Forrest also took several towns and a great many prisoners.[102] We hear nearly every day of a little fight over the river in Madison County. The other day Hambrick and Gurley with about 150 men attacked about 400 Yanks and killed General McCook and took a great many prisoners besides killing a good many.[103]

The Yankee gunboats shelled Vicksburg six weeks and at length concluded it was useless and therefore have withdrawn from the city; however, before they left they had a grand fight with the Confederate ram "Arkansas" who whipped them well, sinking several and damaging the whole fleet.[104]

August 19th

The Ram "Arkansas" was going down the river to cooperate with the land forces but something got out of order about her and being attacked near the same time by the Yankees; our men blew her up to prevent her falling into their hands. It seems that is to be the fate of all our best boats. The "Virginia" first and now the "Arkansas".[105] The Confederate forces under Breckinridge attacked Baton Rouge, Louisiana. They ran the Feds to the river and could have taken the city had the "Arkansas" come up when expected. It was one of the hardest fought battles of the war and crowned General Breckinridge with laurels. But they had to fall back several miles to get out of range of the gunboats. I do not know the loss on either side. Our men captured a great many goods, commissary goods, but had to burn them.[106]

A law has been passed for a general exchange of prisoners, therefore we expect to hear from Wattie soon.[107] I fear he will not be permitted to come home but will have to join the army immediately.

I believe I have never said anything about the Conscript Act. That is: All between the ages of eighteen and thirty-five have to join the army.[108] *I LIKE* THE *LAW*!

Sep 1st

Four weeks ago today, the Feds shelled *Guntersville*, a little town about five miles from here, all day, burned fourteen or fifteen houses, killed one lady, one gentleman and wounded one gentleman.[109] The lady killed was Mrs. Sarah Rayburn, she was greatly beloved by all her acquaintances.[110] The gentleman was a traveler from Nashville; his mother and a young lady were with him, his name I believe was McCray.[111] Mr. Ben Matthews was wounded.[112] The shells passed through several houses up in town but did no other damage. Those that were burnt were down on the bank near the river. The next evening about sunset we were all surprised by hearing cannon right at us or at least that is the way it sounded. Directly after the firing started the negroes came running to the house frightened nearly to death and said they saw the cannon and Yanks and that they were at the steam mill, about half a mile from here but across the river. They shelled the pickets a while and then left, doing no damage. We expected they would throw shells at this house and burn it just for fun as they have burned a great many over the river lately. Our houses is large and white and they could see it very well. It is supposed that our men killed nine or ten at Guntersville and the Yankees reported that they had killed 1,500 Confederates when there were only about 500 men there, but they don't mind telling a lie, that is only a small one to what they tell sometimes.[113] I ought to have written this long ago but I kept forgetting it when I was writing until today.

Received glorious news today. A gentleman arrived here this morning directly from Huntsville and said the Federals had all left there Saturday. He said they seemed very uneasy before they left. They burned a great deal of corn, bacon, guns, tents, etc., before they left.[114] Everybody is rejoicing and I am so happy that I do not know what to do. They took about 600 negroes with them. No one was sorry but glad to get rid of them; a great many want to come back to their masters but they will not let them so the Yankees have to take them.[115]

Bragg (so report says) is coming in on the northeast and Price on the southwest, so the Yankees are in a bad fix.[116] Oh, I do hope they will all be taken or killed. Some of our men (about a hundred) attacked about 4,000 of the Yankees over there a few weeks ago, killing several and taking several prisoners. Among the killed was Brig. Gen. McCook. Such occurrences are not infrequent, our brave men attack when they get ready, no matter what may be the number of the enemy. Capt. Frank Gurley and Hambrick commanded.[117]

Jackson has had another fight up in Virginia. The Yanks say they gained the victory and the Confederates say they gained it. I do not know the particulars but know the Confederates were not beaten. We hear of so many fights that it is almost impossible to write about them all.[118] Lincoln has called out 600,000 more men; he is determined to whip us and that very quickly but I think he will be mistaken for once.[119] Both sides speak of hoisting the black flag (that is, to take no prisoners but to kill all) but I hope that they will not have to do that.[120]

*I heard a few days ago of the death of one of my dear Aunts. It was Aunt Catherine Cobb of Jackson County, Alabama. As the Yankees were there, we had never heard that she was ill until we heard that she was dead. The shock was very sudden but we are able to bear it, knowing that she is better off than if she was in this wicked world. I do not know when she died but she died away from home and her husband was very sick at home and could not go to see her. She had gone on the Mountain for her health. Ma was her sister and is in a great deal of trouble.[121]

Sep 2nd

Morgan and Forrest are still up in Tennessee and Kentucky. Morgan captured Gallatin, Tenn. about the 14th or 15th of August. He took and destroyed four trains, contents valued at $400,000, army stores principally. He then proceeded to destroy railroad bridges between Nashville and Bowling Green. Returning to Gallatin, he found that the Feds had made a dash and captured the guard he had left there. He pursued, recapturing none of his men. His losses were one killed, one wounded and four prisoners. Enemy's loss not known.[122]

Sep 5th

The Federals have evacuated Baton Rouge, Louisiana and it has since been occupied by our forces.[123] Clarksville, Tenn. has been taken by a few Southern Guerillas. Fort Donelson was evacuated by the Feds and afterward occupied by Col. John H. Morgan and not captured by him as I before stated.[124] Maxie (one of our commanders) had a fight with the enemy at Bridgeport, Alabama on August 27th. The enemy was repulsed, none killed on our side but eight or ten wounded.[125] A few days ago our men attacked Stevenson, Alabama, but the Yankees would not fight. They ran and left the town in Southern hands.[126]

Sep 8th

Heard today that Jackson and Pope had fought another hard battle up in Virginia exactly on the same field that the Battle of Bull Run was fought and the Southern Troops were victorious.[127] Stonewall Jackson! How every heart swells with pride and thankfulness when his name is mentioned. I do not know the particulars of the fight yet but will write them as soon as I can. We also heard of a battle up in Kentucky and that our forces had taken Lexington.[128] I hope it is true but it is only a report.

There has been a continuous rush on the river ever since the Yanks left. The people fear they will return and are therefore almost afraid to rejoice.[129] We heard that the Yankees had taken every negro that Uncle Frank Fennell had, men, women, and children.[130] I am sure I don't know what they want with them.[131]

Have not heard from Wattie yet, we fear the Yanks will stop exchanging as soon as they get their officers.

Sep 29th

After a long illness, I am able to write again. A great many battles have been fought and victories won. It is very hard to get a correct account of them. The last time I wrote I spoke of a battle that had been fought in Virginia on exactly the same field that the Battle of Manassas was fought on July 21, 1861. The battle lasted three days; 28th, 29th and 30th of August 1862. The Confederates were gloriously victorious. McClellan, Halleck and Pope were gathered on the same plains and marshaled their mighty hosts for the subjugation of the Rebels.[132] 90,000 Federals, as if by the movement of a spring, were thrown with a thundering force upon our gallant army, men wearied with heavy marches and continuous fight.[133] They attacked our whole line simultaneously and were driven back with a loss almost fabulous. Again they came—again repulsed. Fresh troops of McClellan's chosen divisions came up to meet the fate of their comrades. When at last our troops could be restrained no longer, with a yell they charged on the retreating enemy when a rout ensued equal to that at Bull Run of July 21, 1861. They were pursued for miles. Such a series of battles have never occurred on this continent. Lee's army within a fortnight marched 150 miles, fought four battles and sundry combats. Jackson, Longstreet and Lee commanded our forces.[134] All deserve great praise and they have it from the grateful people of the South. Seven Generals in the Federal army were killed. Their whole loss in killed, wounded and prisoners is estimated at 30 to 40 thousand. They lost five, some say seven to our one.[135] We owe to God a debt of gratitude for all His mercies and for His evident intervention on our behalf as a people. The 18th of this month was appointed by the President of the Confederacy as a day of thanksgiving.[136] After our victory at Manassas the Confederates pushed in and crossed the Potomac River on the 5th and 6th of September. We cannot hear what our forces are doing in Maryland, we know they occupied Fredrick City [Fredericksburg] and thousands were flocking to them.[137] We also heard that there had been a fight at Poolesville in Maryland and another near Baltimore.[138] The people of Baltimore, when they heard that the Confederates were so near, seized the Provost-Marshall of that City and hung him.[139] They also took a fort which had been erected to destroy the city in case the Confederates attacked it.[140] The whole of Maryland, Pennsylvania and Washington is in a blaze of excitement.

The Yankees say that Pope is a coward; McDowell is a traitor and as for McClellan, they scarcely venture an opinion now. They have lost confidence in their high officers and conceive a high opinion of ours.[141] While Lee, Jackson, Longstreet and Hill are gaining laurels in Virginia and Maryland, Kirby Smith and Morgan are winning them in Kentucky.[142] Kirby Smith entered Lexington, Kentucky on the 1st of September.[143] The people rushed to receive him and they poured in all day in the midst of wildest demonstrations of delight. The ladies cried for joy and gratitude.

Scott's Louisiana cavalry took Frankfort, Kentucky on Sept. 3rd. Col. Scott planted his flag on the dome of the State house. The enemy evacuated the city on the night of the 2nd. Our forces went in pursuit the next morning and sent back a number of prisoners and 300 mules.[144] General A. Buford, Confederate, has raised ten regiments, 3,000 were recruited in 24 hours.[145] Kirby Smith has since marched towards Cincinnati and it is presumed that he will soon take that city, in fact we have heard that he did have it once.[146]

Bragg is up in Tennessee threatening Buell who has stolen ten or twelve thousand negroes and working them in fortifications of Nashville. The negroes are starving and many of them have escaped to their owners. Negro women are selling their children to buy bread.[147]

General A. G. Jenkins is making inroads in northwestern Virginia. As he advances, loyal people are flocking to his army by hundreds and it is expected that in a brief period of time he will have a force sufficient to wipe out the remains of Federalism in that part of the country.[148] If there ever was a time when the hearts of our people should swell with pride and gratitude to Heaven, that time is now. The banner of the Confederacy no longer trails in the dust but in the hands of our victorious legions. In Virginia and Kentucky the enemy has been beaten, routed and demoralized and the tide of success turned completely in our favor. Oppressed, downtrodden, and outraged in every conceivable manner, the people of the invaded districts on our borders are rushing to arms and the tears of our women and children whose homes have been made desolate have infused molten fire into the veins of our soldiers to take vengeance upon the enemy who has been made to cower at their feet. I pray Heaven that no evil genius may deter our brave Generals from the immediate invasion of the enemy's country.

Brother William was elected Captain of a cavalry company a few weeks ago and is now up in Tennessee.[149] We are going to send him a negro boy and clothes.

Oct 9th

Received a letter from brother Watkins today. He had been exchanged and arrived at Vicksburg the 17th of September and expected soon to be mustered into service again. He said nothing of coming home and I fear they all will have to go into the army immediately. We were very glad to hear from him. Oh, I do want to see him so much![150]

Cumberland Gap was evacuated by the Federals (commanded by Morgan) the 17th of September.[151] Our forces under Stevenson are in pursuit.[152] We have had some terrible battles in Maryland and the information from there is meager and to some extent, unsatisfactory. It has come from afar with no telegraphic or mail communications of any kind.

General "Stonewall" Jackson has captured Harpers Ferry. The garrison surrendered 10,000 men with all their arms also 20,000 negroes, fifty pieces of artillery, etc. This important conquest was affected without the loss of a man on our side.[153]

It is reported that an engagement took place near Boonsboro. Enemy's loss was 5,000; our loss was heavy.[154]

Price had a fight at Iuka, Mississippi several weeks ago. I do not know the particulars as they have never been given in the paper.[155]

Oct 24th

Price or Van Dorn rather has fought another great battle near Corinth, Mississippi and it was feared that the enemy got the best of it but it has since proven that their loss was almost as great if not equal to the Confederate. Van Dorn was in command and he has been accused of being drunk and if Price had not been there, our whole army would have been killed or captured, as they outnumbered us. Price ordered them to fall back to Ripley.[156] Drunkenness has been the cause of every disaster during this war.

The greatest battle that was fought in Maryland was fought at Sharpsburg. The slaughter there was terrible on both sides. It is generally supposed that the Federal loss was 30 or 40 thousand while the Confederate loss was about half as many. The Confederates took but few prisoners so the number of killed was immense. My brother-in-law, Col. Sam Henry, was wounded two or three times in that battle, but was well when we last heard from him. He was then at Winchester, Virginia whither our army was removed.[157]

General Stuart with about 300 cavalry has penetrated away up into Pennsylvania has captured Mercersburg and Chambersburg, destroyed a large amount of ordinance and army stores and taken a large number of prisoners and horses. On returning to the Potomac River he cut his way through Gen. Stowes Division and arrived at Winchester without the loss of a man.[158]

General Bragg's first pitched battle in Kentucky was fought at Perrysville on the 8th of October. He whipped the enemy badly. Our loss estimated at

1,500; the enemy's double. He captured a great number of prisoners, some say 25,000. I do not know how many.[159]

Oct 26th

The people of the Confederacy are suffering for salt. They do not know what they will do this winter when they have no salt to cure their meat. The citizens of this and adjoining counties have sent to Virginia to get it but the Governor of Virginia has said that no salt shall leave the State, so I don't know what we are to do.[160] Everything brings a high price; calico, for instance, is $1.50 per yard. I suppose it will be $3.00 by next summer. Ma and sister Charity have home spun dresses and I and sister Mary are having some woven. Nearly all of the ladies wear homespun now.[161]

FIVE

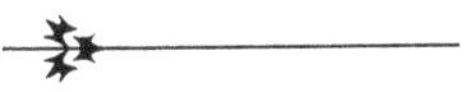

Awful Hard Times: Prices, Shortages, and Stresses on the Home Front, 1863

April 1863

A long time has elapsed since I last wrote. One reason that I stopped writing was that I could not keep up with the news. A great many battles have been fought since October. Murfreesboro, Tenn., one or two attempts to capture Vicksburg, several cavalry fights in Tennessee, fights with gun-boats all along the coast, Charleston, Savannah, etc. The most glorious victory of all was Fredericksburg, Virginia.[1] The Confederates were victorious in all except a cavalry fight in West Tennessee and one at Fort Donelson.[2] The first commanded by Forrest and the second commanded by Wheeler.[3] Cousin Tom Fennell was captured the day of the second fight. We are now expecting him to be exchanged but have our fears as they are not now exchanging officers as President Davis holds all of their officers until "*Brute Butler*" is delivered up to the Confederates to answer for his actions while in New Orleans and also they (the officers) are kept to retaliate for the way they have treated our men.[4]

One of the greatest battles of the war was fought in Maryland last fall. It is called the battle of Sharpsburg. A great many fell there on both sides. Col. Henry (brother-in-law) was slightly wounded there.[5]

Brother Wattie is at Port Hudson, Louisiana. There have been several fights with the gun-boats since he went there.[6] Brother Willie is up in Tennessee. He has been in several fights. He was home in January. Wattie has not been home yet.

*In December I heard of the death of Cousin Isham Fennell, of Texas from a wound received in the fight before Richmond.[7] Tom Hobbs was also killed there.[8]

May 9th

The Confederates gained a glorious victory at Charleston a short time ago. Whipped *nine gunboats* which the *North* boasted could never be beaten.[9] We were very much alarmed last Friday on hearing that the Federals were at Blountsville (30 miles south of here) 16,000 strong. We also heard that they had whipped Roddy and Forrest at Tuscumbia, but I am glad that the report was false, as they were badly whipped by our brave boys. Well, we continued uneasy until we heard that Forrest was after them and then we were satisfied for we thought that he would be sure to capture them and so he did before they got to Rome, Georgia where they were trying to go.[10] I have not yet heard their number nor the place where he captured them, nor do I know whether they fought or not. I shall soon find out all about it and write.

Oh, such awful hard times; I never dreamed anything could be so scarce and dear as they are. Can't get calico for less than $1.50 to $2.00 per yard; one cup and a saucer for $1.00; one plate for $1.00 and everything in proportion. One paper of pins costs $2.50. The fact is, everything is so high that we seldom buy anything but make it at home. Factory thread is so high that few can afford to buy it. It is now only seventy-five cents per dozen.

*My Pa's mother died on the 20th of April, 1863. Pa, Sister Mary and myself were there. She went off so calm as if falling asleep. She was 77 years old and had been sick a long time. They buried her in the garden at her house. She was the only grand-parent I ever saw.[11]

July 4th

It has been so long since I wrote that I hardly know where to begin. I believe I was writing about Forrest capturing the Federal raiders. Well, there were 1,600 of them and only 400 of our men. The Yankees surrendered without a fight to one-fourth their number.[12] There have been two or three big fights up in Virginia. One near Fredericksburg in which we were victorious but the victory was embittered by the death of our great "Stonewall" Jackson, the greatest loss the South has sustained during the war. He was shot by some of his own men who mistook him for the enemy.[13] Van Dorn, one of our best cavalry generals was killed near the same time.[14] Recently, there has been another fight in Virginia near Winchester. Our forces were commanded by General Ewell. He captured nearly all of the Federal army. Our army pursued and is now in Pennsylvania, we heard today that they were in Harrisburg.[15] Have not had a great deal of fighting up in Tennessee; our army is now retreating, supposedly to Bridgeport.[16]

We all expect the yanks here this summer, thought I pray they may not come. Army wagons, etc. have been passing for about two days. It makes me sad, very sad, to think about them overrunning our country, burning our houses and stealing everything else.

There has been a great deal of fighting at and near Vicksburg and Port Hudson. The enemy, 75,000 strong, landed at Grand Gulf on the 29th of April, and were attacked by three brigades who fell back after a gallant resistance. The enemy then advanced in the direction of Jackson, Mississippi.[17] Our forces fought them on the 1st and 13th of April at Canton and Mississippi Springs. They occupied Jackson on the 14th and sacked the place.[18] They entrenched on the 16th and on the 20th Pemberton gave battle at Baker's Creek, our forces falling back, renewed the attack on the 23rd at Big Black Bridge. Again our forces retired, losing a number of guns.[19] On the 24th, Grant laid siege to Vicksburg and on the 29th made an assault on our works and was repulsed every time with immense slaughter. On the 30th, they renewed the assault with the same success and on the 31st their troops refused to renew the assault. The idea of taking the place by storm was abandoned. By ditching siege parallels, they have at present gotten within 300 yards of our works and mounted siege pieces. They opened fire without doing any damage. So far, our losses in the series of attacks are between fifty and sixty thousand.[20] The above I got from a paper of the 13th of June.

They also have been fighting at Port Hudson for a long time. We can hear but little news from there as the place is surrounded by the enemy. The Yanks have negro troops there. A great many have been killed as they put them in the front as a sort of breast work.[21] My brother Wattie was taken prisoner at the battle of Baker's Creek, Miss. but as he did not care to lay another seven months in prison, he jumped overboard and swam to shore 23 miles above Memphis and made his escape to his command.[22] My brother Willie is now at home on "detached service."[23] My brother-in-law, Col. Sam Henry, is also home.[24]

July 14th

News came yesterday that the Yanks were in Huntsville again. The refugees are crowding this side of the river. The Yanks are not doing much damage to the citizens as yet. We also hear that Vicksburg has fallen. Pemberton, who commanded the Confederates, surrendered the city on condition that his forces would be permitted to march from the city unmolested, at least that is the report that we hear of it. There were only 17,000 men in all and they were about half-starved.[25] Everybody is low spirited. It is some consolation to know that if they have Vicksburg, we have recaptured New Orleans. Yes, Magruder has that city—but it is a report too and may be false.[26]

July 15th

Firing heard nearly all day in the direction of Whitesburg. We suppose that the Yanks are trying to cross the river. Cousin John Allison came in a short while ago just from Whitesburg.[27] He says they have been shelling their breastworks all day, they are not completed yet.

Vicksburg surrendered the 4th of July and Port Hudson on the 9th.[28] Both surrendered unconditional. New Orleans has not been taken by Magruder. It was a "grapevine" report.

The greatest battle of the war was fought at Gettysburg, Pennsylvania about the 10th or 11th of this month. Loss on both sides was great and both sides claim the victory. Lee has retreated 15 or 20 miles to protect his trains and wounded.[29]

July 18th

We heard today that Lee had possession of Arlington Heights near Washington and that he has burned that city, but I suspect that is a "grapevine" news too.[30]

I had a great many friends and acquaintances at Port Hudson. I expect that about all of them are prisoners now. Cousin John Rivers is among them.[31] The last we heard from Johnston's army, it was at Jackson, Miss., and had been fighting several days. Brother Watkins is there.

July 23rd

We hear this morning that the Federals have left Huntsville. Oh, I am so glad: I feared they would cross the river. We don't know why they left unless they were afraid of Morgan who is now in Ohio. It is said that 30,000 men have joined them.[32]

(Later) Willie and Johnnie have just got in from Huntsville. They say that the people on that side of the river think that the South had just as well stop fighting as they think the North will whip us. The Yanks took all their horses, pulled down their fences and turned the cattle into the crops. They also took all of their provisions.

July 28th

Received the sad news today of Cousin John River's death. He was killed at Port Hudson while gallantly leading his company on to a charge. I feel so much for his wife and young boy who are left alone in the world, for she has but few relatives.[33] We also hear that Bill Cremer, a distant relation, was killed at the same place.[34]

August 1st

Lee is still retreating or at least he has re-crossed the Potomac River. All are expecting a fight up there soon.

August 5th

The Yanks have reoccupied Huntsville. I understand that the "Bushwhackers" are over there thick. I hope they will not attempt to cross the river. Refugees are coming thick and fast.

August 12th

We are now looking for brother Wattie, several of his company have come home and they say that he will be home soon. I am fearful that he will not. Received a letter from him near two weeks ago, he had been in a seven days fight down in Mississippi near Jackson.[35] Oh, I do hope he will come.

August 15th

Capt. Grayson came over the river this morning.[36] He said the Yankees were in Vienna, about nine miles from here. They are not doing much damage to the citizens.

John H. Morgan and a large number of his men were captured up in Ohio or Kentucky, some where up there.[37] I am very sorry, but it can't be helped.

August 17th

Scouts came in from across the river this morning. One of them was captured near Vienna and the rest had to run for their lives.[38] Brother Willie and several others started over this morning, we will be very uneasy until they return. We are expecting the Federals at the river every day; they can shell us out.

August 20th

Brother Willie returned from over the river this morning. He had been among the Yanks at Camden.[39] They have taken all of Uncle David Allison's horses. It is reported that they expect to attack Guntersville next Sunday. Oh, I do hope they will not cross the river.

August 21st

This is the day appointed by the President of the Confederacy for *fasting* and *prayer.*[40]

August 24th

Yesterday Sunday, about 12 o'clock we heard the report of several guns in quick succession at the river. We knew immediately that the Federals had come in right on the other side. There was a regular fire that kept on for two hours, when the Yanks left. They killed one horse on this side and left a mule which had been wounded which our men went and brought over. The boat was about in the middle of the river when they first fired into them, one boy jumped out and swam to this shore and his horse jumped and swam to the Yanks who took him away.[41] They also captured a citizen (Mr. Poarch). I suppose they will soon release him.[42] I do hope they will never cross. Brother Willie started to his command (which is now at Alexandria, Ala.) yesterday.[43] He did not know whether he would remain long or not, he has to do as he is ordered and not as he pleases. I think he was glad to go as he was tired of the "detached service."

I believe I have never said anything about the troops that are stationed here. They have been here ever since the Yanks came to Huntsville. At first, a part of the 3rd Confederate Regiment under the command of Lieut. Robertson and then two or three companies from the 8th Confederate Regiment in the command of Capt. Williams and next came several companies from the same regiment who were commanded by Lieut. Matthews as the Capt. has been sick. They are still here and the officers stay here *most of the time*. Some of them are very nice gentlemen.[44]

Sep 3rd

Willie has returned from Alexandria.[45] He was ordered there to attend a court martial.

I spoke of the troops who are now here as some of them being very nice gentlemen, well, one of them (Capt. Field) is paying particular attention to cousin Matilda Fennell who has been staying here ever since the Yanks came into Madison County.[46] He is a very fine young man and I think she likes him very much.[47] Nearly all of the troops are from Mississippi.

Sep 5th

We understand that the Yanks are still advancing towards Gadsden. We also hear that the regiment stationed here, the 8th Confederate, has been ordered off.

Sep 8th

We hear that the Federals are in Wills Valley or this side of Gadsden. Troops are preparing to leave this part of the country. I fear we will soon have the Yanks in their place. Several of the officers came down today to tell us goodbye, Capt. Williams, Capt. Fields and Lieut. Matthews. We could not but feel sorry for them, they had been here so long and Capt. Fields hated to leave Cousin Matilda so much. I hope we will all meet after the war.

Sep 18th

Our family is now plunged into grief for the loss of Sister Charity's youngest child, Little Sam Wattie. He was nineteen months old and the sweetest baby I ever saw. He had been sick for some time but we had no fears for his recovery until the whooping cough got into the family. It was hard, hard to see him so pure and innocent consigned to the cold ground, but our Heavenly Father knows what is best for such as he.

Sep 25th

Another great battle has been fought near Chattanooga. It is called the Battle of *Chickamauga*. Loss on both sides was great. Confederate from ten to fifteen thousand; Federal from twenty five to thirty thousand. The Confederates gained a complete victory; driving the enemy back to Chattanooga, capturing a great many prisoners and stores. The battle was fought on the 18th, 19th and 20th of September, 1863. It was one of the hardest battles of the war. General Bragg was in command of the Confederates and General Rosecrans commanded the Federals. Several Confederate generals were killed, among them were Gen. Preston Smith and Gen. Helm.[48]

Sep 27th

We were all agreeably surprised this evening by brother Wattie's return home from the army where he has been for two years. He has not changed much, only looks older; but he has suffered so much that we could but expect that he would look badly. He will only remain at home for 26 days; we feel badly about his having to leave us so soon.

Oct 16th

Cousin Tom Fennell arrived here this morning from Wheeler's command. Cousin Tom was with the cavalry on its raid around through Tennessee, in Sequatchie Valley, Tenn. They captured the whole wagon train of the Federals which was filled with clothing and provisions of all kinds. Every soldier supplied himself with a suit of clothes and filled their haversacks with everything that was good. As they could not bring all the wagons out they were compelled to burn a great many and had to shoot 700 mules to prevent them falling into the hands of the enemy again. I believe they brought out all the ammunition. General Wheeler commanded the Confederates to the Tennessee River.[49] They had several battles, the whole loss of the Confederates was about five or six hundred. Cousin Tom gave me some nice writing paper and Sister Mary a bottle of perfume which he captured. I was glad to get the paper for it is almost impossible to get nice paper now and when we do get it have to pay $3 or $4 a quire for it and then it is not fit to write on, it is so rough. I have seen a great many letters written on brown paper.

Oct 19th

Brother Wattie and Willie both left here today for their commands. We all felt very badly but knew that it was their duty to go though they should both fall and we would never see them again. It seems to me that we can hardly bear it if one of them should get killed—I don't like to think about it, I feel too badly.

Oct 26th

Yesterday (Sunday) we heard that the whole of Wheeler's command had arrived at Warrenton, five miles from here, and it was not long before several soldiers came to press Pa's shop to shoe their horses. Brother Willie came in about sunset and remained until after supper. He is now in command of his old company. Wheeler has three brigades, amounting in all to about 7,000 men. The soldiers are pouring in thick and fast today; they went to buy nearly everything they see, that is, every thing to eat. Ma has kept several women cooking for them all day. Cousin Tom left here today; he is a Lieutenant in Willie's company.

Oct 27th

The cavalry all left here this morning and everybody is glad of it for they are nearly as bad as the Yankees, stealing everything they got a chance at. They were camped about two miles from here between Col. Beard's and Mr. Erwin's.[50] They killed up a good many cows, hogs, etc. for the people who lived near the camp. They dug the potatoes and caught the turkeys and chickens. The Yankees are in Vienna, about nine miles from here. We hear a good deal about General Kirby Smith and General Taylor gaining some great victories on the other side of the Mississippi River but cannot hear the straight of anything.[51] Heard that Gen. Taylor had captured General Banks and staff down in Louisiana but don't know that it is true, but I hope it is.[52]

Dec 25th

This is Christmas and how little like Christmas before the war. We have had a very gay time considering the hard times. Went to a party at Mr. Taylor's in Warrenton tonight.[53] I did not enjoy myself as well as I used to at parties because this awful war is going on and I could not help thinking about it as all the gentlemen who were there were soldiers. Well, it has been a long, long time since I have written any and I have almost given up the idea of trying to keep a journal. So many awful things have occurred that I hardly know where to begin.

The Federal army still have north of the Tennessee River and is treating the citizens as bad as they possibly can. They have taken some eight or ten men from their homes and shot them down like so many hogs. Mr. Mat Riche, four Rhodens, Mr. Hodge and Mr. Lemly are all that I know the names of.[54] Mr. Riche's daughter Mexico was here when she heard the news of her father's death, poor girl; I feel so sorry for her.[55]

There have been several small fights down here across the river at Deposit. The Confederates have had only one man killed; the Yanks have had several wounded but I have not heard of any of them being killed. It is very hard to kill a man from this side of the river as they have the advantage of having a high bluff from which they fire. Our men have only small breastworks to protect them.

The Yanks tried to hang Uncle John Allison and Dr. Sullivan for their gold, which they supposed was hidden, but they did not succeed for they (Dr. and Uncle) would not let them put the rope around their necks. Uncle John told them they might shoot him but hang him, they never would.[56] I hear of them hanging a great many until they are almost dead. They treat the women worse than they do the men. They take everything from them, search their persons and insult them in every way. I have heard of several ladies running to the mountains to get away from them. These three with whom I am acquainted had to jump out of bed at 12 o'clock in the night and run to the mountains nor did they have time to dress and it was a bitter cold night.

A great many negroes are still going to the Feds. They put all of the men who are able in the army and send most of the women and children to Nashville where they die as fast as anyone could wish them. Some are going from this side of the river. I can hardly blame them for going, for the Yanks tell them they will be free but in reality they have to work harder than they would if they would remain at home. Well I wish the Yanks had them all, really, I am very tired of them.[57]

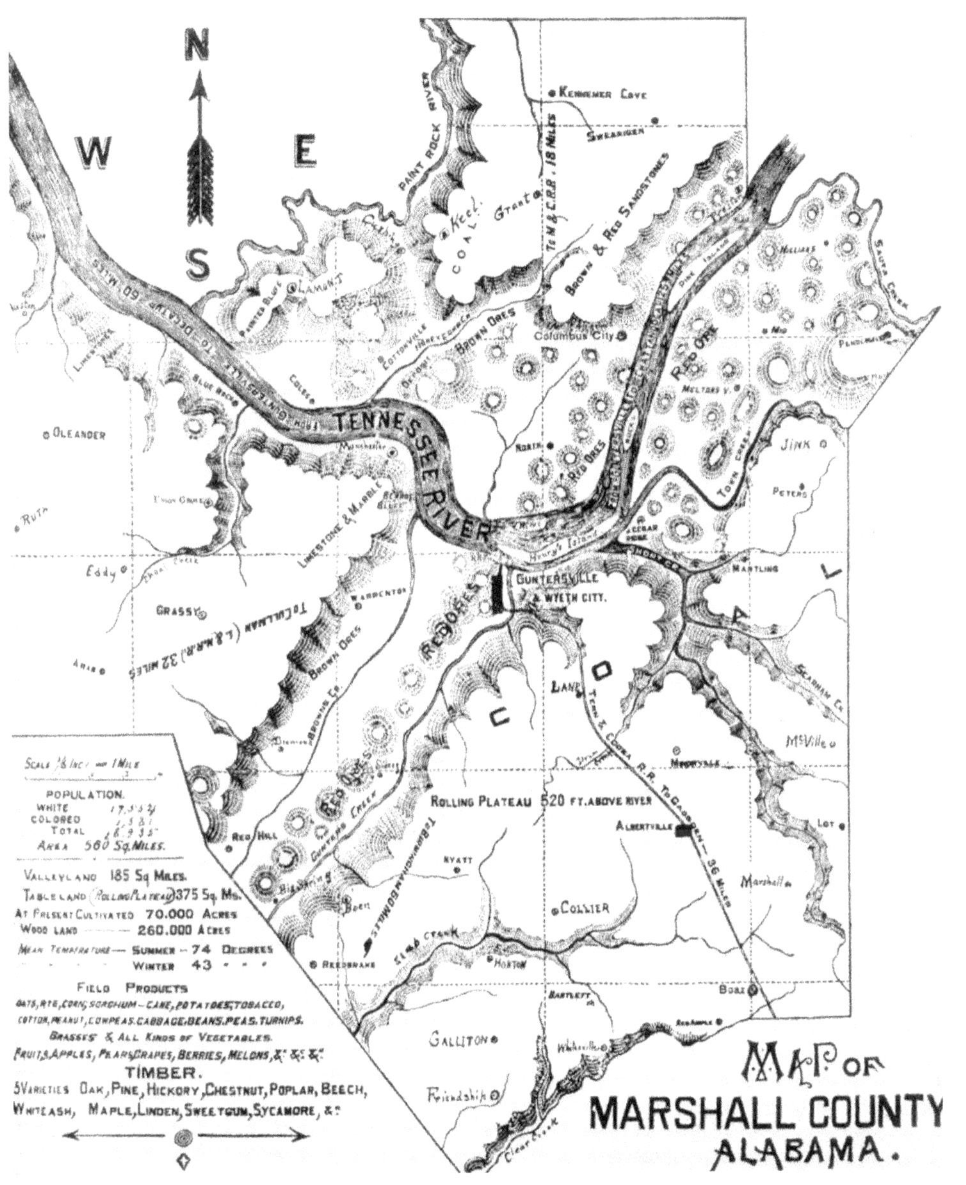

Map of Marshall County, Alabama,
drawn by Ed Neely, circa 1890.
Courtesy of the Marshall County Archives.

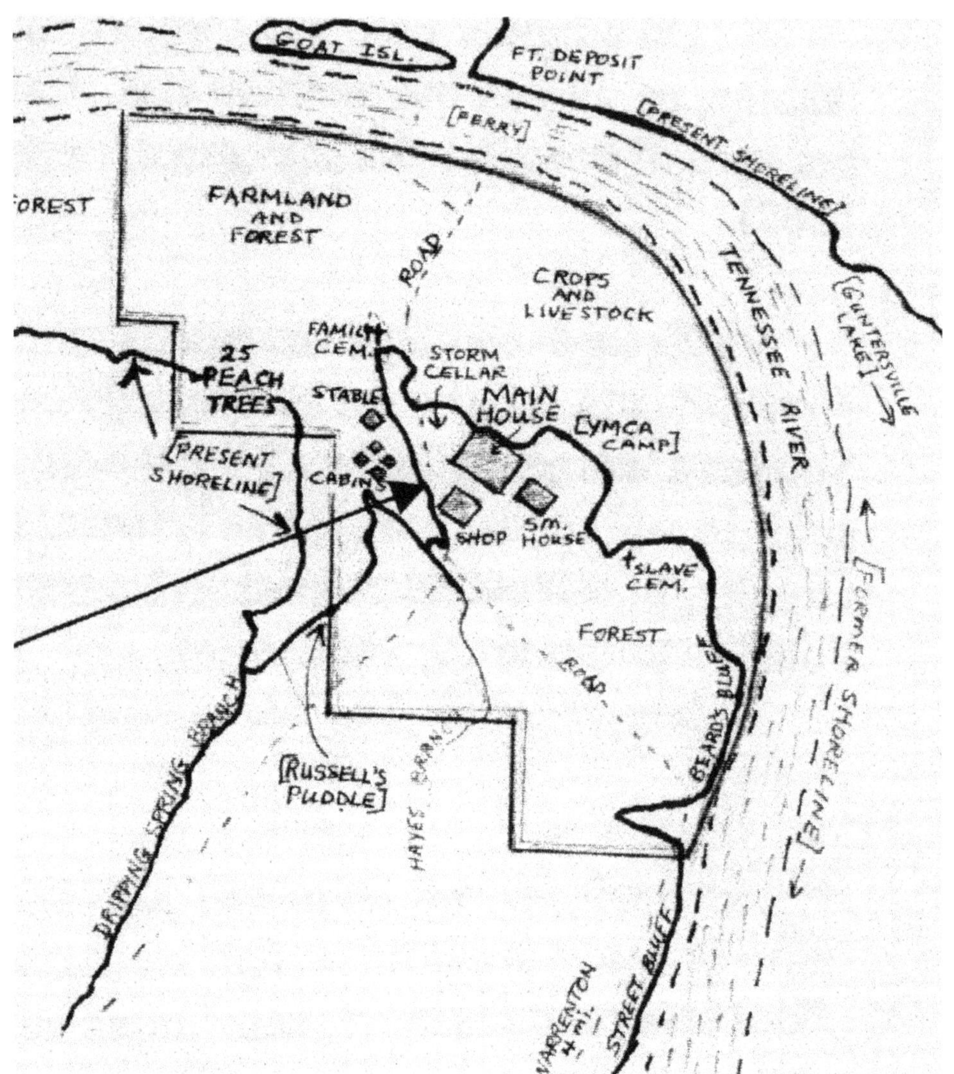

Dr. James W. Fennell's estate. Though a contemporary drawing by Carmen Hurff, it endeavors to depict the estate as it appeared in 1860. Courtesy of Carmen Hurff.

Portrait of Dr. James W. Fennell, circa 1840s. Courtesy of Carmen Hurff.

Portrait of Matilda (Allison) Fennell, circa 1840s. Courtesy of Carmen Hurff.

Matilda (Allison) Fennell, circa 1880s. Courtesy of Carmen Hurff.

Congressman Williamson R. W. Cobb, circa 1860. Courtesy of Marshall County Archives.

The Lea Mansion, the former home of Cassie's maternal aunt Charity (Allison) Cooper Lea. Courtesy of John Rankin.

Catherine "Cassie" Fennell, 1859.
Courtesy of Carmen Hurff.

Grave of Catherine M. Esslinger, circa 2010s. Courtesy of Betty Taylor.

The Andrew Jackson "A. J." Esslinger family, circa 1890s. Back row: Andrew Watkins; Wade Hampton; William Francis; James Houston; and Earnest Alva. Front row: Martha Matilda; Catherine Margaret; Margaret Lucinda Hodges (A. J.'s second wife); Thomas Hodges; Andrew Jackson; Mary Elizabeth; and Arthur Graham. Courtesy of Carmen Hurff.

Willie Fennell, circa 1860. Courtesy of the Marshall County Archives.

Wattie Fennell, circa 1860. Courtesy of the Marshall County Archives.

Mary Jane Fennell, 1859. Courtesy of the Marshall County Archives.

Mary Jane (Fennell) Graham, circa 1890s. Courtesy of the Marshall County Archives.

Johnnie Fennell as a child, circa 1850s. Courtesy of Carmen Hurff.

Johnnie Fennell, circa 1900. Courtesy of the Marshall County Archives.

Belle Fennell, circa 1870s. Courtesy of the Marshall County Archives.

Belle (Fennell) Neill, circa 1890s. Courtesy of the Marshall County Archives.

Caius Fennell, circa 1880s. Courtesy of the Marshall County Archives.

The Caius Fennell Family, 1905. From left to right: Mattie (Foster) Fennell, Caius, and their daughter Mary (Fennell) Hulsey. Courtesy of the Marshall County Archives.

The youngest of Dr. James W. Fennell's ten children, Mattie (Fennell) Jordan, with her daughter Eula, circa 1890. Courtesy of the Marshall County Archives.

Margaret (left) and Beulah, daughters of Sam Henry and Charity Fennell, circa 1871. Courtesy of the Marshall County Archives.

William Francis "Frank" Esslinger, Cassie (Fennell) Esslinger's eldest son, circa 1900. Courtesy of the Marshall County Archives.

Martha Matilda "Mattie" (Esslinger) Prewitt, Cassie (Fennell) Esslinger's only daughter, with her son Marion Prewitt Jr, circa 1879. Courtesy of Carmen Hurff.

Albert Gallatin "A. G." Henry, Sam Henry's cousin and business partner, circa 1870s. Courtesy of the Marshall County Archives.

Arthur C. Beard, neighbor to Dr. James W. Fennell, circa 1860. Courtesy of the Marshall County Archives.

Portrait of John Rayburn. Courtesy of the Alabama Department of Archives and History.

Surgeon and historian John Allan Wyeth (circa 1890s), an eyewitness to the shelling of Guntersville. Courtesy of the Marshall County Archives.

Colonel James L. Sheffield, 1861. Courtesy of the Marshall County Archives.

Portrait of Thomas Hubbard Hobbs, circa 1850s. Courtesy of the Marshall County Archives.

Samuel K. Rayburn, circa 1880s. Courtesy of the Marshall County Archives.

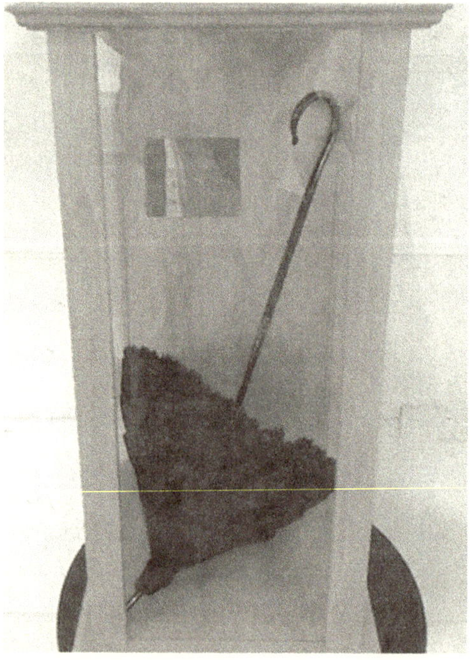

Evergreen Rayburn's parasol, 2019. Courtesy of Larry Smith.

SIX

Plunged into Grief and Silent Suffering: The Death of a Father and Capture of Two Brothers, 1864

*Our family is again plunged in the deepest grief for the death of our dear, dear father, who died January 19th, 1864. It was hard, very hard, to give him up but we knew that he was leaving a world of trouble for a home in Heaven where he will be eternally happy. He had no fears of death, all that troubled him was leaving his large and almost helpless family in this, the time of war. He prayed for his country and for a termination of the war as long as he had breath. Among the last things that he said was, "I put my trust in the Lord" and "I have fought the good fight, I have finished my work, I am ready to be offered up, the day of my departure is near at hand." I have not the power to express our anguish at his loss, but try to bear it with meekness. No one had a better father nor did a woman ever have a better husband than Ma. They had never quarreled and had been married for 27 years.[1]

[Undated]

A very severe battle was fought at Missionary Ridge, near Chattanooga. I think about the 18th of last November. I had forgotten to write about it as our forces were defeated and the Feds captured both Missionary and Lookout Ridges.[2]

Feb 19, 1864

I was in hopes that I had recorded the last death of any of my relations but I have the sad privilege again. Cousin Joe Fennell died at Summit, Ala. yesterday evening. It was a great shock to us. He was here only last week and said he was enjoying better health than he had for three or four years, but he took the pneumonia and was dead before any of us knew that he was seriously ill.[3] I deeply sympathize with his brothers and sisters. It seems to me that the relations are dying rapidly and I know not what moment I will be cut off.

Feb 24th

Today we were sitting talking about the Yanks firing across the river when all at once we heard the guns; BAM-BAM! We knew that they were there again and waited in suspense for the result. It was not long before some of the negroes came running to the house and said that the Yanks had been firing at them. They were down on the river bank ploughing. It frightened the negroes nearly out of their wits. They came near shooting several, among them were three women. The Yanks saw them and tried to shoot them and killed one of our mules; one of the men was lying under it when it was killed. They also killed one of the soldier's horses. I went down to the river after they had stopped firing but I kept an eye over the river for fear they would come up. I believe they would fire at a woman as soon as they would a man.

Directly after Pa's death, I went to Grandpa's about nine miles on the other side of the river.[4] We went over Wednesday and returned Friday. I was afraid to stay any longer as I had heard that several ladies had been taken up as spies and I did not care to spend the spring and summer and perhaps the whole war in prison. I hurried home. The Yanks were at Grandpa's the night or two before I got there, had torn up everything generally. I stayed at Uncle Parker's.[5] That night all of his and Cousin Web's negroes left for the Yanks excepting one old woman. They were all glad to get rid of them for they would not work at home. I did not see any Yankees while there but just as I got out of the canoe one of the soldiers who took us across said, "Just look at the Yanks!" I turned and looked on the other bank and sure enough, there they were. I was right badly frightened for I thought they would fire at the soldiers who were standing around but they did not. I crossed the river about nine miles below here and as I was coming home, I met a soldier who said the Yankees were crossing in a large force above Guntersville. I thought before I could get home the Yanks would have possession of our whole country. Well, the Yanks did cross two or three thousand, I believe, [and] are there yet, that is, about 19 miles above Guntersville.

March 8th

Have not heard any news in so long. We hear a great many reports about Longstreet whipping Burnside in East Tennessee but I don't know what to believe.[6] Have not heard from Willie and Wattie since near the first of January. They have been fighting in both West Tennessee and Mississippi. Willie is with Longstreet's cavalry or rather the cavalry that stays near

Longstreet's infantry.[7] Wattie is in a hospital. I think he ranks as assistant Surgeon. Oh, I do want to see them so much, sometimes I fear I will never have that pleasure again. If they would get killed I believe it would almost break our hearts. It seems to me that I would not stand it.

August 12th

It has been so long since I have written any that I hardly know where to begin. One reason that I have not written in so long is that I have had this book hidden for fear that the Yanks would get it and would think I was too good a "Secesh" to please them and they would tear it up, for I have known a great many instances where they have destroyed a great deal only from finding letters.

Directly after I wrote last Brother Willie came home on a short furlough (24 days). Oh, we were so glad to see him, it seemed we loved him more than we ever did. He was in a great deal of trouble about Pa's death. We were fearful that he would be captured for the Yanks were on the other side of the river all of the time. The Yankee gunboat came down the first time while he was here.[8] I could not keep from being amused at seeing the soldiers running as it was thought that it would land at Deposit. There were four pickets and two soldiers at our house; they left in a hurry but Willie was out on the side of the bank in sight of the boat. One Yank raised his gun and pointed it at him but did not fire. Willie said he was near enough for them to see the bars on his coat collar. Nearly the whole of Roddy's command has camped at Warrenton and Beard's Bluff.[9] They had several pieces of artillery at Warrenton but could not get them to the river in time to stop the boat. After the boat had passed (I went upstairs and saw it from a window), a company came down but could do nothing but fired at the Yanks on the other banks. I never felt so badly about anything hardly as to let one little boat pass unmolested through the very heart of the Confederacy.[10] The boats, I believe there were four, ran regularly after that for a month or two until the water got too low. On May 14th, a gunboat landed at Deposit, stayed there a long time and we were sure they would come to the house but they did not. They cut several large trees down on this bank, I suppose so they could get a clear range at this house and place. After they left, Frank went down to see what they were doing so long and he found a note sticking on the breastworks which said, "If the gunboat GENERAL SHERMAN is fired upon, I will burn Dr. Fennell's place."[11] No name was signed. We were all pretty frightened. We knew very well that we could not keep the soldiers from firing at the boat and we knew that if it was fired upon they would burn the place for they burned Mr. Hollowell's place about nine miles below because our men had fired at them. We thought about it for a while and then concluded that we had better move off some of the goods and clothes. Therefore, we packed up and Sister Charity, her baby, two servant girls and myself moved up to Sister Charity's place, eight miles from Ma's, and we have been here ever since.[12] I have no idea when we will return home or if the enemy is still there. Sister Charity was very glad to come up here as she would then be near Col. Henry's particular friend staying here (Capt. M. G. May) and he is a very nice young gentleman.[13] We had been here nearly two weeks enjoying ourselves in fancied security when we heard that a large force of Yankees were crossing the river away down below and were going to raid through this county. The 23rd of May we heard that they were coming up rapidly and would camp in Warrenton the next night. The Southern soldiers were passing to the Mountains or wherever they could remain in safety. It made me sad to see our few retreating before the mighty foe. Monday night, May 30th, sure enough 30,000 camped in Warrenton. Monday we were looking for them all day out here, we live only two miles from Warrenton, but only one came here that day. He inquired for arms; if any "Bushwhackers" were about; if we were "Secesh", etc., etc. We told the truth in everything. He asked sister if her husband was in the army, she told him he was. He then asked if she had heard from him lately. She told him she had and he wanted to know when. She said, "This morning."

"This morning? You must have had the mails lately."

She told him, "No, I saw my husband."

"Oh, I guess he is what we call a Bushwhacker", said the Yank.

"My husband would not stoop so low as to "Bushwhack", nor was he conscripted, he has been in the army three years."

He sat there and talked with us for a long time. I thought he would have been afraid away out here alone but we found out after he left that he had a squad just below the house waiting for orders. Well, that night I sat up part of the night and Sister part. We feared that they might come in the night but all was quiet until about 9 o'clock Tuesday, when a squad of infantry came up with a rush. They ran into the yard like they were going to tear up everything but the officer called them back. Some ran to the smokehouse and peeped in and said, "There is nothing there but smoked bacon and we have more of that than we can use." Two or three got something from Sister to eat. They did not stay long. Wednesday, they just kept coming all day.

One squad searched the house for arms, ammunition etc. We seemed so willing for them to search that they were ashamed to search closely. They found nothing they wanted but a bag of fruit that the officer said they must take for the wounded. I told him I expected the wounded and sick had a hard time of it over the rough roads and could get so few delicacies and appeared so willing for them to take anything that they wanted that they offered to pay for the fruit but we would not take it as we said it was for the wounded. While I was gone into another part of the house to see what they were doing, the Captain told Sister that he thought the Southern people were brave and generous people and thought we had the best army in the world. He said that General Bob Lee was the best general in America or the world. He behaved so well that we called him the "Good Little Captain". About dinner time, two officers dressed as fine as they could be came up to Mrs. Tyler's (She lives just across the road from us) to get dinner.[14] While she was preparing dinner they came over to talk with us. They appeared to be gentlemen although they were real Yankees. They told us they had been "bushwhacked" ever since they crossed the Tennessee River. Also said they had caught Col. Henry.[15] They also reported that they had captured Capt. M. G. May and a great many more but we would believe nothing they told us for we caught them in several falsehoods. We would pretend to them that we believed everything they said. The last crowd that came here took all of our hams but one, about half our flour and a few knives and forks.[16] The house and yard both were full of them and just us two ladies among so many men. I think we felt pretty badly about that time. Our negroes ran to the mountain and stayed there while the Yanks were in the country. We only had four up here and they had heard that the Yanks were taking all the negroes, so they left and each took a ham with them so we saved four that the Yanks knew nothing about. I asked one Yank if they had not met a great many Union men on this side of the river. He said they had not seen a single Union man since they had crossed the river. He said some pretended to be Union to get their property protected. I told him I knew there were some Union people on the mountain over which they had passed but they were the very lowest class. He said he knew that but they did not want them. I told him we did not care to have them either, so the poor Unionists were thrown over by both parties. One Yank said he liked to see people stand up for their country and for his part, if he had been a Southerner, he would have fought for the South and that he thought that every man in the South who did not fight was a great coward and I agreed with him. The Yankees stayed in our yard all night. I do not know what their reasons were for doing so unless they were looking for Col. Henry to come in. They told us about sunset for no one to leave the house after dark if they did not want to get shot. The morning after, the raid passed on toward Rome. Sister Mary came up to see us, she thought the country was full of Yanks, yet Ma was so uneasy, for she had heard that the Yanks had burned our house so she ventured up on a mule and Frank rode behind her. They were afraid to bring more than one for they knew the Feds would take them if they came across them. Sister Mary said that none of the Yanks had been to Ma's and I was truly glad when I heard it for I feared that they had been there. Sister Mary had not been here long when we saw four soldiers coming. I told Sister Mary that I suspected that they were Yankees in disguise and to be careful of what she said for I did not know that the Yankees were gone. They stopped at the gate and asked me if they could get some milk. I told them they could and they got their canteens to fill. By that time Sister Charity came in from the woods where she had been to see Mr. A. G. Henry, who was hiding from the Yanks, and one of the soldiers asked her if the Yanks had treated her badly.[17] I stepped to the door and told them it was useless to play off on us for I knew that they were Yankees in disguise, but they vowed that they were not that, they were just as good Rebels as we were. I told them it was hard for me to believe that they were Southern soldiers for if I was not mistaken there was one in the crowd who had taken one of our hams the day before. They all laughed a good deal at him for being accused of stealing. He told me he could show me papers that would prove to me that he was a southern man. He convinced me after a while that he was a Southern soldier by telling about my brothers. He used to belong to the same regiment as my brother Willie. When they left we cheered the Southern soldiers and the Confederacy. General Blair commanded that raid.[18]

A few weeks after Blair's raid passed through we heard of the approach of another large force of Yanks. Everybody was in great excitement for all knew there was not Confederate force enough to stop them in this part of the country. We were very glad when we found they had taken the road to Summit and would not pass by here. Clanton's command chased them a long distance capturing a good many and some escaped to Sherman's army.[19] Sister's husband, Sam Henry, now belongs to Clanton's command. The Yanks have been closely picketing the river ever since Blair's raid here. They began to come to Ma's house in June and have been there every two or three days since. The first time that they came they did no mischief and seemed to be gentlemen. They tore down the fortifications on this side of the river at Deposit that day. Since then they have taken all of Ma's horses. I had two horses and one mule up here which they did not get. They left her two mules which they said were for her carriage. I sent the horses I had to Johnny, as he sent me word if we could not keep them to send them to him. The Yanks have taken nearly all of Ma's corn, several hogs and several other things. Three weeks ago two or three hundred crossed the river at Deposit, came up to this side of Warrenton. They were after Capt. Griffin's company, but did not succeed in capturing any of them. Griffin captured two of them.[20] They were fired upon by some of our men at Mr. Atkins's, a mile and half from here.[21] No one on either side was hurt and yet they burned Mr. Atkins's house for it. He is an old harmless man, nearly eighty years old. Nobody was home except Mrs. Atkins and she was not able to save but little. Some of the Yanks would take things out for her and some would throw them back into the fire. I was very glad they did not get out this far for they were drunk and very mad. Thirty took dinner at Ma's that day. They behaved worse than they ever did before. When they left they quietly pocketed knives, forks and spoons but paid her ten dollars in Confederate money, about one third of the usual price. A short time before this, there had been a great stampede among the negroes to the Yanks. Mr. Harris lost 27, Dr. Smith 9 and Mr. Atkins all of his but five and Mr. A. G. Henry lost 7.[22] All of those left one night. The Yanks crossed at Guntersville one night and went over to Warrenton to take the negro men's families who had gone to them. They carried off a great many also a great many horses besides plundering several houses, etc. We have not as yet had but two negroes to go to them. One man went last year and one this year. The Yankees are surprised themselves at our negroes remaining at home when nearly everybody is losing theirs. They are with our negroes nearly every day. I would not be surprised at any time to hear of their leaving for the north side of the river.

August 20th

We have but little fear of the Yankees now as Clanton's command is throughout the country.[23] Sister's husband, Col. Henry, has been to see her but could not remain but about two hours. I do not know what they intend to do here. We hear daily of fighting in Virginia and Georgia. The Federal army has been before Atlanta, Georgia for a long time fighting nearly every day but hear that they have retreated to Marietta.[24] We have our army in Pennsylvania and also one in Kentucky and Missouri. Fighting at Mobile,

Ala.[25] We seldom ever get any Southern papers now and therefore cannot get the particulars of any of the battles. The regiments to which Willie and Wattie belong have both been in several engagements. The 55th Alabama Infantry covered itself with glory and was cut nearly all to pieces. The Captain, Carter of Wattie's company, was killed also two of the lieutenants. The company went to battle with 60 and came out with 5. I suppose Wattie is safe, have not heard for certain. I am very uneasy. The Lieut. Colonel and Major both were killed. It was a desperate fight and crowned with victory. I think the battle was fought on the 20th or 28th of July.[26]

August 28th

One regiment of Clanton's cavalry in the command of Lieut. Col. Chandler has been in here more than a week and are leaving today for Blue Mountain.[27] All of the people are so disappointed for all thought they were to remain here until the Yanks left northern Alabama. They made a raid up to Town Creek to drive out the Tories who have possession of that part of the country. They killed a few Yankees and captured a few Tories. Our armies are victorious wherever they have been fighting and they are fighting all along the line from Virginia to the Mississippi River.[28] I cannot get the particulars of any of the battles. I saw a soldier directly from the regiment to which Willie belongs. He said Willie and Wattie are both well. I was so glad to hear from them, so many have been killed out in Georgia that I feared both of them had not escaped. There have been a good many Confederate soldiers here this morning. I fear the last we will see in a long time.

Dec 5th

My Birthday. Just twenty two today. What changes have taken place since last 5th of December. I then had a father and was living at home. Now, I have no father and am compelled to stay away from home as the Yankees are so near our home. Since I wrote last I had a great many heartaches and few happy moments.

My three brothers, Willie, Wattie and Johnnie have all been at home. I went home in September and remained there until two weeks ago. Willie and Wattie were there in November. Wattie was on his way to Richmond to complete his education.[29] Willie had just returned from the south where he had carried our negroes. Seven of them had gone to the Yanks and we knew the remainder were going. Willie said he had enough to fight without fighting the negroes.[30]

The night of November 22nd, while we were all sitting around the fire, we suddenly heard a noise as the rushing of many feet. Both of the boys sprang to their feet and ran into a back room while I jumped to the door. I saw the yard was full of Yankees. I stepped back and said, "Yankees! Yankees!" The boys disappeared and we did not know where they went. The Yankees came rushing in demanding "those two Rebels that were there". Said "it was useless for us to deny that they had been there for they knew they were there a quarter of an hour ago". We told them they had been there but were gone. But that did not satisfy them, they went plundering about, searching every nook and corner. They searched the house over two or three times when the officer in command came in and told Ma that he had found her sons and said that "*Ladies who pretended to be ladies and could tell such lies as we told, he was ashamed of us*". We did not believe they had found the boys until we stepped to the door and saw them. There they stood, two unarmed "Ragged Rebels", surrounded by a hundred and fifty Yankees armed to the teeth. Oh, my God! Spare me from such another scene! We were all taken completely by surprise. We thought the boys had got out of the house before it was surrounded but they could not for the Yanks were all around the house before we heard them. The officer said, "Come and tell them good-bye if you want to—make haste—no time to lose!"

We all went out where they were. Willie said, "Ma, write to Col. Russell (the Colonel of his regiment) and tell him I have acted honorably all the time and tried to do my duty. I may never see you all again, stand firm to your principles; I think you have so far, continue to do so."[31] The Yanks were so mad at that I was really afraid they would do something to them. Wattie also requested us to write to his commander and tell of his capture. The boys asked if they could get their overcoats, for it was a bitter cold night, but the Yanks said, "No, did not have time". Sister Mary, Ma and I ran into the house and got overcoats, blankets, etc. They hurried for fear some of the Confederates would come down and recapture my brothers. Oh, how desolate we felt; it seemed to us that both had been carried to their graves. I could have died to save them—Ah, I would be willing to lay down my life now to bring my brothers home in safety to my almost broken-hearted mother. It was a terrible blow, never to be forgotten. It seems there is but little happiness left for our poor family or in fact any family in the South. It may be my brothers will live out their tedious imprisonment and return to us once again.

The morning of the 23rd, the same crowd of Yanks returned, surrounded the house before we were up, would not let any of us leave the house to get wood to make fires nor would they let the children. They took off our cotton and plundered about considerably, searched the house for arms but found none.[32] When they first came, they demanded Willie's and Wattie's arms; said they would give us half an hour to get them in. Ma did not know what they would do so we gave Willie's pistol to them, they got his sabre the night before. Wattie had no arms but the Yanks pretended that he told them he had a repeater. I told them he had no repeater and that he never said that he had any. I asked the officer to give me Willie's pistol, that I would promise never to give it to a Rebel nor shoot it at a Yankee, but he would not give it to me. He said, "Yes, you will shoot Yankees, you would shoot them any time you had a chance". He little knew how glad I would have been to shoot *him*. I can never forget that man; a meaner looking man I never saw. He gave me the belt that Willie wore his pistol on. I intend keeping it as long as I live.

The Yankees the night before turned our molasses out. The next morning Ma asked them why they did it. The officer said, "Oh, you might give it to the Rebels". He was mistaken if he thought the Confederates lived on molasses. They took a great many of Ma's and Sister Mary's clothes. I do not think they would have got Willie and Wattie had it not been for one of our negro men (Isham) who had gone to them a year or two ago. He knew all of the doors and windows and they were at every door before we knew they were near. Sister Mary and I wanted to go down to the boat the morning of the 23rd to carry the boys' clothing but the officer would not let us. He said he would carry them so we sent them by him though I have no idea if they ever received them. Not one of us shed a tear or made any noise when they carried my brothers off. I would not have had them see me shed a tear to save the whole Yankee nation. One Yank could not help expressing his surprise. He said had it been his mother and sisters, they could have been heard for miles. I told him the ones that suffered most did not always make the most noise.[33] He asked me if we did not hate to see all of our property going in that way, that they were going to take everything before they stopped. I told him that we had become accustomed to having our property taken and when we saw Yankees coming we always expected to lose something and that we would not have cared what they would take had they not captured my brothers.

So many changes have taken place in the armies that it is impossible to keep up with the movements as we are almost entirely cut off from newspapers. Hood, who had command of our army in Georgia, has left there, passed south of here a few miles, crossed the river below and is now up in Tennessee.[34] They have fought one desperate battle at Franklin, Tennessee in which our forces were victorious.[35] Sherman, the Yankee commander in Georgia, has gone on south, meeting little opposition.[36] Lee still holds his ground in Virginia. Forrest is up between Nashville and Louisville.[37] I hope my next birthday finds me with nothing to write about war and that all my brothers may be at home in PEACE.

SEVEN

"The Worst Can Hurt Us but Little": The Dusk of War and an Anguished Peace, 1865

Jan 7, 1865

Another year has come and gone and yet this cruel war is raging. I can see no prospect for peace, but all things are possible with God and He can make war cease when He thinks best. Christmas and New Years Days, times for joy and festivity, have passed but they brought no joy to me. The day before Christmas we heard that some Tory had shot Willie, my oldest brother. Oh, the anguish we suffered, no words can express. But we doubted the truthfulness of the report, so Sister Charity got on her horse Christmas Day, though it rained all day, and rode twenty eight miles to hear all about it from some soldiers who it was said had brought the news. When she got there they had heard nothing about it and were very much surprised to hear that it was said to have come from them. Oh, how glad and thankful I was to hear it for it seems that I could hardly bear it. She heard that a Tory had tried several times to shoot him, but the Yanks had put a guard around him for they knew that if he were killed the Southern soldiers would retaliate for it, ten to one.

Hood has retreated to this side of the river, we hear. Sherman has marched through Georgia and reached Port Royal, so report says.[1] We have no papers to get the truth. I hear cannonading today, I suppose it to be at Guntersville. I believe I have not said anything about them shelling us at home. They shelled four or five times but not a single ball ever struck the house. They were using twenty four pounders. We all would go into the cellar whenever they would begin to shell us, then they would pass on to shell Col. Beard's family who live a mile and a half from us. We would go out and watch the shells and listen to the report echo down the river from bluff to bluff. It was splendid!

*I have lost another cousin in the army. Cousin Hubbard H. Fennell died in Georgia, July 20th, 1864. Poor fellow, he has suffered greatly and fell nobly at his post. He was the second of that family who has died from disease contracted in camps. I deeply sympathize with his bereaved sisters and hope that their remaining brother may be spared to them after this cruel war.[2]

Jan 20th

We, in this part of the country, know but little of the movements of the armies. We hardly ever see a newspaper and can believe nothing we hear, therefore I can only write what transpires near us.

Three weeks ago, General Lyons with twelve hundred men came up on the river opposite to Guntersville, trying to cross to this side, having been cut off from the main army. The gunboats were determined that they should not cross, so they kept up a continual shelling on both sides of the river. A portion of the command succeeded in crossing with their cannon, the remainder portion of the command went to other places to cross. General Lyons was among the first to cross. He stayed at Ma's a while. The gunboats would shell while he and his staff were there but they felt alright on this side of the river, did not even put out pickets. General Lyons had his cannon planted on Beard's Bluff and every time a boat would pass it would give them a salute. Most of the Confederates succeeded in crossing on the 14th of January, so that night they moved off, going south but alas, the Yanks were too smart for them. They put a large force off at Whitesburg which came up on the Confederates before they knew they were near. The Confederates had gone as far as Red Hill and stopped for the night, had not pickets out as usual, so the Yanks got right on them before they dreamed of such a thing. The Yanks captured the cannon and near a hundred men. They got General Lyons but he killed his guard and got away.[3] On the 15th, the Yanks came out from the boats and burned Col. Beard's house, the church near there and several old stores and negro cabins. They also burned all the houses in Guntersville but nine and it was a desolate looking place.[4] One of the pilots, Mr. Jim Johnson, told a young lady in Guntersville that they were going to burn Ma's house but he had persuaded them not to do it. He was the same man that saved Willie's life, we can never thank him enough.[5] The Yanks that captured the cannon and men came on down through Warrenton but hardly stopped, went on down to Ma's to feed, etc. There were five hundred Yanks and a hundred prisoners. They fed their horses on Ma's corn and took nearly all of her meat. Old Ben Harris and John Dickey, the noted Tories, were in the crowd but as they were not in command they could do no damage.[6] Sister Mary found a Captain among the prisoners who she had become acquainted with while Gen. Lyons had been staying there. She sent for him to come into the house and gave him a great many nice things to eat and put up a snack for him to carry with him. When he left, he just got out of the gate when she saw a Yankee step up and demand it of him and he had to give it up. I believe the Captain was named Nibbett from Kentucky.[7] She saw another Yank step up to one of the prisoners and take off his boots and put them on himself. The Colonel in command seemed to be a gentleman and behaved very well. He got Sister Mary to write brother Wattie and said he would have it sent to him. I was really surprised to learn that Ma's house had not been burned. I heard once that it was but it did not hurt me much as we are getting accustomed to everything and the worst can hurt us but little. Since the 15th of January, the Yanks have been at Ma's nearly every day. The other day there came up a large crowd of negro soldiers, commanded by Harper, a noted Tory.[8] The way they did cut up was dreadful. A crowd went into Sister Mary's room and began to pack off dresses, quilts, beds, etc. She could hardly get in for the crowd but when she did she took a stick and lay it to them right and left and drove them out. One Yankee Lieutenant assisted her in driving them out. He snapped a pistol at one of the negroes. They took all the meat that Ma had left but four pieces, killed all the hogs they could find and killed all the turkeys and chickens. Oh, what do the people of the South suffer to gain our independence. Ah, we can suffer more, ten times more, to be in the end an independent nation. It is now reported that Vice-President Stephens has gone to Washington and old Lincoln has sent General Blair on to Richmond to negotiate for peace.[9] I do hope they will arrange matters so that we can have an honorable *peace*. One of the Captains of the gunboats told a lady at Guntersville that he had letters from Willie and Wattie for us. I sent Ma word so she and Sister Mary went down to the river and hailed the boats as they passed up. A Captain and four men came out to see what they wanted. They told Ma they were not the ones that had the letters but that her sons were well and were in Nashville, Tenn. I hope we will hear from them soon. Have not heard from brothers John and Sam in a long time though they have been in a fight in Southern Alabama somewhere. Confederates were victorious.

May 1st

It has been a long time since I have written. I hardly know where to begin. We have heard from Willie and Wattie. Willie is at Johnson's Island. Wattie is at Camp Douglas, Illinois, the same prison he was in once before.[10]

Received one letter from Willie and three from Wattie. Wattie writes to Mr. Jim Johnson, pilot on one of the gunboats, nearly every time and he send it to us. Mr. Johnson has also sent Wattie some money. We hope to see the boys soon as they are paroling the prisoners. A great many are coming in every day or two. I am now staying at home. The Yankees have been here twice since I came home. The first time they came out they did nothing but shoot at the black boys as they ran when they saw the Yanks coming. I sent a letter by them to Willie and Wattie. They said they would send them. The next bunch that came killed all the hogs they could find. The Yankees have been raiding all through South Alabama. We have heard of the fall of Tuscumbia, Selma, Montgomery, Talladega, etc.[11]

Brother John is at home on parole. He was captured near Talladega on the 22nd of April.[12] Sam Henry has been wounded in the arm but we hear that he is almost entirely recovered.

*Cousin Lou Chandler died the 6th of April, 1865. They sent for me to come up to see her but the summons came too late as she died about two hours before I got there. I could but grieve for her though I know that she is far better off now than here on the wicked earth. It almost makes me weep to look at her poor little babe, only four months old, all unconscious of his great loss. None of her brothers or sisters were with her. Cousin Mag Fennell was over the river and cousin Tom Fennell is in the army so neither could come to see her. She had lost two brothers since the war began, Joe and Hubbard Fennell. She is buried by her father and mother in our family ground.[13]

*Heard a few days ago of the death of cousin Emmet Hobbs. He died in the army down in Mississippi. He was only about 17 years old. I was sorry to hear of his death. He was a good boy and all of his comrades loved him.[14]

May 5th

We heard reports of the surrender of Lee, Johnston and "Dick" Taylor, which takes in all of our army east of the Mississippi River. Lee, down to the last battle was victorious. Yankee loss 60,000 and Lee's from 15,000 to 20,000. But he was overpowered and forced to give it up.[15]

Old Abe Lincoln was shot by an actor by the name of Booth in the theatre at Washington City. So Andy Johnson is president of the United States. Lincoln was killed on the 14th of April.[16]

Everything appears very dark and all think our independence very doubtful. We heard that France, Spain and Russia had recognized us and that France had taken New Orleans and had 20,000 at Galveston, Texas.[17] If these reports be true there is some hope for us yet. I can get no dates as we have no papers; just have to go by what I hear.

May 13th

PEACE HAS BEEN MADE and the South (East of the Mississippi River) has gone back into the Union. There is very little rejoicing, the people know that they must submit but it is hard, after all the blood has been spilled, to go back to submit to Yankee government. All try to take it as cheerful as possible for they know we have no army and by standing on our dignity would only make the burden heavier. It is supposed that the negroes will be freed. The Yankees and southerners have meetings every few days in Guntersville. They hoisted the old Stars and Stripes, the symbol of oppression, amid the cheers of several hundred of our citizens. Yes—they cheered the old flag when their hearts were almost breaking and they felt like tearing it down and trampling it into the dust. If brothers Willie and Wattie were home I would feel a great deal better but it is reported now that no more prisoners will be released until the Texas war ends, for Kirby Smith with a large army is still standing his ground on the west side of the Mississippi River.[18]

May 17th

Yesterday, brothers John and Frank and nearly all of our negroes went up to Guntersville to a meeting which the Yankees had appointed and invited all of the citizens and negroes to come up and talk about the terms of Reconstruction. I don't think they have decided yet just how we are to be treated but think we will go back as we were before the war only *slavery* will be abolished. I am not so sorry for that, for they were so much trouble and now we will not feel the responsibility for their comfort. I have been opposed to slavery for a long time but the poor negro will have to work harder than ever. All who used to belong to us are going to remain, I believe, this year as they have the crops in. Ma will have to pay them wages. One of the men was very much disappointed when the Yanks told him "They were free but better go and work for their masters and receive wages. They did not want any more negroes in the North, there were more now than they wanted". The negro man thought they would tell him "You are free—go home and get a good horse or anything you want from your mistress and live in ease and like a gentleman". Captain Morehead of the U.S. Gunboat told Johnny that any time Ma or his sisters wanted to go anywhere up or down the river to come to his boat. He has been here once.[19]

May 18th

Several persons have told me that no more of the prisoners will be paroled or released until after the Texas war unless they take the oath.[20] I have been advised to write to Willie and Wattie and ask them to take it and come home but I am not "Unionized" enough for that yet. I wrote and told them that I expected they would have to take it to get out. I can't realize that we are whipped and are in the Union. I can't but hope for something to happen that will change affairs. Mead went up to Huntsville a few days ago and surrendered.[21] The Yanks treated his men as well as could be. They can't help but dreading them some and do all they can to get on the good side of them and that is the way they are doing everywhere, trying to gain the friendship of the South while the poor "Rebs" can hardly bear the sight of a Yankee. Some of our most noted "Bushwhackers" have given up and been treated with the greatest kindness.

May 25th

I wrote to Willie and Wattie today to take the oath and come home as that is the only way they can come. I see in the Yankee papers of May 19th that they have killed Booth, the man who killed Lincoln.[22] He tried to get away but was caught and as he was going to resist he was shot. I also saw where they captured Jeff Davis, President of the Confederate States.[23] I hope it is not true. I should like for him to make his escape although I know that he could do us no good. I am going to try to be a good unionist henceforth but it is hard, hard to submit with a good grace. If I thought I was good enough, I would almost wish to die, rather than live to see our beloved South trampled under the foot of the triumphant Northerner. I can't write what I feel, the heart-sickness which oppresses me whenever I think of our being subjugated but alas—it is too true.

May 30th

Ma has gone over the river. Sister Mary went some time ago and we heard she is very sick at Aunt Charity's.[24] I am so uneasy about her. Ma has gone over to see her. I am very lonely. I am uneasy and in trouble and I don't know what else. I am almost sorry that I wrote to the boys to take the Oath of Allegiance as something may turn up yet that they can be released. We hear of fighting in Texas.

June 20th

Kirby Smith has surrendered at last or at least that is the report.[25] There is no hope now, we are certainly gone up. I believe we could have given up slavery at the beginning and it would have been still better if we had abolished slavery and stayed in the Union but it is too late now and we should do the same if it were to be done over again. Received a letter from Willie and he says he has made application for the Oath, so we may expect to see him home soon.

June 22nd

I heard of a man who has threatened Willie's life as soon as he gets home. I have heard the report often and had become very uneasy so I concluded I would go up to see the commander of the post at Guntersville and see what protection a paroled soldier would have as they were bound to protect soldiers as long as they stayed here and he gave me a written order for the man, Marion Berry, to come up and report to him.[26] As his men are infantry, he asked me if I could send it to him. There was an old sergeant who had been to our house several times and he came up and shook hands like he was delighted to see me—bah! But I am a good Unionist now and must not mind such things.

June 23rd

As I came on down from Sister's this morning, a lady stopped me and told me that a man told her he had seen Willie and Wattie both, above here on a raft, coming down the river and she expected they were home by this time. When I got near the house some of the negroes told me they were home. I cannot describe my feelings, I was so overjoyed. And then as both had returned together, which was strange, as they were in separate prisons. They accidentally came together at Nashville where they were parted on their way to prison. They both look very badly as they have been starved nearly to death. Willie has a very bad cough, he is uneasy about it but I think he will soon get over it. They got in yesterday directly after I had started to Sister's.

June 24th

Willie went up to see Captain Dunn today to give him that order for the appearance of Mr. Berry as he has no fear of him and told the Captain if it was to oblige him, Berry could remain at home.[27]

[Editor's note: This is Cassie's last entry in Diary Three.]

APPENDIX 1

Family Biographies

Dr. James Watkins Fennell (1810–1864): Born on November 17, 1810, James spent the first six years of his life in Westmoreland, Virginia. The fifth child of James Clark Fennell (1780–1817) and Elizabeth "Betsy" Hobbs (1785–1863), James had five siblings: Martha M. (Eldridge Rivers), Isham H. (Margaret Bedford) (Sarah Key), Hubbard Hobbs (Mary Smith), John D. (Sarah Kelly), and Francis Marion (Isabella Allison). In 1816, James and his family moved to Madison County, Alabama, then part of Mississippi Territory. His father purchased Section 4, Township 5, Range 1 East "near the western foot of Green Mountain within the Great Bend of the Tennessee River."[1] His father died in 1817, just a year later. James longed to become a physician and graduated from both the University of Virginia and the Medical College of Louisville. After earning his degrees, he returned home and opened a practice in Madison County. He acquired land near Deposit Ferry about five miles west of Guntersville in Marshall County, and on September 26, 1836, he married Matilda Allison. Ultimately, his estate included 178 acres and almost thirty slaves. James fathered five sons and five daughters: Charity Elizabeth (Sam Henry); James William; Isham Watkins (Mary Arnold); Catherine Margaret (Andrew J. Esslinger); Mary Jane (Joseph D. Graham); John Houston (Lucinda R. Sheffield); David Francis; Isabella (William C. Neill); Caius Grattan (Mattie Foster); and Martha Matilda (William G. Jordan). His great-great granddaughter Carmen reports that, in addition to his medical practice, he served as a reverend in the Methodist Episcopal Church. An intellectual, he cherished his private library, which contained works of literature, history, philosophy, and medicine. Though a slave owner, he did not approve of secession and wanted no part of the war, but three of his sons served in the Confederate Army. James died on March 18, 1864, leaving his wife and children much bereaved. His tombstone, which is located at the Guntersville City Cemetery, reads, "Blessed are the Dead that Die in the Lord."[2]

Martha Matilda (Allison) Fennell (1816–1893): Born on November 12, 1816, Matilda spent her first four years in Londonderry, Ireland. Her parents William Allison (1790–1839) and Isabella Moore (1790–1840), both Protestants, had eight children over the course of their marriage. Matilda's siblings were Charity (James Cooper)(Houston Lea); John (Catherine Nancy Cobb); Catherine (W. R. W. Cobb); David (Sarah Smith); William; Mary Jane (Edward Tilley Parker); and Isabella (Francis Marion Fennell). Matilda must have been exceptionally close to her siblings because she later named several of her own children after them. Around 1820, the family immigrated to the United States and ultimately settled in Madison County, Alabama. Given the Allison family's affluence, all the children, except one confirmed bachelor, married well. Matilda married Dr. James W. Fennell, a wealthy physician and planter. She later gave birth to the following children: Charity, Willie, Wattie, Cassie, Mary Jane, Johnnie, Frank, Belle, Caius, and Mattie. Widowed in 1864, Matilda never remarried. Though she faced several postwar lawsuits initiated by her son-in-law Sam Henry, she made ends meet by leasing land. Matilda outlived four of her ten children. In her later years, she resided with her daughter Belle in Nashville, and in January 1893, Matilda fell and broke her hip. Several months later, in June, she visited son Johnnie at No. 5 Avenue I in Birmingham. She died there on December 15, 1893. Her children transported her body back to Deposit Ferry and buried her in the Fennell family cemetery. Caius, her youngest son, later had her tombstone moved to the Guntersville City Cemetery. It reads, "She walked with God."[3]

Charity Elizabeth (Fennell) Henry (1837–1884): Named after her maternal aunt, Charity was born near Deposit Ferry in Marshall County, Alabama. The eldest of ten children, she aided her parents Dr. James W. Fennell and Martha Matilda Allison in seeing after her younger siblings until her marriage to Samuel Henry on September 18, 1856. She and Sam had six children: James F. (1858–); Margaret (1859–1886); unnamed infant (1860–1860); Sam Watkins (1862–1863); Beulah Elizabeth(1863–1929); and Mary (1866–1884). Based on her sister Cassie's diaries, Charity had a close bond with her mother and siblings. Cassie claimed that during the Civil War, Charity rode a horse twenty-eight miles in a thunderstorm to find out if their brother Willie had been killed. In 1866, Charity and Sam moved to nearby Gadsden, Etowah County, where the latter owned a general store. It is unknown how Charity felt about the lawsuits her husband brought against her mother after the war. The most contentious case had to do with her inheritance. Her father had gifted her a number of slaves before the war, and many in the Fennell family claimed that was her share of the estate. Sam, whether due to concerns about honor or money, disagreed and sued after the passage of the Thirteenth Amendment. Sam argued that the family of slaves had been a down payment on her share, not its entirety (a sentiment later echoed by his youngest brother-in-law Caius). Though Charity's mother and her brother Willie fought hard, Sam won the lawsuit and $2,000. It might be tempting to see Charity as passive or browbeaten, given the larger-than-life personality of her husband, who was a well-respected veteran/merchant in Marshall and Etowah Counties. On one hand, she may have seen the loss of her inheritance via Emancipation as her misfortune but respected her father's wishes and wanted to see her siblings receive their fair shares of his estate. On the other hand, it could be surmised that she, as the eldest child, viewed the situation as a gross injustice and believed her father would have wanted her to have a share of the remaining estate, since she had, through no fault of her own, lost what he had allotted. She died in 1884.[4]

Samuel "Sam" Henry (1825–1893): Born on July 17, 1825, in Sevier County, Tennessee, Sam was one of six children belonging to Sam Henry Sr. and Margaret Bryan. Between July 1, 1846, and June 30, 1848, he attended the United States Military Academy. Though receiving few demerits, he struggled in math and French. At the end of his sophomore year, these poor marks led the academic board to seek his dismissal. Before it could make this recommendation to the secretary of war, Sam resigned.[5] During his time at the academy, his parents had moved to Marshall County, Alabama. So, rather than return to Tennessee, Sam headed for Marshall County, where he went into business with Albert Gallatin "A. G." Henry, a first cousin and brother-in-law. The two operated a general store at Gunter's Landing. At age thirty-one, Sam married Charity Fennell, then nineteen, on September 18, 1856. He and his wife had six children. As the owner of Henry Plantation in Henryville and co-owner of a general store, Sam accrued a great deal of wealth. In 1860, the US Federal Census listed him as having real estate valued at $5,500 and personal property worth $22,535.

During the Civil War, he entered service as a captain in the 9th Regiment, Alabama Infantry, and was later promoted to colonel. He was charged with shameful behavior at the Battle of Williamsburg and sustained wounds at the Battle of Antietam. On the incident at Williamsburg, his men came to his defense, even going so far as to sign a petition. Nevertheless, he was suspended and court martialed. After resigning, Sam returned home and then joined Clanton's Brigade, 8th Alabama Cavalry. After the war, on November 1, 1865, Sam received a pardon from President Andrew Johnson.

In 1866, Sam and Charity moved to Gadsden, Alabama, where he opened another general store. Due to his land holdings, his business, and his money loaning, Sam remained one of the wealthiest men in north Alabama. Unfortunately, his business habits made enemies. In the hardscrabble Reconstruction era, many locals resented his calling in loans when people could least afford to pay. Marshall County's court records brim with lawsuits brought by Sam. He sued his own mother-in-law twice. The first instance can be seen under the biography of his wife Charity. The second lawsuit he brought was over his brother-in-law Frank's share of Dr. James W. Fennell's estate. Young Frank had died suddenly in 1867 and, rather than have Frank's "share" redistributed to the remaining siblings, Sam wanted power of attorney over the teen's estate. The case ended with Frank's estate being divided among all of his siblings.

Charity died in 1884, and she must have left a significant impact as Sam never remarried. In his later years, he had eyesight issues to the extent that he traveled to Cincinnati, Ohio, for treatment. In 1889, he suffered a debilitating stroke. He had just begun to recover from the partial paralysis when his past appears to have caught up with him. Someone with a grievance sought revenge. Not once but twice, one or more arsonists set fire to his house. The first attempt in 1888 burned his barn and stable, but the second reduced his house to ashes, though many of his possessions were saved. Neighbors also rescued a bedridden Sam who, unharmed, lived for several more years. He died on March 21, 1893.[6]

James William "Willie" Fennell (1839–1878): The eldest son of Dr. James W. Fennell and Martha Matilda Allison, Willie was born in 1839 in Marshall County, Alabama. Like his father, he became a physician. In March 1859, he earned a medical degree from Columbian College in Washington, DC. He then moved back to Marshall County and later, served as a field surgeon in the Confederacy's 9th Alabama Infantry. He was severely injured at the Battle of Gaines's Mill. Once he recovered, he joined the 4th Regiment, Alabama Cavalry, and became a captain. On November 22, 1864, Willie was captured and sent to a military prison in Louisville, Kentucky. On December 3, 1865, he was transferred to Johnson's Island. Willie survived the war, and in 1865, became administrator of his late father's estate. In 1870, Willie had real estate valued at $3,500 and a personal estate of $300. Sometime before 1878, he moved to Holly Springs, Mississippi, and practiced medicine with his cousin John Fennell, a druggist. During the 1878 yellow fever epidemic, many fled the area, but Willie and John stayed to nurse the sick and paid the ultimate price. Both contracted the illness and died. According to Carmen Hurff, one of his great-grandnieces, "Uncle Frank was told that the Methodist-Episcopal Church of Holly Springs had a beautiful window dedicated to the 'Memory of Dr. William Fennell, who gave his life to help his people.'"[7] Long after his burial at Hillcrest Cemetery, Willie's family sought to recognize his war service. His youngest brother Caius signed an application for a veteran's headstone. The headstone reads "Captain James W. Fennell of the Fourth Alabama Cavalry, Company I." Willie never married and had no children. Caius later sold Willie's share of the Fennell estate at auction.[8]

Isham Watkins "Wattie" Fennell (1841–1918): Born the second son of Dr. James W. Fennell and Martha Matilda Allison, Wattie followed in his father's footsteps to become a physician. An assistant surgeon during the Civil War, he served in the 42nd Tennessee Infantry but was captured at the Battle of Fort Donelson. After being paroled, he returned to service only to be captured at Port Hudson. Once paroled, he joined the 55th Regiment, Alabama Infantry. On November 30, 1864, Wattie was captured yet again and sent to a military prison at Louisville, Kentucky. On December 4, he was transferred to Camp Douglas in Chicago. Although the first name in the record is blurred, he is listed as a hospital steward from Marshall County, Alabama, in the 55th Regiment, Alabama Infantry. The remainder of the name reads Watkins Fennell.

According to his nephew William Francis "Frank" Esslinger, Wattie's POW experience soured him on northerners. In a family history, Frank recalled hearing the following story: "Reading of the great fire in Chicago, in 1871, memories of his [Wattie's] suffering caused him to show he felt like it was just a part of retaliation, for which he felt no sympathy and expressed none for the cruel city."[9]

In this book, Frank repeated a story he had been told by another Camp Douglas POW: "A certain guard, pompous and over-bearing carried a stick while marching lines of prisoners for exercise, or other purpose, feeling free to tap a prisoner with it, if out of line, or slow, so he thought it best. One day,

Dr. Fennell told the others, 'If he hits me with that cane, I am going to give him a whipping.' So, on march, he was ordered to step up, with a prod of the stick added. The guard should have known better than to enrage a red-headed Southerner. Uncle Wattie doubled his fist, gave a well packed punch to his jaw and down he came. Then, he jumped on him, took that stick, and wore him out. The guard took a good beating. Then he said to the other guards, 'Why did you let that Little Johnnie beat me up?' The guards told him he deserved all he got, for he had no right or orders to strike a prisoner."[10] This anecdote amused Frank, but of course, he had only the man's word and no substantiating evidence. Perhaps such tales served Fennell family members as a coping device, soothing the blow of captivity to the family's pride.

After the war, Wattie returned to his schooling. He earned a medical degree from the University of Nashville in 1867 and, for a while, resided with his Aunt Charity (Allison) Cooper Lea in Madison County. He later moved to Florence, Alabama, where he opened a medical practice. On January 31, 1876, he married his second cousin Mary Arnold (1854–1902). He and Mary had three children: James (1879–1883); Mattie Iola (1886–1918); and Lula (1883–). Several years after Mary died, Wattie married Jessie Burckhalter on February 2, 1906. Wattie himself died on September 26, 1918. Wattie was buried in Courtland, Lawrence County, Alabama, and his brother Caius applied for and received a military headstone to mark the grave.[11]

Catherine "Cassie" Margaret Fennell (1842–1884): Born on December 5, 1842, in Deposit Ferry, Alabama, Cassie was the second daughter of Dr. James W. Fennell and Martha Matilda Allison. Of her nine siblings, she expressed a particular fondness for Willie, Wattie, and Charity. Between 1859 and 1861, Cassie attended the Young Ladies' Institute in Washington, DC. In the nation's capital, Cassie began keeping a diary, a habit she maintained at least through the close of the Civil War. On December 27, 1866, she married Confederate veteran Andrew Jackson "A. J." Esslinger, who had been a private in Company K of the 49th Alabama Infantry. For the first few years of their marriage, the newlyweds lived with Cassie's Aunt Charity (Allison) Cooper Lea in Whitesburg, Madison County. While there, Cassie went through three pregnancies, and each time, she chose to give birth at her mother's home. As a result, her first children, William Francis (1868–1951), James Houston (1870–1920), and Earnest Alva (1872–1918), were born at Deposit Ferry. After Earnest's birth, Cassie and A. J. moved to the eastern part of Madison County, where many Esslingers lived. For a few years, they rented land formerly owned by one of Cassie's aunts, Nancy (Cobb) Allison. Eventually, in 1874, Cassie and A. J. bought 215 acres in Berkley, Madison County. Though her first pregnancies had been detrimental to her health, Cassie gave birth to four more children: Andrew Watkins (1874–1951); Wade Hampton (1876–1919); Arthur Graham (1879–1941); and Martha Matilda "Mattie" (1882–1967). These births greatly weakened her constitution, and she frequently stayed with her mother, who attempted to nurse her back to health. During her convalescence at Matilda's home, Cassie and A. J. wrote myriad love letters. In 1884, Cassie died of pneumonia at her home in Berkley. She was buried in the Beason-Esslinger Cemetery.[12]

Mary Jane Fennell (1845–1926): On November 23, 1845, Mary Jane, the third daughter of Dr. James W. Fennell and Martha Matilda Allison, was born at Deposit Ferry, Alabama. From 1859 to 1861, she attended the Young Ladies' Institute in Washington, DC. On May 7, 1872, she married Joseph D. Graham in Marshall County, Alabama, and by 1880, the two lived in nearby Madison County. Eventually, Mary Jane moved to Homestead, Dade County, Florida, where she worked as a bank teller. She died widowed and childless on November 2, 1926. In her will, she left her estate to her surviving siblings, Mattie and Caius, as well as to numerous nieces and nephews.[13]

John "Johnnie" Houston Fennell (1846–1906): Born on September 6, 1846, at Deposit Ferry, Johnnie was the third son of Dr. James W. Fennell and Martha Matilda Allison. On February 12, 1864, at age seventeen, he enlisted in the 8th Regiment, Alabama Cavalry, Company F, as a private. He was captured near Talladega, Alabama, on May 1, 1865, and paroled on May 14, 1865. After the war, he attended school in Warrenton, farmed, and did carpentry work. On February 5, 1868, Johnnie married Lucinda R. Sheffield, the daughter of Col. James L. Sheffield and Mary Ann (Atkins) Street. Johnnie and Lucinda had six children: James W. (1871–1933); Lawrence (1874–1932); John Allison (1876–1946); Lucia (1878–); Mattie (1879–); and Willie (1879–). By 1890, Johnnie lived in Birmingham and, by 1905, resided in Landersville, Lawrence County. After being widowed, he married a woman named Martha. In June 1905, he suffered a stroke that left him partially paralyzed. He died almost a year later, on May 23, 1906.[14]

David Francis "Frank" Fennell (1849–1867): Born on March 27, 1849, Frank was the fourth son born to Dr. James W. Fennell and Martha Matilda Allison.

Little is known about Frank, as he was rarely mentioned in Cassie's diaries and only briefly in the memoirs of his little brother Caius. Though he never served in the Confederate forces, Frank may have participated in the home guard, though he would have been only fourteen when the war ended. He died two years later, on October 17, 1867, at the age of sixteen. The cause of death is unknown. He was buried in the Fennell Family Cemetery, and his mother purchased a rather ornate tombstone. It reads, "Prepare to meet thy God."[15] In the late 1930s, when the Tennessee Valley Authority constructed Guntersville Dam and planned to create Lake Guntersville by flooding many area farms and plantations, Caius arranged for Frank's tombstone to be transferred to the Guntersville City Cemetery.

Isabella "Belle" Fennell (1852–1917): The fourth daughter of Dr. James W. Fennell and Martha Matilda Allison, Belle was born in 1852 at Deposit Ferry, Alabama. As a teenager, she attended Huntsville Female College. On January 8, 1883, she married George William "Bill" Neill (1836–1885). They had one child—Virginia (1888–1970), a.k.a. "Jennie." Belle and her family later lived in Nashville, Tennessee, at 914 Fatherland Street. At one point, she brought a suit—*Belle F. Neill vs. The United States*—for losses incurred by her family during the Civil War. The losses she itemized included 131 bales of cotton, 5,000 pounds of meat, 43 hogs, 150 bushels of corn, 2 mules, 1 horse, 3 oxen, 1 cow, 1 steer, 1 heifer, poultry, and barrels of lard, molasses, honey, and preserves. Belle and her lawyers valued the cotton at $12,400 and the food stuff at $4,002.50. Belle alleged that her parents and siblings had not been advocates of rebellion and had opposed secession. Although the lawsuit stretched on for many years, she finally received a settlement in 1907. The US government granted $1,330 for the descendants of Dr. James W. Fennell. The estates of the noncombatants, those of Cassie, Mary Jane, Frank, Belle, Caius, and Mattie, received $181 each, while the estates of Willie, Wattie, Johnnie, and Charity only got $60 each, as the court said their loyalty had not been proven.[16]

Caius Grattan Fennell (1854–1940): The fifth and youngest son of Dr. James W. Fennell and Martha Matilda Allison, Caius (pronounced "Keys") was born on March 8, 1854, in Deposit Ferry. Caius had a childhood interrupted by war. After the Civil War, Caius attended school on nearby Georgia Mountain. When he reached his teens, his mother sent him to school in Gadsden, Alabama, and made her son-in-law Sam Henry his guardian.

Unhappy with the strictness of the Henry home, Caius ran away. He later returned to work in Sam's general store but was eventually fired. Though his mother had wanted him to go to a university, Caius preferred attending Bryant and Stratton's Business College in Nashville, Tennessee, but he did not remain long. Initially, he purchased a farm in Madison County and, for a time, worked for his brother-in-law Bill Neill. After that, he leased a furniture factory and then dabbled in the lumber trade. For two years, he worked in a machine shop of the Louisville & Nashville Railroad. In 1903, he purchased the *Guntersville Democrat* newspaper and made it his career. He married Mattie Foster (1854–1931) on June 26, 1876, and had three children: Erin (1879–1970); Robert (1881–1950); and Mary Caius (1886–1977). One of his daughters married Sam Henry, son of A. G. Henry and thus, a cousin of Charity's husband Sam. Of note, Caius had bright red hair, a Fennell trait, in his words, "The physical distinction of which we have always been proud" because it "bespeaks a caliber above or below the ordinary."[17] In 1909, Caius was elected president of the Alabama Press Association. He continued to serve as editor of the *Guntersville Democrat* until 1928, when he sold the newspaper. Fond of automobiles, Caius became one of the first Marshall County residents to own a Studebaker. Shattered by his wife's death in 1931, he never remarried. In 1937, the Tennessee Valley Authority purchased his parents' former land, then owned by his brother-in-law Bill Jordan. Caius was most concerned about the Fennell Family Cemetery, which held thirty-two graves. He made it a point to have the tombstones of both his parents and his brother Frank moved to the Guntersville City Cemetery. In his later years, Caius suffered from severe rheumatism. One of the most respected men in Marshall County, he died on February 6, 1940, and was buried at the Guntersville City Cemetery.[18]

Martha Matilda "Mattie" Fennell (1856–1933): The fifth daughter and youngest child of Dr. James W. Fennell and Martha Matilda Allison, Mattie was born on November 15, 1856. After the Civil War, then nine-year-old Mattie went to school on Georgia Mountain. When older, she attended Huntsville Female College. On December 20, 1881, Mattie married farmer William "Bill" D. Jordan (1859–1942). They had four children: David C. (1882–1965); Jack (1884–1967); James Lafayette (1889–1939); and Eula (1889–1946). Ironically, though the youngest of ten children, Mattie bought out her siblings, and she and her husband came to own her late father's land. She died on April 6, 1933.[19]

Catherine Ann (Allison) Cobb (1813–1862): Born in Londonderry, Ireland, Catherine was the elder sister of Martha Matilda (Allison) Fennell. Her parents were William and Isabella (Moore) Allison. On September 1, 1825, Catherine married Williamson Robert Winfield "W. R. W." Cobb. After W. R. W. won election to the US Congress, she and her husband divided their time between Bellefonte, Alabama, and Washington, DC. Though childless, Catherine doted on her many nieces and nephews. During much of the time her nieces Cassie and Mary Jane attended the Young Ladies' Institute, Catherine and W. R. W. boarded next door. Catherine suffered from poor health and frequented Huntsville's Monte Sano Mountain for its supposedly restorative powers. She died in either late August or early September 1862. By that time, Cassie had long ceased mentioning W. R. W. and Catherine in her diary, probably because of the former's unionism. When Catherine died, however, Cassie noted her passing by remarking that Matilda was devastated.[20]

Williamson Robert Winfield "W. R. W." Cobb (1807–1864): Born on June 8, 1807, in Rhea, Tennessee, W. R. W. was the son of David Cobb and Martha Bryant. The 1860 US Federal Census listed him as a farmer with real estate valued at $1,000 and a personal estate worth $70,000.[21] He had earned much of his wealth from peddling clocks, and some political critics labeled him with the pejorative name of tinker. From 1845–1846, W. R. W. served in the Alabama legislature. In 1847, he was elected to the US House of Representatives and remained there until January 1861, when he reluctantly resigned after Alabama seceded. He appeared frequently in his niece Cassie's diary until the Civil War, when she stopped mentioning him altogether. In all likelihood, Cassie, a staunch Confederate, believed that her uncle's sympathies lay with the Union.

In 1861, W. R. W. sought election to the Confederate House of Representatives but lost. In 1863, he ran again and won. For whatever reason, he never took his seat and was later expelled by the Confederate House. According to the *Evening Star*, "We find the following in Tuesday's proceedings of the rebel Congress: Mr. Clinton, (Ala.) from the special committee appointed to investigate the charge of disloyalty against Williamson R. W. Cobb, member of Congress from Alabama, made a report, accompanied by testimony of sundry witnesses, who prove that the accused remained within Yankee lines, of his own accord, when he could easily have left had he so desired: that his conduct and conversations since he has been among them clearly show that he is hostile to the Confederate cause; and that the committee recommend that his seat be declared vacant, and the Governor of the State of Alabama be informed of the action of the House."[22] One of the witnesses, captain Ben Lane Posey, testified that he saw W. R. W. pleasantly conversing with Union soldiers on a Union steamer in December 1863. A Mr. Mullen (VA) described W. R. W. as "a Yankee by birth and education; he was selfish and mercenary."[23] In 2004, a document signed by President Abraham Lincoln was discovered by volunteers in the Jackson County, Alabama, loose records project. The contents were as follows: "The White House, Washington D.C., January 4 1863, To Any United States Depository, Pay on demand to W. R. W. Cobb, Esq the sum of $5000.00, five-thousand and 00/100 for patriotic services to the United States of America as Provisional Governor of the State of Alabama. A. Lincoln."[24] W. R. W. never assumed this office.

In 1864, W. R. W. managed to procure a travel pass from Union general William T. Sherman, and he used it to travel to Kansas to see about some land holdings he and his brother owned. His presence in Leavenworth threw local officials into a tizzy, as they did not quite know what to make of this Confederate congressman who somehow had passes from several noteworthy Union officers. One such official wrote: "Hon. W. R. W. Cobb is now in our city looking up property confiscated by the Government. You are probably as well posted as to his history as myself he has several certificates one from Gen. Sherman and from other officers saying that Mr. Cobb was loyal."[25]

W. R. W. died on November 1, 1864, on his land in Bellefonte, Alabama, of an accidental, self-inflicted gunshot wound. The *Philadelphia Inquirer* reported, "From the *Chattanooga Rebel* we learn that W. R. W. Cobb, member of Congress elect from Alabama, recently expelled for disloyalty was killed a few days ago in north Alabama by the accidental discharge of one of his own pistols. He has for some time past been consorting with the Yankees, and was not long since in Nashville. His Yankee friends had presented him with a pair of pistols, which he wore upon his person. One of them dropped to the ground and went off, the ball penetrating his bowels and coming out of the back, causing death."[26] Ironically, W. R. W. died before he was expelled from the Confederate House on November 17, 1864. Of interest, while local gossip held that he had been murdered, no newspapers, Confederate or Union, suggested foul play. Perhaps the best summation of his death was given by historian Charles Rice: "Cobb had been repairing a fence on his farm and supposedly had been careless enough to use a loaded revolver as a hammer, holding it by the barrel. The pistol had fired, killing Cobb. While W. R. W.'s death was most likely an unfortunate accident, more than a few people wondered if he had not been murdered by a secessionist, angered by his less than enthusiastic support of the Confederacy."[27]

Charity (Allison) Cooper Lea (1801–1872): Born in Londonderry, Ireland, to William and Isabella Allison, Charity (pronounced Chair-a-tay) immigrated to Virginia with her parents and siblings and, with them, made the move to Madison County, Alabama. In 1832, Charity married James Cooper (1793–1834) who set about building them a large white mansion. He committed suicide by drowning two years later. Rumor had it that James placed an iron pot on his head before leaping into the Tennessee River. In his will, James decreed that substantial real estate and personal property, including the house, land, furniture, livestock, and eighteen slaves, be left to his wife. One contemporary newspaper article estimated the value at well over $24,470.51. Charity's plantation grew mostly cotton and indigo. After a lengthy courtship, Charity married her neighbor Houston H. Lea (1805–1853). The nuptials followed a not-uncommon business arrangement—a pre-nuptial agreement. In a court document signed on December 1, 1840, Charity retained her belongings and the right to manage her own finances. If Houston were to predecease her, she would inherit his real estate and personal property. If she predeceased him, he would not inherit her real estate or personal property. As an extra precaution, Charity made her brother-in-law Dr. James W. Fennell a trustee of her estate, selling him the following for one dollar: roughly eight hundred acres; all nineteen slaves; all farm equipment; all household and kitchen furniture; and all livestock. Once wed to Houston, Charity renovated the mansion, even installing a cantilever staircase. Charity outlived her second husband, and settling his estate coupled with managing such vast holdings became a burden as she grew further in debt. In the late 1850s, Charity faced a forced sheriff's sale of her property, including her house. James and his brother Francis Marion Fennell bought the property for $7,745.97. They allowed Charity to continue living on the estate, because evidence shows that she remained in the house during and after the Civil War. Charity had no children, never remarried, and died in 1872.[28] She was buried in the graveyard at the Ebenezer Presbyterian Church; in her will, she left funds to have both her husbands' graves moved there, as well. The Fennell family sold the Lea Mansion in 1882, and it went through a series of owners. In 1941, Redstone Arsenal gained control of the property, and the commanding general used it as his personal residence. Ultimately, the base sold the building to the Darwin family, and, in 1973, they moved it to its present location on Metaire Lane, north of Eastview Drive, in Madison, Alabama. In March 2005, it became part of the Alabama Register of Landmarks and Heritage.[29] While modern-day newspaper articles and the historical marker noting her former home spell Charity's surname "Lee," most legal documents read "Lea." Her second husband Houston signed his name "Lea."

APPENDIX 2

A Letter from Katie Fennell to Cassie Fennell[1]

Katie to Cassie M. Fennell
Confederate States of
America
Bellefonte, Ala. May 29/61

Dear Cassie,

I received your letter a few days ago. I would have answered it sooner but I wanted to wait until I had some news to write.

We have been making uniforms for the volunteers and are not quite done yet. I (in the name of the ladies of Bellefonte) presented to the company a beautiful flag last Saturday. If I have room I would send you my speech, but I expect aunt will want to write to Aunt Matilda.[2]

There were 11 girls dressed in white with blue sashes on to represent the seceded states. We all had the names of the state we represented on our badges. I represented Alabama:

In the new born arch of glory
Lo, where shines the central star,
Alabama, and her radiance,
Never cloud of shame shall mar.

I was standing in the center of the half circle. Tilda was the first one to speak.[3] She represented South Carolina:

First to rise against oppression
In this glorious southern band,
Home of dead and living heroes,
South Carolina takes her stand,

Sarah represented Virginia.[4] I have forgotten her verse except the first two lines which are

> Wave, wave on high your banners
> For the old dominion comes.

Mrs. Shelton composed our verses for us.[5] They all did very well, but they say I did exceedingly well in my speech. I will send it to you soon if I don't in this letter. I have one copy, but I have promised to give that to Mr. Jones to publish.

Mr. John Snodgrass received the flag as soon as he was through, they gave three cheers for the ladies, three for the Jackson Hornets (the name of the company) and three for the Confederate States.[6] Then Sarah played Sons of the South Arise on the Melodeon and we all joined in and helped her sing.

Mr. Swan sang bass.[7] Mr. Swan held the flag while I was making my speech. Pa says he thinks I did better than the lady that presented the flag in Huntsville. But, the worst part of it was that I had to compose my speech myself:

> Gentlemen, Every true and patriotic woman in the South has a deep and thrilling interest in the issue of the conflict in which you are about to engage and we the ladies of Bellefonte, hoping you the Jackson Hornets may bravely assist in repelling the foe and sustaining our country, present to you this flag of our Confederate States and hope it may proudly wave over the brave and victorious.
>
> Although the ordeal may be a more terrible one than has ever been recorded in the annals of history, we will trust in the right. The all-pervading power of the Almighty will aid and sustain you in the war with your treacherous brother of the North. And help you drive from your homes the blood thirsty abolitionists who are now preparing to invade us. With hope and faith our prayers will night and morning ascend to the throne of grace for your welfare while gone from your mothers, sisters, and friends who will await with anxious eyes and beating hearts your return to the proud old hills of Jackson.
>
> If it be that this flag is torn in shreds and trailed in the dust by northern minions as conquerors, long may the brave company of Jackson Hornets be enshrined in the memory of the South as the bravest in battle and the last to leave the field. But the victory will be ours, the flag of our country will wave in the breeze from Virginia's garden spot to the Gulf of Mexico and from

Carolina's fair coast to Texas's border and the flower will bloom, the birds sing only the sweeter for the loss of the Northerners.

Captain Snodgrass we hope to hear of you leading your company to honor and fame and may your name be spread over every hill and dale of the South as the bravest Captain of the bravest company in the army. Take this flag and when you look upon it, remember the prayers of your friends are with you and your followers.

All are well except Pa and Charlie and they are both better.[8] Pa had the headache and Charlie the sore throat and brother John is up here now.[9]

Katie

I don't expect you can read the last page of this. I am in such a hurry I can scarcely write. It is time I was at Mrs. Martin's now making the uniforms. They may have a call soon. I suppose you have heard the Federal troops have taken Alexandria, but I am in hopes it will soon be taken back. Brother John speaks of going with Cousin Sam's company and said it was to leave on Monday, but he was not well enough to go and was in hopes the company would come by here whenever they are going.[10] Give my love to all.

Katie

APPENDIX 3

The Civil War Diary of Willie Fennell[1]

Tuesday Oct 15–1861

Marched from Groveton to across Stink Creek a distance of about 12 miles, took our stand on a high grade 4 miles from Springfield where the main body of the enemy were located.[2]

Our Piquits advanced 1 ½ miles, could plainly hear the Yankee music. Slept on our arms, expecting constantly to be roused up to march either on the Yankees or on retreat ____________ continually arriving.

Wednesday Oct 16

Woke up early cold and chilly, three of us having slept on one blanket in the open air. Went to the fire and warmed, and then lay down again. At daylight's order waked up again by cannon booming, Apparently close at hand, Did'nt rise however until the beat of the "Longroll" summoned us to arms, Stood in rank some time, was taken with Diarea very severly and felt very weak, no medicine to get. Felt grateful to Bill Walters[3] for a drink of Whiskey which would cure the diarea and give me strength for the days march, Took up line of march at 8 o'clock, From the direction we were going, knew that firing of cannon and musket in that direction, After marching 2 miles we stopped to wait orders, Spent the day gathering chestnuts. Provisions all out, Bought up turnip sallads, had nothing to cook our flour in, Before will Borrow the drum head for us to mix ____________ Get a biscuit from a lady, Marched 'till midnight. Taps ______________________ ____________ On fire two R.R. Bridges ______________________ ____________________ and camped near Battlement. Slept on one straw covered with blankets.

Thursday Oct 17th

Remained in camp until 12 o'clock and took up line of march for Centerville, reached there about 3 P.M.[4] Found the whole country white with tense [tents], marched until dark in the direction of Fairfax turn pike, Slept in some bushes covered with my blanket, and it rained but did not make me ________.

Friday Oct 18th

Stayed in camp until about twelve o'clock when all of the Piquits arrived, then marched up the turnpike for about 2 miles and then turned off towards Centerville, country surprisingly beautiful, about 4 miles from Centerville our company was detached as Piquits, Stood my hour without anything occurring.

Saturday Oct 19th

Detail became certain that there was ______ enemy in the vicinity, Spent the day jovially getting plenty to eat ______ bought some honey tomatoes eggs and butter and baked turkey. Marched in our camp late in the evening.

Sunday Oct 20th

Didn't think of it being Sunday until I heard some one say so later. Got a testament and read a few chapters. Drum beat to march to ________ South East of Centerville. Reached the place late, Slept in the Dispensary.

Monday Oct 21st

_______ falling rain. Heavy firing in the direction of Leesburg, Fireing continued off and on nearly all night.[5]

Tuesday Oct 22nd

Rain continued, Fireing continued in the afternoon, 500 prisoners arrived from Leesburg. Reported that 10,000 were shot, drowned and otherwise destroyed, by 2,500 Confederates under command of Gen ______ Evans, Considerable excitement arose.[6]

Wednesday Oct 23rd

200 more prisoners passed enroute for Richmond, weather cold, Received my overcoat, but lost my knapsack, Afternoon word came that Gen Evans was in danger.

Thursday Oct 24th

Waiting orders to march to the relief of Gen. Evans. Out of flour, wrote a letter to Pa and Ma, Received none from for about two months, Received letter from Uncle Frank.[7] Got my knapsack, Afternoon heard that Gen Evans was defeated.

Friday Oct 25th

Inspection of arms, Gen Evans not defeated but made a Brigadier General. Also Col _____ (Knox?).[8]

Saturday Oct 26th

Nothing of importance ________ rather sick at ________.

Sunday Oct 27th

Guarded. Nothing of importance.

Monday Oct 28th

Nothing worth relating ______________________ nor on the two days following.

Thursday Oct 31st

Marched on Piquit for the 2nd time, marched through Centerville. Saw Gen Johnson, I thought he looks rather shabby, continued our march for about four miles, stacked the Bivouach of the Piquits, Slept under a tent in shelter of brush.[9] Rained all night.

Friday Nov 1st

Awoke wet and weary, Spent the morning drying myself and cooking. Afternoon took our turn on guard. Staid in a pile of wet corn tops. Cold and rainy nearly all night, Kept a fire part of the time in spite of orders.

Sunday Nov 3rd

Before day thought we saw two balloons, but could not make them out anything or the stars in the evening ____________________________ to the ______________.[10]

Monday Nov 4th

Weather pleasant, sky clear, The reg which should have relieved us, late to arrive, slept pleasantly as before.

Tuesday Nov 5th

Returned from Piquit, Got along ______________________________ expected letter from home, Generally in a good humor.

Wednesday Nov 6th

Got my clothes that were sent from home. Sam promoted to a Colonelcy and Oneal to a Lieut Colonel.[11] Spirits still up above the weather.

Thursday Nov 7th

Slightly affected with pleurasy, Nothing important occurring, considerable reaction take place, Spirits low.

Friday Nov 8th

Drilled, nothing else important.

Saturday Nov 9th

Nothing.

Sunday Nov 10th

Did all cooking, All of my sick __________ or on guard.

Monday Nov 11th

WM James Ruptured from coughing.

Tuesday Nov 12th

Moved into winter quarters, two miles to Centerville Spring. The afternoon getting wood ______________ scarce articles here.

Friday 15th Nov

Fair day had pretty good __________________________________ had my supper.

Saturday 16th

Nothing of importance occurred.

Sunday 17th

Regiment went on Picquet, Wind very high blowing tents about ___ O'clock ______________________________. My ________________________ left in camp in charge of sick.[12]

Monday Nov 18th

Still blustery, Nothing else.

Wednesday Nov 20th

Very light _______________ of ___________________________________ from __________.

Thursday Nov 21st 1861

Afternoon ____.

Friday Nov 22nd

____.

Saturday March 1st

Went into Manapas [Manassas] in search of my box lost at Simasburg [Strasburg], unsuccessful. Therefore spirits low. Packed up all surplus baggage to send off prepatory to marching.

Sunday March 2nd

Warm but snowing, Evening snowing about 4 inches deep, Read, some in the New Testament, Sam found Whiskey selling at Gen Wilcox's.

Monday March 3rd

Drizzling rain. In the evening Snow melting very fast.

Tuesday Mar 4th

Ground frozen hard, Very cold. Afternoon, mild and muddy, Carried wood half mile.

Wednesday March 5th

Finished reading New Testament, through, G. W. Martin arrived in camp. Learned that we had threshed the Yankees near Winchester, also learned that Quarles reg'te to which Brother W__________belonged was captured at Fort Donaldsen, Had some hopes that they had escaped.[13]

Thursday March 6th

Weather beautiful, Sent off all surplus baggage, Slight sprinkling of snow in the afternoon. News of a battle at Winchester con-____d.[14]

Friday March 7th

Morning fine and clear, but cold. Evening still fine, Looking for orders to march, Which came about midnight.

Saturday March 8th

Got up about 3 A.M. preparing to march, Ready before the time, Started about sun rise and marched to the battle field near the stone house, where we remained until later in the day, Then started down the turnpike towards Winchester, Marched a mile or two and then camped for the night.

Sunday March 9th 1862

Morning, Read eleven chapters in Mathew, The weather fine, All in good spirits but wondering where we are going. Started about 11 o'clock A.M. in a southern direction. Saw Gen Smith for the first time.[15] Marched pretty constantly until afternoon. And camped in a chestnut grove, Slept on the ground but didn't rest well as the ground was not level, and I was seroughed [?], Supped upon Army crackers and dried beef.

Monday March 10th 1862

Started early and marched hard until about 11 A.M., stopped and staid About an hour, eating nothing but crackers, beef was all out. During the march went through Warrenton and near White Sulphur Springs.[16] Got a piece of bacon at night and ___ eat it as I was very hungry, It made me very sick, Worked hard to get a fire started, Others wouldn't work. Went to bed about 2 o'clock and slept ________. Waked _________ow __________ound_______________.

Tuesday March 11th A.M.

Weather pleasant, Started about 7 P.M. passed through Jeffersonton & crossed the Hazel River. Entire reg' detailed to wait upon the wagons, Got my blankets halled [?]. Got the sore throat pretty badly. Camped about 8 miles from Culpepper C.H.[17]

Wednesday March 12th

Walter pretty sick, got _____ about 2 o'clock and got him [to] try some tobacco. Went to bed again but got up early. Ate no breakfast, throat being sore. Started soon after for Culpepper C.H.[18] After a hard, march we arrived at Culpepper C.H. Camped about 2 miles from town, No soldiers allowed to visit town ____________________ ____________________________ _____poon____stand it. Learned that we would stay in camp a day or so. Mighty glad to hear it as I was nearly worn out by marching and carrying my big knapsack.

Thursday March 13th

Awoke after a sound sleep much better, Throat clear and lungs not so sore, Weather warm but cloudy, Evening rainy.

Friday 14th March

Friday still in camp near Culpepper C.H. Raining, Nearly well. Learned that Yankees had reached Bristtow, also that Gen McCulloch was killed.[19]

Sat March 15th

Still raining, Learned that we would move soon, not certain wherefor, Suppose it _____________ Gardinsville, 12 order came to be ready at a moments notice ________. Remained in ________________________ eve_____________________________ Still ________________________ ____________________ht__________.

Sunday March 16th

____________________ still cloudy, _________________, Got ready to march about 9 A.M. Rear Brigades passing by, 10 Started. Allways march on Sundays, Roads very bad, Artillery fireing continually, Infantry stopped

Though ______________ Marked ______________________. The fields entirely. Did not make over five miles during this day.

Monday March 17th

Rose early after a refreshing sleep, Weather cloudy but warm, Started early and Marched to within 14 miles of Orangeburg C.H. Stopped and went into camp, went out in the country, Bought some eggs & sugar, Returned in about 9 o'clock ___________
Very tired _____________________________________.[20]

Tue _________

K____
______________________.

APPENDIX 4

The Memoirs of Caius Grattan Fennell, 1938[1]

In attempting to give my reminiscence for so long a time the face must be borne in mind that my early years fully circumscribed and that the matter must be in first person.

I was quite young [born March 8, 1854] when Mr. Lincoln was elected president. So young in fact that politics involved did not in the least disturb me. My daily associates were negro boys who were slaves, and they were as happy as it is possible to be, and I may add, that perhaps I was happier than I have ever been since. It was before the evil days came.

I well remember the stir that Lincoln's election made. The State would secede from the Union—War would result—and after that the deluge. My father opposed secession but our most trusted neighbor, Mr. Arthur C. Beard, was strongly in favor of withdrawing. Others twittled my father on his loyalty to the state, to which he replied, "It is better to endure the evils that we have, than to rush into others we know not of." But the secession was a fact, and every eligible man was expected to volunteer for service.

My eldest brother was soon convinced that he must go with the State—or go against it. My second brother was in Washington where he was attending Medical College.

A sharp battle occurred while he was there, and his first surgical practice was dressing wounds of the enemy. There was much speculation at home, as to his action, whether he would come south or take service with the enemy.

At this time, troops were being mobilized and drilled. The old river steamer "Lookout" was due from Chattanooga and many soldiers and citizens gathered at Deposit Landing to see the soldiers who came on the boat. While the people watched tensely as the boat rounded into shore, the band on board struck up "The Girl I Left Behind Me." It was like an explosion. The people yelled and shouted, and when the gang plank was put out "Wat" Fennell was the first man ashore. Then everybody went wild.

I am finding it difficult to keep my data in chronological order, but I can state facts and permit my readers to fix dates.

Soon after the landing of the steam boat, groups of volunteers could be seen daily in argument about securing uniforms and arms. Our place appears to have been a favorite rendezvous for the new troops. I well remember that Lieutenant Jack Weatherby was the first man I saw in Confederate uniform, with gold lace and a bright sword evidently shown for moral effect on young men who hesitated to enlist. In passing I may say that Lieut. Weatherby wore his uniform with honor and at last fertilized the soil of Georgia with his life blood at Peach Tree Creek.[2] Things moved rapidly with us after Wat's return. He had already enlisted in the 42nd Tennessee Infantry, while the eldest brother William joined the 9th Alabama Infantry and was sent to Virginia, where he became Field Surgeon of the regiment—but going into action at Gaines' Mill was severely wounded. In the same battle John May, a neighbor boy was mortally wounded and died in the hospital where my brother was confined.[3] As soon as the news of the battle reached us, my father made a hurried trip to Richmond and brought Will home. Will's wounds were such as disqualified him for infantry service, and he at once raised a company of Cavalry Service and was attached to Russell's 4th Alabama Cavalry, Wheeler's Division.

Incidents of the war, which were the leading incidents of my early life are about to supplant all other matters in my narrative.

I was a lonesome boy and always sought to find out things I did not understand. My mentality was always below my age and this fact contributed to my tendency to an inferiority complex which I have never overcome.

Reverting back to the early days of the war. I remember that I wanted to be a soldier, and that desire was greatly augmented when a sand fort was built to defend Deposit Landing from raiding parties who would ferry themselves across the river, and commit petty defraudations. A small garrison was stationed at the fort with orders to prevent crossing. I would slip off to the fort daily. But one day the Yankee Cavalry rode up on the north side and began firing. I was on the fort relieving a boy a little older than I, but I jumped down to the ditch when our men began returning the fire. I was anxious to get out and go home, but the soldiers said it was too dangerous.

Bullets were knocking sand from the top of the fort and crackling corn stalks in the field. I was pretty scared but it was getting dark and I knew I would go home when night came on.

Suddenly one of our men named Bearden, threw up his hands and fell back onto the ditch. Blood spurted from his face and they told me he was dead. Soon after that I took a sneak down a fence row and made the trip home (half mile) in record time. That cured my wish to be a soldier. Tho' I never could stay in the house when firing began.

My daily associates as I have stated were negro boys about my age. I was always the big man among them. There were no schools, and my sisters taught the rudiments of learning and I learned to write. I had no nice pads to scribble on and paper was very scarce. So I used white chips and shingles to form my letters.

A few white boys of questionable loyalty lived nearby but I did not associate with them. The only boy of near my age that I played with was Jim Beard.[4]

There was not a white girl in our neighborhood. My sisters had young lady friends who visited them quite often. Refugees from Madison County were frequent visitors.

As the war progressed the Yankee gun boats began to patrol the river and shell the country at times, and we began to feel that we were at the mercy of Tiberius.

By this time a third brother, John, who under age, had joined Capt. Sam Henry's company "F" in the 8th Confederate Cavalry. For some reason known only to grown folks, the bulk of our negroes were sent to Bibb County where they were employed at Iron Works.

My father died in January 1864 and left mother with the untried problem of managing the farm, the negroes and the livestock. Two older brothers were then in northern prisons—Will at Johnson's Island and Wat at Camp Douglas. We never had a word from them.

Irregular cavalry used to fire at the gun boats and the enemy had no means of putting a stop to this annoyance. It so happened that two neighbor boys had been captured at Baker's Creek in Mississippi, and were on parole at home. To help out scant supplies these boys would fish in Fishing Hollow. This squad closed in on the Wedgeworth brothers and made them prisoners.[5] In vain they protested that they had paroles at home, but the commandant would not let them go for the papers, but took them on to prison in their shirt sleeves. It was July or August and they were thinly clad but were forced to face the rigors of prison in the north with only their summer garb. At the same battle Wat Fennell was captured and started north on "The Star of the West," but before reaching Memphis, Wat jumped over board in the Mississippi River and swam out to the southern shore. At this remote day I can't remember how men fared for fuel, but the negroes were still doing some work. Both the older boys came home to see if the family needed help. While at home on the night of November 14th, the gun boats landed and sent out a company who surrounded the house and captured both the boys, and took 33 bales of cotton that were stored in a shed. They also took livestock, cattle and hogs and all the supplies my mother had provided—meat, meal and molasses.

The officers of the boats had sent word to the people that in order to save their hogs, it would be necessary to have the hogs penned. We took no note of that order, but our neighbor Henry Burnside had his fine hogs rounded up and penned.[6] When the raider came they got Mr. Burnside's hogs without the trouble of hunting them. Our hogs were in the deep woods and so escaped. Mr. Burnside was very wroth, but had to put up with it though, for saving them trouble.

Soon after this when negroes were free, a few of the more intelligent negroes began to cast about for some place to live. They no longer expected to draw their weekly rations, and it looked as if they must go to work. My mother told them that they were free and could go whenever they wanted to go, but explained to them that she was no longer responsible for them, but did not tell them to get out. The foreman, Miles, a negro of good character came to my mother and told her that he understood that they could go when they wished to, but he continued—"where can we go?" A short time after this Miles told her that two nice looking men who came down in a boat asked him to go with them and they would put him on the road to make money. My mother made no objection but cautioned Miles against strangers. But Miles went with them.

It was later in the day and very soon the men suggested that they make camp. They landed on the Foster place and built a fire. They all rolled up in blankets and went to sleep. In the night Miles felt one of the men feeling for his watch and purse. Miles rose up and showed fight, when one of the pirates shot him in the jaw. He was unconscious for a time, but when he got up, his watch, his purse, his blankets, the boat and pirates were gone. He was only a few miles from home, and began his return trip in much pain—but made it. After that episode the negroes were wary of strangers.

About this time northern teachers began coming south and their influence was the worst that could have afflicted the negroes. One teacher located at Warrenton, lived with negroes and went to church with the women. He became so obnoxious that some men who had seen service in the army wrote him, protesting his conduct as being defiance of the oldest traditions of the South. He grew worse—more defiant until one night three ex-soldiers, who assumed the names and characters of well known soldiers who were killed in action took the teacher out and thrashed him soundly and to make him more like his associates, they blackened him with lamp black and turpentine. This incident was used as a pretext to send a company of negro troops as garrison to hold Guntersville and Marshall County in subjection.[7] The Commander was Captain Elliot, who remained and made his home here.[8] Three innocent boys were arrested and held for trial by court martial. They were Will Taylor, Pleas Mitchell and Peter Kilfoyle.[9]

The three guilty men had a private meeting and took a solemn oath that they would rescue these boys if the boys were convicted—or all would die in the attempt. They were not brought to trial.

The teacher who was flogged was named Lang.[10]

The negro garrison remained for some months, and the soldiers would get leave and go into the country where they intimidated citizens. They were often drunk and very noisy. Working negroes did not take to the soldiers. They feared Peter Whitecotton, Jere Cornwell and Jack Weatherby—the three dead soldiers—might make another visit.[11] These were names assumed by whiffers. Everybody knew that these soldiers had been killed, but they were more dreaded dead than they would have been alive. This incident occurred about 1867 when our state was supposed to be back in the Union. Negroes and Tories could vote, but men who served in the Confederate Army were required to sign an oath, and go to the polls through a file of negro soldiers. The oath was not regarded as binding as it was taken under duress.

A cotton buyer at Chattanooga wrote my mother an offer of $20,000 for the cotton seized which he saw at a depot. This note and offer was placed in the hands of Charles Fielder, a well known Tory, who destroyed the note through malice. The writer of the offer was Captain Eaton who was connected with the Federal Army in some capacity. We have fought [for] that cotton ever since, but without avail.

It is impossible to observe events in chronological order.

About this time my youngest brother [Frank] died—the first break in a family of ten.

Two of the boys, John and Frank attended school at Warrenton.[12] My young sister [Mattie] and I had no schooling except such the older sisters gave us. We were not poor in the sense of actual want, but money we did not have and there was no means of making any. Sister and I finally went to school on Georgia Mountain to Miss Susie Alford. The distance was about 2 ½ miles which we walked or rode double on a big mule. The sisters finally went to Huntsville Female College and I despairing of college, begged my mother for $150 to attend Bryant and Stratton's Business College at Nashville. It was my first trip on a train.

Before this Senator Grayson had given me an appointment to the State University, but I had not the means of attending.[13] There was no rail nearer than Decatur, which at that time, seemed like a foreign country, no bus lines, nor scarcely any roads. My failure to go to the University was the "tide in my life that ebbed", and I have never ceased to regret it.

The circumscribed area of my information gives this memoir the character of autobiography.

The home place began filling up with white settlers who rented the land, and that was my mother's means of subsistence. I was at home much of the time and had acquired a taste for reading, and by this means, contributed to my education.

Now, in order to skip nothing that may interest the patient reader I must revert back to 1863, when my eldest brother paid us a passing visit. He and I walked down to the ferry to ask if any refugees were at the Scott house on the north side. Several men came out of the house and hailed us. My brother asked who they were and whether they were trying to get across. My brother told me to go up the bank. He evidently suspected treachery from the number of men. They continued to talk and advance toward the river when one of them made a mistake and his gun came out in full view. The intention appears to have been to get Will (my brother) down to the edge of the water in order to fire on him at close quarters. Will retreated up the bank and joined me. He laughed at the ruse, but it was a serious matter to me. I was quite young, but was tall and at a distance could be taken for a man.

A young soldier, a Lieutenant, scarcely older or larger than I, came to our house with a bad wound in his foot. He lived on the north side of the river and was anxious to go home. It would never do to cross the river in his uniform. He offered to exchange with me and got my brother and myself to help him across the river. He knew it was risky but was determined to take the risk. Walking was painful to his bad foot, but by going over at night, he was sure he could reach his friends safely. We never heard of him again. He was Lieut. Fletcher. But that uniform got me in a tight place when I was driving up the cows. A gun boat sneaked up without attracting my attention and the officer on watch decided that I was not only a soldier, but an officer as well. He had used his field glass and saw the stripes on my collar. The boat immediately opened fire with two 32 lb. guns. If he hoped to stop me, he was disappointed. The first shell went over me, and I tried to out run the next shot. It struck the ground between me and the boat, and made a ditch that would hold a wagon and team. Shelling continued for some hours. The officers were sure that they had found a Confederate camp.[14]

In the spring of 1863 mother sent a half dozen plow hands to prepare for a crop. The field they were in is opposite the high bluff on the north side. The hands were plowing when a column of cavalry came on the bluff and began firing at the negroes who at once took panic and ran to the woods. They killed one fine mule and broke up the work in that section. It was a tragic and appalling attack, and we did not know whether we could make a crop with the hands under fire. Further up the river the field was out of range from the bluff. My mother had to rely on the negro foreman, as I and my brother [Frank] were too young to have an opinion. We grew corn and provender, but I don't think we grew any cotton after my father died.

Mother had secured a bag of green coffee and doled it out sparingly. It was distressing for the old neighbors to beg for some real coffee as "grand pop" was sick and craved coffee. She also had a barrel of yellow sugar, but they did not ask for that. There were two outlaws named Karl Scruggs and Joe De Fer.[15] They had relatives among the tenants and found lodging on our place. I never knew what offense they had committed, but I knew that they were guilty of some crime, when the Yankees sent a squad down and arrested them both, and subjected them to brutal treatment—hanging them till almost dead and then reviving them. I never learned their ultimate fate.

This was after the war, but men were embittered by the treatment their houses had suffered under bayonet rule. An incident showing the feeling about this time occurred in Guntersville when one man named Knight, who had been a Tory, shouted defiance at any "damned rebel" who was not afraid to show himself. We had a near neighbor and special friend who had lost one hand in battle, and nobody doubted his physical courage. That was Hop Beard; after trying to avoid any conflict with Knight, he could stand it no longer, and drawing his heavy army revolver shot Knight dead. It made a stir in the community, but the evidence cleared Hop of murder.

When Hood retreated from Kentucky he knew that it was impossible to transport his whole army across the Tennessee River at any one place with the small ferry boats that were available. He therefore divided his forces and directed brigade commanders to cross at different points. General Lyons, I think, commanded the 6th Kentucky Cavalry and he made Deposit ferry his objective.[16] The Federal gun boats were on guard to prevent his crossing. The boat commander thought Lyons would cross at Deposit, Law's landing or Guntersville to a point from which the commander could see the north bank at Deposit, from which point, after looking for troops on north, he would leisurely run back up the river. The contour of the shore line is such that nothing could be seen from the boat's anchorage, a half mile below Deposit. Hood's engineers and scouts saw the situation at a glance, and determined on the hazard of crossing at a point just out of sight of the boat, a mile or two down the river. It was necessary to open up a road from the highway to the river over the sandy terrain that would make it possible to transport wagons, artillery and cavalry. By working day and night, the engineers opened a road through virgin woods and rocky bluffs till, by use of ropes, chains and skids, they got the wagons and artillery down to the shore. The boat had already been provided and as fast as wagons and guns reached shore, they were loaded onto the ferry boat and carried across. The artillery was only one 12 lb. napoleon gun. It was very long and of course very heavy. It was drawn by four horses that were unequal to the task. With the heavy impediments safely across, the wagons and guns were taken up into the field and began moving up the river, the dense cane growing along the bank, was good protection from observation should the gun boat come down before everything was clear. But the men and horses were ferried rapidly with the men crowding into the boat and holding halters while the horses swam. I don't recall that a horse or man was lost in crossing. When the last boat load was nearing the south shore, the gun boat came dashing down the river, having been apprised by scouts or Tories, that the army was crossing below Deposit at "Last Ferry", a name given the place by the army. It would have been a simple matter for the gun boat to ram the ferry boat, which was little over half way across. Instead, the Commander determined to use his guns to sink the flat boat. He turned his broadside down stream and opened fire with his 32 lb. guns. Every shell he fired passed three or four feet above the heads of the fleeing men. It was a condition the officers could not correct. The guns could be elevated to any degree, but could not be depressed quite to a level. Thus Lyons' brigade made what appeared to be an impossible escape.

General Lyons made my mother's house his headquarters while his army camped around the house. Gen. Lyons had the foolish idea that being south of the river he was perfectly safe. He moved to Red Hill next day, where he camped with no pickets and that night Federal Cavalry charged his camp and captured 100 men and all army impediments. But the artillery had some action before going into camp.

At Beard's Bluff, two miles from Deposit, the gunners planted their one gun so as to command the river, with a view of sinking the gun boat that had annoyed them at the crossing. The gun boat promptly opened fire, but the brow of the bluff was such that their shells could not reach the few gunners, and some obstruction prevented the Confederates from getting a fair shot at the boat until the boat dropped down the river to a point from which it could shell the shore gun.

This move also gave the shore gun a fair shot at the steamer. They had anchored and were preparing for a hot assault on bluff forces, when a lucky shot made a direct hit on the steamer, smashing steam pipes and boiler until escaping steam hid the craft from view. There was a near panic on the boat and cries of distress indicated that the crew were being scalded by steam. I never learned the casualties of the encounter. After this action the gun moved on to Red Hill and was captured with the army.

The Federals had crossed the river above, perhaps at Law's Landing and had attacked Lyons from the south. Next day the enemy returned with prisoners who had been our guests the day before. On their return they burned the house of Mr. (Uncle) Tommy Atkins and the house of Col. Beard.[17] The smoke was plainly seen from our place and we expected the same treatment but they used the house for headquarters and spared it.

The gun boats met the Cavalry at our landing and took them aboard. The Yanks had a dead officer in a spring wagon. His name was Lyons and was said to have been killed by the General of the same name. He went into the General's room and found him fast asleep. He told the General he was a prisoner and ordered him to dress. The General seized his revolver and shot his captor dead. He then made a hasty escape.

I think Gen. Palmer was in command of the Federals.[18] He was very polite to mother and demanded the keys to the crib and smoke house. He placed a guard around the bins and did not permit any soldier to enter the house except to see him. It was raining and the flag was encased in black oil cloth.

When the war ended, my two eldest brothers were in northern prisons. Will being an officer was in Johnson's Island at Lake Erie. Wat immured in Camp Douglas, Chicago. The rigor of weather was very trying on prisoners, who rarely experienced weather below the freezing point and only strong men lived through the war. When they were released in July 1865, the brothers met by accident at Bridgeport, where they secured a large barge and floated down to our landing. Some other prisoners joined them and helped manage the barge. There was great excitement when they arrived.

There were plenty of wild hogs in the woods and there was enough corn for bread so that the main problem was how to get the hogs. Fire arms were taboo, except for negroes and Tories. But the boys got the hogs some way.

My third brother, John, who was captured at Blakely, reached home about this time and all had agreed that he and Frank, a younger brother, should go to school. They attended a good school at Warrenton under Dr. A. E. Russell.[19] Many young soldiers and soldiers' widows attended this school.

It is marvelous that incidents so long ago are as fresh in memory as those a year ago.

I am minded now of my mother's main care. She was not able to give us vocational or business training but she bore down hard on our moral training. Sunday had to be a day of rest and reading. "A Sabbath at home brings a week of discord, and ill prepares us for duty." On that ditty she made us toe the line. Even going in swimming was taboo and fishing out of all reason.

Autobiography is perhaps the dullest reading matter that we have but what must one write who saw little outside the house?

When white settlers came in to take the negro's place, they brought with them a crude religious spirit which found expression in singing sacred songs. After a time they joined with my brothers and built a long church. The men hewed the logs and brothers furnished a wagon team to haul them in place. That was practical Communism but it was quite a success. Mother thought our community was coming to the front. There were some girls and boys among the tenants and they made life more tolerable.

Mother decided to send me to school at Gadsden and made Colonel Sam Henry my monitor and guardian.[20] His dictatorial and arbitrary rules soon destroyed my fondness for school and as a result I made poor progress in studies. It was all so different to my home life. I became deathly homesick but did not know what it was. The upshot was that I ran away and came home. No bus or train to bring me and besides I didn't have a dollar. I walked and found kindly people who let me stay till the night was out. I guess I was about 17 years old and my escape worried mother no little.

I have run ahead of my dates—having already mentioned my trip to Nashville which was after my escape from Gadsden.

Cholera broke out in Nashville and cut my session short. But the trip was worth all it cost. I saw something of the big world of which I had read but had never seen.

On my return home Colonel Henry made me an offer of a place in his store which of course I accepted and became a sales clerk and bookkeeper and had the job some four years.

It was the Colonel's habit to give room to Sand Mountain customers and they were put in our little room in back of the store. I had a roommate named Jack Blair and together we were tired out with our mountain friends.[21] One rainy night in April after we had been asleep some time there was a savage knock at the door. Neither of us got up to open the door. The men were drunk and had beer at the saloon till late. The well behind the store was the only shelter available and they went there and crowding in the small shelter they knocked the bucket into the well which made a noise that sounded like a run-away team. Jack commented, "There's one in the well." But it was only the bucket.

Next day the Colonel was roaring mad. He ordered me to make up my and Jack's accounts adding that he was through with us. Then I protested. "Mr. Henry, I am responsible for not opening up last night and besides I have a home to go to and Jack has not." That struck him as it would any selfish man and he called Jack to one side and said, "Jack, Caius is man enough to take the blame on himself for last night's outrage, you can therefore continue on at work." But Jack replied, "I am anxious to stay on but only on condition that Caius stays too." That was a poser. Rain was pouring down and the store full of customers. The Colonel hated to give up, but finally said, "Both of you go on to work and learn to behave better in the future." I don't think the Colonel ever got over being checkmated and let me go pretty soon.

The Colonel had married my oldest sister, Charity, and before the war my father wished to give them a start and he told Charity that he could make an advance on her share of the estate without waiting for a division. He then gave her two families of negroes and they were well content with their share. But after the war negroes were no property and the Colonel sued my mother for $2,000, an amount he figured to be one tenth of the estate. He got judgment and the Supreme Court sustained him with one Judge (Stone) dissenting. Meeting that judgement and costs were as devastating as the war. We were only recovering from the war when this disaster occurred. We met it but it took all our savings.

Another brother-in-law, G. W. C. Neill [Belle Fennell's husband] acted as go-between our family and the Henrys and there was always a suspicion that Henry and Neill acted in concert and made it hard on mother.

My youngest sister [Mattie] married Will G. Jordan. Then I was single handed against three brothers-in-law. But they did not operate together.

Colonel Henry never came to the place after the suit and Neill and Jordan did not trust each other. Then Neill brought in a "promoter," C. C. NeSmith, and they began to organize the Manchester Land Co.[22] They never mentioned the matter to me. One night I heard Colonel NeSmith and Bill Neill whispering. It was dark and they came out to where I was or near me and whispered. I did not hear their words but went in and told mother what I had heard and told her further that I was going to leave and buy a place elsewhere. I left in a short time and bought a small farm at Madison in Madison County. Mr. Neill gave me a job on the road for a commission. This helped me to get started and I later bought an interest in Wiles's Mercantile Company and became secretary and treasurer of that concern.

When I left Madison I went to Decatur and leased a furniture factory. The most daring act of my life. But I changed it into a hickory chair factory with George S. Richardson as foreman.[23] The chairs we made were popular and the venture was going over in great shape. Then I was notified the building I had spent so much to make tenable had been sold and I had limited time to vacate. That was a blow from which I never recovered. I had two boys, one son and one maverick and all three of us were idle. I secured apprenticeship in L&N Shops for the boys, one in a blacksmith shop and one in a paint shop. I then went in the timber business with Jim Wharton who stole a case of handles and left me with a complete loss. I then took a job in the Machine Shop of L&N and stuck to it for two years.

That brings me to 1903 when I bought the *Guntersville Democrat* newspaper and was as green on the tripod as I had been in manufacturing. The office had the oldest and most archaic equipment that was then in use. The main feature was a Washington Hand Press, one of the first forms of printing paper. I had so much trouble getting the paper out that after one year I installed a Campbell Cylinder Press and found trouble getting the press turned by hand. One year of this and I installed a gasoline engine Fairbanks and Morse. I personally turned the pulley and used a two inch pipe for a shaft. The only help I had was Miss Sallie Hill, in lining up the pulleys to the press.[24] But it worked for 23 years and gave fair service.

When I bought the plant there were three employees, Arthur Kearney, Yancy Burke and Will Willis. The editor was H. W. Wheeler. The trouble I had keeping printers induced me to quit hiring men and boys and use girls and women altogether which was more satisfactory. They never got drunk, did not smoke and were punctual. Mr. Hill remained as long as he lived.

Miss Sallie was foreman eight years. I picked up several girls who did not know the "cases" and gave them a trade by which all earned their living.

After six years on the tripod I was elected President of the Alabama Press Association—an honor that I did not feel that I merited and so expressed myself to the editors, citing the smallness of my paper and obscure section it served, when Mayor Sorews of Montgomery interrupted me by saying, "We are not electing the *Guntersville Democrat*, we have elected you and nominations are closed."[25] That settled it and I knew I had got into deep water.

My philosophy teaches me that the boy is extremely fortunate whose father lives to direct his life's work. That is assuming that the father is honest, competent to direct and has a father's interest in his son's progress. My father possessed all these qualifications but did not live to give any direction. Those who say that heredity shapes a man's character are only partly correct. Heredity gives a moral basis which lives through life but environment does much toward shaping character. This again verges on to autobiography. My father was a man of profound learning, and competent to direct his son in a proper way. But his life with my mother' steady effort made such impressions on me as control my conduct largely today. My inferiority complex has always made me hesitant about directing my children and the children have appreciated my inferiority.

It is next to impossible for a man reared with my environment to write memoirs of long ago and not make it more of an autobiography than a general history.

I seem to have crossed and re-crossed my chronology and after saying that we had practically no roads, I note that I omitted to mention, our one and only means of exit and egress between the people along the river to the outside world; the Tennessee River.

The Tennessee River served us when and if we found it necessary to leave home. The first steam boat I remember was the old "Lookout," named for the famous mountain at Chattanooga. My first sight of the Lookout was early in the war—perhaps 1861 or 1862. It was a curiosity not only to negroes and children but grown ups as well. Guntersville people were apprised of her visit and a great number of people white and black went over to the point of Henry's Island to get first and best view of the oncoming steam boat. When the craft finally found the island everyone stood aghast until the pilot pulled the whistle cord and emitted a horrid shriek. It was too much for the sight seers. Those who had boats hastened to the mainland and those without boats plunged into the water and swam to shore. It was rather ludicrous in view of the fact that many of those present were there to volunteer for service. There were many boats after this but they never became common place as on the coast. Among the steamers I remember after the war were Knoxville, Chattanooga, Anderson, Johnson, Gunter, Emma, Ida, N. B. Forrest, Sam Davis, Joe Wheeler and many more I can not recall. The Federal gun boats were The Grant, Sherman and others.

It was difficult to keep negro boys from leaving the crops and going on any special trip. Such a trip the Anderson made in the 1880s when one of my field hands slipped off and took passage. The boat encountered a storm near Triana, when this boy, Neal, jumped overboard and drowned. His mother was frantic but it was a casualty resulting from his disobedience.

The river was a great convenience in getting away but boat schedules were so irregular that it required long waits in many cases. It was not only a highway for steam boats but we used it for local travel. Guntersville, six miles from our home was our post office. When the creek was up we would take a light boat and a lusty negro and go for the mail at least once a week. There was no bridge across Brown's Creek and often it was not fordable. On one occasion my family (wife and baby) and my brother visited Mrs. Fearn in a small boat.[26] We almost had an accident when the boat hit a sunken log. We waited at Mrs. Fearn's until the steamer came up and brought us home. That was in 1882 or 1883.

In 1877 the Tennessee River froze solidly from bank to bank. I personally saw a drove of mules, 25 or more, cross the river on ice. The ice had jammed until it stood up in spires and peaks and numbers of men with hammers and axes had to break down a road for the mules to cross.

To revert to incidents of early life, when we were first married, I took my wife to an ice cream parlor in Huntsville, there being nothing of the kind in this country. In that Jewish parlor there was a wall motto that caught my interest and I remembered it. It was German. "Gott Segne Dein Ein-und Ausgehen." I learned since that it is translated "God bless your coming in and going out." I cite here to show that 62 years are not sufficient to obliterate a motto that fitted so well into our lives.

Notes

Editorial Decisions

1. Whoever typed this signed it W. H. E., which probably stood for Wade Hampton Esslinger, one of Cassie's sons.

2. W. F. Esslinger, *Two Hundred Years of the Esslinger Family* (Huntsville: W. F. Esslinger, 1950), 59.

3. Steven M. Stowe, *Keep the Days: Reading the Civil War Diaries of Southern Women* (Chapel Hill: Univ. of North Carolina Press, 2018), 11.

4. Sarah E. Gardner, *Blood & Irony: Southern White Women's Narratives of the Civil War, 1861-1937* (Chapel Hill: Univ. of North Carolina Press, 2004), 14; and Kimberly Harrison, *The Rhetoric of Rebel Women: Civil War Diaries and Confederate Persuasion* (Carbondale, IL: Southern Illinois Univ. Press, 2013), 15-17.

5. "Historical News and Notices," *Journal of Southern History* 19, no. 1 (Feb. 1953): 127.

Introduction

1. When Union forces occupied Huntsville, Alabama, on April 11, 1862, the *Huntsville Democrat* ceased publication when its editor John Withers Clay fled the city. After Union forces departed Huntsville that August, Clay returned in October and resumed publication, now calling his weekly paper the *Huntsville Confederate.* In May 1863, he renamed his paper the *Huntsville Daily Confederate.* In July of that same year, Union forces occupied Huntsville again, but this only led an undaunted Clay to move his press to Chattanooga, Tennessee. Due to increasing Union activity in and around Chattanooga, he eventually moved his operations to Marietta, Georgia, and later, Dalton, Georgia. Ultimately, Clay ceased publication but resumed after the war. Even though he died in 1896, his paper, the *Huntsville Democrat,* lasted until 1919. "A Journalist's Perspective on the Invasion of Huntsville," *Huntsville Historical Review* 16, no. 1 & 2 (Spring-Fall 1989): 23; and James Record, *A Dream Come True: The Story of Madison County and Incidentally of Alabama and the United States*, vol. 1 (Huntsville, AL: John Hicklin Printing Co., 1970), 130. According to Huntsville historian Nancy Rohr, "Withers Clay had evacuated his

office and left printing equipment behind. The Federals used it to print their own army newspaper. Apparently, it was discontinued after four weeks." Nancy Rohr, ed., *Incidents of the War: The Civil War Journal of Mary Jane Chadick* (Huntsville: Silver Threads Publishing, 2005), 57. On Huntsville during the Civil War, see also Elise Hopkins Stephens, *Historic Huntsville: A City of New Beginnings* (Woodland Hills, CA: Windsor Publications, 1984), 43–61. On diaries and intended audience, see, for example, Harrison, *The Rhetoric of Rebel Women*, 17.

2. For Tennessee, see Minoa Uffelman et al., eds., *The Diary of Nannie Haskins Williams* (Knoxville: Univ. of Tennessee Press, 2014); William R. Snell, ed., *Myra Inman: A Diary of the Civil War in East Tennessee* (Macon, GA: Mercer Univ. Press, 2000); and Daniel E. Sutherland, *A Very Violent Rebel: The Civil War Diary of Ellen Renshaw House* (Knoxville: Univ. of Tennessee Press, 1996). For Kentucky, see John David Smith and William Cooper Jr., eds., *A Union Woman in Civil War Kentucky: The Diary of Frances Peter* (Lexington, KY: Univ. Press of Kentucky, 2000); and Mary E. Wharton and Ellen E. Williams, eds., *Peach Leather and Rebel Gray: Bluegrass Life and the War, 1860–1865: Farm and Social Life, Famous Horses, Tragedies of War: Diary and Letters of a Confederate Wife* (Lexington, KY: Univ. Press of Kentucky, 1986). For Georgia, see Eliza Frances Andrews, *The Wartime Journal of a Georgia Girl, 1864–1865*, introduction by Jean V. Berlin (New York: D. Appleton and Co., 1908; repr., Lincoln: Univ. of Nebraska Press, 1997); and James C. Bonner, ed., *The Journal of a Milledgeville Girl, 1861–1865* (Athens: Univ. of Georgia Press, 1964). On North Carolina, see Beth G. Crabtree and James W. Patton, eds., *"Journal of a Secesh Lady": The Diary of Catherine Ann Devereux Edmondston, 1860–1866* (Raleigh, NC: Division of Archives and History, 1979); and Karen L. Clinard and Richard Russell, eds., *Fear in North Carolina: The Civil War Journals and Letters of the Henry Family* (Asheville, NC: Reminiscing Books, 2008). For South Carolina, see, for example, Robert T. Oliver, ed., *A Faithful Heart: The Journals of Emmala Reed, 1865 and 1866* (Columbia: Univ. of South Carolina Press, 2004); Marli Weiner, ed., *A Heritage of Woe: The Civil War Diary of Grace Brown Elmore, 1861–1868* (Athens: Univ. of Georgia Press, 1997); and C. Vann Woodward, ed., *Mary Chesnut's Civil War* (New Haven, CT: Yale Univ. Press, 1981). For Virginia, see, for example, Kristen Brill, ed., *The Diary of a Civil War Bride: Lucy Wood Butler of Virginia* (Baton Rouge: Louisiana State Univ. Press, 2017); and Mary D. Robertson, ed., *Lucy Breckinridge of Grove Hill: The Journal of a Virginia Girl, 1862–1864* (Columbia: Univ. of South Carolina Press, 1994).

3. Born in Salem, Massachusetts, Chadick was the daughter of David and Mary Cook. After her parents moved to Lebanon, Tennessee, she became the second wife of Reverend William Davidson Chadick who, in 1855, moved the family to Huntsville. Nancy Rohr, ed., *Incidents of the War: The Civil War Diary of Mary Jane Chadick* (Huntsville, AL: Silver Threads Publishing, 2005), 6-12. Like Cassie, Sarah Lowe Davis, the daughter of Nicholas and Sophia (Lowe) Davis, kept diaries during

her school days. The Alabama Department of Archives and History describes Davis's diaries as follows: "These two diaries, one bound and the other loose pages, date from 1861 Jan. 28 to 1862 Sept. 7. Davis discusses her experiences at school, the subject she is studying, and the weather. She also writes about the Civil War, the military information she receives, and its effects of the conflict on the school. Her entries are particularly valuable for providing insights into the Civil War home front." Sarah Lowe diaries, SPR113, Alabama Dept. of Archives and History. Octavia Wyche Otey kept a diary near Meridianville, Madison County. See Mickey Maroney, ed., "The Civil War Journal of Octavia Wyche Otey," *Huntsville Historical Review* 18, no. 1 (Winter-Spring 1991): 1-30. Two other north Alabama women, Sarah Rousseau Espy and Zillah Haynie Brandon, kept diaries in Cherokee County. Sarah Rousseau Espy diary, SPR2, Alabama Dept. of Archives and History; and Zillah Haynie Brandon diary, SPR262, Alabama Dept. of Archives and History.

4. Leah Rawls Atkins, Joseph H. Harrison Jr., and Sara Hudson, eds., *A Belle of the Fifties: Memoirs of Mrs. Clay of Alabama* (Tuscaloosa: Univ. of Alabama Press, 1999). See also, Carol Bleser and Frederick M. Heath, "The Clays of Alabama: The Impact of the Civil War on a Southern Marriage," in *In Joy and In Sorrow: Women, Family, and Marriage in the Victorian South*, ed. Carol Bleser (New York: Oxford Univ. Press, 1991), 135–53.

5. Faye Acton Axford, ed., *The Journals of Thomas Hubbard Hobbs: A Contemporary Record of an Aristocrat from Athens, Alabama written between 1840, when the diarist was fourteen years old and 1862, when he died serving in the Confederate Army* (Tuscaloosa: Univ. of Alabama Press, 1976); and Jeffrey D. Stocker, ed., *From Huntsville to Appomattox: R. T. Cole's History of 4th Regiment, Alabama Volunteer Infantry, C.S.A., Army of Northern Virginia* (Knoxville: Univ. of Tennessee Press, 1996). See also Charles Rice, ed., "Youthful Innocence Shattered: The Diary of Private George T. Anderson," *Huntsville Historical Review* 18, no. 2 (Summer-Fall 1991): 7-22. Anderson, a native of Huntsville, served in Company I of the 4th Alabama Infantry.

6. Ira E. Hobbs was the brother of Cassie's paternal grandmother Elizabeth (Hobbs) Fennell Childress. His only son captain Thomas Hubbard Hobbs served in the Alabama state legislature and, later, at the Alabama Secession Convention. When the Civil War began, Thomas formed a company in Limestone County and entered the 9th Alabama Infantry as a captain. At the Battle of Gaines's Mill, he was mortally wounded. Family Trees, Ancestry.com.

7. On Guntersville, see, for example, Larry Smith, ed., *Guntersville Remembered* (Albertville, AL: Creative Publishers, Inc., 1989), 30–31; Katherine Duncan and Larry Smith, ed., *History of Marshall County, Alabama,* vol. 1 (Albertville, AL: Thompson Printing Co., 1969); J. F. Sparks, *A River Town's Fight for Life: A History of Guntersville, Alabama in the Civil War* (self-published, 2011); John Robert Kennamer, *The History of Jackson County* (Winchester, TN: Press of Southern Printing & Publishing Co.,

1935); and Louis Wyeth, *The History of Marshall County, Alabama*, transcribed from the *Guntersville Democrat* by Betty Taylor, 1883, Vertical Files, Marshall County Archives, Guntersville, Alabama (hereafter cited as VF, MCA, GA).

8. "Union Officer Geary's Report on the Shelling of Guntersville," July 27–30, 1862, Shelling and Burning of Guntersville, VF, MCA, GA.

9. "Union Officer Geary's Report on the Shelling of Guntersville," July 27–30, 1862; and "Shelling of G'ville: the Union version," Shelling and Burning of Guntersville, VF, MCA, GA.

10. Duncan and Smith, 66; Smith, *Guntersville Remembered*, 33; and C. G. Fennell, "Guntersville Burned by Union Troops," *Guntersville Democrat*, February 9, 1911. Born on May 25, 1845, John Allan Wyeth grew up at Missionary Station, near Guntersville, Alabama. As a teenager, he attended LaGrange Military Academy until its close due to the Civil War. In 1862, he served in General John Hunt Morgan's irregular cavalry and, the following year, joined the 4th Alabama Cavalry. At one point, he was captured and spent time at Camp Morton. After the war, he earned a medical degree at the University of Louisville. For a time, he practiced medicine in Arkansas. In 1872, he moved to New York City, where he later formed the New York Polyclinic Graduate Medical School and Hospital. The country's first post-graduate medical school, it opened its doors in 1881. From 1888 to 1909, Wyeth fostered the growth of Wyeth City, an industrial town best known for the Nedofik Sofa Manufacturing Company. Its product, a surgical sofa designed by Wyeth, sold internationally. In 1902, Wyeth became president of the American Medical Association. In addition to his medical publications, he enjoyed writing histories like *With Sabre and Scalpel: The Autobiography of a Soldier and Surgeon*; *That Devil Forrest: Life of General Nathan Bedford Forrest*; and *History of LaGrange Military Academy and the Cadet Corps, 1857–1862: LaGrange College, 1830–1857*. Wyeth died on May 22, 1922. Roderick Davis, "John Allan Wyeth," *Encyclopedia of Alabama*, http://www.encyclopediaofalabama.org/article/h-3522 (accessed August 7, 2019); and Whitney A. Snow and Barbara J. Snow, *Wyeth City: Alabama's Model Industrial Experiment* (Birmingham, AL: Banner Digital Printing and Publishing, 2019).

11. See, for example, "More Yankee Villainy," *Evening Bulletin* (Charlotte, NC), August 8, 1862; "Town Shelled," *Charlotte-Democrat* (Charlotte, NC), August 12, 1862; "Shelling of Guntersville, Ala.," *Shreveport Semi-Weekly News*, August 22, 1862; "Guntersville (Ala) Shelled," *Chattanooga Daily Rebel*, August 9, 1862; and Untitled, *Evening Bulletin* (Charlotte, NC), August 21, 1862.

12. This statement appeared in a *Tuscaloosa Observer* article, which myriad newspapers reprinted. "Shelling of Guntersville, Ala.," *Shreveport Semi-Weekly*, August 22, 1862.

13. "Town Shelled," *Charlotte Democrat*, August 12, 1862.

14. "It was a creek that you could wade across," *Advertiser-Gleam*, September 19, 1981.

15. In 2009, the Guntersville Historical Society erected a historical marker titled, "Ravine Used for Protection Against Yankee Shelling." The marker reads: "The first major attack on Guntersville during the Civil War occurred on the morning of Monday, July 28, 1862. The Federals had marched by night and had reached a hill on the north side of the Tennessee River and from this vantage point aimed their cannons at the small town of Guntersville. The Federals, led by major J. W. Paramore of the Third Ohio Cavalry, included a regiment of Union infantry, and a section of artillery with two 6 pounder Parrott guns. At 6 a.m., when the Federals began shelling the town, many of its citizens fled to the deep ravine, which extended from main street to present Blount Avenue. More than one hundred women and children huddled here against the slopes of the ravine for twelve hours until the shelling ended at 6 p.m. While considerable damage was inflicted by the shelling, only two people were killed. One was Mrs. Evergreen Findley Rayburn, the wife of Samuel King Rayburn, who was the Confederate general in charge of militia for north Alabama and a later mayor of Guntersville. The shelling incident was reported in John Allan Wyeth's book *With Sabre and Scalpel* and the *Chattanooga Daily Rebel* newspapers."

16. "Shelling of G'ville: the Union version," Shelling and Burning of Guntersville, VF, MCA, GA. On Union forces being fired upon prior to the shelling, see Donald Davidson, *The Tennessee The New River: Civil War to TVA*, vol. 2 (Nashville, TN: JS Sanders & Co., 1992), 110.

17. "John F. Fore, Pine Apple, Ala., writes of Forrest," *Confederate Veteran* 6, no. 1 (Jan. 1898): 24.

18. "Shelling of G'ville: the Union version," Shelling and Burning of Guntersville, VF, MCA, GA.

19. The daughter of Josiah and Elizabeth Decatur Dupree Rainey, Evergreen married Samuel Findley in 1836. They had eight children before his death from pneumonia. On May 15, 1861, she married Samuel K. Rayburn whose wife Sarah had died the previous year. In 1862, the ages of Evergreen's children were as follows: Sarah (21); Lucy (20); Mary (18); Joan (16); Woodson (14); Miriam (11); Samuel (7); and William (5). According to Evergreen's daughter Lucy, she and her siblings were not at the hotel when it was shelled. Instead, their mother had sent them (along with some prized possessions) to take shelter with the other townspeople. In the aftermath of her mother's death, Lucy and her siblings were in a precarious situation. Their stepfather was serving in the war. Given his absence, they were cared for by a slave woman until their uncle Stephen Decatur Rainey, who lived in Marshall, Texas, traveled to Alabama to take them home with him. "This parasol," Guntersville Historical Society, 2014, Shelling and Burning of Guntersville, VF, MCA, GA; Marriage Certificate between Samuel K. Rayburn and Evergreen Findley, May 15, 1861, film # 002203983, Alabama County Marriage, Records, 1805-1967, Ancestry.com; 1860 US Federal Census; and Lucy Findley, Shelling and Burning of Guntersville, VF, MCA, GA. On their uncle, see William S. Speer and Hon. John

Henry Brown, ed., *The Encyclopedia of the New West containing fully authenticated information of the agricultural, mercantile, commercial, manufacturing, mining and grazing industries, and representing the character, development, resources and present conditions of Texas, Arkansas, Colorado, New Mexico and Indian Territory also Biographical Sketches of their representative men and women* (Marshall, TX: The United States Biographical Publishing Co., 1881), 609-611.

20. Sparks, *A River Town's Fight for Life*, 12–13; "Owner of parasol killed in shelling," *Advertiser Gleam*, January 24, 2015; and Obituary Index, 1819-2006, Alabama, Huntsville-Madison County Public Library. Evergreen's lone stepchild John Rayburn served in Company K of the 9th Alabama Infantry and disappeared (presumed dead) in the Battle of Antietam. He began as a sergeant and died as a captain. Over the decades, Guntersville newspapers frequently reprinted one of the letters he had written to his father. In the letter, he wrote, "Let not public faith waver. If you can't get guns fight with spades, picks, axes, and the Jaw-bones of asses. Pray and fight and the good Lord will be with us even unto the end." "John Rayburn's Letter," *Guntersville Democrat*, February 19, 1919. On John's death, see Colonel Sam Henry to General S. K. Rayburn, September 20, 1862, VF, MCA, GA.

21. *Nashville Dispatch*, Shelling and Burning of Guntersville, VF, MCA, GA.

22. "Owner of parasol killed in shelling," *Advertiser-Gleam*, January 24, 2015. Lewis believes that the Rayburn family had a house separate from the hotel, but some local historians disagree. The Rayburn hotel was located on the end of the peninsula, near what is now Lurleen B. Wallace Drive. Its site is currently under water due to the creation of Lake Guntersville in 1939.

23. George Kryder to wife, August 1, 1862, Civil War, VF, MCA, GA.

24. "Shelling of G'ville: the Union version," Shelling and Burning of Guntersville, VF, MCA, GA.

25. On the burning of Guntersville, see Arthur Wyllie, *The Union Navy* (Morrisville, NC: Lulu Press, 2007), 159. Willis M. Hatch later wrote: "Of the forty boys who came with me that day from the Gunboat General Thomas, it is quite safe to say each acted of his own volition, but came under strict military discipline to do that which gave every one pain in the performance and some I know shed bitter tears at the hardships and sorrow that came from their action. And if there was unnecessary cruelty done by any that day, be sure that the one who did has suffered many times more than those who are injured." "Willis M. Hatch," *Guntersville Democrat*, January 22, 1891; and "Here's the letter from Union marine," *Advertiser-Gleam*, January 18, 2017. Originally from Erie County, Pennsylvania, Hatch lived in Decatur, Georgia, at the time he wrote this letter. In the letter, he expressed regret but stated firmly that he had no intention of apologizing because his actions had resulted from military duty. Having recently visited Guntersville, he spent much of his letter praising the town's beauty.

26. Duncan and Smith, 70–72; and Sparks, *A River Town's Fight for Life*, 31–37.

27. USS *General Burnside*, Stack Area 18W4, Row 3, Compartment 19, Shelf 1, Box 1–2, 8/8/1864–1/21/1865; USS *General Sherman*, Stack Area 18W4, Row 3, Compartment 19, Shelf 2, Box 2, 1/1/1865–6/3/1865; USS *General Grant*, Stack Area 18W4, Row 3, Compartment 19, Shelf 1, Box 2, 1/1/1865–6/2/1865; and USS *General Thomas*, Stack Area 18W4, Row 3, Compartment 19, Shelf 2, Box 2 and 3, 12/6/1864–6/3/1865, Navy Ship Logs, RG 24: Records of the Bureau of Naval Personnel, Logs of Ships and Stations, 1801–1946; Logs of US Naval Ships, 1801–1915, National Archives, Washington, DC.

28. USS *General Burnside*, Stack Area 18W4, Row 3, Compartment 19, Shelf 1, Box 1–2, 8/8/1864–6/1/1865; USS *General Sherman*, Stack Area 18W4, Row 3, Compartment 19, Shelf 2, Box 2, 1/1/1865–6/3/1865; USS *General Grant*, Stack Area 18W4, Row 3, Compartment 19, Shelf 1, Box 2, 1/1/1865–6/6/1865; and USS *General Thomas*, Stack Area 18W4, Row 3, Compartment 19, Shelf 2, Box 2 and 3, 12/6/1864–6/3/1865, Navy Ship Logs, RG 24: Records of the Bureau of Naval Personnel, Logs of Ships and Stations, 1801–1946; Logs of US Naval Ships, 1801–1915, National Archives, Washington, DC. See also "Willis M. Hatch," *Guntersville Democrat*, January 22, 1891; and "Here's the letter from Union marine," *Advertiser-Gleam*, January 18, 2017.

29. Duncan and Smith, 72. See also "Guntersville burned by Union troops," *Guntersville Democrat*, February 9, 1911.

30. "A Spunky Little Town," *Daily Confederate*, February 10, 1864.

31. "Cassie Fennell's Diary," Diary 3, p. 49, Carmen Hurff Collection, Guntersville, Alabama (hereafter cited as CHC, GA).

32. Megan Kate Nelson, *Ruin Nation: Destruction and the American Civil War* (Athens: Univ. of Georgia Press, 2012), 67.

33. James Marten, *Civil War America: Voices from the Home Front* (Santa Barbara: ABC Clio, 2003), 54.

34. "Cassie Fennell's Diary," Diary 3, p. 18, CHC, GA.

35. Ibid.

36. James Oakes, *Freedom National: The Destruction of Slavery in the United States, 1861–1865* (New York: W. W. Norton & Co., 2013), 398. On slavery as the primary motivation for secession, see also Charles B. Dew, *Apostles of Disunion: Southern Secession Commissioners and the Causes of the Civil War* (Charlottesville: Univ. of Virginia Press, 2001).

37. Bertram Wyatt-Brown, *The Shaping of Southern Culture: Honor, Grace, and War, 1760s–1880s* (Chapel Hill: Univ. of North Carolina Press, 2001), 179.

38. Ibid., 214.

39. Stowe, xii.

40. Ibid., x.

41. Ibid., 104.

42. Ibid., 116.

43. "Cassie Fennell's Diary," Diary 2, p. 29, CHC, GA. In 1850, the Fennells owned sixteen slaves (seven men and nine women) but only two women, aged sixty and forty-five, were old enough to have been Cassie's "nurse." The editor assumed Queen to have been the sixty-year-old. In 1860, the Fennells owned twenty-seven slaves (twelve men and fifteen women). 1850, 1860 US Federal Census Slave Schedules.

44. Stowe, 115.

45. "Cassie Fennell's Diary," Diary 3, p. 56, CHC, GA. On slaves being used as spies, see, for example, Eugene D. Genovese, *Roll, Jordan, Roll: The World the Slaves Made* (New York: Pantheon Books, 1974), 152.

46. One of the Fennell slaves later gained a great deal of local publicity. In the 1890s, Phoebe Fennell, formerly owned by Dr. James W. Fennell, not only claimed to have been 114 years old but to have once belonged to former vice president John C. Calhoun. If true, she would have been sixty-eight in 1850 and seventy-eight in 1860. In 1850 and 1860, the oldest Fennell slave had been recorded as sixty, so Phoebe may not have known her true age. Caius Fennell claimed his father purchased Phoebe from the Calhoun family, but the editor could not find substantiating evidence. According to the Guntersville newspaper, Phoebe loved to regale listeners with stories of her years with Calhoun. "A Centenarian," *Guntersville Democrat*, June 12, 1890; and untitled, *Guntersville Democrat*, July 16, 1896.

47. Stowe, 106. It is unknown how Cassie's parents perceived and treated their slaves. Her father's letters mentioned slaves in passing and only in regard to health. For example, in one letter primarily concerning the medical profession, he included a single line referencing slaves: "This leaves us in usual health both black and white as also your relations as far as known." Dr. James W. Fennell to Willie Fennell, 1858, FF-Fennell, Vertical Files, Huntsville-Madison County Public Library, Huntsville, Alabama (hereafter cited as VF, HMCPL, HA). After James died, his widow Matilda appointed one of the slaves as overseer. See "The Memoirs of Caius Grattan Fennell," VF, MCA, GA.

48. Catherine Clinton, *The Plantation Mistress: Woman's World in the Old South* (New York: Pantheon Books, 1982), 26.

49. "Cassie Fennell's Diary," Diary 3, p. 21, CHC, GA.

50. "Cassie Fennell's Diary," Diary 3, p. 18, CHC, GA.

51. Clinton, *The Plantation Mistress*, 185. On "rhetorics of denial," see Harrison, *The Rhetoric of Rebel Women*, 111.

52. Clinton, *The Plantation Mistress*, 185.

53. Deposit Ferry, otherwise known as Fort Deposit, should not be confused with the Fort Deposit in Lowndes County, Alabama. While marching to Horseshoe Bend, Andrew Jackson's militia camped briefly at Warrenton, near Guntersville. To improve his supply lines, Jackson stored goods at a site near the Tennessee River.

Locals later called it Fort Deposit. During the Civil War, Union gunboats referred to it as Port Deposit. Duncan and Smith, 23.

54. The fifty-seven acres had been part of his inheritance. Elizabeth Fennell, Bragg Collection, 1827, #5123, VF, MCA, GA.

55. Carmen Hurff, *Within the Great Bend: Our Families of Alabama's Tennessee River Valley: The Fennells of Marshall County, the Esslingers of Madison County, the Russells & Austins of Jackson County* (Guntersville: Carmen Russell Hurff, 2000), 1–22; and 1850, 1860 US Federal Census, Ancestry.com.

56. On education for southern women, see, for example, Sarah L. Hyde, *Schooling in the Antebellum South: The Rise of Private Education in Louisiana, Mississippi, and Alabama* (Baton Rouge: Louisiana State Univ. Press, 2016), 25; Candace Bailey, *Music and the Southern Belle: From Accomplished Lady to Confederate Composer* (Carbondale: Southern Illinois Univ. Press, 2010), 15; and Harrison, *The Rhetoric of Rebel Women*, 10.

57. "Cassie Fennell's Diary," Diary 2, p. 70, CHC, GA.

58. Wyatt-Brown, 187.

59. "Cassie Fennell's Diary," Diary 2, p. 74, CHC, GA.

60. Daniel W. Crofts, *Reluctant Confederates: Upper South Unionists in the Secession Crisis* (Chapel Hill: Univ. of North Carolina Press, 1989), 99.

61. Michael W. Fitzgerald, *Reconstruction in Alabama: From Civil War to Redemption in the Cotton South* (Baton Rouge: Louisiana State Univ. Press, 2017), 19.

62. "The Memoirs of Caius Grattan Fennell," VF, MCA, GA. Dr. James Fennell was a bibliophile and evidently, enjoyed the works of William Shakespeare.

63. Crofts, 111.

64. Dr. James W. Fennell to W. R. W. Cobb, February 23, 1860, CHC, GA.

65. "Cassie Fennell's Diary," Diary 2, p. 76, CHC, GA. Slavery was intrinsic to secession. See, for example, James Oakes, *The Scorpion's Sting: Antislavery and the Coming of the Civil War* (New York: W. W. Norton & Co., 2014), 51–76.

66. "The Memoirs of Caius Grattan Fennell," VF, MCA, GA. When Wattie enlisted, he brought along a slave named Jackson who he planned to use as a "body servant." Caius Fennell, "A Faithful Slave's Death," *Guntersville Democrat*, February 1, 1912.

67. "Cassie Fennell's Diary," Diary 3, p. 64, CHC, GA.

68. Ibid.

69. Ibid., 63.

70. "Speeches of Paroled Rebel Officers," *Salem Observer*, June 3, 1865.

71. Ibid.

72. "Cassie Fennell's Diary," Diary 3, p. 64, CHC, GA.

73. Ibid.

74. Ibid., 65.

75. Cassie's diaries included many entries on raids by Union troops. Evidently, she repeated these experiences to her children, because her son Frank later recalled them in a family history he authored. In his words, "Stock was driven off, a large clay-bank horse, in exchange, they named Gunboat was left, all ribs and angles. Shots from 25 pound cannon, on gunboats, were fired at the house, but none happened to burn the house . . . One of these rounds, promptly emptied, was given my mother, and for years was in our front yard being used part of the time as a weight to hold a front gate shut." Esslinger, 59.

76. *Belle F. Neill, administratrix of the estate of James Watkins Fennell v. The United States*, 59th Congress, 2nd Session, Document 355, Congressional Number 10609, Fennell Family, VF, MCA, GA.

77. "The Memoirs of Caius Grattan Fennell," VF, MCA, GA.

78. Fennell, no. 522, Box 133, State of Alabama, Probate Court of Marshall County, Marshall County Archives, Guntersville, Alabama.

79. Clinton, *The Plantation Mistress*, 44.

80. "In Re Estate of David Francis Fennell Deceased, Application for Appointment of Administration, filed in office this 30th day of May 1879," Frank Fennell, VF, MCA, GA; Fennells, VF, MCA, GA; and Fennell, Probate Court of Marshall County, no. 689, MCA, GA.

81. "The Memoirs of Caius Grattan Fennell," VF, MCA, GA.

82. Fennell, Probate Court of Marshall County, no. 689, MCA, GA.

83. Ann Cochrane, "Fennells—Always on the Move," *Valley Leaves: Tennessee Valley Genealogical Society* 2, no. 2 (Dec 1976): 91–93; and Family Trees, Ancestry.com. Cochrane was one of Cassie's granddaughters.

84. Cassie devoted one page of Diary 3 to a decorative arrangement of squares, rectangles, and triangles containing the names of soldiers/officers she had met during the Civil War. On another page, one much fainter, appeared an array of names in no particular order. She tended to write the individual's name, affiliation, origin, and occasionally noted whether or not they had died. Those mentioned are as follows, as she described them: Col. M. G. May; Cor. Alex Simpson, 4th Alabama Infantry (Madison County); Captain H. J. Hughes, 11th Texas Regiment; Lieut. Joe Graham, detached service (Pond Beat); Tom A. Street, [undiscernible] Alabama Regiment (Warrenton); L. B. Moran, 5th Alabama Regiment; Lieut. Graham, 4th Alabama Cav. (Madison County); Lieut. Jack Harris, Roddey's Command (Tuscumbia); Capt. James Richards (Arkansas); Capt. Joe H. Fields, 8th Confederate Regiment (Columbus); Lieut. J. A. Matthews, 8th Confederate Regiment (Columbus); Capt. Tom Williams, 8th Confederate Regiment (Columbus); Lieut. A. Ledbetter, 9th Alabama Regiment; Lieut. S. Mitchell, 56th Alabama Regiment; Capt. Jas Jones (Bellefonte, Ala.), dead; Lieut. T. Fennell, 4th Regiment Ala. Cav; Capt. W. Fennell (Guntersville); Lieut. H. Beard (Marshall, Ala.); Capt. A. Carter, 56th Alabama Regiment, dead; Sgt. Marcus Erwin, 2nd Georgia Cav. Reg. (Warrenton); Cor. Frank

Erwin, 4th Alabama Cav; Capt. Ashburn, 4th Regm Ala. Cav (Madison Co., Ala); Adj. Ben Snody, 56th Ala Reg Infantry (Bellefonte), dead; Wallace Henry, 9th Ala; Hop Beard; Julian Beard; George Caperton; Dr. Hugh Hollis; Adjc. Gen Snodgrass; and William Perry, 8th Texas Reg.

85. Victoria E. Ott, "Love in Battle: The Meaning of Courtships in the Civil War and Lost Cause," in *Children and Youth during the Civil War*, ed. James Marten (New York: New York University Press, 2012), 129.

86. A poem by Charles Colton.

87. They had been granted a marriage license on December 19. Marriage license, CHC, GA.

88. Esslinger, 59.

89. 1860 US Federal Census; and 1860 US Federal Census Slave Schedules, Ancestry.com. By 1870, A. J.'s father William had $600 in real estate and $5,000 in personal wealth. 1870 US Federal Census, Ancestry.com.

90. Esslinger, 63.

91. Only the first page of this hand-written letter remains. Written by one of Cassie's sons, probably Frank, the eldest, it is addressed to "Mrs. M. M. Fennell" and begins, "Dear GrandMa." Grandson to M. M. Fennell, September 30, 1884, CHC, GA.

92. Ibid.

93. "Died," *Huntsville Independent*, October 6, 1884.

94. Hurff; and Tombstone of Catherine Esslinger.

95. Elliott Ashkenazi, ed., *The Civil War Diary of Clara Solomon: Growing Up in New Orleans, 1861–1862* (Baton Rouge: Louisiana State Univ. Press, 1995), 16.

96. For more information on female espionage and military service during the Civil War, see, for example, Catherine Clinton, *Stepdaughters of History: Southern Women and the American Civil War* (Baton Rouge: Louisiana State Univ. Press, 2016); and Elizabeth Leonard, *All the Daring of the Soldier: Women of the Civil War Armies* (New York: W.W. Norton & Co., 1999).

1. *When the Sun Shone Brightly*

1. At ages seventeen and fourteen, respectively, Cassie and Mary Jane came to the Norton household. Located at No. 490 East Street, this school had Charles H. Norton as principal, and in advertisements, he referred to it as "Young Ladies' Institute, A Boarding and Day School." For more information, see advertisements in the *Evening Star*, May 24, 1853, December 5, 1853, August 14, 1857, October 1, 1858, November 11, 1858, and September 8, 1859.

2. Cassie mentioned Mr. McJ___ twelve times but deliberately left out the bulk of his surname. In one case, she called him Mr. McJ___ Jr. Given that Cassie had several male acquaintances from Columbian College, the editor scoured its student listings. During Cassie's time in Washington, DC, only one student had a surname beginning with "Mc": Townsend Jesse McVeigh Jr. (1840–circa pre-1880), who went

by Jesse. Jesse attended Columbian College from 1858 to 1861. US Catalogs, 1765–1935, Ancestry.com.

3. These were likely Clara Blanche Naylor (1847–1915) and Isabella Naylor (1841–1914), daughters of Charles and Ruth (Price) Naylor of Philadelphia, Pennsylvania. Hattie Lindsley was probably Harriet Lovenia Lindsley, the daughter of Silas and Elizabeth (Grim) Lindsley of Whiteside County, Illinois; she would have been eight years old in 1859. 1850, 1860, US Federal Census; and Family Trees, both at Ancestry .com.

4. Home, meaning Deposit Ferry.

5. Laura V. Tayman operated a boarding house in Washington, DC's Fourth Ward. She and her husband Richard had a daughter named Molly. When referring to Mrs. Tayman, Cassie later mentioned a "Mollie." 1850, 1860 US Federal Census, Ancestry.com.

6. Cassie belonged to the Methodist Episcopal Church. Ball served as reverend at the Methodist Church Wesley Chapel located at the corner of 5th and F Streets. The church's assembly room stood on Louisiana Avenue between 4 ½ and 6th Streets. "The Ladies of Wesley Chapel," *Evening Star*, February 7, 1859. Reverend Ball spoke at a revival on the evening of September 13, 1859. "The Revival," *Evening Star*, September 14, 1859.

7. Catherine Ann (Allison) Cobb, Cassie's maternal aunt, had married Williamson Robert Winfield "W. R. W." Cobb, who had become a US congressman. When Congress was in session, the Cobbs lived in Washington, DC, but in the off season, they resided in Bellefonte, Alabama. For more information about the Cobbs, see appendix 1: Family Biographies.

8. Vashti Town, the daughter of John and Sarah Town, had attended Kimball Union Academy and worked as a teacher. 1860 US Federal Census; US High School Student Lists, 1821–1923; and US, Find A Grave Index, 1600s–Current, all at Ancestry .com.

9. Mary Jane Fennell (1845–1926), Cassie's younger sister. For more information, see appendix 1: Family Biographies. On September 15, 1859, seventy-three-year-old Sarah Cochrane Polk died of asthma. US Federal Census Mortality Schedules, 1850–1885, Ancestry.com. Laura Tayman had a daughter named Molly. 1860 US Federal Census.

10. See chap. 1, note 9.

11. Julia Norton (1831–) was twenty-eight years old at the time. The editor has been unable to discern her maiden name. Census records listed her as "Julia D." and "Julia G." Julia and her husband Charles had three children: Charles Jr. (1859–); Harwood (1863–); and Nettie (1865–). 1860, 1880 US Federal Census, Ancestry.com.

12. For more information on Martha Matilda (Allison) Fennell, see appendix 1: Family Biographies. The son of David and Sarah (Smith) Allison, William Benjamin

Allison (1837–1861) had four siblings: Jane (1825–), Isabella (1835–), John A. (1840–), and Sarah (1843–). 1850, 1860 US Federal Census, Ancestry.com.

13. The son of Edward Tilley Parker (1798–) and Mary Jane (Allison) Parker, twenty-seven-year-old Daniel Webster Parker (1832–1882) lived in New Hope, Alabama. Mary Jane was Cassie's maternal aunt. 1850, 1860 US Federal Census, Ancestry.com.

14. Untitled, *Evening Star*, April 9, 1859.

15. Reverend Gurley served as pastor at the F Street Presbyterian Church in 1859. Untitled, *Evening Star*, January 3, 1859.

16. Originally from New Jersey, Reverend J. Spencer Kennard became pastor of the East Street Baptist Church when Reverend Dr. George W. Samson became the fifth president of Columbian College in 1859. "Called," *Evening Star*, September 29, 1859; and G. David Anderson, "Columbian College and the Civil War," *GW Magazine* (Spring/Summer 2006), https://www2.gwu.edu/~magazine/archive/2006_spring/docs/feature_civilwar.html (accessed January 8, 2020).

17. Rather than refer to her as Miss Charlotte, the pupils called Charles Norton's sister "Lottie." Unlike her brother, who was born in New York, Charlotte Norton was born in Connecticut. Prior to moving to Washington, DC, she lived in New Orleans. Charlotte never married and still resided with Charles and Julia as late as 1880. 1860, 1880 US Federal Census, Ancestry.com.

18. "Lou Whorton," a day student at Norton's school, may have been Laura Whorton, the daughter of Robert and P. J. Whorton, who resided in Washington, DC's Second Ward. In 1860, Robert, who worked as a clerk, had real estate valued at $40,000 and personal worth estimated at $10,000. His two children, eighteen-year-old Frank and fourteen-year-old Laura were born in Alabama. This Alabama connection may have been how they became acquainted with Congressman and Mrs. Cobb, with whom they socialized. 1860 US Federal Census, Ancestry.com.

19. Then sixteen, Margaret J. Fennell (1843–1919) was the daughter of Cassie's paternal uncle Hubbard Hobbs Fennell (1807–1855) and Mary Irene Smith (1810–). 1860 US Federal Census; and Family Trees, both at Ancestry.com.

20. Cassie often referred to Charles Norton's then sixty-one-year-old mother as "Old Mrs. Norton." Ann Amelia Flint Norton (1798–1874) was born in Hartford, Connecticut, to Reverend Abel Flint (1766–1825) and Amelia Bissell (1765–1810). She married Herman Norton (1782–) on October 10, 1826, and the couple had two children, Charles and Charlotte. 1860 US Federal Census; and *The New England Historical & Genealogical Register, 1847–2011*, both at Ancestry.com. See also "In the Supreme Court of the District of Columbia," *Evening Star*, August 15, 1874.

21. Mary Todd, a day student at Norton's school, may have been the sixteen-year-old daughter of Lydia C. Todd, a resident of Washington, DC, and the sister of

fourteen-year-old Willie Todd. 1860 US Federal Census, Ancestry.com; and untitled, *Evening Star*, July 2, 1860.

22. Reverend Jos. Proctor preached at the Methodist Church South on October 2, 1859. "Local News," *Evening Star*, October 3, 1859.

23. Reverend Byron Sunderland (1820–). 1860 US Federal Census, Ancestry.com; "Local News," *Evening Star*, May 9, 1859; and "The Union Festival," *Evening Star*, June 7, 1859.

24. Cassie's paternal uncle Francis Marion Fennell (1818–1872) and his wife Isabella (Allison) Fennell (1815–1881) had a fifteen-year-old daughter named Katharine (1844–1887). Their other children included Martha (1841–1880); Sarah (1846–); Matilda (1848–1926); Arthur (1851–1887); William R. W. (1852–1853); and Charles (1855–1891). The family lived in Bellefonte, Jackson County, Alabama. 1850, 1860, 1870 US Federal Census; US Federal Census Mortality Schedules, 1850–1885; US, Find A Grave Index, 1600s–Current; and Family Trees, all at Ancestry.com.

25. Cassie frequented this singing school. In order to make them more attractive to potential suitors, many southern women were encouraged from youth to pursue singing and/or playing an instrument. Bailey, 15.

26. Dr. James William "Willie" Fennell (1839–1878), Cassie's eldest brother. In March 1859, Willie received a medical degree from Columbian College. "Creation of M.D.'s," *Washington Union*, March 5, 1859. Cassie may have meant LaGrange Military Academy in Leighton, Alabama, near Florence. This academy, which offered medical courses, operated from 1857–1862. Union forces burned it in 1863. Prior to becoming a military academy, it had operated as a college from 1830–1857. John A. Wyeth, *History of LaGrange Military Academy and the Cadet Corps, 1857–1862* (New York: The Brewer Press, 1907). For more information on Willie, see appendix 1: Family Biographies.

27. Cassie's parents owned a piano, the price of which may have ranged from $180 to over $1,000. On piano prices, see, for example, Bailey, 92.

28. Mr. Huggans may have been H. A. Huggins who, with his wife M. E., lived in a boarding house in Washington, DC's Third Ward. Originally from Alabama, H. E. worked as a clerk in a law office. In 1860, he had real estate estimated at $6,000. He and his wife had a daughter named Katie. 1860 US Federal Census, Ancestry.com.

29. The elephant had probably been part of Dan Rice's Great Show, which gave two performances in Washington, DC, on October 10, 1859. "Dan Rice's Great Show," *Evening Star*, October 5, 1859. Cassie likely witnessed the pachyderm as the show departed town.

30. There are two possibilities for Mrs. Hoyle. Rebecca Hoyle (1824–) and her husband Henry lived in Washington, DC's Third District. Sarah Hoyle (1789–) and her husband Jacob lived in Washington, DC's Fourth District. 1860 US Federal Census, Ancestry.com.

31. Martha Matilda Fennell (1856–1933), Cassie's youngest sister. For more information, see appendix 1: Family Biographies.

32. John Allison (1802–1866) and Catherine Nancy Cobb (1811–1872). Family Trees, Ancestry.com.

33. Dr. A. Y. P. Garnett, professor of clinical medicine at the National Medical College, was the son-in-law of then Virginia governor Henry A. Wise and lived on 9th Street. "Personal," *Evening Star*, January 30, 1857; "A Mass Meeting," *Evening Star*, June 4, 1860; "District Court," *Evening Star*, July 22, 1863; and "National Medical College," *National Republican*, March 22, 1861.

34. At boarding schools, especially in times of illness, having a sibling present provided a great comfort. Hyde, 42.

35. At age twenty-two, Jennie Granberry died while giving birth in October 1859. Her daughter lived and was also named Jennie. In 1860, then eight-month-old baby Jennie Granberry lived in the household of Sarah Mapes, who resided in Washington, DC's Second Ward. US Federal Census Mortality Schedules, 1850–1885; and 1860 US Federal Census, both at Ancestry.com.

36. John Brown's raid of Harpers Ferry transpired on October 16–18, 1859. On October 17, the *Evening Star* referred to it as a "Negro Insurrection." "Washington News and Gossip," *Evening Star*, October 17, 1859. For more information on Brown's raid, see, for example, Tony Horwitz, *Midnight Rising: John Brown and the Raid that Sparked the Civil War* (2011; repr., New York: Picador, 2012); and Robert E. McGlone, *John Brown's War Against Slavery* (New York: Cambridge Univ. Press, 2009).

37. Three companies were sent from Fort Monroe to squash the raid on Harpers Ferry. Col. Robert E. Lee served as their commander. Eighty marines under lieutenant Israel Green were also sent. "Washington News and Gossip," *Evening Star*, October 17, 1859. Harpers Ferry raid casualties included Marine private Luke Quinn, ten raiders, and four civilians. A total of seven raiders were captured, five then and two later. Fergus M. Bordewich, "John Brown's Day of Reckoning," *Smithsonian Magazine* (October 2009), https://www.smithsonianmag.com/history/john-browns-day-of-reckoning-139165084/ (accessed October 8, 2018); and "Marine Private Luke Quinn Killed," *Charleston Gazette-Mail*, May 26, 2001.

38. Charity (Allison) Cooper Lea (1801–1872), Cassie's maternal aunt, lived in Madison County, Alabama. For more information, see appendix 1: Family Biographies.

39. Angeline Anderson, a seventeen-year-old from Pennsylvania, lived with Thomas and Eliza Anderson in Washington, DC. Thomas and Eliza may have been her parents, but given their advanced ages, were probably her grandparents. 1860 US Federal Census, Ancestry.com.

40. In an earlier entry, Cassie said Ben Allison was engaged to a Mollie Gardener. Web married Elizabeth "Lizzie" Gardiner. Family Trees, Ancestry.com.

41. Maggie Pickett (1844–) may have been fifteen-year-old Margaret R. Pickett, daughter of James and Martha Pickett of Marshall County, Alabama. 1850 US Federal Census, Ancestry.com.

42. John "Johnnie" Houston Fennell (1846–1906), one of Cassie's brothers. For more information, see appendix 1: Family Biographies.

43. Brown was sentenced to death for treason, first-degree murder, and attempting to foment a slave rebellion. His trial took place in Charles Town, Virginia, and lasted from October 26 to November 2. Brown was executed on December 2, 1859. Fergus M. Bordewich, "John Brown's Day of Reckoning," *Smithsonian Magazine* (October 2009), https://www.smithsonianmag.com/history/john-browns-day-of-reckoning-139165084/ (accessed October 8, 2018). See also Louis DeCaro Jr., *Freedom's Dawn: The Last Days of John Brown in Virginia* (Lanham, MD: Rowman & Littlefield Publishers, 2015); and Stephen B. Oates, *To Purge This Land with Blood: A Biography of John Brown* (Amherst: Univ. of Massachusetts Press, 1984).

44. Mary Jane Parker, Web's mother.

45. Henrietta Townsend may have been the ten-month-old daughter of Edward and Ann Townsend, who lived in Washington, DC. In 1859, however, Henrietta's brothers Thomas and Edward would only have been eight and six, respectively. Cassie could have been referring to Ann Townsend's younger brother. 1860 US Federal Census, Ancestry.com.

46. Charles Herman Norton Jr. The editor found nothing on Charles Jr. after 1860. He may have died young. 1860 US Federal Census, Ancestry.com.

47. Dr. Beale's Panopticon of India appeared at the Oddfellows' Hall during that week. "Dr. E. Beale's Wonderful Panopticon of India," *Evening Star*, November 10, 1859.

48. Reverend S. M. Dill of Ballymena, Antrim County, Ireland. "The Union Prayer Meeting," *Evening Star*, November 11, 1859; and "The General Interest," *Evening Star*, November 8, 1859.

49. In her diary, Cassie wrote that Charity Elizabeth (Fennell) Henry (1837–1884) was her favorite sister. For more information, see appendix 1: Family Biographies.

50. Reverend George W. Samson served as president of Columbian College. "Christian Association," *Evening Star*, March 14, 1859; and "The Washington Art Association," *Evening Star*, March 12, 1859.

51. According to the *Evening Star*, Virginia governor Henry Wise had arrived in Harpers Ferry with four hundred soldiers. Many remained while he and the rest made their way to Charles Town to keep order until Brown's execution. It was feared that sympathizers might attempt to rescue Brown. "Harpers Ferry," *Evening Star*, November 21, 1859. There had been a great deal of chaos and arson, to the extent that, according to the *Richmond Enquirer*, "Night after night the heavens are illuminated by the lurid glare of burning property." "The Charlestown Reports," *Evening Star*, November 21, 1858.

52. When attending medical school at Columbian College, Willie made it a point to visit his sisters Cassie and Mary Jane. Their father had instructed, "Don't fail to see the girls as often as you can to give them all the attention you can." Dr. James W. Fennell to Willie Fennell, 1858, FF-Fennell, VF, HMCPL, HA.

53. Morgan was a presiding elder at Wesley Chapel. "The Revival," *Evening Star*, September 13, 1859.

54. A Mrs. E. Holmead operated a boarding house in Washington, DC's Fourth Ward. Catherine's Aunt and Uncle Cobb selected other accommodations. 1860 US Federal Census, Ancestry.com.

55. An advertisement in the *Evening Star* read as follows: "The original and celebrated Peak Family of Swiss Bell Ringers, of twelve members, This popular Troupe having closed a successful engagement at Baltimore respectfully announces a series of their Great Original Entertainment as above on which occasion they will be assisted by a strong corps of instrumental sole performers. Tickets 25 cents." "Odd Fellows' Hall for One Week Only," *Evening Star*, November 22, 1859. Among the performers was Julia A. Peake, "the great American harpist," Miss Fannie "with her splendid staff of 12 Silver Bells," Gustave Kaufman, "solo violinist and pianist from the Academy of Music, N.Y.," and Master Eddie and La Petite Lizette, "two wonderful prodigies." "Peak Family," *Alexandria Gazette*, November 21, 1859.

56. Sarah Irving, then thirty-five years old, ran a boarding house at 28 4 ½ Street in Washington, DC's Fourth Ward. Right next door to Norton's school, this boarding house attracted W. R. W. and Catherine Cobb. It provided a convenient abode from which to watch over their nieces Cassie, Mary Jane, Katie, and Sarah. 1860 US Federal Census, Ancestry.com; and "Alphabetical List and Residencies of xxxvith Congress," *Evening Star*, March 3, 1860.

57. James Rood Doolittle (1815–1897) and his wife Mary Lovina Cutting boarded with the Norton family. Doolittle (R-WI) served in the Senate from 1857–1869. "Alphabetical List and Residencies of the Members of the xxxvith Congress," *Evening Star*, March 3, 1860.

58. See chap. 1, note 43.

59. Francis and Isabella (Allison) Fennell of Bellefonte, Alabama, sent their daughters Katie and Sarah (1847–post-1900) to Norton's school. 1850, 1860 US Federal Census, Ancestry.com.

60. "Next door" meant Sarah Irving's boarding house.

61. Charity (Fennell) Henry, Cassie's older sister.

62. Among the possible ambrotype galleries that may have taken Cassie's picture were McClees' at 303 Pennsylvania Avenue and Whitehurst's at 434 Pennsylvania Avenue. "Business Directory," *Evening Star*, November 11, 1858.

63. In one undated letter written to the girls during their time at Norton's school, their father wrote, "I am anxious that you should complete your studies before you leave, but I wish to enjoin on you the importance of exercise in open air, as also the

bath, to keep you in good health. Without health you can not learn fast long. It is best for you then to proportion your times between study, eating, and exercise." Dr. James W. Fennell to Cassie and Mary Jane Fennell, CHC, GA.

64. Four of Brown's co-conspirators—Edwin Coppoc, John Anthony Copeland, Shields Green, and John Cook—were executed on December 16, 1859. Steven Lubet, *The 'Colored Hero' of Harper's Ferry: John Anthony Copeland and the War Against Slavery* (Cambridge Univ. Press, 2015), 197-199. Two more, Aaron Stevens and Albert E. Hazlett, were executed on March 16, 1860. Lubet, 210.

65. Willard Saulsbury Sr. (1820–1892) (D-DE) served as a US senator from 1858 to 1871. In 1860, Saulsbury lived at Mrs. Irving's boarding house. "Alphabetical List and Residencies of the xxxvith Congress," *Evening Star*, March 3, 1860.

66. Congressman John Henninger Reagan (1818–1905) (D-TX). "Reagan, John Henninger," Biographical Directory of the United States Congress, 1774–Present, http://bioguide.congress.gov/scripts/biodisplay.pl?index=r000098 (accessed July 2, 2018); and "John Henninger Reagan," Biographical Directory of the United States Congress, 1774–Present, https://tshaonline.org/handbook/online/articles/fre02 (accessed July 2, 2018).

67. Twenty-year-old Adelaide Marion Coltart (1840–1904) lived with her parents in Pittsburgh, Pennsylvania. In 1850, her father Joseph had a personal worth of $15,000 and by 1864 was listed in the City Directory as a "gentleman." 1850, 1860 US Federal Census; US City Directories, 1822–1995; and Family Trees, all at Ancestry .com.

68. Mr. Bradley may have been eighteen-year-old Charles Bradley or his sixteen-year-old brother Andrew. They had a fourteen-year-old sister named Elizabeth, and Cassie sometimes mentioned a "Lizzie Bradley." Charles, Andrew, and Elizabeth lived with their parents Charles and Catherine in Washington, DC's Fourth Ward. Their father worked as a clerk and had real estate valued at $8,000 and a personal estate worth $3,500. 1850, 1860 US Federal Census, Ancestry.com.

69. John B. Haskin (1821–1895) either dropped or brandished a pistol during session on January 12, 1860. Haskin (D-NY) and several colleagues had been debating slavery when the incident occurred. Haskin claimed that the gun fell and that he carried it for protection because he lived in a bad part of town—English Hill. Eyewitnesses, however, believed he waved the weapon. "The Pistol Dropping," *Evening Star*, January 13, 1860.

70. The Pemberton Mill Disaster took place on January 10, 1860, in Lawrence, Massachusetts. The mill, originally built by John Lowell and J. Pickering Putnam, collapsed suddenly and, shortly thereafter, a fire broke out. The mill employed eight hundred workers, and sources differ as to the number of casualties. In the immediate aftermath, newspapers had the death toll in the hundreds. Historian Alvin F. Oickle hazarded that 83–96 were killed and 275 hurt. Alvin F. Oickle, *Disaster in*

Lawrence: The Fall of the Pemberton Mill (Charleston: The History Press, 2008); and "The Pemberton Mill Disaster," New England Historical Society website, http://www.newenglandhistoricalsociety.com/pemberton-mill-disaster/ (accessed October 8, 2018).

71. Lewis Cass (1782–1866) served as US secretary of state (March 1857–December 1860) under President James Buchanan. Willard Carl Klunder, *Lewis Cass and the Politics of Moderation* (Kent, OH: Kent State Univ. Press, 1996); and "Cass, Lewis," Biographical Directory of the United States Congress, 1774–Present, http://bioguide.congress.gov/scripts/biodsiplay.pl?index=c000233 (accessed October 8, 2018).

72. Annie (Ponder) Saulsbury (1825–1912), the wife of Senator Willard Saulsbury Sr. US, Find A Grave Index, 1600s–Current, Ancestry.com.

73. Julia A. Kesley, then fifty-five years old, lived in Washington, DC's Third Ward and worked as a teacher. Her son William worked as a Senate page, while her daughter Lydia found employment as a music teacher. 1860 US Federal Census, Ancestry.com.

74. Adele (Cutts) Douglas (1835–1899) was the second wife of Senator Stephen Douglas, one of the most important nineteenth-century political figures in US history. By this time, her husband had long since gained fame through his stance on popular sovereignty as well as his role in the Compromise of 1850, the Kansas-Nebraska Act, and the Lincoln-Douglas Debates. For further information on Stephen Douglas, see, for example, Roy Morris Jr., *The Long Pursuit: Abraham Lincoln's Thirty-Year Struggle with Stephen Douglas for the Heart and Soul of America* (New York: HarperCollins, 2008); and Robert W. Johannsen, *Stephen A. Douglas* (New York: Oxford University Press; 1973; repr., Chicago: Univ. of Illinois Press, 1997).

75. Congressman William Pennington (1796–1862) (R-NJ). Steven O'Brien, *American Political Leaders from Colonial Times to the Present* (Santa Barbara, CA: ABC-Clio, 1991), 315–16.

76. Congressman John Durant Ashmore (D-SC) and Congressman John Jones McRae (D-MS). "Durant, John Ashmore," Biographical Directory of the United States Congress, 1774–Present, https://bioguide.congress.gov/scripts/biodisplay.pl?index=A000316 (accessed October 8, 2018); and "McRae, John Jones," Biographical Directory of the United States Congress, 1774–Present, http://bioguide.congress.gov/scripts/biodisplay.pl?index=M000596 (accessed October 8, 2018).

77. Cassie went to see the Russian Panorama on February 3, 1860. Untitled, *Evening Star*, February 2, 1860.

78. This entry was written on the back cover of Diary 1.

79. Written in the back of Diary 1. Cassie wrote this essay for school.

2. *Discord and Distance*

1. Mary H. Murray, then twenty-six years old, lived with her mother Sarah in Washington DC's Third Ward. A music teacher by trade, Mary had a personal estate of $300 in 1860. 1860 US Federal Census, Ancestry.com.

2. Annie (Ponder) Saulsbury, the wife of Senator Willard Saulsbury Sr. (D-DE).

3. They visited the Fourth Annual Exhibition of the Washington Art Association. It took place at the gallery on Pennsylvania Avenue between 10th and 11th Streets. According to the *Evening Star*, "This Exhibition of American Art contains works by nearly all of our Eminent Artists." "Paintings and Statuary," *Evening Star*, March 2, 1860.

4. Annie Sturgess, the seventeen-year-old daughter of Thad and Anne Sturgess, lived with her parents and siblings in Washington, DC's Second Ward. 1860 US Federal Census, Ancestry.com.

5. Between 1841 and 1845, Benjamin Fitzpatrick (1802–1869) served two terms as governor of Alabama. He served as a senator (D-AL) from 1853 to 1861. "Fitzpatrick, Benjamin," Biographical Directory of the United States Congress, 1774–Present, http://bioguide.congress.gov/scripts/biodisplay.pl?index=F000174 (accessed October 8, 2018).

6. The *Evening Star* announced, "Messrs. Fowler and Wells of New York announce a course of Lectures on Phrenology and Physiology to be given by Prof. L. N. Fowler, of their establishment, at Philharmonic Hall, Washington, D.C., commencing on Wednesday Evening, March 21st, at 7 ½ o'clock, and continuing six evenings." "Phrenology," *Evening Star*, March 19, 1860. Another article stated, "Now is the time to get your heads examined to find out what manner of men ye are." "Phrenology and Physiology," *Evening Star*, March 20, 1860.

7. Both juniors at Columbian College in 1860, Samuel Kirkland Sorsby and Charles P. Harmon came from Hinds County, Mississippi, and Alexandria, Virginia, respectively. Prior to attending Columbian College, Sorsby had spent time at Mississippi College. "Undergraduates," Columbian College, 1860, US School Catalogs, 1765–1935; and "Mississippi College, at Clinton," Mississippi College, 1860, US School Catalogs, 1765–1935, both at Ancestry.com. Of note, both Sorsby and Harmon were in the same class as Cassie's mysterious Townsend Jesse McVeigh Jr.

8. Fourteen-year-old Elizabeth Bradley, the daughter of Charles and Catherine Bradley, lived in Washington, DC's Fourth Ward. 1850, 1860 US Federal Census, Ancestry.com.

9. Originally from New York, M. M. May, then twenty-three years old, lived in a Georgetown boarding house. 1860 US Federal Census, Ancestry.com.

10. On April 12, 1860, the Columbian College's "Enosinian and Philophrenian Literary Societies" hosted a scholarship celebration at the Smithsonian Institute. At the event, Reverend Byron Sunderland read a poem, and the Honorable Jabez Lamar Monroe Curry, a native of Talladega, Alabama, delivered the address. A

veteran of the Mexican-American War, Curry (D-AL) represented Alabama in the House of Representatives. "Curry, Jabez Lamar Monroe," Biographical Directory of the United States Congress, 1774–Present, http://bioguide.congress.gov/scripts/biodisplay.pl?index=C001003 (accessed October 8, 2018); and "Scholarship Celebrated this Evening," *Evening Star*, April 12, 1860. On Curry, see also Edwin A. Alderman and Armistead Gordon, *J. L. M. Curry: A Biography* (New York: The Macmillan Company, 1911).

11. Five women named Alice Adams lived in Washington, DC, at the time, but assuming the subject to have been close in age to Cassie, the realm of possibilities may be limited to two. The first was a nineteen-year-old who lived in Washington, DC's Fourth Ward with her parents J. (a cashier) and C. Adams. The second was a twenty-two-year-old who lived in Washington, DC's First Ward with parents James (a stenographer) and Alice Adams. 1860 US Federal Census, Ancestry.com.

12. Senator James A. Pearce (1805–1862) (W/D-MD) took rooms at Mrs. Irving's boarding house. "Pearce, James Alfred," Biographical Directory of the United States Congress, 1774–Present, http://bioguide.congress.gov/scripts/biodisplay.pl?index=P000161 (accessed October 8, 2018).

13. Eighteen-year-old Susan R. Ingle lived with her parents and siblings in Washington, DC's Fourth Ward. 1860 US Federal Census, Ancestry.com.

14. Located between 7th and 8th Streets, W. M. Shuster & Co. carried dresses, robes, silks, cloaks, and shawls. "Cheap French Work," *Evening Star*, January 1, 1857; "Extensive Sale of Dry Goods," *Evening Star*, December 30, 1859; and "New Goods," *Evening Star*, April 4, 1861. Situated between 9th and 10th Streets, Ellis's Music Store was operated by John F. Ellis. "Two Very Fine Second Hand Pianos," *Evening Star*, January 9, 1858.

15. Miss McCollar was Mrs. Saulsbury's cousin.

16. Cassie spelled Mrs. Saulsbury's cousin's surname as McCollar, MacCaslin, and McColla. As such, the editor remained unable to discern her identity. Cassie misspelled other names, so the surname could have been McCullough.

17. Mrs. M. J. Harrover, then thirty-one years old, worked as a teacher and lived in a boarding house in Georgetown. The previously mentioned teacher Minnie May resided at the same boarding house. 1860 US Federal Census, Ancestry.com.

18. This may have been twenty-one-year-old T. C. M. Hatcher, a student who lived in Washington, DC's Second Ward, or it may have been Thomas C. L. Hatcher, a senior at Columbian College. This latter Thomas came from Purcellville, Loudoun County, Virginia. 1860 US Federal Census; and Columbian College, 1860, US School Catalogs, 1765–1935, both at Ancestry.com.

19. Methodist Reverend Thomas Hewlings Stockton (1808–1868) served as chaplain of the House of Representatives in 1833, 1835, and 1861. "Chaplains of the House," Office of the Chaplain: House of Representatives, https://chaplain.house.gov/chaplaincy/history.html (accessed October 8, 2018).

20. Senator James Rood Doolittle and his wife Mary.

21. Captain J. H. Simpson lectured on Utah. Sponsored by the Young Men's Christian Association, the talk took place at the Smithsonian. "Lecture on Exploration in Utah," *Evening Star*, April 12, 1860.

22. This was probably Ella McRae, the daughter of Sherwin and Sarah McRae, who lived in Henrico, Virginia. Sherwin listed his occupation as farmer/lawyer with a real estate worth $10,000 and a personal estate estimated at $19,570. 1860 US Federal Census, Ancestry.com.

23. Cassie went to see Dan Rice's Great Show at Judiciary Square on April 25–27, 1860. Performing animals included horses, mules, and ponies as well as an elephant and a black rhinoceros. "Dan Rice's Great Show," *Evening Star*, April 25, 1860.

24. The junior class at Columbian College held an exhibition at the Smithsonian, and Charles P. Harmon served as a speaker. "College Exhibition at the Smithsonian," *Evening Star*, April 28, 1860. The following month, Harmon gave a talk "on the vanity of human grandeur." "Elocutionary Contest," *Evening Star*, June 26, 1860.

25. John E. Bouligny (1824–1864) was a New Orleans lawyer and American Party member who served in the House of Representatives from 1859 to 1861. He married Mary Elizabeth Parker on April 25, 1860, in Washington, DC, at a ceremony attended by President James Buchanan. District of Columbia Marriage Records, 1810–1953, Ancestry.com; and "Bouligny, John Edward," Biographical Directory of United States Congress, 1774–Present, http://bioguide.congress.gov/scripts/biodisplay.pl?index=B000665 (accessed October 8, 2018). According to historian Ernest B. Furgurson, "Many of those invited to the wedding of John E. Bouligny of Louisiana to Mary Parker, daughter of the capital's most prosperous grocer, realized that it might be the last social fling before disunion." Ernest B. Furgurson, *Freedom Rising: Washington in the Civil War* (New York: Vintage, 2005), 17.

26. The New Orleans and Metropolitan Burlesque Opera Troupe performed at the Odd Fellows' Hall in Washington, DC, on May 2–5, 1860. "Double Minstrel Troupe," *Evening Star*, May 5, 1860.

27. The Marine Band performed on Wednesdays at President's Square and at the Capitol on Saturdays. "Music at the President's Grounds," *Evening Star*, April 25, 1860.

28. The Japanese Embassy arrived in Washington, DC, on May 14, 1860. "The Japanese Embassy to the United States," *Evening Star*, May 14, 1860.

29. On July 30, 1850, Alex Penland (1819–1896) had married Isabella Jane Allison, the daughter of Cassie's uncle David Allison. In 1860, Alex, Isabella, and their four children lived with David. 1860 US Federal Census; and Alabama, Select Marriages, 1816–1957, both at Ancestry.com.

30. On May 12, 1860, magician Robert Heller performed at the Washington Theater. "Washington Theater," *Evening Star*, May 12, 1860. Heller claimed to have

second sight and claimed expertise in witchcraft, necromancy, and demonology. "The 'Seer' has Come," *Evening Star*, January 26, 1855.

31. The *Evening Star* included an article which scolded the behavior of onlookers, especially children, who had gawked at and attempted to touch the Japanese as they might "do to our Indians." Whoever authored the article suggested that the honor and dignity of the Japanese had been insulted, while the United States had been embarrassed. "The Japanese Embassy," *Evening Star*, May 15, 1860.

32. Cornelia Munson lived in Washington, DC's Fourth Ward. She and her husband Owen, a dentist by trade, had three daughters: Cornelia, Addie, and S. A. In 1860, their daughters would have been nineteen, eighteen, and seventeen, respectively. 1860 US Federal Census, Ancestry.com.

33. This may have been Leonidas E. Coyle, the son of merchant Leonidas Coyle and his wife Harriet. The younger Leonidas attended Columbian College as a sophomore, while Charles P. Harmon was in the junior class. "Undergraduates," Columbian College, 1860, US School Catalogs, 1765–1935; and 1860 US Federal Census, both at Ancestry.com.

34. According to the *Evening Star*, "The Japanese Embassy was represented on Saturday evening at the open air concert by the Marine Band, in the President's grounds, by some eight or ten of their number. During the performance of the music they occupied the balcony of the semi-circular colonnade on the south side of the house, where they continued seated most of the time. Several of them were busily employed in sketching the scene before them, of which the Virginia hills were in the farther and the Potomac river in the nearer distance, with the red-coated band and five or six thousand of the sovereign people of both sexes and all ages and sizes gathered immediately in the pleasure grounds below. In the course of their sitting for the double purpose of seeing and being seen, the President and Miss Lane paid them a brief visit, during which mutual felicitations and courtesies were exchanged, the members of the Embassy conducting themselves throughout with equal dignity, politeness, and grace. The principal Embassadors were not present—only some of their head officers and attaches." "The Promenade Concert on Saturday Evening," *Evening Star*, May 21, 1860. Since her uncle had no wife, Harriet Lane served as pseudo–first lady of the United States.

35. "The Sabbath School Celebration," *Evening Star*, May 19, 1860.

36. Waugh's Italia opened at the Philharmonic Hall in Washington, DC, on May 23, 1860. It included myriad paintings and a lecture. "Waugh's Italia," *Evening Sun*, May 21, 1860; and "Waugh's Italia," *Evening Star*, May 24, 1860.

37. The city had more than one strawberry festival. One, which took place on June 1, 1860, was sponsored by the women of the New York Avenue Presbyterian Church. "The New-York Avenue Church Concert," *Evening Star*, June 5, 1860.

38. A lawyer by profession, Senator Stephen Mallory (1813–1873) (D-FL) spent much of his life in Key West, Florida. During the Civil War, he served as secretary of the Navy for the Confederacy. "Mallory, Stephen Russell," Biographical Directory of the United States Congress, 1774–Present, http://bioguide.congress.gov/scripts/biodisplay.pl?index=M000084 (accessed October 8, 2018).

39. The election between incumbent Mayor James G. Berret (Democrat) and Richard Wallach (Independent) had been extremely contentious. In the end, Berret won by twenty-four votes, and Wallach cried foul. Wallach's brother W. D., editor of the *Evening Star*, suggested voter fraud. Furgurson, 39; and "The Election Yesterday," *Evening Star*, June 5, 1860. A mob erupted the night of the election. See following endnote.

40. Several mob activities took place on election night. Rioters threw stones and bricks, fired guns, and created general havoc. Several people suffered injuries. The *Evening Star* implied that the rabble-rousers had supported the incumbent. The incident Cassie referred to transpired between Thomas J. Magruder and James Mahoney. Evidently, as Magruder stood in line to vote, he casually expressed his belief that Wallach would win. Perhaps provoked by that statement, Mahoney shoved Magruder out of the line. When Magruder protested, Mahoney slugged him in the face. Shocked, Magruder reached out and clasped him by the collar as he shouted for the man to be arrested. Several came to Mahoney's defense and bombarded Magruder with their fists. Mahoney was never charged. Initially, Magruder was held for disturbing the peace but was released that same evening. "Incidents of the Election Yesterday," *Evening Star*, June 5, 1860.

41. A Baltimore nativist political group/gang, the Plug Uglies had a reputation for rioting and violence. See Tracy Matthew Melton, *Hanging Henry Gambrill: The Violent Career of Baltimore's Plug Uglies, 1854–1860* (Baltimore: Maryland Historical Association, 2004).

42. On July 2, 1860, the *Evening Star* mentioned this commencement, including prizes: "First prize to Miss Susie K. Ingle; second to Misses Cassie M., Mary J., and Kate A. Fennell, of the senior department; middle department, first prize to Miss Kate L. Dunnington, second to Miss M. E. Todd." Untitled, *Evening Star*, July 2, 1860.

43. The editor attempted to discover the fates of the Nortons and could find only bits and pieces. In May 1861, the Young Ladies' Institute contributed $40.00 for "volunteers" and agreed to do so without butter for three months. Untitled, *Evening Star*, May 4, 1861. By May 1862, Charles had left the school and worked at the nearby Cavalry Mission, which had forty-one teachers and over two hundred students. D. C. Whitman served as superintendent, while Charles worked as his assistant. "Anniversary Celebration of the Sabbath," *Evening Star*, May 26, 1862. Ann Amelia Norton died on June 10, 1874, at the age of seventy-six. "The Courts," *Evening Star*, August 18, 1874. At that time, Charles, Julia, and Charlotte lived at 17 H Street Northwest. Untitled, *National Republican*, June 12, 1874. By 1880, Charles had

changed career fields, having become a clerk with the US Treasury Department. 1880 US Federal Census, Ancestry.com. On August 6, 1884, Charles died at the age of fifty-one. "Deaths," *Critic and Record*, August 7, 1884. The editor had no success in her attempt to find additional information on Julia or Charlotte.

44. Francis Marion Fennell, Cassie's paternal uncle. Family Trees, Ancestry.com.

45. Thomas Street and John Rayburn, young men from Guntersville, had recently graduated from Cumberland University. Rayburn Family, Vertical Files, MCA, GA.

46. This may have been reference to a miscarriage. At the time, Charity and her husband Sam Henry had two children, James (1858–) and Margaret (1859–1886). For more information, see appendix 1: Family Biographies.

47. Martha Matilda "Mattie" Fennell, Cassie's youngest sister. See appendix 1: Family Biographies.

3. *Home in Marshall County, Alabama*

1. The candidates were John Breckinridge (Southern Democrat); Stephen Douglas (Democrat); John Bell (Constitutional Union Party); and Abraham Lincoln (Republican).

2. Breckinridge, President James Buchanan's vice president and the youngest man ever to hold that office, had a pro-property rights stance when it came to the western territories and believed strongly in "equality of states" as a means to preserve the union. William C. Davis, *Breckinridge: Statesman, Soldier, Symbol* (1974; repr., Lexington: Univ. Press of Kentucky, 2010), 231. Douglas, famed Illinois senator, believed in unionism, congressional non-interference, and local government. Douglas R. Egerton, *Year of Meteors: Stephen Douglas, Abraham Lincoln, and the Election that Brought on the Civil War* (New York: Bloomsbury Press, 2010), 32; and Martin H. Quitt, *Stephen A. Douglas and Antebellum Democracy* (New York: Cambridge Univ. Press, 2012), 154–57.

3. The future King Edward VII began his American tour on September 20. He stopped in major cities ranging from Detroit and Chicago to Cincinnati and Philadelphia. On this historic trip, he also visited Washington, DC, and Richmond. Christopher Hibbert, *Edward VII: The Last Victorian King* (1976; repr., New York: Palgrave Macmillan, 2007), 32–33.

4. This may have been anti-royal sentiment, or it could have stemmed from the fact that many southerners believed the Prince of Wales more sympathetic to northern political viewpoints on slavery. Hibbert, 33.

5. Stephen Douglas's train arrived in Huntsville at 8:00 a.m. on October 25, 1860. An open carriage transported him to a local hotel. Though scheduled to appear at 11:00 a.m., he did so at noon and spoke for over two hours. Due to the large size of the audience, roughly ten thousand, most in attendance had difficulty hearing him. In an attempt to counter Douglas, fire-eater William Lowndes Yancey spoke in Huntsville that evening. Raneé Pruitt, ed., *Eden of the South: A Chronology*

of Huntsville, Alabama, 1805–2005 (Huntsville: Huntsville-Madison County Public Library, 2005), 39; Quitt, 163; and "Hon. Stephen A. Douglas' Southern Appointments," *Autauga Citizen* (Prattville, AL), October 18, 1860. On Yancey, see J. Mills Thornton III, *Politics and Power in a Slave Society: Alabama 1800–1860* (Baton Rouge: Louisiana State Univ. Press, 1978), 397; and William H. Freehling, *The Road to Disunion*, vol. 2, *Secessionists Triumphant, 1854–1861* (New York: Oxford Univ. Press, 2007), 271–87.

6. Web Parker had a sister named Matilda E. and a brother named Edward Tilley. Family Trees, Ancestry.com.

7. Edward Tilley Parker. Family Trees, Ancestry.com.

8. In the 1860 presidential election, Lincoln received 180 electoral votes and 1,865,908 popular votes. Breckinridge received 72 electoral votes and 848,019 popular votes. Douglas received 12 electoral votes and 1,380,202 popular votes. Bell received 39 electoral votes and 590,901 popular votes. "Election of 1860," The American Presidency Project, www.presidency.ucsb.edu/showelection.php?year=1860 (accessed September 2, 2018). Douglas carried eleven of the sixty-seven Alabama counties, including Madison County, the location of Huntsville. Breckinridge, Cassie's favorite candidate, won the majority of Alabama votes as a whole. Thornton, 411–13. For more information on the 1860 election, see Michael F. Holt, *The Election of 1860: "A Campaign Fraught with Consequences"* (Lawrence: Univ. of Kansas Press, 2017); and A. James Fuller, ed., *The Election of 1860 Reconsidered* (Kent: Kent State Univ. Press, 2013).

9. Advocates of secession often wore cockades or rosettes. Made of ribbon, popular colors included blue and red.

10. Many northern Alabamians opposed secession whereas most southern Alabamians favored it. Fitzgerald, *Reconstruction in Alabama*, 19; and Thornton, 437–42.

11. Major Robert Anderson.

12. In addition to Carrie, Absalom Weedon Arnold and Elizabeth Minerva (Moore) Arnold had the following children: George (1841–); William (1843-1861); Sarah (1844–); Mariah Jane (1846–); James (1848–1927); John (1852–); Mary (1854–1902); C. H. (1856–); and Martha (1858–). 1850, 1860 US Federal Census; and Family Trees, both at Ancestry.com.

13. Thomas Jefferson Watkins, a teacher in 1860, lived in the household of the Arnold family. After marrying Carrie Arnold, he moved with his wife to Kentucky and later became a judge. 1860 US Federal Census; and Family Trees, both at Ancestry.com. Carrie's sister Mary Arnold later married Cassie's brother Wattie.

14. Mariah Jane Arnold, Carrie's sister.

15. According to historian Candace Bailey, "The idea of singing appealed to the natural simplicity that was inherent in how young women were supposed to behave." Bailey, 119.

16. William Lowndes Yancey (1814–1863) represented Alabama in the US House of Representatives from 1844 to 1848. A noted orator and fire-eater, he had significant influence on the debate on the extension of slavery into the western territories. In a highly simplified explanation, he proposed that the Constitution protected all property, whether in a state or territory. The opposing view, supported by many northerners, allowed each territory to decide for itself on the issue of slavery. After Lincoln's election, Yancey was instrumental in Alabama's secession. Seeking recognition for the Confederacy, he served on a diplomatic mission to France and England. He also represented Alabama in the Confederate Congress from 1862 to 1863. Yancey died from Bright's disease in 1863. Lucille Griffith, *Alabama: A Documentary History to 1900* (Tuscaloosa: Univ. of Alabama Press, 1968), 338–43, 379–80; and Malcolm C. McMillan, *The Land Called Alabama* (Austin, TX: Steck-Vaughn Co., 1968), 176–77.

17. Florida seceded on January 10, but Georgia did not secede until January 19. George Justice, "Georgia Secession Convention of 1861," *New Georgia Encyclopedia*, https://www.georgiaencyclopedia.org/articles/government-politics/georgia-secession-convention-1861 (accessed September 2, 2018).

18. Mississippi seceded on January 9, and Louisiana seceded on January 26. On Mississippi, see Timothy B. Smith, *The Mississippi Secession Convention: Delegates and Deliberations in Politics and War, 1861–1865* (Jackson: Univ. Press of Mississippi, 2014), xi. On Louisiana, see John M. Sacher, "Louisiana's Secession from the Union," *64 Parishes*, https://64parishes.org/entry/louisianas-secession-from-the-union (accessed September 2, 2018).

19. Cassie's neighbors Arthur Campbell Beard and James Lawrence Sheffield, both cooperationists, represented Marshall County. Duncan and Smith, 45–51.

20. Jefferson Davis, a former US senator (D-MS) and secretary of war (1853–1857), became provisional president when inaugurated on February 18. Emory Thomas, *The Confederate Nation, 1861–1865* (New York: Harper & Row, 1979), 87; and "Important from Montgomery; Inauguration of Jefferson Davis as President of the Southern Confederacy," *New York Times*, February 19, 1861.

21. Texas seceded on February 1, 1861. Eight delegates opposed secession at the Texas convention. Thomas, *The Confederate Nation*, 55–56; and Walter L. Buenger, *Secession and the Union in Texas* (Austin: Univ. of Texas Press, 1984).

22. President Lincoln had not ordered its evacuation.

23. Alexander H. Stephens had formerly represented Georgia in the US Congress. For more information, see Thomas E. Schott, *Alexander H. Stephens of Georgia: A Biography* (Baton Rouge: Louisiana State Univ. Press, 1988).

24. The Madison Rifles left for Mobile and Pensacola on March 26, 1861. The unit comprised Company D of the 7th Alabama Infantry Regiment. Dennis Partridge, "Confederate Units of Madison, Alabama," AlGenWeb: Southern Genealogy, https://algw.genealogyvillage.com/madison.confunit.htm (accessed September 2, 2018). On the Madison Rifles, see also Rohr, 77.

25. Southern artillery bombarded Fort Sumter on April 12. Union major Robert Anderson surrendered on April 13, 1861. Jayne E. Blair, *The Essential War: A Handbook to the Battles, Armies, Navies, and Commanders* (Jefferson, NC: McFarland & Co., 2006), 59–60; and E. A. Pollard, *The Lost Cause: A New Southern History of the War of the Confederates* (New York: E. B. Treat Co. Publishers, 1866), 109–11.

26. Frank Fennell, Cassie's younger brother. For more information, see appendix 1: Family Biographies.

27. Cassie's brother-in-law Sam Henry. The Confederates bombarded the fort for thirty-four hours. No Confederate or Union soldiers were killed prior to surrender. However, during a cannonade the following day on April 14, two Union soldiers were accidentally killed by one of the cannons. Fergus Bordewich, "Fort Sumter: The Civil War Begins," *Smithsonian Magazine* (April 2011), https://www.smithsonainmag.com/history/fort-sumter-the-civil-war-begins-1018791/ (accessed January 8, 2020).

28. Pierre Gustave Toutant Beauregard, better known as P. G. T. Beauregard, served as a brigadier general in the provisional army of the Confederacy.

29. Virginia seceded on April 17. See Thomas, *The Confederate Nation*, 93; William W. Freehling and Craig M. Simpson, eds., *Showdown in Virginia: The 1861 Convention and the Fate of the Union* (Charlottesville: Univ. of Virginia Press, 2010); and Nelson D. Lankford, "Virginia Convention of 1861," *Encyclopedia Virginia*, Virginia Humanities, https://www.encyclopediavirginia.org/Virginia_Constitutional_Convention_of_1861 (accessed September 2, 2018).

30. Fort Pickens was relieved and reinforced on April 11–13, 1861, when the USS *Brooklyn* arrived. Russell McClintock, *Lincoln and the Decision for War: The Northern Response to Secession* (Chapel Hill: Univ. of North Carolina Press, 2008), 134; and George F. Pearce, *Pensacola during the Civil War: A Thorn in the Side of the Confederacy* (Gainesville: Univ. Press of Florida, 2000).

31. On June 5, 1861, the Marshall Boys, a hodgepodge of volunteers from Marshall County, and the Railroad Guards, comprised of the Irish railroad crew, left Guntersville to join the 9th Alabama Infantry. Duncan and Smith, 62.

32. Isham Joseph Fennell (1842–1864), the son of Hubbard Hobbs Fennell and Mary Irene Smith. Family Trees, Ancestry.com.

33. Lieutenant general Winfield Scott remained true to the Union. For more information, see Timothy D. Johnson, *Winfield Scott: The Quest for Military Glory* (Lawrence: Univ. Press of Kansas, 1998).

34. On its way to the nation's capital, the 6th Massachusetts Regiment was attacked by Baltimore residents sympathetic to the Confederate cause. Twelve people, including three soldiers, were killed. On the Pratt Street Riot, see Harry A. Ezratty, *Baltimore in the Civil War: The Pratt Street Riot and a City Occupied* (Charleston: The History Press, 2010).

35. Both casualties at Fort Sumter occurred after the official surrender.

36. John, the son of David and Sarah (Smith) Allison. Family Trees, Ancestry.com.

37. Captain Sam Henry, Cassie's brother-in-law, led the Marshall Boys. Once in Richmond, Sam received a promotion to lieutenant colonel. In November 1861, he became a full colonel. Sam Henry, VF, MCA, GA.

38. Teacher Mary H. Murray lived in Washington, DC. 1860 US Federal Census, Ancestry.com.

39. Neither major Robert Anderson nor lieutenant general Winfield Scott were tried for treason.

40. Above this entry, Cassie wrote, "Captured, 800 of the Massachusetts Regiment with 800 stand of arms." She must have learned this to be false as she later scribbled over this line.

41. Davis did not resign.

42. On April 27, 1861, Lincoln declared martial law in Baltimore. Ezratty, 87.

43. Fort Pickens remained in Union control for the duration of the Civil War. Pollard, 109–11.

44. Lieutenant general Winfield Scott.

45. This is untrue. Union major general Benjamin Butler occupied Annapolis on April 21, 1861, and had his troops repair the railroad track destroyed by secessionists. Ezratty, 76.

46. Twelve people died in the Pratt Street Riot. See chap. 3, note 34.

47. Henry attended but did not graduate from the US Military Academy. See appendix 1: Family Biographies.

48. John D. Phelan wrote this stanza, part of his poem "Ye Men of Alabama!" It first appeared in the *Montgomery Advertiser* in October 1860. Bob Blaisdell, ed., *Civil War Short Stories and Poems* (Mineola, NY: Dover Publications, Inc., 2011), 6–7.

49. Emory and Henry College in Emory, Virginia.

50. Most of the people in Washington, DC, were southern, likely from Maryland or Virginia, or had southern roots. See, for example, Lucinda Prout Janke, *A Guide to Civil War Washington, D.C.: The Capital of the Union* (Charleston: The History Press, 2013).

51. Lee became a brigadier general and, later, a general. On Lee, see Douglas Southall Freeman, *Lee*, with a new forward by James M. McPherson (New York: Touchstone, 1997).

52. Commander John Rodgers led the Union flotilla of three paddle wheelers headquartered at Cairo, Illinois, during the summer of 1861. The thrust to control the Mississippi River helped keep Kentucky and Missouri from seceding. Sam Smith, "Winning the West," American Battlefield Trust, https://www.battlefields.org/learn/articles/river-war (accessed September 2, 2018). Over this particular entry, Cassie wrote, "All false reports."

53. Because England purchased the bulk of southern cotton, Confederates assumed that connection would lead to a wartime alliance. They overestimated their importance, however, because England resorted to its stockpiled cotton and also procured the crop from locations like India and Egypt during the war. On the importance of cotton to the South, see Thomas, *The Confederate Nation*, 81–82; and Sven Beckert, "Cotton and the US South" in *Plantation Kingdom: The American South and Its Global Commodities*, ed. Richard Follett et al. (Baltimore: Johns Hopkins Univ. Press, 2016), 39–55.

54. North Carolina seceded on May 20. See Michael C. Hardy, *North Carolina and the Civil War* (Charleston: The History Press, 2011), 16. Tennessee's General Assembly voted to secede on May 6, and a referendum reaffirmed this decision on June 8. On Tennessee, see Kent T. Dollar, Larry H. Whiteaker, and W. Calvin Dickinson, eds., *Border Wars: The Civil War in Tennessee and Kentucky* (Kent: Kent State Univ. Press, 2015).

55. Born in Alabama, Jeremiah H. J. Williams (1831–1911) served in the 9th Regiment, Alabama Infantry, Companies F and S, as a captain and, later, a major. In the 1850 census, Williams was listed as a twenty-one-year-old engineer living with his parents James and Catherine. However, a "James" H. J. Williams graduated from the University of Alabama that same year. By 1860, Williams resided in Jackson County, Alabama, worked as a civil engineer, and was involved in railroad construction, specifically that of the Tennessee & Coosa. He owned real estate valued at $1,440 and had a personal worth of $2,000. At the dawn of the Civil War, Williams recruited Company B, which was nicknamed the "Irish Guards" or "Railroad Guards." Between 1881 and 1909, he worked as a postmaster in Jackson County. College Student Lists, 1763–1924; Civil War Soldiers, 1861–1865, Film M374, Roll 48; 1850, 1860 US Federal Census; "A Virtual Cemetery Created by Hutch 9th Alabama Infantry," US, Find A Grave Index, 1600s–Current; and All Appointments of US Postmasters, 1863–1959, all at Ancestry.com. See also Kennamer, 134–35; and Duncan and Smith, 49, 63.

56. On May 23, 1861, at Harpers Ferry, Confederate colonel Thomas Jackson managed to take 42 locomotives and 386 railcars. He also destroyed thirty-six miles of track. See Blair, 62. Throughout the war, Culpeper, Virginia, hosted several skirmishes between the Union and the Confederacy, culminating in the Battle of Culpeper Courthouse on September 13, 1863. See Daniel E. Sutherland, "Culpeper County during the Civil War," *Encyclopedia Virginia*, Virginia Humanities, https://www.encyclopediavirginia.org/Culpeper_County_During_the_Civil_War#start_entry (accessed September 2, 2018). The Hampton affair Cassie referenced should not be confused with the Battle of Hampton Roads, which transpired on March 8–9, 1862.

57. Willie Fennell, Sam Henry, and John Allison.

58. In 1860, Henrietta "Hennie" Walpole (1840–c. 1877), then twenty-one years old, and her mother Mary Ann Lynes Walpole resided with the W. W. Coleman

family in Guntersville. Prior to living in Guntersville, Hennie, her parents Mary and John, and her siblings Sophronia, Emma, and John, lived in Huntsville. 1850, 1860 US Federal Census; and Family Trees, both at Ancestry.com. Hennie married Samuel B. Jackson on October 16, 1867. Alabama County Marriages, 1805–1967, Ancestry.com. During the Civil War, Samuel served as a private in Company D of the 5th Alabama Regiment. Alabama Civil War Muster Rolls, 1861–1865, Ancestry.com. In 1870, Sam practiced law. He had real estate valued at $1,000 and a personal estate worth $750. 1870 US Federal Census, Ancestry.com.

59. Thomas J. Eubanks worked as editor of the *Marshall News*, Guntersville's newspaper. The speeches were brief because *Paint Rock*, a steamer, waited to take the troops to Bridgeport, Alabama. Duncan and Smith, 62.

60. Virginians voted to secede on May 23, and the following day, in Alexandria, Union colonel Elmer Ellsworth was killed while trying to take down a Confederate flag at a hotel. On these skirmishes in Virginia, see Brady Dennis, "The Federal Occupation of Alexandria in the Civil War changed and spared city," *Washington Post*, April 7, 2011; and Charles P. Poland Jr., *The Glories of War: Small Battles and Early Heroes of 1861* (Bloomington, IN: Author House, 2004). There was a Union camp at Hampton. See Blair, 63.

61. On May 20, the provisional Confederate Congress voted to move the Confederate capitol from Montgomery to Richmond, Virginia. See Thomas, *The Confederate Nation*, 100–102; and Christopher Lyle McIlwain, *Civil War Alabama* (Tuscaloosa: Univ. of Alabama Press, 2016), 45.

62. The Camp Jackson Affair took place near St. Louis on May 10, 1861. Brigadier general Nathaniel Lyon took prisoners from the Missouri National Guard, and when his men fired on angry civilians, killing twenty-eight of them, a riot ensued. "Nathaniel Lyon," State Historical Society of Missouri Historic Missourians website, https://shsmo.org/historicmissourians/name/l/lyon/#references (accessed September 2, 2018). For more on Lyon, see Christopher Phillips, *Damned Yankee: The Life of General Nathaniel Lyon* (Baton Rouge: Louisiana State Univ. Press, 1996).

63. The Battle of Philippi, which took place on June 3, 1861, in Philippi, Virginia, stemmed from Union troops attempting to protect the Baltimore & Ohio Railroad from Confederates. Only ten men sustained wounds in this brief battle. The Confederates, led by colonel George Porterfield, retreated. John W. Shaffer, *Clash of Loyalties: A Border County in the Civil War* (Morgantown: West Virginia Univ. Press, 2003), 64–66.

64. On June 10, 1861, a battle took place at Bethel Church, Virginia. The combatants included the troops of Union major general Benjamin Butler and those of Confederate colonel John B. Magruder. Butler wanted to keep the Confederates away from Yorktown and Fort Monroe, while Magruder sought to stop the Union progress to Richmond. There were 4,500 Union troops and 1,408 Confederate troops in the battle. The Union lost eighteen men while the Confederacy lost one.

Blair, 63. On the Battle of Bethel Church, see J. Michael Cobb, Edward B. Hicks, and Wythe Holt, *Battle of Big Bethel: Crucial Clash in Early Civil War Virginia* (El Dorado Hills, CA: Savas Beatie, 2013); and John V. Quarstein, *Big Bethel: The First Battle* (Charleston: The History Press, 2011).

65. The Senate of the 37th Congress convened from March 4–27 before adjourning. On April 15, Lincoln called Congress back into session. Heeding his call, Congress met from July 4-August 6. During this time, its members endorsed Lincoln's war plans. "37th Congress," History, Art & Archives, United States House of Representatives, https://history.house.gov/Congressional-Overview/Profiles/37th/ (accessed September 3, 2018).

66. On April 15, Lincoln called for 75,000 troops. Nelson D. Lankford, *Cry Havoc: The Crooked Road to Civil War, 1861* (New York: Penguin, 2007), 105. As of July 1, the Union army had 186,751 men. E. B. Long with Barbara Long, *The Civil War Day by Day: An Almanac, 1861–1865* (1971; repr., New York: Da Capo, 1985), 706. By January 1, 1862, the Confederate army had 209,852 men while the Union army had 527,204. Thomas, *The Confederate Nation*, 155. For information on army numbers prior to the Civil War, see Clayton Newell, *The Regular Army before the Civil War, 1845–1860* (Washington, DC: Center of Military History, United States Army, 2014); and George T. Ness Jr., *Regular Army on the Eve of the Civil War* (Baltimore: Toomey Press, 1990).

67. The Battle of Vienna took place in Vienna, Virginia, on June 17, 1861. Confederates, led by colonel Maxey Gregg, fired on a train of Union troops under the command of general Robert Schenck. When attacked, the train had been traveling on the Loudoun & Hampshire Railroad. Eight Union soldiers were killed, and four were wounded. There were no Confederate casualties. Poland, 45–46; and William C. Davis, *Battle at Bull Run: A History of the First Major Campaign of the Civil War* (New York: Doubleday & Co., 1977).

68. The Battle of Boonville took place in St. Louis, Missouri, on June 17, 1861. Led by brigadier general Nathaniel Lyon, Union troops forced the Missouri State Guard, led by colonel John S. Marmaduke, to retreat. This helped prevent Missouri, a state whose governor wanted to secede, from joining the Confederacy. There were thirty-one Union casualties and fifty Missouri State Guard casualties. "The Battle of Boonville," National Park Service website, https://www.nps.gov/parkhistory/online_books/civil_war_series/26/sec3.htm (accessed September 3, 2018); and Thomas L. Snead, *The Fight for Missouri: From the Election of Lincoln to the Death of Lyon* (New York: Scribner's Sons, 1888), 172–73.

69. On June 13, the Battle of Romney took place in Romney, Virginia. The 11th Indiana Regiment, led by colonel Lewis Wallace, defeated the Confederates. "The Battle of Romney," *Harper's Weekly*, July 6, 1861.

70. See chap. 3, note 64.

71. This is likely Confederate brigadier general Benjamin McCulloch. On August 10, he defeated Union brigadier general Nathaniel Lyon at the Battle of Wilson's Creek. Thomas W. Cutrer, "Benjamin McCulloch," *The Handbook of Texas Online,* https://tshaonline.org/handbook/online/articles/fmc34 (accessed September 3, 2018).

72. The Confederates fled Harpers Ferry, burning a nearby bridge and setting fire to one in Martinsburg and at Shepherdstown. To prevent Union forces from benefitting, provisions were discarded in the river. "Evacuation of Harper's Ferry," *Harper's Weekly*, June 29, 1861.

73. See Paul Quigley, "Independence Day Dilemmas in the American South, 1848–1865," *Journal of Southern History* 75, no. 2 (2009): 235–66; Paul Quigley, *Shifting Grounds: Nationalism and the American South, 1848–1865* (New York: Oxford Univ. Press, 2012); James Jefferson Bond, "Competing Visions of America: The Fourth of July During the Civil War" (master's thesis, Virginia Polytechnic Institute and State Univ., 2007); and Brian Resnick, "Would the Confederacy Have Celebrated the Fourth of July," *The Atlantic*, July 3, 2014, https://www.theatlantic.com/politics/archive/2014/07/would-the-confederacy-have-celebrated-the-fourt-of-july/454464 (accessed September 7, 2018).

74. In a special message to Congress, Lincoln asked that its members "place at the control of the Government for the work at least 400,000 men and $400,000,000." Abraham Lincoln, "Special Session Message," July 4, 1861, The American Presidency Project, https://www.presidency.ucsb.edu/documents/special-session-message-5 (accessed September 3, 2018). For more information on Union army numbers, see Clayton R. Newell and Charles R. Shrader, *Of Duty Well and Faithfully Done: A History of the Regular Army in the Civil War* (Lincoln: Univ. of Nebraska Press, 2011).

75. On August 8, 1861, Davis called for 400,000 volunteers to serve one to three years. On March 28, 1862, he requested that the Confederate Congress pass the Conscription Act, and they did so on April 16. Allen Tate, *Jefferson Davis: His Rise and Fall* (Nashville, TN: J. S. Sanders & Co., 1998), 114; and R. Jarrod Atchison, *A War of Words: Rhetorical Leadership of Jefferson Davis* (Tuscaloosa: Univ. of Alabama Press, 2017), 48.

76. Confederate brigadier general Joseph E. Johnston, along with twelve thousand men, guarded access to the Shenandoah Valley. Thomas, *The Confederate Nation*, 110. On Winchester, Virginia, during the Civil War, see Richard R. Duncan, *Beleaguered Winchester: A Virginia Community at War, 1861–1865* (Baton Rouge: Louisiana State Univ. Press, 2007).

77. On July 5, 1861, at Carthage, Missouri, brigadier general Nathaniel Lyon and major general Franz Siegel fought a force of secessionists led by governor Claiborne Jackson and brigadier general Ben McCulloch. Though they caused severe damage with their artillery, Union forces retreated. While the Union lost thirteen of

its roughly one thousand men, the Confederates, who had about four thousand combatants, lost forty to fifty men. The Union reported 31 injuries, while the Confederates had 120. Long, 91.

78. At Martinsburg, Virginia, in the Shenandoah Valley, the Confederate military leaders at that time were brigadier generals Joseph E. Johnston and Thomas J. Jackson. Long, 94–95.

79. Hoping to protect western Virginia, which had a great deal of Union loyalists, Confederate brigadier general Robert S. Garnett took control of roads at Rich Mountain and Laurel Hill. Between July 7 and July 11, he led his men against Union troops under the command of general George McClellan, and on July 11, he lost the Battle of Rich Mountain. While retreating, Garnett was killed at Corrick's Ford on July 13. "Laurel Hill and the First Land Battles of the Civil War," The Battle of Laurel Hill, http://www.battleoflaurelhill.org/history.html (accessed September 4, 2018); "Robert S. Garnett," American Battlefield Trust, https://www.battlefields.org/learn/biographies/robert-s-garnett (accessed September 4, 2018); and Long, 92–94.

80. This is in reference to a battle or skirmish at Blackburn's Ford, Virginia, on July 18. Union brigadier general Irvin McDowell ordered brigadier general Daniel Tyler to seek a place to cross Bull Run Creek. Tyler and his men were repelled by the troops of Confederate lieutenant general James Longstreet, who served under brigadier general P. G. T. Beauregard. Reported deaths: eighty-three Union and sixty-eight Confederate. Davis, *Battle of Bull Run*, 112–31; and "The Skirmish at Blackburns Ford," National Park Service website, http://www.nps.gov/mana/learn/historyculture/the-skirmish-at-blackburns-ford.htm (accessed September 4, 2018).

81. The earliest significant battle of the war, the First Battle of Bull Run resulted in a Confederate victory. The officers mentioned include Confederate brigadier general Joseph E. Johnston, Confederate brigadier general P. G. T. Beauregard, Union brigadier general Irvin McDowell, and Union major general Robert Patterson. Thomas, *The Confederate Nation*, 110–16.

82. Confederate forces, including the 6th North Carolina Infantry Regiment and the 4th Alabama Infantry Regiment, overran the six-gun batteries led by Union captains J. B. Ricketts and Charles Griffin. Richard W. Iobst, *The Bloody Sixth: The Sixth North Carolina Regiment, Confederate States of America* (Durham, NC: Christina Printing Company, 1965), 23, http://archive.org/details/bloodysixthooiobs (accessed September 4, 2018).

83. Estimates placed Union and Confederate losses at 481 and 387 men, respectively. The Confederates secured 1,200 prisoners. Allan Nevins, *War for the Union*, vol. 1, *The Improvised War, 1861–1862* (1940; repr., New York: Konecky & Konecky, 1971), 221.

84. According to historian Allan Nevins, Confederates took "28 fieldpieces of good quality, 8 of them rifled, with more than 100 rounds for each gun; some 500

muskets and 500,000 rounds of ammunition; and horses, wagons, caissons, and ambulances." Ibid.

85. On July 21, Davis boarded a train in Richmond and arrived at Manassas Junction, where he took a horse to brigadier general Joseph E. Johnston's field headquarters. By the time he arrived, Confederates had won the battle, and that evening, Davis met with Johnston and brigadier general P. G. T. Beauregard. William J. Cooper Jr., *Jefferson Davis: American* (New York: Vintage, 2001), 374; and Thomas, *The Confederate Nation*, 115–16.

86. The Union forces included roughly eighteen thousand men, while the Confederates had an estimated twelve thousand. See Ernest B. Furgurson, "The Battle of Bull Run: The End of Illusions," *Smithsonian Magazine* (August 2011), https://www.smithsonianmag.com/history/the-battle-of-bull-run-the-end-of-illusions-17525927/ (accessed September 4, 2018). For more information on the First Battle of Bull Run, see Davis, *Battle at Bull Run*.

87. At the First Battle of Bull Run, the 4th Alabama Infantry suffered dramatic losses, but played a crucial part in the attack on the artillery units. Of the 4th Alabama regiment's 750 men, 208 were wounded, 38 were killed (including four officers), and 3 were missing. For many friends and relatives in Marshall County, these casualties were their first personal losses in the war. Blair, 66; "Fourth Alabama Infantry Regiment," Alabama Archives, https://archives.alabama.gov/referenc/alamilor/4thinf.html (accessed September 5, 2018); Charles Rice, *Hard Times: The Civil War in Huntsville and North Alabama, 1861–1865* (Boaz, AL: Boaz Printing Co., 1995), 41–43; Stewart Sifakis, *Compendium of the Confederate Armies: Alabama* (New York Facts on File, 1992), 58–59; and Douglas Southall Freeman, *Lee's Lieutenants: A Study in Command*, vol. 1, *Manassas to Malvern Hill* (New York: Charles Scribner's Sons, 1946), 79. During the First Battle of Bull Run, Confederate brigadier general Barnard E. Bee said, "Look, there is Jackson with his Virginians standing like a stone wall against the enemy." This statement led to Thomas Jackson's nickname "Stonewall." Nevins, *War for the Union*, vol. 1, *The Improvised War*, 218.

88. William Arnold (1843–1861), the brother of the previously mentioned Carrie Arnold, enlisted at Huntsville, Alabama, in the 4th Alabama Infantry, Company I, on May 2, 1861. He died in the First Battle of Bull Run on July 21, 1861, and was buried in Virginia. See Alabama Civil War Soldiers, 1861–1865, film #M374, Roll 2; Global, Find A Grave Index for Burials at Sea and Other Select Locations, 1300s–Current; and 1850, 1860 US Federal Census, all at Ancestry.com. Cassie's cousin and fellow diarist Thomas Hubbard Hobbs gave a graphic description of the battlefield, including the scavenging of shoes, clothes, and weapons. Sifakis, *Compendium of the Confederate Armies: Alabama*, 68–69; and Axford, 238–39.

89. Willie, attached to the medical corps of the 9th Alabama Infantry, arrived too late for the First Battle of Bull Run.

90. The Battle of Wilson's Creek took place at Springfield, Missouri, on August 10, 1861. Confederate brigadier general Benjamin McCulloch engaged Union brigadier general Nathaniel Lyon, who became the first general killed during the Civil War. The Confederates prevailed. Many called this "The Bull Run of the West." There were 258 Union casualties and 279 Confederate casualties. Long, 107. For information on Lyon, see Phillips, *Damned Yankee*, 255–56. Brigadier general William J. Hardee organized troops in Arkansas. See Nathaniel C. Hughes Jr., *General William J. Hardee: Old Reliable* (1965; repr., Baton Rouge: Louisiana State Univ. Press, 1992).

91. Captain Isaac "Ike" Henry, a cousin of Cassie's brother-in-law Sam Henry, joined the 42nd Tennessee Infantry. "U.S. Civil War Soldiers, 1861–1865," M231, Roll 20, Ancestry.com. Archibald W. Ledbetter joined the 9th Regiment Alabama Infantry. Wounded at Salem, he was captured at Petersburg. See Alabama Civil War Centennial Commission, *Brief Historical Sketches of Military Organizations Raised in Alabama in the Civil War* (Tuscaloosa: Univ. of Alabama Press, 1961), 604; and US Civil War Soldiers, 1860–1865, Ancestry.com. An engineer by trade, captain George Ames lived with his wife Ettie and son Harry at a Guntersville hotel owned by Alabama militia general Samuel Rayburn. 1860 US Federal Census, Ancestry.com.

92. A private in the 55th Alabama Infantry, Hubbard Hobbs Fennell was the son of Dr. James W. Fennell's brother Hubbard Hobbs Fennell Sr. Family Trees, Ancestry.com.

93. A first lieutenant upon enlisting, Arthur Beard Carter later received a promotion to captain. He served in the 55th Alabama Infantry and was killed at the Battle of Peach Tree Creek, near Atlanta, on July 20, 1864. US Civil War Soldiers, 1861–1865; US Confederate Army Casualty Lists and Reports, 1861–1865; 1850 US Federal Census; US Civil War Soldier Records and Profiles, 1861–1865; and US, Find A Grave Index, 1600s–Current, all at Ancestry.com. See also *Brief Historical Sketches of Military Organizations Raised in Alabama in the Civil War*, 667.

94. On divided loyalties in Kentucky, see Anne E. Marshall, *Creating a Confederate Kentucky: The Lost Cause and Civil War Memory in a Border State* (Chapel Hill: Univ. of North Carolina Press, 2010).

95. In July, a state convention voted to remain with the Union, but Missouri's secessionist governor Claiborne Jackson set up a conflicting government in the state. Both the United States and the Confederacy coveted Missouri, but it was largely controlled by the former. Christopher Philips, *Missouri's Confederate: Claiborne Fox Jackson and the Creation of Southern Identity in the Border West* (Columbia: Univ. of Missouri Press, 2000).

96. The Battle of Ball's Bluff took place at Leesburg, Virginia, on October 21, 1861, and resulted in a Confederate victory. The Union had 49 dead, 158 injured, and 714 missing while the Confederacy had 36 dead, 117 injured, and 2 missing. Casualties included Union colonel Edward D. Baker. Long, 129.

97. The Battle of Belmont took place on November 7, 1861, in Mississippi County, Missouri. When Union brigadier general Ulysses Grant and his men entered the area, fighting broke out between them and the Confederates led by major general Leonidas Polk. When Confederate brigadier general Benjamin F. Cheatham arrived with reinforcements, Grant and his men retreated. Even so, Grant claimed victory, but Confederates retained control of the area. The dead included 120 Union and 105 Confederate soldiers. Long, 136.

98. On November 7, 1861, the Union navy sailed into Port Royal Sound in South Carolina and forced Confederates to abandon their positions at Fort Beauregard and Fort Walker. Thomas, *The Confederate Nation*, 125. See also Michael D. Coker, *The Battle of Port Royal* (Charleston: The History Press, 2009); and James M. McPherson, *War on the Waters: The Union and Confederate Navies, 1861–1865* (Chapel Hill: Univ. of North Carolina Press, 2012).

99. "Notice," *Wilmington Daily Journal*, November 14, 1861; and Pruitt, 43.

100. Cassie already mentioned the Battle of Bethel Church, the First Battle of Bull Run, the Battle of Leesburg, the Battle of Wilson's Creek, and the Battle of Belmont. Manassas is what Confederates called Bull Run, but Cassie might have been referring to a skirmish in the area. The Battle of Carnifex took place at Carnifex Ferry, Virginia, on September 10, 1861. The Confederates, led by brigadier general John B. Floyd, prevented Union general William Rosecrans's men from gaining ground and lost fewer men. However, given that his troops faced overwhelming numbers, Floyd retreated. Terry Lowry, *September Blood: The Battle of Carnifex Ferry* (Charleston, WV: Quarrier Press, 2011).

101. Cassie's figures are scuttlebutt.

102. Cassie had previously mentioned the Battle of Laurel Hill. "Tory" referred to someone who opposed the Confederacy and/or supported the United States. On Tories, see, for example, David Williams, "Civil War Dissent," *New Georgia Encyclopedia*,https://www.georgiaencyclopedia.org/articles/history-achaeoogy/civil-war-dissent (accessed September 7, 2018).

103. Led by major general Benjamin Butler and flag officer Silas Stringham, Union forces took Fort Hatteras in the Battle of Hatteras Inlet Batteries on August 28–29, 1861. Thomas, *The Confederate Nation*, 120; and "Hatteras Inlet Batteries," CWSAC Battle Summaries, American Battlefield Protection Program, https://www.nps.gov/abpp/battles/nc001.htm (accessed September 8, 2018).

104. On the Battle of Laurel Hill, see chap. 3, note 79.

105. The inauguration of Jefferson Davis and Alexander Stephens occurred at Richmond, Virginia, on February 22, 1862. Thomas, *The Confederate Nation*, 143.

106. On November 1, 1861, Winfield Scott, commanding general of the United States Army, retired. Already at an advanced age, he suffered from dropsy and vertigo. "Order Retiring Winfield Scott from Command," in *The Collected Works*

of Abraham Lincoln, vol. 5, ed. Roy P. Basler (New Brunswick, NJ: Rutgers Univ. Press, 1953), 10; and Nevins, *War for the Union*, vol. 1, *The Improvised War*, 297. In November, Union major general Henry W. Halleck was sent to Missouri to replace major general John Fremont. For more information on Halleck, see John F. Marszalek, *Commander of All Lincoln's Armies: A Life of General Henry W. Halleck* (Cambridge, MA: Belknap Press, 2004); and Stephen E. Ambrose, *Halleck: Lincoln's Chief of Staff* (1962; repr., Baton Rouge: Louisiana State Univ. Press, 1996).

107. Scott's long and distinguished military career spanned over fifty years, from 1808 to 1861. Pollard, 185–186.

108. On October 9, 1861, Confederate brigadier general Richard Anderson led 1,200 men to Union-held Santa Rosa Island. Hoping to force Union troops to exit the fort and fight, they attacked the 6th Regiment New York Volunteers. Union colonel Harvey Brown received reinforcements, and the Confederates fled. All of this derived from a Confederate attempt to take Fort Pickens. "Santa Rosa Island," American Battlefield Trust, https://www.battlefields.org/learn/maps/santa-rosa-island-october-9–1861 (accessed September 8, 2018). The Union lost sixty-seven men, while the Confederates lost eighty-seven. "Santa Rosa Island," CWSAC Battle Summaries, American Battlefield Protection Program, https://www.nps.gov/abpp/battles/fl001.htm (accessed September 8, 2018).

109. Though born in Alabama to Hubbard Hobbs Fennell and Mary Irene Smith, Thomas McDonough Fennell (1837–1907) had been living in Caldwell County, Texas, before the war. He served as a lieutenant in the 4th Regiment, Alabama Cavalry (Russell's), Companies C and D. Family Trees, Ancestry.com.

110. Isham Joseph Fennell (1842–1864), the son of Hubbard Hobbs Fennell and Mary Irene Smith. Family Trees, Ancestry.com.

111. In the original diaries, Cassie edged family deaths in black marks. Cassie's first cousin William B. Allison, a private in Company F of the 4th Alabama Infantry, died on October 16, 1861. US Find A Grave, 1600s–Current, Ancestry.com; and "Allison, William B.," Search for Soldiers, Civil War, National Park Service, https://www.nps.gov/civilwar/search-soldiers-detail.htm?soldierId=52C39C7A-DC7A-DF11-BF36-B8AC6F5D926A (accessed September 8, 2018). See also chap. 1, note 12.

112. The bombardment of Fort McRee took place on November 22–23, 1861, on Pensacola Bay. Union forces at Fort Pickens exchanged fire with Confederates at Fort McRee and Fort Barrancas. Fort Pickens remained under Union control for the duration of the war. "Fort McRee," National Park Service, https://www.nps.gov/guis/learn/historyculture/fort-mcree.htm (accessed September 8, 2018); and "Fort Pickens, Gulf Islands National Seashore," American Battlefield Trust, http://www.battlefields.org/visit/heritage-sites/fort-pickens-gulf-islands-national-seashore (accessed September 8, 2018).

113. Sam Henry, Cassie's brother-in-law.

114. According to historian James M. McPherson, "At the end of October the

Tennessee Unionists began burning bridges, attacking Confederate supply lines, and softening up the opposition for their Northern liberators." In November, "Confederate soldiers rounded up scores of Unionists, executed five, and imprisoned the rest." James M. McPherson, *Ordeal by Fire: The Civil War and Reconstruction* (New York: Alfred A. Knopf, 1982), 162.

115. On November 8, 1861, James Mason and John Slidell, Confederate commissioners traveling to Europe on the British sloop *Trent,* were captured by Union captain Charles Wilkes of the USS *San Jacinto*. After jail time in Boston and much diplomatic wrangling between the United States and Britain, the two were permitted to continue their journey. They were unsuccessful in persuading Britain to recognize the Confederacy as a nation. In John Allan Wyeth's book, *With Sabre and Scalpel,* he mentioned wild gossip about the Trent Affair. The grapevine had it that Slidell was returning with Emperor Napoleon and a million French soldiers to invade from the west by marching to Moscow and traveling to America via the Bering Strait. While it sounds farcical to contemporary ears, many such rumors were widely believed at the time. John A. Wyeth, *With Sabre and Scalpel: The Autobiography of a Soldier and Surgeon* (Charleston, SC: Bibliolife, 2009), 143. On the Trent Affair, see also Blair, 72; Axford, 249; and Pollard, 194–97.

116. George Eustis Jr. was secretary to Slidell, and James McFarland was secretary to Mason. See previous note.

117. The Battle of Rowlett's Station took place on December 17, 1861, near Munfordville, Kentucky. The 32nd Indiana Volunteer Infantry Regiment faced off with the 7th Texas Cavalry and the 1st Arkansas Battalion. While there was no clear winner, Union forces kept control of a Louisville & Nashville Railroad bridge across the Green River. There were forty Union dead and ninety-one Confederate dead. Among the casualties was Confederate colonel Benjamin Franklin Terry of the 8th Texas Cavalry. "Rowlett's Station," CWSAC Battle Summaries, American Battlefield Protection Program, https://www.nps.gov/abpp/battles/ky004.htm (accessed September 8, 2018); and Blair, 73.

118. This was part of the campaign in western Virginia and took place on December 13. Union brigadier general Robert H. Milroy attacked the Confederate troops at Camp Allegheny, who were led by colonel Edward Johnson. It was more or less a draw, as both retreated. There were 137 Union casualties and 146 Confederate casualties. Milroy was not among the dead. "Cheat Mountain," CWSAC Battle Summaries, American Battlefield Protection Program, https://www.nps.gov/abpp/battles/wv005.htm (accessed September 8, 2018); and Long, 148.

119. On December 25, 1861, Lincoln reluctantly agreed to release Mason and Slidell, and the two reached Britain on January 29, 1862. This was Lincoln's attempt to smooth things over with the English, who had been affronted by the Union capture of commissioners aboard a British vessel. Thomas, *The Confederate Nation*, 174. For information on the views the British and French had on the American Civil

War, see Don H. Doyle, *The Cause of All Nations: An International History of the American Civil War* (New York: Basic Books, 2015).

120. As historian James Marten explained, "The war deprived some children of even the simplest Christmas." Marten, *The Children's Civil War*, 121. On depression during Christmas, see, for example, "Christmas, 1861," *New York Times*, December 25, 1861.

4. *"Yonder Come the Yankees"*

1. In the Battle of Dranesville, which occurred on December 20, 1861, Confederate major general J. E. B. Stuart engaged brigadier general Edward Ord in a skirmish on the road to Georgetown, Virginia. Although the Confederate force had only 1,200 men, it suffered greater losses, specifically 71 deaths. The Union had 1,600 troops, and only lost 7. Blair, 74; Freeman, *Lee's Lieutenants*, vol. 1, 17; and Thomas W. Cutrer, "Ord, Edward Otho Cresap," *The Handbook of Texas Online*, https://tshaonline.org/handbook/online/articles/foro1 (accessed September 9, 2018). Lieutenant colonel James Benson Martin (1825–1861), a lawyer from Jacksonville, Alabama, served as a field and staff officer in the 10th Regiment, Alabama Infantry. Diarist Thomas Hubbard Hobbs called him Judge because Martin had served as a judge in the tenth judicial district in 1860. According to Hobbs, Martin predicted his own death and "expressed the conviction that the last day of his life had dawned." Axford, 249. See also 1850, 1860 US Federal Census; Alabama Civil War Soldiers, 1860–1865, both at Ancestry.com; and *Brief Historical Sketches of Military Organizations Raised in Alabama in the Civil War*, 605.

2. At Provincetown, they boarded the *HMS Rinaldo*, a British sloop. Long, 156.

3. On the contrary, the blockade proved quite effective, as by February 1862, the Confederacy only had thirty-three ships. Thomas, *The Confederate Nation*, 129. For further information on the blockade, see, for example, Robert B. Ekelund Jr. and Mark Thornton, *Tariffs, Blockades, and Inflation: The Economics of the Civil War* (Wilmington, DE: Scholarly Resources, Inc., 2004); and Dawson Carr, *Gray Phantoms of the Cape Fear: Running the Civil War Blockade* (Winston-Salem, NC: John F. Blair Publisher, 1998).

4. The Battle of Mill Springs (or Battle of Fishing Creek) took place in Kentucky on January 19–20, 1862, and resulted in a Union victory. Among the 125 Confederate dead lay brigadier general Felix Zollicoffer. Zollicoffer was shot and killed when he rode into enemy lines under the assumption that they were his own. Blair, 74; Axford, 251–52; Pollard, 199–201; Reverend Milus Eddings Johnston, *The Sword of Bushwhacker Johnston*, ed. Charles Rice (Huntsville, AL: Flint River Press, 1998), 24; and Clement Eaton, *A History of the Southern Confederacy* (New York: The Free Press, 1954), 156–57.

5. Sam Henry's brother John Bryan Henry (1830–1882) had married Martha C. Fennell, the daughter of Francis Marion Fennell and Isabella Allison of Bellefonte, Alabama. During the Civil War, John served as a private in the 9th Regiment, Alabama Infantry, Company K. 1850, 1860 US Federal Census; Alabama Civil War Muster Rolls, Roll 104, Archive Collection, SG025018–11; and US Civil War Soldiers, 1861–1865, Film #34, Roll 20, all at Ancestry.com.

6. The son of Margaret and Washington S. May of Marshall County, Alabama, Washington Webster May (1841–1862) enlisted in the 42nd Regiment, Tennessee Volunteers (captain Isaac Henry's unit). He died on January 17, 1862, in Clarksville, Tennessee. 1860 US Federal Census; US, Find A Grave Index, 1600s–Current; and US Confederate Soldiers Compiled Service Records, 1861–1865, all at Ancestry.com.

7. Prior to the war, Albert Russell practiced law in Huntsville, Alabama. He died on September 1, 1861, in Pensacola, Florida. The editor had no success identifying Richards. A private named John Gardner belonged to the 4th Regiment, Alabama Infantry. US Civil War Soldiers, 1861–1865; and US, Find A Grave Index, 1600s–Current, both at Ancestry.com.

8. Led by colonel James Garfield, the Union forces at Prestonsburg, Kentucky, forced the Confederates, led by brigadier general Humphrey Marshall, to move toward Virginia. Essentially, this stopped the campaign in eastern Kentucky. There were 2,100 Union troops and 2,500 Confederate troops. The Union lost one man, while the Confederacy lost ten. Blair, 75; and "Middle Creek," CWSAC Battle Summaries, American Battlefield Protection Program, https://www.nps.gov/abpp/battles/ky005.htm (accessed September 9, 2018). Colonel Robert C. Trigg (1830–1872) served in the 54th Virginia Infantry Regiment. David A. Powell, *The Chickamauga Campaign—A Mad Irregular Battle: From the Crossing of the Tennessee River Through the Second Day, August 22–September 19, 1863* (El Dorado Hills, CA: Savas Beatie, LLC, 2014). Cassie referenced brigadier general John C. Moore.

9. Battle of Mill Creek.

10. Union brigadier general Frederick W. Lander, leading roughly four thousand men, did evacuate but then successfully attacked Confederates at Blooming Gap, some thirty-two miles away. Frank Moore, ed., *Biographical Sketches of the Military and Naval Heroes, Statesmen, and Orators, Distinguished in the American Crisis of 1861–62* (New York: G. P. Putnam, 1862), 172.

11. Then seventy-two-year-old Tyler had supported secession. Long, 161; Eaton, 39; and Nevins, *War for the Union*, vol. 1, *The Improvised War*, 93–94. For more information on Tyler, see, for example, Edward P. Crapol, *John Tyler, The Accidental President*, rev. ed. (Chapel Hill: Univ. of North Carolina Press, 2012).

12. Queen Victoria's husband Prince Albert died on December 14, 1861. He had been heavily invested in the Trent Affair and, above all, had wanted a peaceful end

to the matter. Stanley Weintraub, *Uncrowned King: The Life of Prince Albert* (New York: The Free Press, 1997), 408, 433, 439; and Norman B. Ferris, *The Trent Affair: A Diplomatic Crisis* (Knoxville: Univ. of Tennessee Press, 1977). Queen Victoria's mother, also named Victoria, died on March 16, 1861. Julia Baird, *Victoria the Queen: An Intimate Biography of the Woman Who Ruled an Empire* (New York: Random House, 2016), 297–98.

13. Fort Henry was manned by Confederate brigadier general Lloyd Tilghman, who, in expectation of the Union approach, sent most of his garrison to Fort Donelson. On February 6, Union flag officer Andrew Foote came with four ironclads and three wooden gunboats. Tilghman and his remaining force fought but surrendered within two hours. Five Confederates died, as did eleven Union men. An enormous coup, possessing Fort Henry meant the United States could continue its advance further south. Long, 167; McIlwain, 73; Donald Stoker, *The Grand Design: Strategy of the U.S. Civil War* (New York: Oxford Univ. Press, 2010), 107–8; Eaton, 157–58; and Thomas, *The Confederate Nation*, 126–27.

14. In his inaugural address, Davis stated his belief that Maryland would join the Confederacy. He also maintained that the United States could not indefinitely fund the war. Stoker, 120–21.

15. John B. Floyd, formerly Virginia's governor, commanded fifteen thousand troops at Fort Donelson. These soldiers were in the divisions of brigadier generals Simon B. Buckner and Gideon J. Pillow. Ultimately, Floyd, Buckner, and Pillow decided to surrender. Floyd and Pillow retreated, while Buckner remained to negotiate terms. Buckner ended up surrendering unconditionally because Union brigadier general Ulysses Grant refused to accept anything less. The battle started on February 14, and Buckner surrendered on February 16. Thomas, *The Confederate Nation*, 127; and Freeman, 134. Brigadier general Thomas Hindman was not at Fort Donelson during this battle. Diane Neal and Thomas W. Kremm, *Lion of the South: General Thomas C. Hindman* (Macon: Mercer Univ. Press, 1997), 101–2.

16. Buckner had given up 11,500 troops in his unconditional surrender. Thomas, *The Confederate Nation*, 127. Estimates placed Union and Confederate losses at 507 and 327 men, respectively. "Fort Donelson," American Battlefield Trust, https://www.battlefields.org/learn/civil-war/battles/fort-donelson (accessed September 9, 2018). Wattie served in the 42nd Regiment, Tennessee Infantry. See, "Fennell, Isham W.," Search for Soldiers, Civil War, National Park Service, https://www.nps.gov/civilwar/search-soldiers.htm#q=%2242nd+Regiment,+Tennessee+Infantry&22&sort=Last_Name+asc,First_Name+asc (accessed September 9, 2018). Captain Henry Milner served in Company H of the 3rd Tennessee Regiment under lieutenant colonel Nathan Bedford Forrest. "H. Milner," US Civil War Soldiers, 1862–1865, Ancestry.com.

17. See chap. 3, note 83.

18. The Battle of Roanoke Island transpired on February 8, 1861, and Union forces won. Confederate general Henry Wise had just under two thousand men. The Confederacy lost twenty-three men, while the Union lost thirty-seven. Long, 168; and Eaton, 213.

19. The Battle of Hampton Roads took place on March 8–9, 1862, between the ironclads CSS *Virginia* (formerly the USS *Merrimack*) and the USS *Monitor*. It ended in a draw. See Thomas, *The Confederate Nation*, 131–32. At one point, the CSS *Virginia* sank the Union ship *Cumberland*. For more information on this battle, see, for example, Richard Snow, *Iron Dawn: The Monitor, the Merrimack, and the Civil War Sea Battle that Changed History* (New York: Scribner, 2017).

20. The Battle of Pea Ridge occurred at Elkhorn Tavern, Arkansas, on March 7–8, 1862, and the Confederates lost. Eaton claimed Confederate general Earl Van Dorn had 16,202 men, while Union general Samuel Curtis had 12,000. Nevins wrote that Van Dorn had 14,000, and Curtis had 11,000. During the battle, brigadier generals Benjamin McCulloch and James McIntosh were killed. Eaton, 155; Allan Nevins, *War for the Union*, vol. 2, *War Becomes Revolution, 1862–1863* (1940; repr., New York: Konecky & Konecky, 1960), 27; and Long 179–80. For more information on the Battle of Pea Ridge, see William L. Shea and Earl J. Hess, *Pea Ridge: Civil War Campaign in the West* (Chapel Hill: Univ. of North Carolina Press, 1992). Cassie referenced major general Sterling Price.

21. See previous note.

22. Cassie simplified a complex matter. Concerning Lee's role, a great deal of tension simmered between Davis and the Confederate Congress. Many Confederate congressmen wanted Davis to name Lee secretary of war. Rebelling against this pressure while asserting his own power, Davis instead charged Lee with management of the Confederate military. In this arrangement, Lee answered directly to Davis. Freeman, 163.

23. The Confederate Congress had voted to authorize the president to appoint a commanding general. Believing such a position threatened his own authority as commander in chief, Davis vetoed the act. Ibid.

24. On April 11, 1862, Union general Ormsby MacKnight Mitchel, commander of the 3rd Division of the Army of Ohio, captured Huntsville, Alabama, with relative ease. According to archivist Raneé Pruitt, "By 6 am his occupying troops consisted of Turchin's brigade, Kennett's cavalry, and Simonson's battery. It was a complete surprise. The Union captured about 200 prisoners, 15 locomotives, a large number of passenger, box, and platform cars, the telegraphic apparatus and offices, and two Southern mail trains." Pruitt, 43. One of Mitchel's primary motivations had been to take control of the city's stretch of the Memphis & Charleston Railroad. Mitchel also managed to capture 200 prisoners. See also, Malcolm C. McMillan, *The Alabama Confederate Reader* (Tuscaloosa: University of Alabama Press, 1963), 144-147.

When Mitchel's forces fired on a train trying to elude capture, a black man was shot in the neck and died. Rohr, 32. Of interest, Leroy Pope Walker (former C.S.A. Secretary of War) and John Bell (former Constitutional Union presidential candidate) were in Huntsville at the time of this occupation, and both managed to flee. Rohr, 30-33. Shortly after arriving in Huntsville, Mitchel arrested twelve prominent citizens: Bishop Henry C. Lay; John G. Wilson; George P. Beirne; Samuel Cruse; William McDowell; Dr. Thomas Fearn; Stephen W. Harris; William H. Moore; Gus Lyle Mastin; Thomas S. McCalley; William Acklen; and A.J. Withers. Rohr, 39; and Record, *A Dream Come True*, vol. 1, pp. 130. Even though many Huntsville residents were extremely unhappy with Mitchel's occupation, countless others had unionist sympathies. McIlwain, 81–82; John S. Sledge, *These Rugged Days in Alabama in the Civil War* (Tuscaloosa: Univ. of Alabama Press, 2017), 44; and Stephen D. Engle, *Don Carlos Buell: Most Promising of All* (Chapel Hill: Univ. of North Carolina Press, 1999), 243.

25. A Union victory and one of the bloodiest battles of the entire war, the Battle of Shiloh took place on April 6–7, 1862, near Pittsburgh Landing, Tennessee. Union general Ulysses Grant had roughly 42,000 troops, and Union general Don Carlos Buell had 20,000. Confederate general Albert Johnston had 45,000 soldiers at nearby Corinth, Mississippi, which was some twenty miles south. Grant wanted Corinth for its strategic railroad location. Johnston was killed at Shiloh, and though P. G. T. Beauregard took over command, he led a retreat back to Corinth. At Shiloh, there were an estimated 1,754 Union dead and 1,723 Confederate dead. Nathan Bedford Forrest sustained wounds in a rearguard action. Pollard, 237–42; and Long, 194–97. For more information about the Battle of Shiloh, see Jay Luvaas, Leonard Fullenkamp, and Stephen Bowman, eds., *Guide to the Battle of Shiloh* (Lawrence: Univ. Press of Kansas, 1996); D. W. Reed, *The Battle of Shiloh and the Organizations Engaged* (Knoxville: Univ. of Tennessee Press, 2008); and Timothy B. Smith, *The Untold Story of Shiloh: The Battle and the Battlefield* (Knoxville: Univ. of Tennessee Press, 2006).

26. A prosperous farmer, Cassie's uncle John Allison lived on Cave Spring Road near Maysville, Madison County, Alabama. On April 9–10, 1862, occupying Union forces from Huntsville arrested him. After being held a brief time, he was released. Katherine Duncan, "Chronology of the Fennells during the Civil War," VF, MCA, GA.

27. The editor scoured the soldier list of the 3rd Regiment Tennessee Cavalry and found no Ogden. Similar sounding names included Ogilvie and Oglesby. Search for Soldiers, Civil War, National Park Service, https://www.nps.gov/civilwar/search-soldiers.htm#q=ogden&fq%5B%5D=Slide%3A%22Confederacy%22&fq%5B%5D=State%3A%22Kentucky%22 (accessed September 8, 2018).

28. The Battle of Dam Number One happened at Lee's Mill, Virginia, on April 16, 1862. Confederate major general John Magruder managed to hold the

line. The Union lost 165 men, while the Confederacy lost 75. Long, 200; John V. Quarstein, *Yorktown's Civil War Siege: Drums Along the Warwick* (Charleston: The History Press, 2012), 97; and Thomas Settles, *John Bankhead Magruder: A Military Reappraisal* (Baton Rouge: Louisiana State Univ. Press, 2009), 174.

29. In the Battle of Valverde, which took place on February 20–21, 1862, Confederate brigadier general Henry Hopkins Sibley and his men managed to wrest Fort Craig from Union forces led by colonel Edward R. S. Canby. See, for example, Walter Pittman, *New Mexico and the Civil War* (Charleston: The History Press, 2011); Ray C. Colton, *The Civil War in the Western Territories: Arizona, Colorado, New Mexico, and Utah* (Norman: Univ. of Oklahoma Press, 1984); and Marion C. Grinstead, *Life and Death of a Frontier Fort: Fort Craig, New Mexico, 1854–1885* (Socorro, NM: Socorro County Historical Society, 1973).

30. Although Cassie exaggerated, instances of Union soldiers behaving atrociously toward blacks did occur in the area. For example, in nearby Athens, Union colonel Ivan Turchin turned a blind eye while his men ransacked the city, causing damage in excess of $55,000. It was said that during this marauding, they raped a fourteen-year-old slave. Christopher B. Paysinger, "Sack of Athens," *Encyclopedia of Alabama*, http://www.encyclopediaofalabama.org/article/h-1819 (accessed February 1, 2020); and Rice, *Hard Times*, 224–25. Locals deemed Turchin a monster, and his methods were frowned upon by many of his peers. In the aftermath, Turchin was court-martialed for the sack of Athens. However, Lincoln, following a meeting with Turchin's wife, set aside the guilty verdict and promoted him to brigadier general. Pruitt, 48; and McMillan, *Alabama Confederate Reader*, 147. At Lewis's Bluff in 1862, some of Ormsby MacKnight Mitchel's troops had "forced Matt [Gray]," a slave, "and a captured Confederate soldier to mount a mule and tied their feet together beneath the animal." They then scared the mule into the Tennessee River. Gray later reflected, "I don't know how we ever got out alive. They musta just misfiggered that mule, 'cause it swum right out on the other bank. I didn't swoller so much water, but I ain't had no use for Yankees since." Rice, *Hard Times*, 224–25.

31. On March 21–22, Union forces attempted but failed to conquer the Cumberland Gap. Dallas Bogan, "Official Records of Civil War Recount Various Skirmishes in Powell's Valley, Cumberland Gap," History of Campbell County, Tennessee, https://www.tngenweb.org/campbell/hist-bogan/skirmish.html (accessed September 9, 2018).

32. The son of John D. and Sarah Fennell who lived in Holly Springs, Mississippi, John P. Fennell (1836–1878), had enlisted in the 9th Regiment, Mississippi Infantry, Company B, as a private in 1861. His unit fought battles in Kentucky, Tennessee, and Georgia. In 1862, he served in the 2nd Kentucky Cavalry (Duke's Cavalry). US, Find A Grave Index, 1600s–Current; US Civil War Soldiers, 1861–1865, Film #M232, Roll 13; All US, Confederate Soldiers Compiled Service Records, 1861–1865; and US Civil

War Prisoner of War Records, 1861–1865, Roll M598–53, all at Ancestry.com. See also Pollard, 638.

33. The editor found no evidence that Huntsville's occupying forces killed slaves. See chap. 4, note 30.

34. On May 1, 1862, Union admiral David Farragut occupied New Orleans after shelling the city. The largest trade center in North America, New Orleans was vital to control of the Mississippi River. Its loss spread a feeling of dejection across the Confederacy. Pollard, 246–54; Thomas, *The Confederate Nation*, 147; Stoker, 133–38; and Eaton, 176.

35. South Carolina remained under Confederate control, and not until November 1862 did rampant support for the Confederacy began to wane among its inhabitants. Of note, the western part of South Carolina had many unionists. Stoker, 74. Cassie may have been referring to the loss of Fort Macon, North Carolina, to Union brigadier general John Parke on April 25, 1862. Long, 204.

36. Two railroads converged at Corinth, Mississippi, where the Mobile & Ohio Railroad met the Memphis & Charleston Railroad. The Siege of Corinth, which lasted from April 29 to May 30, resulted in a Confederate retreat. The city fell without a fight. Union forces took over Corinth and, thus, control of its railroads. Blair, 81; and Timothy B. Smith, *Corinth 1862: Siege, Battle, Occupation* (Lawrence: Univ. Press of Kansas, 2012), xii.

37. There had been skirmishes at Bridgeport, Alabama, and Paint Rock, Alabama. Long, 204–5. Colonel John Beatty, general Ormsby MacKnight Mitchel's provost marshal, became furious over an attack near Paint Rock. Confederates had shot at train cars and, in doing so, injured six Union soldiers. Afterward, Beatty threatened the locals by warning that for every telegraph line cut, a home would be burned, and for every round fired at a train, a man would be hanged. If such actions persisted, Beatty announced that he had no qualms about burning everything from Decatur to Bridgeport. Sledge, 48. On the history of Bridgeport, see Kennamer, 171-173; and *History of Jackson County, Alabama* (Clanton, AL: Heritage Publishing Consultants, Inc., 1998), 1-2. On the history of Paint Rock, see Kennamer, 157-159; and *History of Jackson County, Alabama*, 7-8.

38. On April 16, 1862, the 24th Illinois Infantry occupied Decatur, Alabama. Those Confederates who were guarding Decatur raised a drawbridge to prevent the Union forces from crossing. Threatened with shelling, however, they lowered the bridge. McIlwain, 82. According to Dr. William Wagner, a surgeon with the 24th Illinois Regiment, these Confederates even tried to burn the bridge but failed. Mitchel later ordered his own men to burn the bridge. Dr. William Wagner, *History of the 24th Illinois Volunteer Infantry Regiment* (Chicago: Illinois Staats Zeitung, 1864). For more information on Decatur, see Robert Dunnavant, *Decatur, Alabama: Yankee Foothold in Dixie, 1861–1865* (Athens, AL: Pea Ridge Press, 1995).

39. Camden, then located in Madison County, Alabama, no longer exists. "Low Dutch" may have meant those with ancestry from Germany or the Netherlands. In Huntsville, occupying Union troops had varied ethnicities.

40. On April 28–29, skirmishes occurred at Bridgeport, Alabama. Long, 204–5.

41. On April 29, fighting took place in the Cumberland Gap. Long, 205.

42. Union major general Ormsby MacKnight Mitchel and Confederate major general Sterling Price. Many Huntsville residents loathed Mitchel to the extent that, when he left the city in July, they rejoiced. When Mitchel died later that year, the *Huntsville Daily Confederate* published the following: "No man ever had more winning ways to excite the people's hatred than he. We have no space to do justice to his vices—virtues he showed none, in dealing with the people of North Alabama." Deborah Storey, "Civil War: 150th Anniversary of the Union Occupation in Huntsville," *Huntsville Times*, April 15, 2002. Much of the acrimony aimed at Mitchel had to do with his insistence that an oath of allegiance be given in order to enter or leave town and even to buy provisions. At first, Mitchel had released captured Confederate soldiers who took the oath of allegiance. After two rebels managed to escape, however, he ceased the practice. Rohr, 36-37.

43. As historian Drew Gilpin Faust explained, "God's punishment, expressed in interim defeats or failures, did not mean that ultimate success was impossible." Drew Gilpin Faust, *Mothers of Invention: Women of the Slaveholding South in the American Civil War* (Chapel Hill: Univ. of North Carolina Press, 1996), 182. For more information on women and religion during the Civil War, see Faust, 179–95.

44. On April 25, New Orleans surrendered to Union admiral David G. Farragut. McPherson, *Ordeal by Fire*, 231. Mobile had yet to surrender.

45. On April 28, 1862, military engagement occurred at the rail bridge at Paint Rock (Camden), Alabama, in Jackson County. A Confederate force of 250 soldiers and some home guard battled a small detachment of 27 men belonging to the 19th Wisconsin Infantry. Losses were light. Six of the Union men were injured. One Confederate was injured and another was killed. "History of the Town of Paint Rock, Alabama," *Paint Rock News*, https://paintrockal.webs.com/historyofpaintrock.htm (accessed September 13, 2018).

46. Hubbard H. Fennell served in Company G of the 55th Regiment, Alabama Infantry. Search for Soldiers," Civil War, National Park Service, https://www.nps.gov/civilwar/search-soldiers-detail.htm?soldierId=DDD2289C-DC7A-DF11-BF36-B8AC6F5D926A (accessed September 13, 2018).

47. Whitesburg is south of Huntsville, Alabama, near Ditto's Landing on the Tennessee River.

48. This entry is on a page full of various-sized doodles and scribbles. On this page, Cassie wrote many versions of her name ranging from "C.M.F." and "C.M. Fennell" to "Cassie M. Fennell, Guntersville, Marshall, Alabama," "Cassie

M. Fennell of Alabama," and "Cassie M. Fennell on the road from Bellefonte, 1860." On this page, written inside a drawn box, Cassie wrote, "April 24th 1862, The Yankees are now in Guntersville, have been at Warrenton and are coming back this evening." At the top left of the page, she wrote, "J. H. Moore, 1862." At the bottom left, she wrote, "End of 2d Vo., July 10, 1862."

49. The Battle of South Mills, between Confederate colonel Ambrose Wright and Union brigadier general Jesse Reno, took place in Camden County, North Carolina, on April 19, 1862. Though outnumbered, the Confederates held their own, and Reno withdrew. On the Battle of South Mills, see John G. Barrett, *The Civil War in North Carolina* (1963; repr., Chapel Hill: Univ. of North Carolina Press, 1995), 113.

50. Two men named James Scott lived in nearby Claysville. The first, James C. Scott, took in boarders. The second, John M. Scott, lived with a wife and seven children. 1850, 1860 US Federal Census, Ancestry.com.

51. According to an April 28th entry by Huntsville diarist Mary Jane Chadick, "General Mitchell has been in a rage all the week on account of the cutting of the telegraph wires, the tearing up of the railroad tracks, firing into trains, and holds the citizens responsible for the same, having had 12 of the most prominent arrested." Rohr, 37-38.

52. Isham Jordan Fennell (1811–1891) was born in North Carolina to Isham Fennell (1784–1832) and Temperance Jordan (1789–1843). By 1860, he farmed in Madison County, Alabama, had an estimated worth of $130,000, and owned eighty-three slaves. 1850, 1860 US Federal Census; and US, Find A Grave Index, 1600s–Current, both at Ancestry.com.

53. On April 8, 1862, Confederates surrendered Island No. 10. They had been using the strategically located island to prevent Union forces from navigating the Mississippi River. Prior to this surrender, the Confederate garrison there had seven thousand men. McPherson, *Ordeal by Fire*, 229–30.

54. This may have been news related to the Siege of Corinth.

55. The first battle of the Peninsula Campaign and a Confederate loss, the Battle of Williamsburg transpired on May 5, 1862, in Williamsburg, Virginia. Confederate lieutenant general James Longstreet led a counterattack against Union brigadier general Joseph Hooker. Accounts varied, but the Union lost roughly 466 men, while the Confederacy lost 354. Drew A. Gruber, "The Battle of Williamsburg," *Encyclopedia Virginia*, Virginia Humanities, https://www.encylopediavirginia.org/Williamsburg_The_Battle_of#start_entry (accessed September 13, 2018); Sifakis, *Compendium of the Confederate Armies: Alabama*, 68; Blair, 84; McPherson, *Ordeal by Fire*, 238; and Pollard, 267–68.

56. On May 4, 1862, Confederate lieutenant general Thomas "Stonewall" Jackson and his troops arrived in Staunton, Virginia. For more information on Staunton, see Catherine M. Wright, "Staunton During the Civil War," *Encyclopedia Virginia*, Virginia Humanities, https://www.encyclopediavirginia.org/Staunton

_During_the_Civil_War (accessed September 13, 2018); and James Robertson, *Stonewall Jackson: The Man, The Soldier, The Legend* (New York: MacMillan Publishing, 1997).

57. Confederate brigadier general John Hunt Morgan had garnered fame for raiding in Ohio, Kentucky, Tennessee, and Indiana. Essentially, Kentucky had two governments, one Union and one Confederate. The latter was in Bowling Green. The Battle of Lebanon took place in Lebanon, Tennessee, on May 5, 1862, when Union colonel Frank Wolford attacked and forced Morgan to flee. Thomas, *The Confederate Nation*, 249; and James A. Ramage, *Rebel Raider: The Life of General John Hunt Morgan* (Lexington: Univ. Press of Kentucky, 1986), 51; 84.

58. The Siege of Yorktown took place from April 5–May 4, 1862, and resulted in a Confederate withdrawal. McPherson, *Ordeal by Fire*, 237–38.

59. In 1862, prices escalated in north Alabama. Salt was $80 per sack; butter was $3 per pound; pork was 10 cents per pound; and cotton was 8 cents per pound. Inflation was commonplace. Record, 131–37; and McMillan, *The Land Called Alabama*, 198–99.

60. Union forces took Fort Pulaski on April 11, 1862. Consequently, they gained control of the Savannah River. Thomas, *The Confederate Nation*, 147.

61. Sam Henry was accused of "misbehavior" at the Battle of Williamsburg and court-martialed. Rumor held that he had acted with cowardice by hiding behind some logs while his men fought. His troops, however, believed him much wronged and blamed political intrigue. They respected him so much that, after these accusations and Sam's ultimate resignation, many of his troops deserted the 9th Alabama Infantry and joined new regiments back home. An undaunted Sam joined a cavalry unit shortly after his return to Marshall County. Bessie Martin, *A Rich Man's War, A Poor Man's Fight: Desertion of Alabama Troops from the Confederate Army*, introduction by Mark A. Weitz (Tuscaloosa: Univ. of Alabama Press, 2003), 67; and Spencer Clack to John Clack, February 15, 1863, VF, MCA, GA.

62. The Confederates retreated at the Battle of Williamsburg. Confederates lost 354 men. Long, 207.

63. Willie served as a field surgeon in the 9th Alabama Infantry. Wattie served in the 42nd Regiment, Tennessee Infantry, and was taken prisoner at the Battle of Fort Donelson. "Fennell, Isham W.," Search for Soldiers, Civil War, National Park Service, https://www.nps.gov/civilwar/search-soldiers.htm#q=%2242nd+Regiment,+Tennessee+Infantry%22&sort=Last_Name+asc,First_Name+asc (accessed September 13, 2018); and "J. W. Fennell," Alabama Civil War Soldiers, 1860–1865, Ancestry.com.

64. Confederate propaganda claimed that women better exhibited honor by wearing homespun, homemade textile goods. Though many women may have been embarrassed to wear homespun, the blockade left them little choice. Many men struggled with seeing their wives and daughters make homespun because such work had traditionally been done by slaves. Faust, *Mothers of Invention*, 46–47.

65. Calico was a popular cotton fabric, usually a print, used to make an array of clothing. Shoes were few and far between, to the extent that many went barefooted. Faust, *Mothers of Invention*, 222.

66. Located near Warrenton on the north side of the Tennessee River, "Beard's Bluff" is called "Street's Bluff" today.

67. The Battle of Front Royal took place at Front Royal, Virginia, on May 23, 1862. Lieutenant general Thomas "Stonewall" Jackson, along with sixteen thousand troops, took back Front Royal from Union forces led by colonel John R. Kenly. Long, 215. For more information on Front Royal, see S. C. Gwynne, *Rebel Yell: The Violence, Passion, and Redemption of Stonewall Jackson* (New York: Scribner, 2015).

68. The Battle of Winchester occurred at Winchester, Virginia, on May 25, 1862, between the forces of Confederate lieutenant general Thomas "Stonewall" Jackson and Union major general Nathaniel P. Banks. The Union forces retreated. Of the 16,000 Confederate troops, 68 were killed. Of the roughly 8,000 Union troops, 1,714 were either missing or taken prisoner. Long, 216.

69. The editor had difficulty identifying captain Taylor of Huntsville.

70. See chap. 4, note 32.

71. Joseph Turner (J. T.) Hollowell (1838–1885) was born in Madison County, Alabama, to a wealthy farmer/merchant who later moved the family to Holly Springs, Mississippi. J. T. graduated from the University of Virginia and, by 1858, had a home in Huntsville. In 1862, he enlisted in the 9th Regiment, Mississippi Infantry, Company G, as a private. He was later listed as a sergeant in the 2nd Kentucky Cavalry (Duke's Cavalry), Company F. By war's end, he had become a second lieutenant. 1850, 1860, 1880 US Federal Census; US, Find A Grave Index, 1600s–Current; US School Catalogs, 1765–1935; US Civil War Soldiers, 1861–1865; and US, Confederate Soldiers Compiled Service Records, 1861–1865, all at Ancestry.com.

72. The Jackson County Courthouse at Bellefonte, Alabama, was burned sometime during the war. Union forces burned the town of Bellefonte in 1863. According to Union colonel William P. Lyon, his 13th Wisconsin Cavalry was blamed for the 1863 burning, but he disclaimed credit, insisting the arsonists had been general William T. Sherman's troops. "Excerpts from Writings of Col. William P. Lyon and the 13th Wisconsin Cavalry Reports and Letters," Civil War, VF, MCA, GA. It should be noted, however, that local historian John Robert Kennamer Sr. wrote that Federals may have set fire to the town, but did not target the courthouse. In fact, Kennamer believed the courthouse had fallen victim to a local arsonist whose name he refused to reveal. Kennamer, 134-35. Near Larkinsville at Sauta Cave, the Confederates mined nitre. During April 1862, Union general Ormsby MacKnight Mitchel burned and destroyed the mining operations in Larkinsville. Kennamer, 48–49. Woodville, located close to a railroad bridge over the Paint Rock River, endured a number of military encounters. The first took place on April 28, 1862,

between the 10th Wisconsin Infantry and Confederate troops. The Union forces managed to keep control of the bridge. Rice, *Hard Times*, 302–3.

73. Major general Benjamin Butler arrived in New Orleans on May 1, 1862, and occupied this vital port city. He became increasingly frustrated with how rudely local women treated his men. Women avoided the Union troops, spit at them, and even mooned them. Chester G. Hearn, *When the Devil Came Down to Dixie: Ben Butler in New Orleans* (Baton Rouge: Louisiana State Univ. Press, 1997), 101. Some women threw the contents of chamber pots out windows and onto unsuspecting men below. One such victim was Admiral David Farragut. Hearn, 102. In response to what he deemed trashy, unladylike behavior, Butler issued General Order No. 28, which proclaimed that if any woman "by word, gesture, or movement, insult or show contempt for any officer or soldier of the United States, she shall be regarded and held liable to be treated as a woman of the town plying her avocation." Hearn, 103. Butler's order sparked outrage in the United States, abroad, and especially in the Confederacy. On top of the women's order, Butler had commanded the execution of William Mumford, who was accused of "desecrating the flag." Hearn, 134–38. In addition, Butler had given residents a choice of taking the oath of allegiance or losing their property. Hearn, 166. In New Orleans, the vitriol aimed at Butler became so great that some Confederates placed his portrait at the base of their chamber pots. Hearn, 108. Due to his actions in New Orleans, Confederates began referring to him as Benjamin "Beast" Butler.

74. Many Huntsville citizens faced search and seizures from the occupying Union troops, and according to Mitchel himself, "the most terrible outrages—robberies, rapes, arson and plundering—are being committed by lawless brigands and vagabonds connected with the army." Rohr, 38.

75. On May 30, 1862, major general Henry Halleck's Union forces shelled Corinth, but Confederate general P. G. T. Beauregard had already ordered his men to vacate the city. By the time Halleck discovered their absence, he had expended much time and effort. While embarrassed, Halleck at least had Corinth and its railroads. Engle, 251. Disease had inflicted great damage to those in Corinth, both military and civilian. The city also had a great number of soldiers who had been wounded at Shiloh. Larry J. Daniel, *Soldiering in the Army of Tennessee: A Portrait of Life in a Confederate Army* (Chapel Hill: Univ. of North Carolina Press, 1991), 66–69.

76. Such confiscations happened frequently. Though Cassie failed to mention it, on May 10, Union troops had burned Confederate supplies and stolen horses in Guntersville. Local ladies complained that these soldiers had used profane language and offended sensibilities. Untitled, *Augusta Chronicle*, May 10, 1862.

77. On June 7, 1862, major Ormsby MacKnight Mitchel shelled and attacked Chattanooga, Tennessee, but failed to take the city. Long, 223.

78. Cassie may have been thinking of the Battle of Seven Pines, which transpired on May 31–June 1 and resulted in a Union retreat. Although under investigation for

his questionable behavior at the Battle of Williamsburg, Sam Henry fought in the Battle of Seven Pines. US American Civil War Regiments, 1861–1866, Ancestry.com. She may also have been speaking of the Battle of Cross Keys, which took place on June 8, 1862, in Rockingham County, Virginia, or the Battle of Port Republic, which occurred the following day. McPherson, *Ordeal by Fire*, 241–42.

79. Union forces took Memphis on June 6, 1862. Eaton, 180; and Thomas, *The Confederate Nation*, 162.

80. Brigadier general James Shields and major general Nathaniel P. Banks.

81. Colonel Turner Ashby, a cavalry officer under Thomas "Stonewall" Jackson, was killed on June 6, 1862, near Harrisburg, Virginia. Curt Anders, *Fighting Confederates* (New York: G. P. Putnam's Sons, 1968), 210. For more information, see Paul Christopher Anderson, *Blood Image: Turner Ashby in the Civil War and the Southern Mind* (Baton Rouge: Louisiana State Univ. Press, 2006), 10.

82. Johnston sustained a bad shoulder wound at the Battle of Seven Pines. Anders, 67–68.

83. Soldier motivation ranged from adventure and money to duty and honor. There were also soldiers motivated by the quest to free slaves. Bell Irvin Wiley, *The Life of Billy Yank: The Common Soldier of the Union* (Indianapolis: The Bobbs-Merrill Co., 1952; Baton Rouge: Louisiana State Univ. Press, 1998), 36–40.

84. Charity (Allison) Cooper Lea (1801–1872), Cassie's maternal aunt who lived in Madison County, Alabama. For more information, see appendix 1: Family Biographies.

85. Cassie may have been referring to the Battle of Mechanicsville, which took place on June 26, 1862, in Hanover County, Virginia. The Confederates lost 1,484 of their roughly 14,000 men. The Union lost 361 of their roughly 15,000 men. Long, 230–31.

86. The Confederacy repeatedly attempted to secure an alliance by enticing France with the promise of trade. Confederate politicians hoped that the French might break the Union blockade, but France did not want to risk war with the United States. Doyle, 203. France remained neutral for the duration of the war and never recognized the Confederacy, although French citizens had varied stances. For more information on the French position, see, for example, Charles Adams, *Slavery, Secession, & Civil War: Views from the United Kingdom and Europe, 1856–1865* (Lanham, MD: The Scarecrow Press, Inc., 2007), 469–82.

87. France hoped to expand its empire by developing a foothold in Latin America. French forces had failed to take Puebla, Mexico, on May 5, 1862. Edward Shawcross, *France, Mexico and Informal Empire in Latin America, 1820–1867: Equilibrium in the New World* (New York: Palgrave MacMillan, 2018), 2.

88. Fought near Charleston on June 16, 1862, the Battle of Secessionville ended with the Confederates maintaining control of the harbor. Long, 227.

89. Union admiral David Farragut reached Vicksburg on May 18, 1862, with five warships, a few transporters, and roughly 1,400 men under the command of brigadier general Thomas Williams. Several days later, on May 25, Union forces began firing on Vicksburg, but the city refused to surrender. Farragut used batteries on June 28, but the townspeople remained defiant. Sam Mitcham, *Vicksburg: The Bloody Siege that Turned the Tide of the Civil War* (Washington, DC: Regnery History, 2018), 5–9.

90. On June 6, 1862, the United States issued General Orders No. 60 categorizing medical officers as non-combatants, and it was recognized by general Robert E. Lee on June 17. On June 26, the Confederacy issued General Orders No. 45, a similar mandate that allowed for the unconditional release of medical officers. Cunningham, 130; and "Exchange Prisoners in the Civil War," Shotgun's Home of the American Civil War, https://civilwarhome.com/prisonerexchange.html (accessed September 16, 2018). This agreement ceased in mid-summer 1863 but resumed that November. Cunningham, 131–32. Because he was an assistant surgeon, Willie fell under the category of non-combatant. Using Cassie's diary entries, the autobiography of Dr. John Allan Wyeth, and Ancestry.com, the editor found discrepancies about Willie. Cassie claimed that Willie had been taken prisoner at the Battle of Williamsburg and did not attain release until shortly before the Battle of Gaines's Mill which took place on June 27, 1862. However, Wyeth wrote that Willie exhibited great valor at the Battle of Seven Pines which transpired May 31–June 1, 1862. In his words, Willie "had borrowed a gun and gone into the fight" because "the wounded were not coming in fast enough to suit him." Wyeth indicated that Willie sustained severe injuries at the Battle of Seven Pines, but Cassie made no mention of her brother being seriously hurt until Gaines's Mill. Wyeth, *With Sabre and* Scalpel, 202–3. In Alabama, Civil War Soldiers, Willie's engagement information is listed as follows: "Absent on duty: Seizure of Yorktown 1862/04/00, Williamsburg 1862/05/05; Absent Captured: Seven Pines 1862/06/01; Absent Wounded: Gaines Mill 1862/06/27, Fraziers Farm 1862/06/30, Manassas #2 1862/08/30." "J.W. Fennell," Alabama, Civil War Soldiers, 1860-1865, Ancestry .com. Fort Monroe is in Hampton Roads, Virginia. "Mrs. Clare" may have been Margaretta Clair, a forty-four-year-old who lived in Washington, DC's Fourth Ward. She resided with her daughter Adell and son-in-law William H. Clegett. This family may have had links to Alabama, as Margaretta named one of her daughters Alabama. Years before, when Cassie attended the Young Ladies' Institute, she mentioned meeting a "Mrs. Claget," a "Mrs. Clare," and a "Miss Clare." 1860 US Federal Census, Ancestry.com.

91. Definitions of "bushwhacker" vary, but on the whole, the word was used to describe guerillas, snipers, and thieves who, often with stealth, robbed, terrorized, and killed victims. As explained by historian W. Hunter Lesser, "Soldiers were an

easy mark for these cold-blooded killers—known derisively as 'bushwhackers.'" W. Hunter Lesser, *Rebels at the Gate: Lee and McClellan on the Front Line of a Nation Divided* (Naperville, IL: Sourcebooks, Inc., 2004), 150.

92. Originally from Tennessee, Jere C. Cornwell (1820–1862) lived in Guntersville with his wife Mary. In 1860, he had real estate valued at $4,000 and a personal estate worth $29,700. 1850, 1860 US Federal Census, Ancestry.com.

93. Union general Don Carlos Buell, along with roughly forty thousand troops, arrived in Huntsville in late June. For a variety of reasons, Buell and Mitchel did not get along. For one thing, Mitchel thought Buell too reserved and hesitant a commander. After failing to come to any agreement with Buell, Mitchel asked for a short period of leave. Shortly thereafter, Secretary of War Stanton called Mitchel to Washington, DC. Many Huntsville locals loathed both Mitchel and Buell but thought the latter a smidge more tolerable because he exhibited more leniency. Engle, 264–67; and Pruitt, 44. According to historian Stephen D. Engle, "While his army occupied Huntsville, Buell insisted that his soldiers not interfere with the ordinary business and trade of the town, except where marked disloyalty forfeited individual rights and transactions." Engle, 267.

94. The Battle of Gaines's Mill took place on June 27, 1862. This Confederate victory deterred McClellan from continuing to Richmond. McPherson, *Ordeal by Fire*, 246–48. This battle was part of the Seven Days Battles that, as a whole, resulted in 20,000 Confederate casualties and 16,500 Union casualties. McPherson, *Ordeal by Fire*, 248.

95. Colonel Cadmus Wilcox served as the brigade commander for the 9th Alabama Infantry. Sifakis, *Compendium of the Confederate Armies: Alabama*, 68. Wilcox's brigade was under lieutenant general James Longstreet.

96. Arthur Hopkins (Hop) Beard (1843–1928), the son of Arthur C. Beard and Pheriba Jane Moore (1816–1853), lived at Beard's Bluff (now Street's Bluff) on the Tennessee River. In 1862, he enlisted in the Confederate Army as a sergeant. After a later discharge, he became a first lieutenant in the 4th Regiment, Alabama Cavalry, Company, I, the same unit raised by Cassie's brother Willie. At some point, Hop lost a hand in the war. In January 1865, Hop's sister Julia Ann wrote a poem titled "The Burning of Our Home." This was in response to Union forces burning the family home. 1850, 1860, 1870, 1880 US Federal Census; Tennessee, Deaths and Burials Index, 1874–1955; Civil War Records & Profiles, 1861–1865; and US Civil War Soldiers, 1861–1865, all at Ancestry.com.

97. On July 1, 1862, Union and Confederate forces engaged in a skirmish near Holly Springs, Mississippi. Union brigadier general James W. Denver had been ordered to halt the advance. One Union soldier was killed and three were wounded. "J. W. Denver to Major General William T. Sherman," Moscow, Tennessee, July 15, 1862, Working on and guarding the Railroad then on to Memphis (June 2-July 21, 1862), https://www.48ovvi.org/oh48hd1.html (accessed September 15, 2018); and "About Holly

Springs," City of Holly Springs, Mississippi, website, http://www.hollyspringsmsus .com/about-holly-springs/ (accessed September 15, 2018).

98. Cassie's figures referred to the Seven Days Battles. Brigadier general George McCall had been taken prisoner at the Battle of Frayser's Farm (Battle of Glendale), which occurred on June 30, 1862, in Henrico County, Virginia. Brian K. Burton, *Extraordinary Circumstances: The Seven Days Battles* (Bloomington: Indiana Univ. Press, 2001), 297.

99. John Allison, the son of David and Sarah Smith Allison.

100. The son of Ira and Rebecca Hobbs of Limestone County, Alabama, Thomas Hubbard Hobbs served as a captain in the Limestone Troopers and eventually joined the 9th Regiment, Alabama Infantry, as a first lieutenant. According to field surgeon's notes, he was injured at the Battle of Gaines's Mill and succumbed to his wounds in September. He was buried at Lynchburg, Virginia, but his family erected a marker at a graveyard in Athens, Alabama. 1850, 1860 US Federal Census; US, Find A Grave Index, 1600s–Current; Alabama Civil War Muster Rolls, 1861–1865, Roll #100, Archive Collection SGO205018-7; and US Find A Grave Index, 1607–2012, all at Ancestry.com. See also *Brief Historical Sketches of Military Organizations raised in Alabama in the Civil War*, 604; and Axford, 253–54. See also introduction, note 5.

101. Isham Fennell, the son of Isham Harrison Fennell (1806–1880) and Margaret Bedford (1807–1845), was a first cousin to Cassie. Though born in Alabama, by 1860, he and his family lived in Guadeloupe, Texas. In 1861, he enlisted in the 4th Regiment, Texas Infantry, Company D, as a private. Wounded at the Battle of Gaines's Mill, he died on October 25, 1862. 1850 US Federal Census; US Civil War Soldiers, 1861, 1865; and US Civil War Soldier War Records and Profiles, 1861–1865, all at Ancestry.com. See also Axford, 69; and Louis Wyeth, "The History of Marshall County," Civil War, VF, MCA, GA.

102. Beginning on July 4, 1862, Confederate general John Hunt Morgan led raids across Kentucky. Nathan Bedford Forrest had been conducting raids in middle Tennessee that July. Anders, 124; and McPherson, *Ordeal by Fire*, 288–90. In a July 22, 1862, letter addressed to George Dunlap, Morgan wrote that he had "captured sixteen cities" and "destroyed millions of dollars' worth of United States property." Jacquelyn Proctor Reeves, "Thunderbolt of the Confederacy," in *North Alabama Civil War Generals: 13 Wore Gray, the Rest Blue: A Selection of Essays from the Authors of the Tennessee Valley Civil War Round Table* (Madison, AL: Tennessee Valley Civil War Roundtable), 61.

103. Union brigadier general Robert Latimer McCook (1827–1862) had been shot on August 5, 1862, in a skirmish near Huntsville. Newspaper reports varied. In the Union version, a dysentery-stricken McCook, being transported by ambulance, was shot by guerillas. In this scenario, one hundred to two hundred Confederate guerillas fired into the ambulance. One shot entered his hat, missing his head, while another hit his stomach. In the Confederate version, regulars attacked the Union

caravan. Though general Don Carlos Buell ordered no reprisals except to hang any and all guerillas, locals believed that Union forces sought revenge for McCook's death by burning five plantations and performing other acts of terror on civilians. McMillan, 206; Engle, 281; and "The Death of General Robert McCook," Warfare History Network, https://warfarehistorynetwork.com/2018/12/20/the-death-of-general-robert-mccook/ (accessed September 16, 2018). As to Joseph M. Hambrick and Frank Gurley, in 1862, the former was elected captain in the 4th Alabama Cavalry's Company K, while the latter was mustered into the 4th Alabama Cavalry. The Union labeled the members of the 4th Alabama Cavalry as mere guerillas. However, Union captain Hunter Brooke said otherwise and avowed that the 4th Alabama Cavalry were regulars, not guerillas. Once a captive of the Confederates, Brooke had been traded for Hambrick's brother. Brooke claimed that Gurley fired the bullet that led to McCook's death. Donald H. Steenburn, *A Man Called Gurley* (Meridianville, AL: Elk River Press, 1999), 140–42; and "The Death of General Robert McCook."

104. Under the command of lieutenant Isaac Brown, the CSS *Arkansas* arrived in Vicksburg on July 15. That day, Union admiral David Farragut's forces attacked, but the CSS *Arkansas* managed to damage three Union vessels. This was claimed as a Confederate victory. Eighteen Union soldiers were killed. On the CSS *Arkansas*, see, for example, Oliver Wood McClinton, "The Career of the Confederate States Ram Arkansas," *Arkansas Historical Quarterly* 7 (Winter 1948): 329–33.

105. Following orders, Brown took the ironclad CSS *Arkansas* to Baton Rouge to help the forces of major general John C. Breckinridge. Eaton, 181. On August 6, the CSS *Arkansas* was attacked by the USS *Essex*. When a fire broke out, the men evacuated and destroyed the ship rather than see it fall into Union hands. Long, 240, 248.

106. On August 5, Confederate major general John C. Breckinridge's men had engaged in battle with forces under Union brigadier general Thomas Williams. Both the Union and Confederacy lost eighty-four men in the battle. Williams was among the dead. Long, 248.

107. In the words of historian Clement Eaton, "A cartel for the exchange of all prisoners, rank for rank, was ratified on July 22, 1862. If one side should acquire an excess of prisoners over the other, the cartel provided, they should be paroled until they could be exchanged." Eaton, 108. Neither side was very good about adhering to the terms of this agreement.

108. On April 16, 1862, the Confederate Congress passed a conscription law under which men aged eighteen to thirty-five were required to serve three years in the armed forces. Some men, like educators and clergymen, were excluded. McPherson, *Ordeal by Fire*, 181. Throughout the Confederacy, many responded with frustration, because they believed this mandate violated individual free will and represented an undesired growth of big government. Yet another conscription act was passed in October. This one allowed for the exemption of men who owned twenty or more slaves. It also permitted draftees to send substitutes. This outraged poor men who

could not afford to hire a substitute. As such, conscription widened the rift between economic classes in the rebelling states. McPherson, *Ordeal by Fire*, 181–82; and Eaton, 89–90.

109. On July 29, 1862, Union forces shelled Guntersville. Duncan and Smith, 70; and untitled, *Chattanooga Daily Rebel*, August 9, 1862.

110. Sarah Rayburn, the first wife of Alabama militia general Samuel Rayburn, died in 1860, before the Civil War began. Evergreen Findley Rayburn, Sam's second wife, was killed in the shelling of Guntersville. Cassie confused the two women. Sparks, *A River Town's Fight for Life*, 18; and Duncan and Smith, 65–70. An article about the shelling described Evergreen Rayburn as "a most estimable lady." Untitled, *Chattanooga Daily Rebel*, August 9, 1862.

111. According to a correspondent of the *Chattanooga Daily Rebel*, "Mr. McNairy, a gentleman from Nashville, who was accompanying his mother, an aged and decrepit lady, was also killed." "Guntersville (Ala.) Shelled," *Chattanooga Daily Rebel*, August 9, 1862. The victim, Henry Clay McNairy was reported to have been the "son of the late Dr. Boyd McNairy, of Nashville, and brother of Major Frank McNairy, aid to Maj. Gen. Cheatham." Untitled, *Chattanooga Daily Rebel*, August 9, 1862. McNairy and his mother had recently been to visit his sister in New Orleans. The two were on their way back to Nashville when they arrived in Guntersville on July 25. According to the *Nashville Dispatch*, "here their way was hedged up, and they were compelled to wait in patience. They found themselves among the soldiers and in the midst of skirmishing, the Confederates were in the town and the Federals on the opposite bank of the Tennessee River. They took rooms at the hotel kept by Mrs. Rayburn." Untitled, *Nashville Dispatch*, August 14, 1862. McNairy suffered mortal injuries during the same shell strike that killed Evergreen Rayburn. He died less than thirty minutes later. Shelling and Burning of Guntersville, VF, MCA, GA.

112. The *Chattanooga Daily Rebel* reported, "Mr. B. Matthews was slightly wounded." "Guntersville, Ala. Shelled by Yankees," *Chattanooga Daily Rebel*, August 9, 1862. Ben Matthews was a native of Henryville, Alabama. Shelling and Burning of Guntersville, VF, MCA, GA.

113. Beginning at 7:00 a.m., Union troops fired on Guntersville and did not cease until 6:00 p.m. According to Union major J. W. Paramore of the 3rd Ohio Cavalry, "I found the town strongly garrisoned by Forrest's Cavalry and some independent companies of guerillas and bushwhackers raised in the vicinity." Duncan and Smith, 66. Paramore continued, "All this was accomplished without any loss on our side except one man of the artillery slightly wounded in the foot. The loss to the enemy we could not ascertain definitely, but I learned from a citizen who crossed the river the next day that their loss was about 30 killed or wounded. Their camp and town was badly damaged by our shells and about ten buildings, including the warehouse filled with forage and commissary stores were burned." Duncan and Smith, 68. Historian Larry Smith noted, "Maj. Paramore reported that the town was strongly fortified by

Forrest's Cavalry, but this was refuted by John Allan Wyeth, an eye-witness to the event, who said there were no regular Confederate troops here at the time, only a few old men and boys. Only two civilians were killed during the bombardment, not '30 killed or wounded' as Maj. Paramore reported." Smith, *Guntersville Remembered*, 33. John F. Fore, a private in the 42nd Alabama Infantry, claimed he and his company had been in Guntersville the day of its shelling: "We were then ordered to Guntersville, Ala. During the summer the Federals came up on the opposite side of the Tennessee River and opened fire on Guntersville, across the river, with the artillery. I was ordered to take a posse of men out to a cross-roads south of town to keep the enemy from coming into town on that side. The citizens had to leave town during the fight." "John F. Fore, Pine Apple, Ala., writes of Forrest," *Confederate Veteran* 6, no. 1 (Jan 1898): 24.

114. Union forces left Huntsville on August 31, 1862. They confiscated horses, mules, and 1,500 slaves. Rohr, 101; Pruitt, 45; Sledge, 57–58; and McMillan, *Alabama Confederate Reader*, 179-180. According to historian Christopher McIlwain, "Buell's departure from Huntsville and most of northeast Alabama, which began in late August, left a vacuum that Confederate military and political authorities were quick to fill." McIlwain, 96. First arriving in Huntsville in 1862, Union forces occupied it off and on for the duration of the war and even in Reconstruction years. Union forces occupied Huntsville a total of four times. Sledge, 59; and Deborah Storey, "Civil War: 150th anniversary of the Union occupation of Huntsville," *Huntsville Times*, April 15, 2012, Civil War Talk website, https://civilwartalk.com/threads/occupation-of-huntsville-150-years-ago.72209/#post-453500 (accessed September 16, 2018).

115. While general Ormsby MacKnight Mitchel had once written, "The negroes are our only friends," Buell tended to think of them as burdensome. Mitchel 318–19.

116. General Braxton Bragg and major general Sterling Price.

117. See chap. 4, note 103.

118. The Second Battle of Bull Run took place on August 28–30. Lee's forces defeated Union forces led by major general John Pope. Long, 257–58.

119. On July 30, 1862, President Abraham Lincoln issued an executive order calling for 150,000 more troops. "Executive Order—Call for Troops," American Presidency Project, http://www.presidency.ucsb.edu/ws/index.php?pid=69810 (accessed September 16, 2018). On August 4, Edwin Stanton, Lincoln's secretary of war, called for 300,000 men to serve nine months in the militia. McPherson, *Ordeal by Fire*, 251.

120. In one letter, major general John C. Breckinridge spoke of Union troops committing outrages against civilians, specifically arson, theft, and imprisonment. He continued, "I am instructed by Major General Van Dorn, commanding this department, to inform you that the above acts are regarded as in violation of the usages of civilized warfare; and that in future, upon any departure from these usages, 'he will raise the black flag, and neither given nor ask quarter.'" "Headquartered in

the Field Near Baton Rouge, August 14," *Washington Daily Intelligencer*, September 1, 1862.

121. Cassie's aunt Catherine (Allison) Cobb had gone to Monte Sano for health purposes. The air and climate on Monte Sano were said to have curative powers, and patrons saw it as a spa-like environment. Atkins et al., 157; and Sledge, 54.

122. On August 12, Confederate brigadier general John Hunt Morgan took the garrison at Gallatin and trashed two bridges as well as a tunnel, which severed the Union supply lines depending on the functionality of the Louisville & Nashville Railroad. Stanley F. Horn, *The Army of Tennessee: A Military History* (New York: The Bobbs-Merrill Company, 1941), 161; Engle, 280; and Edison H. Thomas, *John Hunt Morgan and His Raiders* (Lexington: Univ. Press of Kentucky, 1985).

123. Union major general Benjamin Butler had Baton Rouge evacuated so he could focus all of his attention on maintaining control of New Orleans. The last Union forces left Baton Rouge on August 21. Lawrence Lee Hewitt, *Port Hudson, Confederate Bastion on the Mississippi* (Baton Rouge: Louisiana State Univ. Press, 1994), 12.

124. Clarksville, the home of Fort Defiance, had surrendered to Union forces in February 1862. The Confederates, led by Adam Rankin Johnson and T. G. Woodward, managed to seize control that August, but Union colonel William W. Lowe later retook Clarksville. Fort Donelson had surrendered to Union forces on February 16, 1862. The Confederates tried several times to retake Fort Donelson but failed. Engle, 171; Uffelman, xxiv, 2–3; and Benjamin Franklin Cooling, *Forts Henry and Donelson: The Key to the Confederate Heartland* (Knoxville: Univ. of Tennessee Pres, 1987), 200–223, 268. On Clarksville, see also Carolyn Stier Ferrell, *Occupied: The Story of Clarksville, Tennessee, During the Civil War* (Nashville, TN: Westview, 2013).

125. Confederate brigadier general Samuel B. Maxey's troops caused the 4th Ohio Cavalry to retreat in this Bridgeport skirmish on August 27, 1862. Stuart Salling, *Louisianians in the Western Confederacy: The Adams-Gibson Brigade in the Civil War* (Jefferson, NC: McFarlan & Co., 2010), 82.

126. Heavily prized for its railroad where the Memphis & Charleston met the Louisville and Nashville, Stevenson had proximity to the following ferries: Caperton's, Shallow Ford, and Cameron's. After Union forces occupied, they built Fort Harker just outside the city. Rice, *Hard Times*, 106–7; Thomas Lawrence Connelly, *Autumn of Glory: The Army of Tennessee, 1862–1865* (Baton Rouge: Louisiana State Univ. Press, 1971), 143; and Eliza B. Woodall, *The Stevenson Story* (Stevenson, AL: Stevenson Depot Museum, 1982), 109-110. On August 31, a skirmish broke out between Confederate and Union forces. *The War of Rebellion: A Compilation of the Official Records of the Union and Confederate Armies* series 1, vol. 16-in 2 parts, part 1-reports (Washington DC: Government Printing Office, 1886), 952.

127. The Second Battle of Bull Run took place on August 28–30 and, like the first, was a Confederate victory. Long, 260.

128. Lexington's mayor surrendered to Confederates on September 1, and Confederate general Edmund Kirby Smith reached the city the following day. Joseph H. Parks, *General Edmund Kirby Smith, C.S.A.* (1954; repr., Baton Rouge: Louisiana State Univ. Press, 1992), 218.

129. The occupying Union forces had caused Huntsville's newspapers, the *Huntsville Democrat, Southern Advocate*, and the *Huntsville Independent*, to cease publication. Rohr, 5; and Pruitt, 45. When the *Southern Advocate* resumed publication on September 11, its editor William B. Figures described the recent occupation: "We were under absolute military rule, subject to the orders of provost marshals, having to obtain passes to go outside of town, and at times to pass from place to place in town; pledges and oaths were extracted under dire compulsion; marketing was prohibited, provisions not allowed to come in; citizens ordered to be off the streets; arrested, kept in prison for days and weeks, not tried, and then discharged on pledges; negro evidence threatened against them, and arrests made on such evidence. Citizens were sent off to Camp Chase without trial or notice; houses searched, property taken without compensation or even receipted for; houses robbed, horses stolen, negroes decoyed off, wanton injury indicted upon many of our people and no redress given . . . They burnt a large number of arms, bacon, flour, salt, etc., which could not be carried off." Untitled, *Southern Advocate*, September 11, 1862. On October 8, the *Huntsville Democrat* resumed activity as the *Huntsville Confederate*. Friction existed between the *Huntsville Confederate* and the *Southern Advocate*. On February 4, 1863, "The editor of the *Confederate* accused the *Advocate* of printing passes for the Union soldiers during their Huntsville occupation. The *Advocate* responded that 'passes, orders, &c were printed at the *Advocate* office by order of the Federals, under the threat of seizing the *Advocate* office.' The *Advocate* further stated that former Governor Clay sold corn and other provisions to the Federals, under similar coercion." Pruitt, 46. See also "A Journalist's Perspective on the Invasion of Huntsville," 36.

130. Cassie's uncle Francis Marion Fennell owned thirty slaves. 1860 US Federal Census—Slave Schedules, Ancestry.com.

131. Cassie diminished the importance of slaves to her family's finances. Using the Confiscation Act, Union troops took the slaves and often impressed them into work. Margaret M. Storey, *Loyalty and Loss: Alabama's Unionists in the Civil War and Reconstruction* (Baton Rouge: Louisiana State Univ. Press, 2004), 88–89.

132. Major generals George McClellan, Henry Halleck, and John Pope. McClellan had been in Alexandria during this battle, and his failure to send Pope reinforcements was heavily criticized. Though pressured to dismiss McClellan, Lincoln refused. As pseudo-punishment for his poor performance, Pope was sent to Minnesota to serve in the Dakota War of 1862. His Army of Virginia was gobbled up by the Army of the Potomac. McPherson, *Ordeal by Fire*, 260.

133. In this battle, the Union had roughly 75,000 men, while the Confederates had about 48,500. Long, 258.

134. Lieutenant general Thomas "Stonewall" Jackson, lieutenant general James Longstreet, and general Robert E. Lee.

135. Union casualties reached 14,462, while Confederate casualties amounted to 7,244. Eaton, 169. No generals were among the dead.

136. Davis declared September 18 "as a day of thanksgiving to Almighty God." He went on: "I do hereby invite the people of the Confederate States to meet on that day at their respective places of public worship, and to unite in rendering thanks and praise to God for these great mercies, now and to implore Him to conduct our country safely through the perils which surround us to the final attainment of the blessings of peace and security." Rev. J. Williams, *Christ in Camp or Religion in the Confederate Army* (Atlanta: The Martin & Hoyt Co., 1904), 44–45.

137. On September 6, lieutenant general Thomas "Stonewall" Jackson and his men arrived in Fredericksburg, where they were treated in a "chilly" fashion by pro-Union townspeople and cheered by those with Confederate sympathies. Gwynne, 449, 452.

138. No battles ever took place in Poolesville, Maryland, but both Union and Confederate troops occasionally passed through the city and camped nearby. "Historic Poolesville," The Blue Hearth, http://thebluehearth.com/find-us/historic-poolesville/ (accessed September 17, 2018).

139. Baltimore's provost-marshal George H. Dodge was not hanged. *The War of The Rebellion: A Compilation of Official Records of the Union and Confederate Armies, Prepared under the Direction of the Secretary of War, by BVT. Lieut. Col. Robert N. Scott, Third U.S. Artillery, and Published Pursuant to Act of Congress Approved June 16, 1880* (Washington, DC: Government Printing Office, 1883).

140. Rumors abounded that "fighting had broken out in the streets of Baltimore." Joseph L. Harsh, *Taken at the Flood: Robert E. Lee and the Confederate Strategy in the Maryland Campaign of 1862* (Kent: Kent State Univ. Press, 1999), 124.

141. Union major generals John Pope, Irvin McDowell, and George McClellan had been heavily criticized for losing the Second Battle of Bull Run. McPherson, *Ordeal by Fire*, 260.

142. General Robert E. Lee, lieutenant general Thomas "Stonewall" Jackson, lieutenant general James Longstreet, brigadier general John Hunt Morgan, and general Edmund Kirby Smith. "Hill" may have been brigadier general Ambrose P. Hill or major general Daniel H. Hill. The likelier candidate, the former served as a major player in the Second Battle of Bull Run.

143. With "liberation" of Kentucky on their minds, general Edmund Kirby Smith and general Braxton Bragg had launched a two-prong invasion of the state. On August 30, Smith and his ten thousand troops ventured north from Knoxville to

the middle of Kentucky and "captured most of the Union garrison at Richmond." McPherson, *Ordeal by Fire*, 289. Smith then occupied the city of Lexington but received a mixed reception from locals. Eaton, 188.

144. Confederate colonel John Scott of the 1st Louisiana Cavalry chased Union forces as they retreated from Smith's forces at Richmond, Kentucky. Consequently, Confederates occupied Frankfort on September 3. Lowell H. Harrison, *The Civil War in Kentucky* (Lexington: Univ. Press of Kentucky, 1975), 41–42.

145. Brigadier general Abraham Buford had attempted to remain neutral for the first part of the Civil War, but with the invasion of John Hunt Morgan and Braxton Bragg into Kentucky, he committed to the Confederacy. After being commissioned, he recruited around Lexington. The men he enrolled "were designated the Third, Fifth, and Sixth Kentucky Cavalry regiments." Marshall D. Krolick, "Brig. Gen. Abraham H. Buford," in *Kentuckians in Gray: Confederate Generals and Field Officers of the Bluegrass State*, ed. Bruce S. Allardice and Lawrence Lee Hewitt (Lexington: Univ. Press of Kentucky, 2008), 51.

146. Union major general Lewis Wallace feared that Kirby Smith intended to target Cincinnati, Ohio. Nevins, *The War for the Union*, vol. 2, *War Becomes Revolution, 1862–1863*, 281.

147. Runaway slaves had been a problem for Buell since he first arrived in Nashville that February. As explained by historian Stephen D. Engle, "Federal policy precluded interference with slaves, and most Federal officers complied, many believing slaves were a nuisance anyway. Buell never had or desired to have a chance to deal effectively with the slavery issue. Though he thought loyal men should have their slaves, he turned away all slaves from his camps, even those belonging to secessionists, since their presence not only demoralized the army but also caused a drain on supplies." Engle, 201. Mitchel's 3rd Division welcomed runaways, much to the ire of Buell, who ultimately instructed Mitchel to return the slaves to their masters and rebuff any others from camp. Given his policy of returning slaves to masters, his men suspected he had Confederate sympathies. Much displeased by Buell's stance, Mitchel saw slaves as useful informants. Engle, 202–3.

148. In southwest Virginia, brigadier general Albert G. Jenkins had "three large regiments and five battalions of horse." Douglas Southall Freeman, *Lee's Lieutenants: A Study in Command*, vol. 2, *Cedar Mountain to Chancellorsville* (New York: Charles Scribner's Sons, 1946), 708.

149. Willie had been made a captain in the 4th Regiment, Alabama Cavalry. It was often referred to as Russell's Cavalry because colonel Alfred A. Russell served as its commander. US Civil War Soldiers, 1861–1865, Ancestry.com.

150. A member of the 42nd Tennessee Infantry Regiment, Wattie had been captured at Fort Donelson on February 16, 1862. In September 1862, he received parole at Vicksburg, Mississippi. On October 9, he entered the 55th Alabama Infantry Regiment, which had been organized from several remaining units. Stewart Sifakis,

Compendium of the Confederate Armies: Tennessee (New York: Facts on File, 1992), 151–52.

151. Union brigadier general George Morgan evacuated the Cumberland Gap on September 17. Horn, 165.

152. Confederate major general Carter L. Stevenson. Horn, 163.

153. Harpers Ferry, manned by thirteen thousand, surrendered to Jackson on September 15. Eaton, 187.

154. Twenty miles from Harpers Ferry, Boonsboro, Maryland, became the site of the Battle of South Mountain on September 14. Harsh, 256–67. Estimates placed the Union and Confederate dead at 443 and 325, respectively. Long, 266.

155. On September 19, Confederate major general Sterling Price lost the Battle of Iuka in Iuka, Mississippi. McPherson, *Ordeal by Fire*, 292.

156. On October 3, the Battle of Corinth took place in Corinth, Mississippi. Confederate major generals Earl Van Dorn and Sterling Price lost to Union forces led by major general William Rosecrans. For the Iuka and Corinth battles combined, Confederate casualties reached 5,700, while Union casualties amounted to 3,300. McPherson, *Ordeal by Fire*, 292. According to historian Stanley F. Horn, "Press and public castigated General Van Dorn for the Corinth defeat. It was said that his attack was ill-advised, improperly organized and poorly conducted; that his soldiers, particularly his wounded, were neglected; that he was drunk on duty; that he did not even have a proper map of the country roundabout." Horn, 175. "Ripley" meant Ripley, Mississippi.

157. The Battle of Antietam took place close to Sharpsburg, Maryland, on September 17, 1862. Lee had roughly thirty thousand men, while McClellan had about sixty thousand. In the end, there were 2,700 Confederate deaths, 2,100 Union deaths, and 18,500 wounded. McPherson, *Ordeal by Fire*, 280–88. As described by historian James McPherson, "The battle was a tactical draw; but for the Confederates it was a strategic defeat." McPherson, *Ordeal by Fire*, 288. Sam Henry's 9th Alabama Infantry saw action in the Battle of Antietam. Sifakis, *Compendium of the Confederate Armies: Alabama*, 68–69.

158. After the defeat at Antietam, Lee tried to salvage some of the objectives of the Maryland Campaign. During October 10–12, general J. E. B. Stuart and his cavalry raided into Maryland and then up to Mercersburg and Chambersburg, Pennsylvania. Stuart damaged rail/telegraph lines; confiscated 1,200 horses; captured both enemy soldiers and civilians for exchange; and gained weapons and supplies. Although the Confederates did not destroy Chambersburg, the mere fact that Stuart managed to get that far into Union territory was frightfully embarrassing for Lincoln, so much so that it contributed to Lincoln's decision to relieve McClellan from the command of the Army of the Potomac. McPherson, *Ordeal by Fire*, 300; and Freeman, *Lee's Lieutenants*, vol. 2, pp. 287–309. Cassie may have meant Union major general Julius H. Stahel-Szamwald.

159. On October 8, the Battle of Perryville took place in Perryville, Kentucky, where Don Carlos Buell and his men forced Braxton Bragg's Confederates to retreat. Of the 15,000 Confederate troops, 3,400 were killed. Of the 23,000 Union troops, 4,200 were killed. After this loss, Bragg decided to leave Kentucky. McPherson, *Ordeal by Fire*, 290–91.

160. The Union blockade led to increasing salt shortages, especially after the occupation of New Orleans. Before the war, most of the southern states had depended greatly on Virginia, Texas, Kentucky, and Florida for salt, but war disrupted its transport. As a result, southern states began trying to produce it themselves. In the case of Alabama, salt was harvested in Clarke and Washington Counties in the southern part of the state. Some people became so desperate for salt that they tried to secure what they could from the soil beneath smokehouses. In 1862, a sack of salt sold for $80. Storey, *Loyalty and Loss*, 94–95; Record, *A Dream Come True*, vol. 1, pp. 131, 137; and McMillan, 198–99.

161. In 1862, prices escalated throughout north Alabama. Butter sold for $3.00 a pound, and pork fetched ten cents a pound. Clothing prices continued to rise. Record, *A Dream Come True*, vol. 1, pp. 131, 137.

5. *Awful Hard Times*

1. The Battle of Fredericksburg happened on December 13, 1862, and was deemed a Confederate victory. In the aftermath, both Confederate Robert E. Lee and Union major general Ambrose Burnside received criticism for strategic errors. Long, 295–96; and Catton, 186–90. Prized as a port city, Charleston also had great value for its railroads and saltworks. In April, Confederate general P. G. T. Beauregard managed to ward off a Union attack of Charleston. Thomas, *The Confederate Nation*, 157. In order to guard the harbors of the Atlantic, the Confederacy used soldiers from Maryland to Georgia. Douglas Southall Freeman, *Lee's Lieutenants: A Study in Command*, vol. 3, *Gettysburg to Appomattox* (New York: Charles Scribner's Sons, 1946), 314.

2. The "cavalry fight in West Tennessee" meant the Battle of Stones River which took place in Murfreesboro between December 31, 1862, and January 2, 1863. The primary commanders were Union major general William Rosecrans and Confederate general Braxton Bragg. This Union victory proved a much-needed morale booster for Lincoln, especially after the Battle of Fredericksburg. Eaton, 190; and McPherson, *Ordeal by Fire*, 309–11.

3. Major general Joseph Wheeler's cavalry made itself helpful at the Battle of Stones River. A Georgian by birth and raised mostly in Connecticut, Wheeler received an education at the United States Military Academy. When the Civil War began, he enlisted in the 19th Alabama Cavalry. By 1862, he had become chief of cavalry for the Army of the Tennessee. In 1863, Wheeler authored a cavalry tactics manual, one of many. Though a strict disciplinarian, Wheeler earned a great deal

of respect from his men. Long after the war, from 1893 to 1900, he served in the US House of Representatives. During the Spanish-American War, Wheeler served in both Cuba and the Philippines, earning the rank of brigadier general. Wheeler died in New York City in 1906. Horn, 193, 198; and John Witherspoon DuBose, *General Joseph Wheeler and The Army of the Tennessee* (New York: The Neale Publishing Co., 1912). Bragg best utilized Nathan Bedford Forrest by sending his cavalry on raids in middle and west Tennessee. Horn, 194–95.

4. Davis had been outraged by Butler's Order No. 28 and especially by the execution of William Mumford. On December 24, 1862, Davis declared, "I do order that he [Butler] be no longer considered or treated simply as a public enemy of the Confederate States of America, but as an outlaw and common enemy of mankind, and that in the event of his capture the officer in command of the capturing force do cause him to be immediately executed by hanging; and I do further order that no commissioned officer of the United States taken captive shall be released on parole before exchange until the said Butler shall have met with due punishment for his crimes." Hearn, 140. According to historian Chester G. Hearn, "Butler shrugged off the proclamation." Hearn, 220.

5. On Antietam, see chap. 4, note 157.

6. At that time, Wattie belonged to the 55th Alabama Infantry Regiment. This regiment was created on February 23, 1863, by combining the remnants of the 6th and 16th Infantry Battalions at Port Hudson. Sifakis, *Compendium of the Confederate Armies: Alabama*, 123. Union forces had targeted Port Hudson and secured it on July 9, 1863. Bruce Levine, *The Fall of the House of Dixie: The Civil War and the Social Revolution that Transformed the South* (New York: Random House, 2014), 147; and Bruce Catton, *This Hallowed Ground: The Story of the Union Side of the Civil War* (Edison, NJ: Castle Books, 2002), 264.

7. On Isham Fennell, see chap. 4, note 101. 1850 US Federal Census; and US Civil War Soldier War Records and Profiles, 1861–1865, both at Ancestry.com. See also Axford, 69; and Louis Wyeth, "The History of Marshall County," Civil War, VF, MCA, GA.

8. See chap. 4, note 100.

9. The Confederates won the First Battle of Charleston Harbor. The Union had nine ironclads, five of which were badly damaged by Confederate artillery. One of the ironclads, the USS *Keokuk*, sank that night. Stephen R. Wise, *Gate of Hell: Campaign for Charleston Harbor, 1863* (Columbia: Univ. of South Carolina Press, 1994), 31. For more information on this battle, see Robert M. Browning, *Success Is All That Was Expected: The South Atlantic Blockading Squadron during the Civil War* (Dulles, VA: Brassey's Inc., 2002).

10. Union brigadier general Grenville M. Dodge and colonel Abel D. Streight traveled from Eastport, Mississippi, and arrived in Tuscumbia in late April. Intending to give Streight time to begin a march across Alabama, Dodge occupied the troops

of Forrest and colonel Philip Roddey. When he realized he had been duped, Forrest pursued Streight, then about thirty miles away. Forrest trailed Streight all the way to the Alabama-Georgia line, where he finally caught up on May 3. Streight, erroneously thinking Forrest's forces outnumbered his own, surrendered. Forrest captured 1,666 men. Robert M. Browning, *Forrest: The Confederacy's Relentless Warrior* (Washington, DC: Potomac Books, 2004), 33–37.

11. Cassie's paternal grandmother, Elizabeth "Betty" (Hobbs) Fennell Childress (1783–1863) lived in New Hope, Madison County, Alabama. Born to William Hubbard Hobbs (1746–1817) and Martha Meredith (1750–1785), Betty married James Clark Fennell (1780–1817) in Virginia in 1803. They moved near Huntsville, Alabama, and reared six children: Martha (Eldridge Rivers); Isham (Margaret Bedford); John (Sarah Kelly); James (Matilda Allison); Francis (Isabella Allison); and Hubbard (Mary Irene Smith). Many years after her husband James passed away, Betty married Joel Childress (1796–1870). Betty died on April 20, 1863, and was buried at Northside Cemetery in Madison County. 1850, 1860, 1870, 1880 US Federal Census; and Virginia, Select Marriages, 1785–1940, all at Ancestry.com.

12. Forrest had fewer than six hundred men, a fraction of the number Streight possessed. Walter L. Fleming, *Civil War and Reconstruction in Alabama* (New York: Columbia Univ. Press, 1905), 67–68. See also John Allan Wyeth, *Life of General Nathan Bedford Forrest* (New York: Harper & Brothers, 1899), 220.

13. Jackson had been shot by friendly fire (18th North Carolina Infantry) in the Battle of Chancellorsville (April 30–May 6, 1863). While the battle resulted in a Confederate victory, Jackson's wounds were such that an arm had to be amputated. On May 10, he died of pneumonia. Gwynne, 540–50. An exceptionally bloody battle, the Battle of Chancellorsville resulted in 17,197 Union deaths and 13,303 Confederate deaths. Gwynne, 545.

14. On May 7, 1863, Dr. George Peters murdered general Earl Van Dorn in Spring Hill, Tennessee. Evidently, Peters suspected his wife and the general had some sort of untoward relationship. Horn, 453; and Long, 350. For more information on Van Dorn, see Arthur B. Carter, *Tarnished Cavalier: Major General Earl Van Dorn* (Knoxville: Univ. of Tennessee Press, 2013); and Robert J. Hartje, *Van Dorn: The Life and Times of a Confederate General* (Nashville: Vanderbilt Univ. Press, 1967).

15. Richard Ewell "captured or scattered Union garrisons at Winchester and elsewhere in the Shenandoah Valley, and crossed the Potomac in mid-June." McPherson, *Ordeal by Fire*, 325. Some of Ewell's forces had gone to Harrisburg.

16. Its bridges made Bridgeport, Alabama, a target. Horn, 278.

17. Grand Gulf, which had a road leading to Jackson, had been attacked by Union forces on April 29. Confederates repelled the Union gunboats. Stoker, 262–64.

18. Union forces occupied Jackson on May 14, 1863. Stoker, 266.

19. "Baker's Creek" referenced the Battle of Champion Hill, which took place on May 16. Lieutenant general John C. Pemberton led the Confederates. The Battle of

Big Black River Bridge took place on May 17. Both battles occurred in Hinds County, Mississippi, and both resulted in Union victories. Long, 354; and Blair, 116–17.

20. Vicksburg surrendered on July 4. Stoker, 275.

21. The Union navy already had some black sailors, and as early as August 25, 1862, US secretary of war Edwin Stanton allowed some South Carolina freedmen to serve as soldiers. Initially, Lincoln was hesitant about making troops of black men, because he feared alienating residents in the Border States. He changed his mind for two main reasons. One was a need for manpower. Another was psychologically strategic. He rightly imagined that blacks in Union blue would terrify and demoralize Confederates. Black soldiers had myriad complaints, however, primarily that they had little chance of commission and promotion, received less pay than their white counterparts, and were relegated to grunt work. Roughly 180,000 blacks served in the Union armed forces during the Civil War. McPherson, *Ordeal by Fire*, 350–51; and Thomas, *The Confederate Nation*, 237.

22. The Battle of Champion Hill.

23. According to the *Merriam-Webster* dictionary, detached service refers to "military service away from one's assigned organization." "Detached service," *Merriam-Webster*, https://www.merriam-webster.com/dictionary/detached%20service (accessed January 14, 2020). Sometimes such men were deemed guerillas because they wore civilian attire. Sean Michael O'Brien, *Mountain Partisans: Guerilla Warfare in the Southern Appalachians, 1861-1865* (Westport: Praeger, 1999), 137–39.

24. After the summer and fall of 1863, Sam Henry served in Clanton's Brigade, 8th Alabama Cavalry. Sifakis, *Compendium of the Confederate Armies: Alabama*, 37.

25. Actually, Grant initially sought unconditional surrender from Pemberton but, on second thought, decided he did not want the burden of feeding and transporting the roughly thirty thousand Confederates he would have had to take prisoner. So, instead, he agreed to parole the Confederates. Stoker, 275.

26. New Orleans remained under Union control, but Confederate major general John B. Magruder had skillfully retaken Galveston, Texas, in early 1863. Thomas M. Settles, *John Bankhead Magruder: A Military Reappraisal* (Baton Rouge: Louisiana State Univ. Press, 2009), 250–54; and Paul D. Casdorph, *Prince John Magruder: His Life and Campaigns* (New York: Wiley, 1996).

27. John Allison, the son of David and Sarah (Smith) Allison.

28. On July 9, Confederates surrendered Port Hudson along with 6,300 troops, 7,500 guns, and 51 field pieces. Horn, 219.

29. The Battle of Gettysburg, waged between the forces of Union major general George Meade and Lee, took place on July 1–3, 1863. Meade had roughly 23,000 men, while Lee had 28,000. By July 4, Lee had set off for Virginia with a caravan of wagons and a slew of exhausted, depressed soldiers. While applauded for the victory, Meade received criticism for allowing Lee to retreat. In the aftermath, Lee, disheartened by the loss, attempted to resign his command, but Davis refused to

accept the request. Eaton, 198–99; Thomas, *The Confederate Nation*, 242–43; Pollard, 406–15; and Douglas Southall Freeman, *Lee's Lieutenants*, vol. 3, p. 190.

30. Rumors abounded after Gettysburg. On July 5, headlines led to further confusion. Some said Confederate forces had taken forty thousand Union prisoners and occupied Washington, DC. Others reported that Baltimore lay in ashes and that Lee had begun peace negotiations in Philadelphia. Joseph E. Stevens, *1863: The Rebirth of a Nation* (New York: Bantam Books, 1999), 293.

31. The son of Martha Fennell (1805–1845) and Eldridge Rivers (1789–1836), John Douglas Rivers (1836–1863) farmed in Madison County, Alabama. During the Civil War, he served in the 49th Regiment, Alabama Infantry. His unit saw action at Shiloh, Vicksburg, Corinth, Baton Rouge, and Port Hudson. Alabama, Texas, and Virginia, Confederate Pensions, 1884–1958; Alabama, Select Marriages, 1816–1942; 1850 US Federal Census; and US, Confederate Soldiers Compiled Service Records, 1861–1865, all at Ancestry.com. See also US, Confederate Army Casualty Lists and Reports, 1861–1865; and *Brief Historical Sketches of Military Organizations Raised in Alabama in the Civil War*, 663.

32. Confederate brigadier general John Hunt Morgan. Stevens, 311, 399–401.

33. In the winter of 1862–1863, Rivers's regiment had been decimated with significant casualties. The remainder of the force was taken prisoner at Port Hudson. Surgeon's notes for May 24, 1863, through June 2, 1863, described John D. Rivers (49th Alabama) as "severely wounded." Officially, his death was reported as June 18, 1863, the date his wife Mary Ellen (Kennabrough) Rivers (1839–1913) later used when applying for a Confederate pension. Alabama, Texas, and Virginia, Confederate Pensions, 1884–1958; Alabama, Select Marriages, 1816–1942; 1850 US Federal Census; US, Confederate Solidiers Compiled Service Records, 1861–1865; and US, Confederate Army Casualty Lists and Reports, 1861–1865, all at Ancestry.com. See also *Brief Historical Sketches of Military Organizations Raised in Alabama in the Civil War*, 663.

34. William "Bill" Frederick Creamer (1840–1863) resided in western Marshall County, Alabama, near Guntersville. In 1860, he and his wife Caroline (Carter) Creamer had a one-year-old daughter named Caroline, real estate valued at $1,000, and personal property worth $6,715. Bill later enlisted as a private in the 49th Regiment, Alabama Infantry, Company A. He died on July 9, 1863, and was buried at the Port Hudson Battlefield in Louisiana. 1860 US Federal Census; Alabama, Select Marriage Records, 1816–1842; US Civil War Soldiers, 1861–1865, M374, Roll 10; Global Find A Grave Index for Non-Burials at Sea, and Other Select Burial Locations, 1300s–Current; and US, Find A Grave Index, 1600s–Current, all at Ancestry.com.

35. Beginning on July 9, 1863, near Jackson, Mississippi, general Joseph E. Johnston endured assault by William T. Sherman's artillery. When Johnston withdrew on July 16, Sherman's troops entered Jackson with devastating results. By the

time Sherman's men left for Vicksburg, the Mississippi capital had been virtually leveled. Horn, 220; and Stevens, 294–95.

36. John W. Grayson (1838–1917) had married Cassie's cousin Sarah Smith Allison. He enlisted in the 37th Regiment, Tennessee Infantry (East Tennessee Rifle Regiment) on October 8, 1861. Listed as a farmer from Paint Rock, Alabama, Grayson became a first lieutenant. By the war's end, he had achieved the rank of captain. After the war, he and his wife lived near New Hope and had six children. Grayson served in the Alabama House of Representatives in 1870–1872 and 1884–1885. He served in the Alabama Senate from 1873–1875. 1860 US Federal Census; All Confederate Soldiers, Compiled Service Records, 1861–1865; and US Civil War Soldier Records and Profiles, 1861–1865, all at Ancestry.com. See also Record, vol. 1, pp. 268; and Captain John W. Grayson, "Alabamians in a Tennessee Regiment," *Confederate Veteran* 19, no. 8 (August 1911): 375.

37. Confederate brigadier general John Hunt Morgan was captured in Youngstown, Ohio, on July 26. Though imprisoned, he escaped on November 27. Stevens, 311, 399–401.

38. Vienna was eventually burned. After the war, its residents rebuilt the city, renaming it New Hope.

39. Camden was located at Paint Rock, Alabama.

40. Davis selected August 21 as a day of fasting. James W. Silver, *Confederate Morale and Church Propaganda* (Tuscaloosa, AL: Confederate Publishing Co., Inc., 1957), 64–65.

41. On August 24, a skirmish took place at Fort Deposit. Duncan and Smith, 77.

42. Forty-eight-year-old Reverend Henry E. Poarch boarded with the James Scott family near Claysville. 1850, 1860 US Federal Census, Ancestry.com.

43. Willie served in the 4th Alabama Cavalry, Company I, which was attached to Russell's Regiment.

44. Though the editor could not discern the identity of lieutenant Robertson, James M. Williams enlisted on July 17, 1861, while Joseph A. Matthews enlisted on May 1, 1862. Both served in the 8th Confederate Infantry. US, Confederate Soldiers Compiled Service Records, 1861–1865, Ancestry.com.

45. Alexandria, Alabama.

46. The daughter of Francis Marion Fennell and Isabella Allison, Matilda "Maud" Fennell (1847–1926) lived in Bellefonte, Alabama. US, Find A Grave Index, 1600s–Current; and 1860 US Federal Census, both at Ancestry.com.

47. The editor had no luck identifying captain Field, who Cassie called captain Fields in another entry.

48. In the Battle of Chickamauga, the Union had 58,000 men, while the Confederacy had 66,000. The Union lost 1,657 men while the Confederacy lost 2,312. Combined casualties reached about 35,000. Long, 412. Though Bragg thought it a much-needed victory, Union major general William Rosecrans believed it "the

worst defeat sustained by the Union military since Chancellorsville." Stevens, 240. Confederate brigadier general Benjamin Hardin Helm was injured on September 20 and died the following day. Allardice, 138–44; and David Herbert Donald, *Lincoln* (London: Jonathan Cape, 1995), 475. Confederate brigadier general Preston Smith was killed on September 19. Clement A. Evans, *Confederate Military History*, vol. 3 (Atlanta: Confederate Publishing Co., 1899), 332.

49. In early October, Wheeler and his 1,900 men took a Union caravan consisting of thirty-two wagons and two hundred mules. Shortly thereafter, Wheeler's force conquered a Union wagon train consisting of eight hundred wagons and four thousand mules. He ordered most of the wagons burned and the bulk of mules killed. After the Sequatchie Raid, Wheeler made his way across the Tennessee River to Mussels' Shoals (now spelled Muscle Shoals). DuBose, 209–10.

50. Arthur C. Beard and his wife Pheriba lived at Beard's Bluff (now Street's Bluff) on the Tennessee River. Family Trees, Ancestry.com. Though Beard was a major in the 4th Alabama Infantry, Cassie called him a colonel because he had once held that rank in the Alabama militia. On April 22, 1862, Beard resigned from the military. He served briefly on the staff of Alabama governor John G. Shorter but then returned home to his farm. Duncan and Smith, 45. Of note, Beard had purchased his property at Beard's Bluff by using intimidation and duress. In his own words, "I bought it, I paid for it, I fought for it, cut Jesse Cheek nearly in two with a Bowie Knife, and cut Matthews nearly open with the same knife!" Ferrell Sparks and Charles McClendon, *Country Grave Yards: Part Two; Cooley, Ridgeway* (self-published, 1996). A teacher from Virginia, John E. Irwin was seventy-three. Irwin's first wife was a Moore, and Beard's wife was a Moore. Note, the Fennells were also related to the Moore family. 1860 US Federal Census; and Family Trees, both at Ancestry.com.

51. Due to Union control of the Mississippi River, Kirby Smith had been cut off from communication with Richmond, so the Confederates had a feeble hold on the Trans-Mississippi area. Parks, 280–81.

52. Confederate brigadier general Richard Taylor had certainly tried to defeat the forces of Nathaniel P. Banks, commander of the Army of the Gulf, but had failed. He and Banks had warred over Bayou Teche at the Battle of Fort Bisland (April 12–13, 1863) and Battle of Irish Bend (April 14, 1863). The Union won both battles. T. Michael Parish, *Richard Taylor: Soldier Prince of Dixie* (Chapel Hill: Univ. of North Carolina Press, 1992).

53. Creed Taylor, a tanner by trade, lived in Warrenton, Alabama, with his wife Mary and their five children. In 1868, Creed's son Creed L. and Cassie's brother Johnnie married sisters Mary and Lucinda Sheffield. Family Trees, Ancestry.com.

54. The Buck Island Massacre took placed on December 27, 1863, when Vienna, Alabama, native and guerilla Ben Harris, a man well known for Union scouting,

targeted cattle on Buck Island. It all began with C. L. Hardcastle, who belonged to the 50th Alabama Regiment and was home on furlough. Fearful of guerillas, Hardcastle, along with James M., F. M., and Porter Roden, had taken sanctuary in Ben Roden's cabin on Buck Island. That morning, Harris appeared at the door with a group of Union cavalrymen. He threatened to kill Hardcastle and the three Rodens unless they helped take the Roden cattle across the river. Having little choice, the Confederates complied but were shot anyway. All were killed except Hardcastle, who, when shot, played dead. The bodies were tossed into the Tennessee River, and Hardcastle, though suffering a bullet in the arm, managed to swim to shore and lived to tell the tale. After this, Harris and his men went to Paint Rock, where they murdered Mat V. Riche, David Lemly, William McClay, and a man named Hodge. Locals feared Harris, and his death on March 5, 1865, provided no small relief. Though his cause of death remains a mystery, at the time a rumor spread that he had been murdered by a relative of one of his many victims. Duncan and Smith, 74–75; and Rice, *Hard Times,* 166–68. Riche had a fourteen-year-old daughter named Atha Mexico. 1860 US Federal Census, Ancestry.com.

55. Atha Mexico Riche was born in Marshall County, Alabama, on August 11, 1846, to Mat V. Riche (1830–1863) and Nancy Ricketts (1827–1850). She married Peter Allen on December 19, 1867, and the couple later had three children: David (1869–), William (1872–1931), and Coe (1878–1953). 1850, 1860, 1870 US Federal Census; Alabama Select Marriage Index, 1816–1943; and US Headstone Applications for Military Veterans, 1925–1963, all at Ancestry.com.

56. Cassie's uncle John Allison (1802–1866) lived on Cave Spring Road near Maysville, Alabama. Rice, *The Sword of Bushwhacker Johnston*, 102.

57. Huntsville's occupying Union soldiers had mixed feelings about slaves. Back when Ormsby MacKnight Mitchel had first occupied the city, Huntsville diarist Mary Jane Chadick wrote of a conversation she had with captain William N. Doughty, a member of the 37th Indiana Infantry. In her words, "Had a conversation with a Federal officer, Capt. Doughty, in the course of which he remarked that the 'Western men who form Mitchel's division are fighting for the right of secession, and whenever we become convinced that the slavery question is involved, we shall lay down our arms and go home.'" Rohr, 35. In any event, the Union forces were not above making use of what runaway slaves came their way. Runaways were used as grunt laborers, spies, and later, as enlisted soldiers. However, many Union officers and enlisted men saw runaway slaves as extra mouths to feed. Cassie's remarks about slaves being shipped off to Nashville were echoed by Chadick. On August 4, 1862, Chadick commented, "500 blacks were sent off on the train this morning toward Nashville to erect fortifications. There is a great panic among the Negroes. But few are willing to go, and they are running and hiding generally." Rohr, 85.

6. Plunged into Grief and Silent Suffering

1. Cassie never mentioned the fifty-four-year-old's cause of death.

2. The Battle of Orchard Knob transpired on November 23, 1863. Led by major general George Thomas, Union forces took the hill. Stevens, 383. A Union victory, the Battle of Lookout Mountain was fought on November 23, 1863, between Union major general Joseph Hooker and Confederate major general Carter Stevenson. Stevens, 386–87.

3. Isham Joseph Fennell (1842–1864), the son of Hubbard Hobbs Fennell and Mary Irene Smith.

4. The second husband of Cassie's paternal grandmother Elizabeth "Betty" Hobbs, Joel Childress (1796–1870) lived in New Hope, Alabama. In 1860, he had an estimated value of $44,160. 1860 US Federal Census; and Family Trees, both at Ancestry.com.

5. Edward Tilley Parker, the father of Web.

6. The Battle of Bean's Station occurred on December 14, 1863, in Grainger County, Tennessee. Part of the Knoxville Campaign, the battle's main combatants were Confederate general James Longstreet and Union major general John Parke. The Union forces retreated. Prior to this battle, Longstreet lost two battles with Union major general Ambrose Burnside: the Battle of Campbell's Station (November 16) and the Battle of Fort Sanders (November 29). Earl J. Hess, *The Knoxville Campaign: Burnside and Longstreet in East Tennessee* (Knoxville: Univ. of Tennessee Press, 2013), 207–20.

7. Willie's 4th Alabama Cavalry had been at Chickamauga, the Chattanooga Siege, Wheeler's Sequatchie Raid, and Knoxville Siege. Sifakis, *Compendium of the Confederate Armies: Alabama*, 33–34.

8. A 187-ton Union gunboat, the USS *General Sherman*, began patrolling the Tennessee River in July 1864. One of lieutenant Moreau Forrest's gunboats, its mission included locating deserters and preventing Confederate general John Bell Hood's forces from getting to Tennessee. Blair, 258; and "General Sherman," Naval History and Heritage Command, https://www.history.navy.mil/research/histories/ship-histories/danfs/g/general-sherman.html (accessed September 22, 2018).

9. In spring 1864, the Confederacy initiated an "offensive against the guerillas in northwest Alabama" and, as a result, targeted counties like Winston, Fayette, Marion, and Walker. They hoped to locate deserters, and that is where Confederate brigadier general Philip D. Roddey played a significant role. He and his cavalry monitored the Tennessee River to "block off exit to the Federal army and pick up the deserters." In fact, they were the "only permanent Confederate force in the Tennessee Valley." Roddey was known to act like a guerilla, and he was nicknamed the "Swamp Fox of the Tennessee Valley." O'Brien, *Mountain Partisans*, 92.

10. Union gunboats had been in the vicinity for months. The gunboat USS *General Grant* was near Fort Deposit as early as January 11. According to the ship's

log, on that day, it "cast loose and steamed down the river. Seen fire on both sides of the river below Port Deposit. Fired three shells." That same day, the gunboat reached Guntersville and when the "enemy opened a battery on us," Commander Jas. Watson retaliated. On January 15, the gunboat burned homes at Beard's Bluff. Later that day, it "landed at Guntersville and sent out a landing party and burnt the town." Civil War, VF, MCA, GA. See introduction, notes 26 and 27.

11. Cassie's younger brother Frank Fennell.

12. Beulah Elizabeth Henry (1863–1929), the daughter of Sam and Charity Henry, was less than a year old. Family Trees, Ancestry.com.

13. Originally from Oleander, Marshall County, Alabama, Malachi Gould May (1833–1912) had been a clerk in Lawrence County before the war. Active in recruiting, May and others helped Lawrence County form three full companies for the Confederacy. May enlisted on May 24, 1861, in the 9th Regiment, Alabama Infantry, Company C, as a lieutenant. By the end of his service, he had been promoted to captain. May received wounds at Antietam on September 17, 1862, and again at Salem Church, Virginia, on May 8, 1863. Severely wounded at Gettysburg, he remained absent wounded until officially dropped from the roster on December 31, 1864. 1850, 1860 US Federal Census; Alabama, Civil War Soldiers, 1860–1865; Alabama Civil War Muster Rolls, 1861–1865, Roll #97, Archive Collection, SGO25018-4; US, Confederate Army Casualty Lists and Reports, 1861–1865; and US, Find A Grave Index, 1600s–Current, all at Ancestry.com. See also, *Brief Historical Sketches of Military Organizations Raised in Alabama During the Civil War*, 604.

14. Mary Jane (Kitchens) Tyler, the widow of Spencer Tyler, lived across from Sam and Charity Henry. Spencer (1824–June 24, 1864) had been a teacher and a lieutenant in the Union army. Mary Jane had three children: Sam (9), Richard (6), and Mahala (2). 1850, 1860 US Federal Census; Alabama County Marriage Records, 1805–1867; and US Army Register of Enlistments, 1798–1914, all at Ancestry.com.

15. Charity's husband Sam Henry.

16. In December 1863, Union general William T. Sherman ordered that all the forage and provisions in the country around Bridgeport and Bellefonte be collected and stored. Fleming, *War and Reconstruction in Alabama*, 75.

17. A cousin to Sam Henry, Albert Gallatin "A. G." Henry (1816–1897) lived in the same neighborhood as Sam and Charity. He and his wife Mary Ann had eight children. A. G. owned a mercantile store in Guntersville. Vehemently opposed to secession, he was rumored to have spent two years hiding in a cave to avoid conscription. If that were the case, Charity had probably taken him food. A. G. later claimed to have operated his store all but two years of the war. During the burning of Guntersville, flames destroyed his store, but he rebuilt. Of interest, one poignant story dealt with two Confederate veterans, both of whom had lost a leg in the war. Supposedly, they met once a year at A. G.'s store, where they would buy one pair of shoes; one took the right shoe and the other the left. Another version of the story

had the men being given shoes by A. G. each year. 1850, 1860, 1870, 1880 US Federal Census; Alabama, Wills and Probate Records, 1790–2002; US, Find A Grave Index, 1600s–Current; and Tennessee, Marriage Records, 1780–2002, all at Ancestry.com. See also *Northern Alabama, Historical and Biographical* (Birmingham, AL: Smith and DeLand, 1888), 394; *Memorial Record of Alabama*, vol. 2 (Madison, WI: Brant and Fuller Publishers, 1893), 495; and Duncan and Smith, 112–13.

18. In May 1864, Union major general Francis Blair and 10,500 troops marched through the northeastern part of Alabama on their way to Rome, Georgia. Fleming, *War and Reconstruction in Alabama*, 68.

19. Confederate brigadier general James H. Clanton had failed to stop Union general Lovell Rosseau on July 14 at Coosa River. This was devastating, as Rosseau, in order to sever supplies to general Joe Johnston's forces, had set out from Decatur on July 10 with the express intent to "destroy the Montgomery and West Point Railway below Opelika." Note that in March 1864 Clanton penned that the Confederate cavalry had been "a great terror" to the area residents. O'Brien, *Mountain Partisans*, 91; and Fleming, *War and Reconstruction in Alabama*, 69.

20. On May 7, 1861, in Montgomery, Alabama, Jonas Griffin was commissioned a captain in the 4th Alabama Infantry, G-N. By the time of this entry, he had joined the 54th Alabama Regiment, Company C (Griffin Rifles). Alabama, Civil War Soldiers, 1860–1865, Ancestry.com.

21. Thomas Atkins (1792–1870) and his wife Rebecca (1800–1870) lived in Warrenton, Alabama. Their daughter Mary Ann married Oliver D. Street (1811–1842) and gave birth to Thomas Atkins Street, who later served four terms as probate judge of Marshall County. After being widowed, Mary Ann married James Lawrence Sheffield (1819–1892) and had five children, including Lucinda (1846–1906), who married Cassie's brother Johnnie. 1850, 1860, 1870 US Federal Census; US, Find A Grave Index, 1600s–Current; Alabama State Census, 1866; and Alabama, Compiled Marriages, 1802–1825, all at Ancestry.com. See also Duncan and Smith, 51; and Sparks, *Country Graveyards, Cooley Ridgeway*, 11–12.

22. A. S. Harris, an extremely wealthy planter in Claysville, had real estate and personal holdings worth $99,000 in 1860. Harris, a neighbor to Sam and Charity Henry, owned thirty-five slaves. 1860 US Federal Census; and 1860 US Federal Census-Slave Schedules, both at Ancestry.com. One of the first physicians in the area, Dr. William Green Smith (1809–1890) lived in Warrenton. 1850, 1860, 1870, 1880 US Federal Census, Ancestry.com; Duncan and Smith, 40; and Ferrell Sparks, Charlie McClendon, and J. F. Sparks Jr., *Country Grave Yards, Warrenton and Bennett*, rev. ed. (Birmingham, AL: Banner Digital Printing and Publishing, 2013).

23. Confederate brigadier general James Holt Clanton had been a Montgomery lawyer and aide to Alabama governor John G. Shorter. McIlwain, 188–92, 202, 260–61.

24. A Union victory, the Battle of Atlanta occurred on July 22, 1864. Marc Wortman, *The Bonfire: The Siege and Burning of Atlanta* (New York: Public Affairs, 2009), 271–84.

25. The Battle of Mobile began on August 5 when Union admiral David Farragut entered Mobile Bay with eighteen ships and won a battle against Confederate admiral Franklin Buchanan. While the Union had gained control of Mobile Bay, the city of Mobile remained in Confederate hands. McPherson, *Ordeal by Fire*, 442; Long, 551–52; and Thomas, 279.

26. In February 1863, at Port Hudson, the 55th Alabama Infantry, which included nine hundred members, reorganized. The force saw action in Mississippi and with the Army of Tennessee during the spring of 1864. They fought at Peachtree Creek near Atlanta on June 20, 1864. They lost 14 of their remaining 22 officers and 155 of their 256 men. The campaigns at Franklin and Nashville consumed many of the remaining members. Sifakis, *Compendium of The Confederate Armies: Alabama*, 123–24; and "Fifty-Fifth Alabama Infantry Regiment," https://archives.alabama.gov/referenc/alamilor/55thinf.html (accessed September 23, 2018); and Kennamer, 49-50.

27. Lieutenant colonel Jonathan L. Chandler of the 8th Regiment, Alabama Cavalry. US Civil War Soldiers, 1861–1865, Ancestry.com; and Sifakis, *Compendium of the Confederate Armies: Alabama*, 37.

28. Since the Confederacy lost myriad battles and had increasingly diminished forces, Cassie exhibited ignorance or denial.

29. Given the decimation of his unit, Wattie had chosen furthering his medical training over joining another regiment.

30. According to Cassie's youngest brother Caius, "For some reason known only to grown folks, the bulk of our negroes were sent to Bibb County where they were employed at Iron Works." "The Memoirs of Caius Grattan Fennell," VF, MCA, GA. However, Willie may have taken these slaves to Selma, Alabama. The Selma Ordnance and Navy Foundry (1861–1865), which depended heavily on slave labor, produced cartridges, shells, rifles, and gunpowder. Estimates of the workforce ranged from six thousand to ten thousand laborers. Herbert J. "Jim" Lewis, "Selma Ordnance and Navy Foundry," *Encyclopedia of Alabama*, http://www.encycloepdiaofalabama.org/article/h-2331 (accessed September 23, 2018).

31. Men from the Union gunboat USS *General Grant* captured Willie and Wattie. Russell was in reference to colonel Alfred A. Russell of the 4th Alabama Cavalry. Sifakis, *Compendium of Confederate Armies: Alabama*, 33. For southerners, honor meant "valor, courtesy, duty, loyalty," and "virtue" and was the "very foundation of the slaveholding ethic." Wyatt-Brown, 208.

32. Years later, when Belle (Fennell) Neill sued the US government for restitution, part of the findings read, "During the war for the suppression of the rebellion

there were taken by the military and naval forces of the United States from the unsettled estate of said decedent from his said plantation 31 bales of cotton, without marks, which, as reported by the Treasury Department, was captured November 23, 1864, by the *U.S.S. General Grant*, in Marshall County, Ala., as the property of Capt. J. W. Fennell, a Confederate officer, who was captured at the same time, which cotton was afterwards transported to Cincinnati, Ohio, where 304 bales were sold by W. P. Mellen, a Treasury agent, and the net proceeds, $4,960.59, arising therefrom were accounted for to the Treasury." *Belle F. Neill, administratrix of the estate of James Watkins Fennell v. The United States*, 59th Congress, 2nd Session, Document 355, Congressional Number 10609, Fennell Family, VF, MC, GA.

33. For southern women, "Silence was frequently a conscious rhetorical strategy for self-protection and a way to preserve dignity and exert their self-control when overt persuasion would likely elicit no result." Harrison, *The Rhetoric of Rebel Women*, 47. Silence also provided a "strategy for communicating bravery, self-control, and by extension, Southern honor when verbal appeals were likely useless and in themselves could signal weakness." Harrison, *The Rhetoric of Rebel Women*, 49.

34. In July 1864, Davis replaced general Joe Johnston, head of the Army of Tennessee, with lieutenant general John Bell Hood, whom he believed to be more aggressive. Consequently, Hood was made provisional general. Horn, 187, 345. Although Hood intended to have his men cross the Tennessee River at Guntersville, high water levels forced the troops to cross at Decatur on October 26–28, 1864. Rice, *The Sword of Bushwhacker Johnston*, 122.

35. The Battle of Franklin took place on November 30, 1864. While Confederates maintained control of Franklin, Hood's forces were greatly reduced in number. Estimates placed Hood's losses between 6,000 and 7,500 men. Twelve generals had been killed, wounded, or taken prisoner. Horn, 395–404.

36. Union major general William T. Sherman began his Atlanta Campaign that summer and occupied Atlanta in early September, after Hood's forces withdrew. Sherman and his 62,000 men began their March to the Sea on November 15. Eaton, 279–83. See also general Jacob D. Cox, *Sherman's Battle for Atlanta* (Cambridge: De Capo Books, 1994).

37. During the fall of 1864, major general Nathan Bedford Forrest conducted several raids in Tennessee. In Johnsonville, for example, he took "two gunboats and five army transports," all of which he destroyed. Horn, 383.

7. "The Worst Can Hurt Us but Little"

1. Sherman arrived in Port Royal on December 20, 1865. Noah Andre Trudeau, *Southern Storm: Sherman's March to the Sea* (Harper Collins e-book, 2009), 486.

2. Hubbard H. Fennell (1844–1864), the son of Hubbard Hobbs Fennell and Mary Irene Smith, served as a private in the 55th Regiment, Alabama Infantry, Company G. He died in Georgia and was buried at the Stonewall Confederate

Cemetery at LaGrange. US, Find A Grave Index, 1600s–Current; and US Civil War Soldiers, 1861–1865, both at Ancestry.com. His brother Isham had already died in the war.

3. On January 14, 1865, Confederate general Hylan B. Lyon, while moving south from Kentucky, stopped at Guntersville with about three hundred troops. From the top of Beard's Bluff, he used two twelve-pound guns to harass Union gunboats. As he marched to Blount County, near Red Hill, Lyon selected a campsite near the home of Thomas Noble but failed to post sentinels. While the Confederates slept, Union cavalry (15th Pennsylvania) surprised them and took roughly one hundred men as prisoners. The Union forces apprehended Lyon in the Noble home. At one point, an underwear-clad Lyon asked to put on his uniform. While dressing, he managed to procure a gun, which he used to shoot Union sergeant Arthur Lyon, no relation, point blank in the head before escaping. Duncan and Smith, 70–72; Barbara Snow, "Flames Along the Tennessee River," *Huntsville Historical Review* 44, no. 2 (Fall 2019): 52; and Sparks, *A River Town's Fight for Life*, 31–37.

4. Union forces burned a path between the Thomas Noble home and Guntersville. On January 15, 1865, Union men from the USS *General Thomas* and USS *General Grant* burned Guntersville. Their motive lay with the gunboats having been peppered with gunshots over a number of days. Local historians Katherine Duncan and Larry Smith claimed seven buildings were left standing. These buildings included the courthouse, the hotel, the jail, the Masonic Lodge, a school, and two houses. Duncan and Smith, 72. See also Sparks, *A River Town's Fight for Life*, 36; and Snow, "Flames Along the Tennessee River," 51-61. Stories vary, however, on just what buildings were targeted. While Duncan and Smith believed the courthouse was spared, some evidence indicates otherwise. In fact, one North Carolina newspaper indicated that the Guntersville courthouse had been burned the previous year. It read, "We learn from a citizen of Marshall County, that the Yankees came down to Guntersville, Ala., last week in a gunboat and burned several houses, among them the Court House and the Masonic Hall." Untitled, *Daily Conservative* (Raleigh, NC), May 4, 1864. The Guntersville courthouse, which had been built of brick in 1848, still stood after the 1862 shelling, but one wall had been destroyed. Wyeth, 72; and Duncan and Smith, 37. According to an April 1870 deed written by Guntersville attorney L.D. Lusk, the courthouse had been burned in 1865. This deed transferred ownership of the "old courthouse lot" to Judge Louis Wyeth, the father of Dr. John Allan Wyeth. Book M, Deed Books, p.47, MCA, GA. After the war, court proceedings were being held under a tree in the yard of A.G. Henry. "Address of Hon. J.A. Lusk Delivered at Recent Meeting of Marshall County Bar Association," *Guntersville Advertiser and Democrat*, September 7, 1932. Whatever befell the courthouse, locals managed to salvage its records as they are currently housed at the Marshall County Archives. A new courthouse was constructed around 1870.

5. Evidently, Union captain Jim Johnson knew many people from Guntersville and had extensive knowledge of the city's design. Duncan and Smith, 72.

6. As previously mentioned in chap. 5, note 54, bushwhacker Ben Harris lived in nearby Vienna, Alabama. John Dickey worked as a paid scout for the Union army and like Harris, incited fear in locals. Rice, *Hard Times*, 168–69.

7. The editor had no success discerning the identity of the captain.

8. In Alabama, roughly 4,969 blacks enlisted in the Union army. Some also came to Alabama when the 15th US Colored Infantry became the first regiment of African descent to be stationed in Huntsville on March 5, 1864. Pruitt, 50. The editor attempted to find information on Harper but to no avail.

9. With the intent of negotiating for peace or a cease-fire, Confederate vice president Alexander Stephens journeyed to Hampton Roads, near Washington, DC, in March 1865. Francis P. Blair, also present and representing the Union, put forth two non-negotiable conditions: abolition and a constitutional union. Due to irreconcilable differences, this meeting came to naught. McPherson, *Ordeal by Fire*, 467–68; and Catton, 380.

10. Willie (captain, 4th Alabama Cavalry) and Wattie (private, 55th Alabama Infantry) were captured at their mother's home on November 22, 1864. While Wattie was sent to Camp Douglas (Chicago, Illinois) on December 4, Willie was sent to Johnson's Island (on Lake Erie) on December 8. US Civil War Prisoner of War Records, 1861–1865; and Confederate-Selected Records of the War Department Relating to Confederate Prisoners of War, 1861–1865, both at Ancestry.com. Only shaped to hold 1,000 prisoners, Johnson's Island ultimately held 3,256 prisoners. Initially, it was to hold Confederate officers but ended up housing all types of POWs. Lonnie R. Speer, *Portals to Hell: Military Prisons of the Civil War* (Mechanicsburg, VA: Stackpole Books, 1997), 77–79, 139–40. On Johnson's Island, see, Roger Pickenpaugh, *Johnson's Island: A Prison for Confederate Officers* (Kent: Kent State Univ. Press, 2016). Camp Douglas, a former training camp for Union recruits, encompassed sixty acres on Chicago's south side. While only designed to hold about six thousand prisoners, numbers reached twelve thousand. As early as mid-1862, the US Sanitation Commission had noted its high death rate and poor conditions, especially when it came to hygiene. Speer, 71–73, 324. On Camp Douglas, see also David L. Keller, *The Story of Camp Douglas: Chicago's Forgotten Civil War Prison* (Charleston: The History Press, 2015); and George Levy, *To Die in Chicago: Confederate Prisoners at Camp Douglas, 1862–65* (Evanston, IL: Evanston Publishing, Inc., 1994; repr., Gretna, LA: Pelican Publishing, 1999).

11. Beginning on March 2, 1865, Union general J. H. Wilson and his approximately fourteen thousand troops marched through Alabama in what became known as Wilson's Raid. He wanted to destroy myriad cities like Elyton (Birmingham), Tuscaloosa, and Selma, all towns involved in manufacturing and with ironworks.

On April 10, Wilson left Selma to travel to Montgomery, which surrendered on April 12. Fleming, *War and Reconstruction in Alabama*, 72–73.

12. Cassie's brother Johnnie served in the 8th Alabama Cavalry, Company F. US Civil War Records and Profiles, 1861–1865; and *Selected Records of the War Department Relating to Confederate Prisoners of War, 1861–1865*, both at Ancestry.com.

13. Louisa E. (Fennell) Chandler (1830–1865), the daughter of Hubbard Hobbs Fennell and Mary Irene Smith, and her husband Elisha lived near Guntersville. Her siblings included Mag, short for Margaret, Thomas, Isham Joseph, and Hubbard. Family Trees, Ancestry.com.

14. Emmet Hobbs may have been E. M. Hobbs, who served in the 31st Alabama Infantry, Company F. He was twenty-eight years old at the time of his enlistment on May 8, 1862. Alternatively, he could have been E. Hobbs, who served in the 7th Texas Regiment, Company G and lived near Nacogdoches, Texas. Alabama Civil War Soldiers, 1860–1865; and Texas Muster Roll Index Cards, 1838–1900.

15. At Appomattox, Virginia, on April 9, 1865, Lee surrendered his remaining army. By that time, Lee's force of twenty-eight thousand had been reduced to eight thousand infantrymen and five thousand cavalry/artillery men. Eaton, 287–88. On April 18, general Joseph E. Johnston surrendered at Durham, North Carolina. Thomas, *The Confederate Nation*, 304; and Eaton, 288. On May 4, general Richard Taylor surrendered at Citronelle, Alabama. Eaton, 288.

16. Famed stage actor John Wilkes Booth shot President Lincoln at Ford's Theater in Washington, DC, on April 14, 1865. Lincoln died early the following morning. Doris Kearns Goodwin, *Team of Rivals: The Political Genius of Abraham Lincoln* (New York: Simon & Schuster, 2006), 738–43; and Donald, 594–99. Upon Lincoln's death, Vice President Andrew Johnson assumed the office of president.

17. Fanciful gossip, these rumors had no foundation.

18. Supposedly, Kirby Smith had thirty-six thousand troops. Shelby Foote, *The Civil War, A Narrative: Red River to Appomattox* (New York: Random House, 1974; New York: Vintage Books, 1986), 1,019; and Jeffrey S. Prushankin, *A Crisis in Confederate Command: Edmund Kirby Smith, Richard Taylor, and the Army of the Trans-Mississippi* (Baton Rouge: Louisiana State Univ. Press, 2005), 213.

19. Captain Joseph W. Morehead commanded the USS *General Sherman*. "General Sherman," Naval History and Heritage Command, https://www.history.naval.mil/reseach/histories/danfs/g/general-sherman.html (accessed October 2, 2018).

20. This talk referred to Trans-Mississippi forces under Kirby Smith.

21. The 25th Battalion, Alabama Cavalry, also referred to as Mead's Battalion, surrendered on May 11 in Huntsville. Joseph W. Wheeler, *Confederate Military History—Alabama* (Cartersville, GA: Eastern Digital Resources, 2003), 284. However, there

are conflicting accounts as to whether its leader, colonel Lemuel Green Mead (1830–1878), appeared at the surrender. Huntsville historian Charles Rice wrote, "Colonel Mead was last seen by the Yankees swimming his horse across the Tennessee River. He held out for a while longer on Brindlee Mountain, but finally took the oath of allegiance at Montgomery in September." Rice, *Hard Times*, 290.

22. Near Port Royal, Virginia, on April 26, 1865, Booth died after being found and shot by pursuers in the form of New York cavalrymen. Foote, 996–97.

23. On May 10, the 4th Michigan Cavalry captured Davis in Georgia. Anne Sarah Rubin, *A Shattered Nation: The Rise & Fall of the Confederacy, 1861–1868* (Chapel Hill: Univ. of North Carolina Press, 2005), 136.

24. Cassie's aunt Charity (Allison) Cooper Lea.

25. While on the ship USS *Fort Jackson* off the coast of Galveston on June 2, Kirby Smith signed the surrender forms sent him by Union major general Edward R. S. Canby. Prushankin, 214.

26. Isaac Marion Berry (1831–1895) lived in the western part of Marshall County, likely at Warrenton or Claysville, with his wife and four young children in 1860. When the war began, he sided with the Confederacy, serving in Company I of the 4th Alabama Cavalry Regiment. However, at some point, he switched allegiance and became one of "Dickey's Scouts." Members of this group scouted for the Union army, and their tactics frightened locals, many of whom thought Berry a ruthless killer. On the basis of having been a scout, Berry later applied for a Union pension but was denied. 1860 US Federal Census; US Civil War Solider Records and Profiles, 1861–1865; and US Civil War Pension Index: General Index to Pension Files, 1861–1934, all at Ancestry.com. On John Dickey, the namesake of Dickey's Scouts, see Rice, *Hard Times*, 168–69.

27. The editor had no success in identifying captain Dunn. See previous note.

Appendix 1

1. Hurff, 14

2. 1860 US Federal Census; Alabama Marriage Index, Ancestry.com; Hurff, 13–14; and Cochrane, 91–93. See also Thomas McAdory Owen, *History of Alabama and Dictionary of Alabama Biography*, vol. 3 (Chicago: S.J. Clarke Publishing Co., 1921), 571-572.

3. "Martha Matilda"; and "William and Isabella Allison," FF-Fennell-2, VF, HMCPL, HA. See also Cochrane, 91–93. On Matilda's broken thigh, see untitled, *Guntersville Democrat*, January 26, 1893; untitled, *Guntersville Democrat*, March 30, 1893; untitled, *Guntersville Democrat*, June 22, 1893; untitled, *Guntersville Democrat*, September 14, 1893; and "Death of Mrs. M. M. Fennell," *Guntersville Democrat*, December 21, 1893.

4. Alabama, Select Marriages, FHL Film No. 1035275; 1860, 1870, 1880 US Federal Census; US, Find A Grave Index, 1600s–Current; and Alabama Death Index, all at

Ancestry.com. See also "On the Death of Mrs. Sam Henry," *Guntersville Democrat*, October 23, 1884.

5. 1847 Official Register of Officers and Cadets, http://digital-library.usma.edu/cdm/compoundobject/collection/p16919coll3/1031/rec/30 (accessed February 11, 2019); 1848 Official Register of Officers and Cadets, http://digital-library.usma.edu/cdm/compoundobject/collection/p16919coll3/id/1031/rec/30 (accessed February 11, 2019); and Suzanne Christoff (Associate Director for Unique Resources, United States Military Academic Library) to Whitney Snow, email, January 7, 2019.

6. List of Cadets Admitted into the US Military Academy; US School Catalogs, 1765–1935; 1860 US Federal Census; Alabama Civil War Muster Rolls, 1861–1865 #104, Archive Collection; US Civil War Soldiers, 1861–1865, Film #M374, Roll 20; US Civil War Regiments, 1861–1865; and Alabama, Civil War Soldiers, 1861–1865, all at Ancestry.com. On Sam Henry, see also *Northern Alabama: Historical and Biographical* (Birmingham, AL: Smith & DeLand, 1888), 372; *Brief Sketches of Military Organizations Raised in Alabama During the Civil War*, 602–3; "The Memoirs of Caius Grattan Fennell," VF, MCA, GA; Hurff, 21; untitled, *Guntersville Democrat*, November 8, 1888; "Col. Sam Henry's House Burned," *Guntersville Democrat*, September 12, 1889; untitled, *Guntersville Democrat*, March 30, 1893; untitled, *Montgomery Advertiser*, December 26, 1886; untitled, *Montgomery Advertiser*, August 22, 1886; untitled, *Montgomery Advertiser*, December 10, 1888; "Col. Sam Henry Dead," *Montgomery Advertiser*, March 23, 1893; and "Samuel Henry Came Here in 1848," *Guntersville Democrat*, February 4, 1948. It was claimed Sam had hidden behind logs while his men fought. In his book *General Lee's Army*, historian Joseph Glatthaar used Sam's case as an example of cowardice exhibited by Confederate officers. Joseph Glatthaar, *General Lee's Army: From Victory to Collapse* (New York: Free Press, 2008), 193. On Sam's support from his men, see, for example, Spencer Clack to John Clack, February 15, 1863, VF, MCA, GA. Sam received a pardon on November 1, 1865. "Samuel Henry," All U.S., Pardons Under Amnesty Proclamations, 1865-1869," Ancestry.com.

7. Hurff, 21. See also "Holly Springs: Continuation of the Death Roll from our Last," *Clarion-Ledger*, October 2, 1878.

8. "Creation of M.D.'s," *Washington Union*, March 5, 1859; Sparks, *A River Town's Fight for Life*, 82; Hurff, 21; and "Administrator's Sale," *Guntersville Democrat*, December 16, 1886. See also 1860 US Federal Census; US Civil War Soldiers, 1861–1865; US Headstone, Application for Military Veterans, 1925–1963; and US, Find A Grave Index, 1600s–Current, all at Ancestry.com.

9. Esslinger, 61–62.

10. Ibid., 62.

11. 1860, 1880, 1900, 1910 US Federal Census; Alabama County Marriage Index; "Directory of Deceased American Physicians, 1804–1929"; US Civil War Soldiers, 1861–1865; Alabama Confederate Pension and Service Records, 1862–1947; US

Civil War Prisoner of War Records, 1861–1865; US, Confederate Soldiers Compiled Service Records, 1861–1865; US Civil War Prisoner of War Records, 1861–1865; US Headstone Applications for Military Veterans, 1925–1963; Lawrence County, Alabama, Burial Index, 1835–2014; and US, Find A Grave Index, 1600s–Current, all at Ancestry.com. See also "Fennells—Always on the Move," FF-Fennell-2, VF, HMCPL, HA. On Wattie's death, see untitled, *Guntersville Advertiser*, October 1, 1918.

12. Hurff, 1–22; and William and Isabella Allison, FF-Fennell-2, VF, HMCPL, HA. One of nine children born to Madison County farmers William Wright Esslinger (1815–1889) and Martha Caroline Neel (1821–1893), Andrew Jackson "A. J." Esslinger (1844–1929) had a modest upbringing. In 1860, his parents had real estate valued at $800 and a personal wealth of $550. When the Civil War began, A. J. enlisted in the Confederate army. In March 1862, he contracted measles and pneumonia. When he recovered, he returned to his regiment, which had become Company K of the 49th Alabama Infantry. A. J. was captured at Port Hudson, paroled, and never returned to service. He survived the war unscathed, and on December 27, 1866, married Cassie Fennell. The two had seven children before Cassie succumbed to pneumonia in 1884. Roughly one year later, A. J. married Margaret Lucinda Hodges (1851–1932). With Margaret, A. J. fathered five more children: Ethel (died in infancy); Julia (died in infancy); Mary Elizabeth "Bessie" (1886–); Catherine Margaret "Cassie" (1889–); and Thomas Hodges (1891–). In 1892, A. J. became tax assessor for Madison County and held the position for four years. In 1915, he sold his farm and ran a store in Chase, Alabama. In March 1929, he died at the age of eighty-five. On A. J. Esslinger, see Hurff; untitled, *Huntsville Weekly Democrat*, January 24, 1894; and Alabama, Census of Confederate Soldiers, 1906, 1921 . . . , Ancestry.com.

13. 1860, 1880 US Federal Census; Alabama County Marriages, 1805–1867; Deaths and Burials Index, 1881–1974; and Alabama, Wills and Probate Records, 1753–1999, all at Ancestry.com. See also untitled, *Guntersville Democrat*, October 1, 1924; and "Madison County," *Montgomery Advertiser*, May 14, 1872.

14. US Civil War Soldiers, 1861–1865, Film No. 374, Roll 14; US Civil War Records and Profiles, 1861–1865; Selected Records of the War Department Relating to Confederate Prisoners of War, 1861–1865; and US Civil War Prisoners, 1861–1865, all at Ancestry.com. Also untitled, *Guntersville Democrat*, June 29, 1905; and "Mortuary," *Guntersville Democrat*, May 31, 1906. Johnnie's first wife Lucinda and her sister Andrew (yes, though female, she was given a boy's name) were the daughters of Confederate colonel James Lawrence Sheffield. At the inducement of her physician boyfriend who had been plying her with opium, Andrew set fire to the house of one of his nemeses. In response, colonel Sheffield killed the doctor and committed Andrew to Bryce, a mental hospital in Tuscaloosa. This bit of family drama became renowned in Marshall County. On Andrew Sheffield, see John S. Hughes, ed., *The Letters of a Victorian Madwoman* (Columbia: Univ. of South Carolina Press, 1993).

15. Cochrane, 91–93. Also 1860 US Federal Census; and US, Find A Grave Index, 1600s–Current, both at Ancestry.com.

16. 1860, 1870, 1880, 1900, 1919 US Federal Census; and Alabama County Marriages, 1805–1967, both at Ancestry.com. See also *Belle F. Neill, administratrix of the estate of James Watkins Fennell v. The United States*, 59th Congress, 2nd Session, Document 355, Congressional Number 10609, Fennell Family, VF, MCA, GA; and "The Memoirs of Caius Grattan Fennell," VF, MCA, GA. The school Belle attended, Huntsville Female College, had been transformed into a hospital by Union occupiers in November 1864. It was reopened in the autumn of 1866. Rohr, 222, 308.

17. "Editor Fennell," *Guntersville Democrat*, November 16, 1905.

18. 1850, 1860, 1870, 1880, 1900 US Federal Census; and Alabama County Marriages, 1805–1967, both at Ancestry.com. Also "The Memoirs of Caius Grattan Fennell," VF, MCA, GA; Hurff, 21; "Caius G. Fennell," *Guntersville Democrat*, April 9, 1903; "Editor Fennell," *Guntersville Advertiser*, June 20, 1916; untitled, *Guntersville Advertiser*, January 3, 1922; "Mrs. C. G. Fennell," *Huntsville Times*, March 8, 1931; and "Guntersville Papers Merged," *Huntsville Times*, April 5, 1928.

19. 1860, 1870, 1880, 1900 US Federal Census; Alabama County Marriages, 1805–1967; and US, Find A Grave Index, 1600s–Current, all at Ancestry.com.

20. Alabama Marriage Index, 1800–1969, Ancestry.com.

21. 1860 US Federal Census; and Web: RootsWeb Death Index, 1796–2010, both at Ancestry.com.

22. "Expulsion of W. R. W. Cobb," *Evening Star*, November 19, 1864; and "Confederate Congress Senate," *Richmond Examiner*, June 1, 1864.

23. "Confederate Congress Senate," *Richmond Examiner*, June 1, 1864.

24. Abraham Lincoln to Any United States Depository, January 4, 1863, copy, VF, MCA, GA; and "Jackson County Volunteers find rare Lincoln signature," *State & Local Records News* 8, no. 1 (May 2003): 2.

25. James L. McDowell to Major Heath, August 8, 1864; and Major Heath to Whom it May Concern, August 9, 1864, copies, W. R. W. Cobb, VF, MCA, GA. On Cobb's loyalty to the Union, see also "Cobb, Williamson RW-State: Kansas-Year: 1864," Series: Papers Relating to Citizens, 1861–1867, Record Group 109: War Department Collection of Confederate Records, 1825–1927, National Archives Identifier 27656106, National Archives, https://catalog.archives.gov/id/27656106 (accessed September 16, 2018).

26. "Latest from Rebeldom!" *Philadelphia Inquirer*, December 2, 1864.

27. Charles Rice, "W. R. W. Cobb—Jackson County Giant Killer," *Old Huntsville* no. 55 (1995), 53.

28. Will of James Cooper, Madison County, Alabama Probate Record Book 7, p. 51; 1870 US Federal Census, Ancestry.com; Houston Lee and Charity Cooper, Marriage Contract, Madison County, Alabama Estate File, Madison County, Alabama Deed Book S, December 1, 1840, pp. 173–74; and "The Lee Home," Historic

Scrapbook, vol. 2, March 5, 1933, VF, HMCPL, HA. On nineteenth-century women, marriage, and law, see Marie S. Molloy, *Single, White, Slaveholding Women in the Nineteenth-Century South* (Columbia: Univ. of South Carolina Press, 2018).

29. Beverly S. Curry, "The People Who Lived on the Land that is now Redstone Arsenal," Huntsville History Collection, December 2006, http://huntsvillehistorycollection.org/hh/hhpics/pdf/book2/People_of_Redstone_Arsenal.pdf (accessed June 11, 2019).

Appendix 2

1. Katie Fennell, the daughter of Francis Marion Fennell and Isabella Allison, was Cassie's double-first cousin.

2. Cassie's mother Martha Matilda Fennell.

3. Katie's sister Matilda (1847–1926). Family Trees, Ancestry.com.

4. Katie's sister Sarah (1846–1900). Family Trees, Ancestry.com.

5. Many Shelton families lived in Marshall, Jackson, and Madison Counties.

6. John Snodgrass (1836–1888) lived in Scottsboro, Alabama. He was commissioned as a captain in Company S, Alabama 16th Infantry Battalion. He later became part of Company S, Alabama 55th Infantry Regiment. US, Civil War Soldier Records and Profiles, 1861–1865, Ancestry.com.

7. James Swan and his wife Hamly lived in Marshall County, Alabama. He was twenty-nine years old in 1861. 1860 US Federal Census, Ancestry.com.

8. Katie's brother Charles (1857–1891). Family Trees, Ancestry.com.

9. Katie did not have a brother named John, so there are three possibilities. She may have been referring to Cassie's brother Johnnie. Or, she may have been speaking of their cousin John Andrew Allison, the son of their uncle David Allison and aunt Sarah (Smith) Allison. David and Sarah Allison also lived in Bellefonte, Alabama. John Andrew Allison later joined the 49th Alabama Infantry in December 1861. Family Tree, CHC, GA. See also Alabama Civil War Muster Rolls, 1861–1865; and Family Trees, both at Ancestry.com. Katie also had a paternal uncle named John D. Fennell (1809–1879), but she probably called him Uncle John, since she referred to Cassie's mother as "Aunt." Hurff, 25.

10. Sam Henry, Cassie's brother-in-law.

Appendix 3

1. This is from a typed transcription of the original diary. At the top, it reads, "Confederate Soldiers Diary—Isham (Wattie) Watkins Fennell, M.D., Surgeon 55th Alabama Infantry, C.S.A." At the bottom of the transcription is the following: "This diary was copied from a pocket memorandum book, very much damaged from water, wet, and moths. The family spoke of this as being Uncle Wattie's diary, and very likely was his, a good part of its [sic] gone, and [neither] his nor any name is on

it. There were three brothers that served in the Confederate Army, Isham Watkins (Wattie) Fennell M.D. Surgeon 55th Ala Infantry, C.S.A. Capt' James William Fennell M.D. Capt' Co. I 4th Alabama Cavalry, C.S.A. John Houston Fennell Private Co. F 8th Confederate Cavalry, C.S.A. There is a picture in the family of two of these brothers in Ku Klux Klan regalia, but not known which they are. This was copied by H. P. Alves as best that could be made out. 1949 Guntersville, Ala." Fennell, VF, MCA, GA. Though Alves believed this to be Wattie's diary, the editor has deduced that this cannot be the case. Wattie never served in Virginia. Willie, on the other hand, was present in Virginia at the time this was written. If, as Alves thought, the diary belonged to one of the Fennell brothers, it must have been Willie's.

2. Springfield, Virginia, is in Fairfax County.

3. Benjamin F. Walters, a native of Marshall County, served as a private in the 8th Regiment, Alabama Infantry. "B. F. Walters," Search for Soldiers, Civil War, National Park Service, https://www.nps.gov/civilwar/search-soldiers-detail.htm?soldierId=059108DD-DC7A-DF11-BF36-B8A06F5D926A (accessed February 27, 2019). See also US, Civil War Soldier Records and Profiles, 1861–1865; and Alabama, Select Marriage Indexes, 1816–1942, both at Ancestry.com.

4. Centreville, Virginia, is near Manassas Junction and the Orange & Alexandria Railroad. Brendan Wolfe, "Centreville During the Civil War," *Encyclopedia Virginia*, www.encyclopediavirignia.org/Centreville-During-the-Civil-War (accessed October 29, 2018).

5. The Battle of Ball's Bluff took place on October 21, 1861, at Leesburg, Virginia. Long, 136.

6. General Nathan G. Evans. The Union leaders were brigadier general Charles P. Stone and colonel Edward Baker.

7. Willie's uncle Francis Marion Fennell.

8. Due to his stellar performance at Ball's Bluff, Nathan G. Evans received a promotion to brigadier general. "Nathan G. Evans," American Battlefield Trust, https://battlefields.org/learn/biographies/nathan-g-evans (accessed October 29, 2018).

9. Probably general Joseph E. Johnston.

10. In 1861, Thaddeus Lowe constructed seven balloons to monitor enemy movements. From October 1861 to the early part of 1862, Lowe placed balloons along the Potomac River. Dr. James L. Green, "Civil War Balloons During the Seven Days Campaign," American Battlefield Trust, www.battlefields.org/learn/articles/civil-war-ballooning-during-seven-days-campaign (accessed October 29, 2018).

11. Willie's brother-in-law Sam Henry received a promotion to colonel on October 21, 1861. Major Edward O'Neal received a promotion to lieutenant colonel. Both men were in the 9th Alabama Infantry.

12. Given that he was left to tend the sick, this diary's author obviously had some connection to healthcare. This gives further evidence that this diary was written

by Willie. Confederate physicians were often overwhelmed. As historian Shauna Devine explained, "While the North expelled competing sects, the southern physicians served alongside slaves, eclectics, homeopathists, and wise women. Even if physicians wanted to research or perform medical experiments, there was little opportunity—physicians struggled most of the time trying to offer comfort and proper treatment. The central goal, then, was to provide immediate care to the troops in order to preserve manpower." Shauna Devine, *Learning from the Wounded: The Civil War and the Rise of American Medical Science* (Chapel Hill: Univ. of North Carolina Press, 2014), 9.

13. Fort Donelson fell on February 16, 1862. "Fort Donelson," American Battlefield Trust, https://www.battlefields.org/learn/civil-war/battles/fort-donelson (accessed October 29, 2018). Willie's younger brother Wattie was taken prisoner at Fort Donelson.

14. In all likelihood, this referred to skirmishing because the first Battle of Winchester did not take place until May 25, 1862.

15. General Edmund Kirby Smith

16. Warrenton and White Sulphur Springs were both in Virginia.

17. The Hazel River is a tributary of the Rappahannock River. C.H. is the Culpeper Courthouse.

18. The Confederate army used the Culpeper Courthouse as a place to train and supply its troops. Daniel E. Sutherland, "Culpeper County During the Civil War," *Encyclopedia Virginia*, Virginia Humanities, https://www.encyclopediavirginia.org/Culpeper_County_During_the_Civil_War (accessed October 29, 2018).

19. On March 7, 1862, brigadier general Benjamin McCulloch died at the Battle of Pea Ridge. Eaton, 155; and Long, 179–80.

20. From March 1862 to May 1864, Orange, Virginia, along the Rapidan River, was the most northern part of the Confederacy. General Robert E. Lee used Orange as his headquarters around this time. "Orange, Virginia," Journey Through Hallowed Ground National Heritage Area website, https://hallowedground.org/Explore-the-Journey/Historic-Towns-Villages/Orange-VA (accessed October 29, 2018).

Appendix 4

1. "The Memoirs of Caius Grattan Fennell," VF, MCA, GA. Some of his recollections conflict with Cassie's dairies. Given that Caius was seven years old when the Civil War began, Cassie is a more reliable source for those years. However, Caius's memoirs reveal a great deal about what happened to the family after the war.

2. John T. Weatherby (1841–1864) served as a private in the 9th Alabama Infantry. US Civil War Soldiers, 1861–1865; and Alabama Civil War Muster Rolls, 1861–1865, both at Ancestry.com.

3. John May (1845–1862), the son of Judge Washington T. May and Margaret Wyeth Johnson, served as a private in the 9th Alabama Infantry. Virginia, Deaths and Burials Index, 1953–1917, Ancestry.com.

4. James "Jim" Beard, the son of Arthur C. Beard, one of Dr. James W. Fennell's neighbors. Family Trees, Ancestry.com.

5. These might have been the sons of Francis and Nancy Wedgeworth, who lived in Marshall County, Alabama. Family Trees, Ancestry.com.

6. William Henry Burnside farmed in Marshall County, Alabama. He and his wife Martha lived near the Fennells. 1850, 1860 US Federal Census, Ancestry.com.

7. 44th US Colored Infantry. US Civil War Pension Index: General Index to Pension Files, 1861–1934 for James W. Elliott, Ancestry.com.

8. During the Civil War, James W. Elliott (1834–1895) served in Company G of the 10th Indiana Regiment until 1864. He then became a lieutenant in the 44th US Colored Infantry. He later received a promotion to captain. After leaving the military, he practiced law in Guntersville. Though not from the area, he had married a local girl named Betty, hence his choice of city. 1870, 1880, 1890 US Federal Census; and Indiana Civil War Soldier Database Index, 1861–1865, both at Ancestry.com.

9. Peter Kilfoyle (1855–1916) and Pleasant Mitchell (1855–1892) resided in Marshall County, Alabama, and moved to Texas before 1880. Kilfoyle died in Smith County, Texas, while Mitchell lived and died in Gregg County, Texas. William Taylor may have been the brother of Kilfoyle's mother Mary. 1860, 1870 US Federal Census; and Family Trees, both at Ancestry.com.

10. There were several Langs in Guntersville. The census listed each as a farmer. As such, the editor remained unable to verify a teacher named Lang. Of course, if the man came to Marshall County after the war, he may not have stayed after this beating and would not have been in Guntersville for the 1870 US Federal Census.

11. Peter Whitecotton, a local guerilla in Marshall County, Alabama, was killed in March 1865. Official Records of the Union and Confederate Armies, 1861–1865, series 1, no. 057, vol. 32, part 1, p. 665; and Robin Sterling, *People and Things from Marshall County, Alabama, Guntersville Democrat, 1901–1908* (Raleigh, NC: Lulu Press, 2016), 340. For Jack Weatherby, see appendix 4, note 2. On Jere Cornwell, see chap. 4, note 92.

12. Johnnie and Frank Fennell, his brothers.

13. John W. Grayson (1838–1917) served in the Alabama House of Representatives from 1870–1872 and from 1884–1885. He served as a state senator from 1873–1875. Captain John W. Grayson, "Alabamians in a Tennessee Regiment," *Confederate Veteran* 19, no. 8 (August 1911): 375. A family connection existed, as Grayson married Caius's cousin Sarah Smith Allison.

14. This story is incredibly suspect given that Caius was seven years old when the Civil War started and eleven when it ended. It is doubtful a Confederate soldier

would have been able to wear his clothes. Caius's older brother Frank, however, would have been fourteen years old in 1865, and it is feasible that he might have exchanged clothes with a soldier.

15. The editor found nothing on Karl Scruggs or Joe De Fer.

16. By 1864, Confederate brigadier general Hylan Lyon led what remained of the 3rd, 7th, 8th, and 12th Kentucky regiments. "Hylan Benton Lyon," American Civil War Officers, *Confederate Military History*, vol. 11, p. 247, Ancestry.com.

17. Thomas Atkins (1792–1870), a veteran of the War of 1812, lived in Warrenton, Alabama. 1850, 1860, 1870 US Federal Census; and US, War of 1812 Service Records, 1812–1815, all at Ancestry.com.

18. Col. William J. Palmer of the 15th Pennsylvania Cavalry.

19. Alexander Erskine Russell (1827–1896). 1870 US Federal Census; and US, Find A Grave Index, 1600s–Current, both at Ancestry.com.

20. Caius's brother-in-law Sam Henry.

21. Perhaps John Stone Blair (1848–1922) from Cherokee County, Alabama. 1880 US Federal Census, Ancestry.com.

22. This may have been Christopher Columbus NeSmith (1835–1906) of neighboring Morgan County, Alabama. He served in the 35th Regiment, Mississippi Infantry. US Civil War Soldiers, 1861–1865, Ancestry.com.

23. George Richardson (1835–1900) lived in Decatur, Alabama, and in his later life, worked as a cabinet maker. 1900 US Federal Census, Ancestry.com.

24. Sallie A. Hill (1889–) lived with her father Henry on Broad Street in Guntersville. The census listed her occupation as printer. 1910 US Federal Census, Ancestry.com.

25. Montgomery never had a mayor by that name or any derivation thereof. Caius became president of the Alabama Press Association in 1909, so the mayor would have been William M. Teague (1905–1909) or Gaston Gunter (1909–1910). Thomas McAdory Owen, *History of Alabama and Dictionary of Alabama Biography*, vol. 2 (Chicago: S. J. Clarke Publishing Company, 1921), 1,040.

26. Guntersville had several Fearn families. 1850, 1860, 1870, 1880, 1890 US Federal Census, Ancestry.com.

Bibliography

PRIMARY SOURCES

Newspapers

Advertiser-Gleam (Guntersville, AL)
Alexandria Gazette
The Atlantic
Autauga Citizen
Charleston Gazette
Charlotte Democrat
Chattanooga Daily Rebel
Clarion-Ledger (Jackson, MS)
Critic and Record (Washington, DC)
Daily Confederate (Raleigh, NC)
Daily Huntsville Confederate
Evening Bulletin (Charlotte, NC)
Evening Star (Washington, DC)
Guntersville Advertiser
Guntersville Advertiser and Democrat
Guntersville Democrat
Huntsville Democrat
Huntsville Independent
Huntsville Times
National Republican
New York Times
Philadelphia Inquirer
Richmond Examiner
Salem Observer
Shreveport Semi-Weekly
Southern Advocate (Huntsville, AL)
Washington Daily Intelligencer
Washington Post

Washington Union
Wilmington Daily Journal

State/Federal Government and Military Records

Alabama Burial Index, 1935–2014
Alabama, Civil Appointments, 1818–1939
Alabama Civil War Muster Rolls, 1861–1865
Alabama, Civil War Soldiers, 1861–1865
Alabama Confederate Pension and Service Records, 1862–1947
Alabama County Marriage Records, 1805–1867
Alabama Death Index
Alabama Marriages, 1809–1920
Alabama, Probate Court of Marshall County, Guntersville, State of Alabama.
Alabama, Select Marriages Indexes, 1816–1942
Alabama, Texas, and Virginia, Confederate Pensions, 1884–1958
Alabama, Wills and Probate Records, 1753–1999
All US, Pardons Under Proclamations, 1865–1869
Indiana Civil War Soldier Database Index, 1861–1865
List of Cadets Admitted into US Military Academy
Logs of Ships and Stations, 1801–1946; and Logs of U.S. Naval Ships, 1801–1915, National Archives.
Marshall County Archives, Guntersville, Alabama.
Official Records of the Union and Confederate Armies.
Selected Records of the War Department Relating to Confederate Prisoners of War, 1861–1865
Tennessee, Deaths and Burials Index, 1874–1955
Tennessee, Marriage Records, 1780–2002
Texas Muster Roll Index Cards, 1838–1900
Texas, Select County Marriage Records, 1837–2015
US Army Register of Enlistments, 1798–1914
US Civil War Pension Index, General Index to Pension Files, 1861–1934
US Civil War Prisoner of War Records, 1861–1865
US Civil War Soldier War Records and Profiles, 1861–1865
US, Confederate Army Casualty Lists and Reports, 1861–1865
US, Confederate Soldiers Compiled Service Records, 1861–1865
US Federal Census, 1850, 1860, 1870, 1880, 1900, 1910
US Federal Census Mortality Schedules, 1850–1885
US Headstone Applications for Military Veterans, 1925–1963
US Slave Schedules, 1850, 1860
Virginia, Deaths and Burials Index, 1953–1917
War Department Collection of Confederate Records, 1825–1927, National Archives.

The War of The Rebellion: A Compilation of Official Records of the Union and Confederate Armies, Prepared under the Direction of the Secretary of War, by BVT. Lieut. Col. Robert N. Scott, Third U.S. Artillery, and Published Pursuant to Act of Congress Approved June 16, 1880. Washington, DC: Government Printing Office, 1883.

Other

"30th to 39th Congresses, 1847–1867." History, Art & Archives, United States House of Representatives. Accessed September 3, 2018. http://history.house.gov/Institution/Session-Dates/30-39/.

Carmen Hurff Collection, Private Collection, Guntersville, Alabama.

Confederate Veteran

"Executive Order—Call for Troops." The American Presidency Project. Accessed September 16, 2018. http://www.presidency.ucsb.edu/ws/index.php?pid=69810.

Finley, Keith R. The Diary of Miss Catherine Margaret Fennell, transcription. Guntersville: Keith Finley, 2012.

GW Magazine

Harper's Weekly

"J. W. Denver to Major General William T. Sherman." Moscow, Tennessee, July 15, 1862. Accessed September 15, 2018. https://www.48ovvi.org/oh48hd1.htm.

Lincoln, Abraham. "Special Session Message," July 4, 1861. The American Presidency Project. Accessed September 3, 2018. http://www.presidency.ucsb.edu/ws/index.php?pid=69802&st=&st1=.

Memorial Record of Alabama, vol. 2. Madison, WI: Brant and Fuller Publishers, 1893.

Moore, Frank, ed. *Biographical Sketches of the Military and Naval Heroes, Statesmen, and Orators, Distinguished in the American Crisis of 1861–62.* New York: G. P. Putnam, 1862.

Northern Alabama, Historical and Biographical. Birmingham: Smith & DeLand, 1888.

Old Huntsville Magazine

"Order Retiring Winfield Scott from Command." In *The Collected Works of Abraham Lincoln*, vol. 5. Edited by Roy P. Basler. New Brunswick, NJ: Rutgers University Press, 1953.

Speer, William S. and Hon. John Henry Brown, ed. *The Encyclopedia of the New West containing fully authenticated information of the agricultural, mercantile, commercial, manufacturing, mining and grazing industries, and representing the character, development, resources and present conditions of Texas, Arkansas, Colorado, New Mexico and Indian Territory also Biographical Sketches of their representative men and women.* Marshall, TX: The United States Biographical Publishing Co., 1881.

"Undergraduates." Columbian College, 1860, US School Catalogs, 1765–1935.
US High School Student Lists, 1821–1923.
US School Catalogs, 1765–1935.
Wagner, Dr. William. *History of the 24th Illinois Volunteer Infantry Regiment.* Chicago, 1864.

SECONDARY SOURCES

"About Holly Springs." City of Holly Springs, Mississippi, website. Accessed September 10, 2018. http://www.hollyspringsmsus.com/about-holly-springs/.
Adams, Charles. *Slavery, Secession & Civil War: Views from the United Kingdom and Europe, 1856–1865*. Lanham, MD: The Scarecrow Press, Inc., 2007.
Alabama Civil War Centennial Commission. *Brief Historical Sketches of Military Organizations Raised in Alabama in the Civil War* reproduced from William Brewer's *Alabama: Her History, Resources, War Record, and Public men from 1540–1872*. Tuscaloosa: University of Alabama Press, 1962.
Alderman, Edwin A., and Armistead Gordon. *J. L. M. Curry: A Biography*. New York: The MacMillan Company, 1911.
Ambrose, Stephen E. *Halleck: Lincoln's Chief of Staff*. 1962. Reprint, Baton Rouge: Louisiana State University Press, 1996.
Anders, Curt. *Fighting Confederates*. New York: G. P. Putnam's Sons, 1968.
Anderson, Paul Christopher. *Blood Image: Turner Ashby in the Civil War and the Southern Mind*. Baton Rouge: Louisiana State University Press, 2006.
Andrews, Eliza Frances. *The Wartime Journal of a Georgia Girl, 1864–1865*. Introduced by Jean V. Berlin. New York: D. Appleton and Co., 1908. Reprint, Lincoln: University of Nebraska Press, 1997.
Ashkenazi, Elliott, ed. *The Civil War Diary of Clara Solomon: Growing Up in New Orleans, 1861–1862*. Baton Rouge: Louisiana State University Press, 1995.
Atchison, R. Jarrod. *A War of Words: Rhetorical Leadership of Jefferson Davis*. Tuscaloosa: University of Alabama Press, 2017.
Atkins, Leah Rawls, Joseph H. Harrison Jr., and Sara A. Hudson, eds. *Belle of the Fifties: Memoirs of Mrs. Clay of Alabama by Virginia Clay-Clopton*. Tuscaloosa: University of Alabama Press, 1999.
Axford, Faye Acton, ed. *Thomas Hubbard Hobbs: The Journal of Thomas Hubbard Hobbs*. Tuscaloosa: University of Alabama Press, 1976.
Bailey, Candace. *Music and the Southern Belle: From Accomplished Lady to Confederate Composer*. Carbondale: Southern Illinois University Press, 2010.
Baird, Julia. *Victoria the Queen: An Intimate Biography of the Woman Who Ruled an Empire*. New York: Random House, 2016.
Barrett, John G. *The Civil War in North Carolina*. 1963. Reprint, Chapel Hill: University of North Carolina Press, 1995.

Beckert, Sven. "Cotton and the US South." In *Plantation Kingdom: The American South and Its Global Commodities*, edited by Richard Follett, Sven Beckert, Peter Coclanis, and Barbara Hahn, 39-60. Baltimore: Johns Hopkins University Press, 2016.

Bernath, Michael T. *Confederate Minds: The Struggle for Intellectual Independence in the Civil War South*. Chapel Hill: University of North Carolina Press, 2010.

Blair, Jayne E. *The Essential War: A Handbook to the Battles, Armies, Navies, and Commanders*. Jefferson, NC: McFarland & Co., 2006.

Blaisdell, Bob, ed. *Civil War Short Stories and Poems*. Mineola, NY: Dover Publications, Inc., 2011.

Bleser, Carol, and Frederick M. Heath. "The Clays of Alabama: The Impact of the Civil War on a Southern Marriage." In *In Joy and In Sorrow: Women, Family, and Marriage in the Victorian South*, edited by Carol Bleser, 135–53. New York: Oxford University Press, 1991.

Bogan, Dallas. "Official Records of Civil War Recount Various Skirmishes in Powell's Valley, Cumberland Gap." History of Campbell County Tennessee. Accessed September 9, 2018. https://www.tngenweb.org/campbell/hist-bogan/skirmish.html.

Bond, James Jefferson. "Competing Visions of America: The Fourth of July During the Civil War." Master's thesis, Virginia Polytechnic Institute and State University, 2007.

Bonner, James C., ed. *The Journal of a Milledgeville Girl, 1861–1865*. Athens: University of Georgia Press, 1964.

"Boonville." CWSAC Battle Summaries. American Battlefield Protection Program. Accessed September 3, 2018. https://www.nps.gov/abpp/battles/mo001.htm.

Bordewich, Fergus. "Fort Sumter: The Civil War Begins." *Smithsonian Magazine*, April 2011. Accessed September 2, 2018. https://www.smithsonian.com/history/fort-sumter-the-civil-war-begins-1018791.

———. "John Brown's Day of Reckoning." *Smithsonian Magazine*, October 2009. Accessed October 8, 2018. https://www.smithsonianmag.com/history/john-browns-day-of-reckoning-139165084.

"Bouligny, John Edward." Biographical Directory of the United States Congress, 1774–present. Accessed September 8, 2018. http://bioguide.congress.gov/scripts/biodisplay.pl?index=B000665.

Brill, Kristen, ed. *The Diary of a Civil War Bride: Lucy Wood Butler of Virginia*. Baton Rouge: Louisiana State University Press, 2017.

Browning, Robert M. *Forrest: The Confederacy's Relentless Warrior*. Washington, DC: Potomac Books, 2004.

———. *Success Is All That Was Expected: The South Atlantic Blockading Squadron during the Civil War*. Dulles, VA: Brassey's Inc., 2002.

Buenger, Walter L. *Secession and the Union in Texas*. Austin: University of Texas Press, 1984.

Burton, Brian K. *Extraordinary Circumstances: The Seven Days Battles*. Bloomington: Indiana University Press, 2001.

Carr, Dawson. *Gray Phantoms of the Cape Fear: Running the Civil War Blockade*. Winston-Salem, NC: John F. Blair Publishers, 1998.

Carter, Arthur B. *Tarnished Cavalier: Major General Earl Van Dorn*. Knoxville: University of Tennessee Press, 2013.

Casdorph, Paul D. *Prince John Magruder: His Life and Campaigns*. Hoboken, NJ: Wiley, 1996.

"Cass, Lewis." Biographical Directory of the United States Congress, 1774–present. Accessed October 8, 2018. http://bioguide.congress.gov/scripts/biodisplay.pl?index=c000233.

Catton, Bruce. *This Hallowed Ground: The Story of the Union Side of the Civil War*. Edison, NJ: Castle Books, 2002.

"Chaplains of the House." Office of the Chaplain: House of Representatives. Accessed October 8, 2018. https://chaplain.house.gov/chaplaincy/history.html.

"Cheat Mountain." CWSAC Battle Summaries. American Battlefield Protection Program. Accessed September 8, 2018. https://www.nps.gov/abpp/battles/wv005.htm.

Clinard, Karen L., and Richard Russell, ed. *Fear in North Carolina: The Civil War Journals and Letters of the Henry Family*. Asheville, NC: Reminiscing Books, 2008.

Clinton, Catherine. *The Plantation Mistress: Woman's World in the Old South*. New York: Pantheon Books, 1982.

———. *Stepdaughters of History: Southern Women and the American Civil War*. Baton Rouge: Louisiana State University Press, 2016.

Cobb, J. Michael, Edward B. Hicks, and Wythe Holt. *Battle of Big Bethel: Crucial Clash in Early Civil War Virginia*. El Dorado Hills, CA: Savas Beatie, 2013.

Cochrane, Ann. "Fennells—Always on the Move." *Valley Leaves: Tennessee Valley Genealogical Society* 2, no. 2 (Dec 1976): 91–93.

Coddington, Ronald S. *Faces of the Confederacy: An Album of Southern Soldiers and Their Stories*. Baltimore: Johns Hopkins University Press, 2008.

Coker, Michael D. *The Battle of Port Roya*l. Charleston: The History Press, 2009.

Colton, Ray C. *Confederate Units of Madison, Alabama*. Norman: University of Oklahoma Press, 1984.

"Confederate Units of Madison, Alabama." AlGenWeb: Southern Genealogy. Accessed September 10, 2018. https://algw.genealogyvillage.com/madison/confunit.htm.

Connelly, Thomas Lawrence. *Autumn Glory: The Army of Tennessee, 1862–1865*. Baton Rouge: Louisiana State University Press, 1971.

Cooling, Benjamin Franklin. *Forts Henry and Donelson: The Key to the Confederate Heartland*. Knoxville: University of Tennessee Press, 1987.

Cooper, William J. *Jefferson Davis: American*. New York: Vintage, 2001.

Cox, General Jacob D. *Sherman's Battle for Atlanta*. Cambridge: De Capo Books, 1994.

Crabtree, Beth G., and James W. Patton, eds. *"Journal of a Secesh Lady": The Diary of Catherine Ann Devereux Edmondston, 1860–1866*. Raleigh, NC: Division of Archives and History, 1979.

Crapol, Edward P. *John Tyler: The Accidental President*, rev. ed. Chapel Hill: University of North Carolina Press, 2012.

Crofts, Daniel W. *Reluctant Confederates: Upper South Unionists in the Secession Crisis*. Chapel Hill: University of North Carolina Press, 1989.

Curry, Beverly S. "The People Who Lived on the Land that is now Redstone Arsenal." Accessed June 11, 2019. Huntsville History Collection. http://huntsvillehistorycollection.org/hh/hhpics/pdf/books2/People_of_Redstone_Arsenal.pdf.

"Curry, Jabez Lamar Monroe." Biographical Directory of the United States Congress, 1774–present. Accessed September 8, 2018. http://bioguide.congress.gov/scripts/biodisplay.pl?index=C001003.

Cutrer, Thomas W. "Benjamin McCulloch." *The Handbook of Texas Online*. Accessed September 3, 2018. https://tshaonline.org/handbook/online/articles/fmc34.

———. "Ord, Edward Otho Cresap." *The Handbook of Texas Online*. Accessed September 9, 2018. https://tshaonline.org/handbook/online/articles/foro1.

Daniel, Larry J. *Soldiering in the Army of Tennessee: A Portrait of Life in a Confederate Army*. Chapel Hill: University of North Carolina Press, 1991.

Davidson, Donald. *The Tennessee The New River: Civil War to TVA*, vol. 2. Nashville, TN: JS Sanders & Co., 1992.

Davis, Roderick. "John Allan Wyeth." *Encyclopedia of Alabama*. Accessed August 7, 2019. http://www.encyclopediaofalabama.org/article/h-3522.

Davis, William C. *Battle at Bull Run: A History of the First Major Campaign of the Civil War*. New York: Doubleday & Co., 1977.

———. *Breckinridge: Statesman, Soldier, Symbol*. 1974. Reprint, Lexington: University Press of Kentucky, 2010.

"The Death of General Robert McCook." Warfare History Network. Accessed September 16, 2018. https://warfarehistorynetwork.com/2018/12/20/the-death-of-general-robert-mccook/.

DeCaro Jr., Louis. *Freedom's Dawn: The Last Days of John Brown in Virginia*. Rowman & Littlefield Publishers, 2015.

Devine, Shauna. *Learning from the Wounded: The Civil War and the Rise of American Medical Science*. Chapel Hill: University of North Carolina Press, 2014.

Dew, Charles B. *Apostles of Disunion: Southern Secession Commissioners and the Causes of the Civil War*. Charlottesville: University of Virginia Press, 2001.

Dollar, Kent T., Larry H. Whiteaker, and W. Calvin Dickinson, eds. *Border Wars: The Civil War in Tennessee and Kentucky*. Kent, OH: Kent State University Press, 2015.

Donald, David Herbert. *Lincoln*. London: Jonathan Cape, 1995.

Doyle, Don H. *The Cause of All Nations: An International History of the American Civil War*. New York: Basic Books, 2015.

DuBose, John Witherspoon. *General Joseph Wheeler and the Army of Tennessee*. New York: The Neale Publishing Co., 1912.

Duncan, Katherine, and Larry Smith. *The History of Marshall County, Alabama*, vol. 1. Albertville, AL: Thompson Printing Co., 1969.

Duncan, Richard R. *Beleaguered Winchester: A Virginia Community at War, 1861–1865*. Baton Rouge: Louisiana State University Press, 2007.

Dunnavant, Robert. *Decatur, Alabama: Yankee Foothold in Dixie, 1861–1865*. Athens, AL: Pea Ridge Press, 1995.

"Durant, John Ashmore." Biographical Directory of the United States Congress, 1774–present. Accessed October 8, 2018. http://bioguide.congress.gov/scripts/biodisplay.pl?index=A000316.

Eaton, Clement. *A History of the Southern Confederacy*. New York: The Free Press, 1954.

Egerton, Douglas R. *Year of Meteors: Stephen Douglas, Abraham Lincoln, and the Election that Brought on the Civil War*. New York: Bloomsbury Press, 2010.

Ekelund Jr., Robert B. and Mark Thornton. *Tariffs, Blockades, and Inflation: The Economics of the Civil War*. Wilmington, DE: Scholarly Resources, Inc., 2004.

"Election of 1860." The American Presidency Project. Accessed September 2, 2018. www.presidency.ucsb.edu/showelection.php?year=1860.

Engle, Stephen D. *Don Carlos Buell: Most Promising of All*. Chapel Hill: University of North Carolina Press, 1999.

Esslinger, William F. *Two Hundred Years of the Esslinger Family*. Huntsville: W. F. Esslinger, 1950.

Evans, Clement A. *Confederate Military History*, vol. 3. Atlanta: Confederate Publishing Company, 1899.

"Exchange Prisoners in the Civil War." Accessed September 16, 2018. www.civilwarhome.com/prisonerexchange.html.

Ezratty, Harry A. *Baltimore in the Civil War: The Pratt Street Riot and a City Occupied*. Charleston: The History Press, 2010.

Faust, Drew Gilpin. *Mothers of Invention: Women of the Slaveholding South in the American Civil War*. Chapel Hill: University of North Carolina Press, 1996.

Ferrell, Carolyn Stier. *Occupied: The Story of Clarksville, Tennessee, During the Civil War*. Nashville, TN: Westview, 2013.

Ferris, Norman B. *The Trent Affair: A Diplomatic Crisis*. Knoxville: University of Tennessee Press, 1977.

"Fifty-Fifth Alabama Infantry Regiment." Alabama Archives. Accessed September 23, 2018. https://archives.alabama.gov/referenc/alamilor/55thinf.html.

"Fitzgerald, Benjamin." Biographical Directory of the United States Congress, 1774–present. Accessed September 8, 2018. http://bioguide.congress.gov/scripts/biodisplay.pl?index=F000174.

Fitzgerald, Michael. *Reconstruction in Alabama: From Civil War to Redemption in the Cotton South*. Baton Rouge: Louisiana State University Press, 2017.

Fleming, Walter L. *Civil War and Reconstruction in Alabama*. New York: Columbia University Press, 1905.

Foote, Shelby. *The Civil War, a Narrative: Red River to Appomattox*. New York: Random House, 1974. Reprint, New York: Vintage Books, 1986.

"Fort Donelson." American Battlefield Trust. Accessed September 9, 2018. https: www.battlefields.org/learn/civil-war/battles/fort-donelson.

"Fort McRee." National Park Service. Accessed September 8, 2018. https://www.nps.gov/guis/learn/historyculture/fort-mcree.htm.

"Fort Pickens, Gulf Islands National Seashore." American Battlefield Trust. Accessed September 8, 2018. http://www.battlefields.org/visit/heritage-sites/fort-pickens-gulf-islands-national-seashore.

"Fourth Alabama Infantry Regiment." Alabama Archives. Accessed September 5, 2018. www.archives.alabama.gov/reference/alamilor/4thinf.html.

Freehling, William W., and Craig M. Simpson, eds. *Showdown in Virginia: The 1861 Convention and the Fate of the Union*. Charlottesville: University of Virginia Press, 2010.

Freeman, Douglas Southall. *Lee*, with a new forward by James M. McPherson. New York: Touchstone, 1997.

———. *Lee's Lieutenants: A Study in Command*, vol. 1, *Manassas to Malvern Hill*. New York: Charles Scribner's Sons, 1946.

———. *Lee's Lieutenants: A Study in Command*, vol. 2, *Cedar Mountain to Chancellorsville*. New York: Charles Scribner's Sons, 1946.

———. *Lee's Lieutenants: A Study in Command*, vol. 3, *Gettysburg to Appomattox*. New York: Charles Scribner's Sons, 1946.

Fuller, A. James, ed. *The Election of 1860 Reconsidered*. Kent, OH: Kent State University Press, 2013.

Furgurson, Ernest B. "The Battle of Bull Run: The End of Illusions." *Smithsonian Magazine*, August 2011. Accessed September 4, 2018. https://www.smithsonianmag.com/history/the-battle-of-bull-run-the-end-of-illusions-17525927/.

———. *Freedom Rising: Washington in the Civil War*. New York: Vintage, 2005.

Gardner, Sarah E. *Blood & Irony: Southern White Women's Narratives of the Civil War, 1861-1937*. Chapel Hill: University of North Carolina Press, 2004.

"General Sherman." Naval History and Heritage Command. Accessed September 22, 2018. https://www.history.navy.mil/research/histories/ship-histories/danfs/g/general-sherman.html.

Genovese, Eugene D. *Roll, Jordan, Roll: The World the Slaves Made*. New York: Pantheon Books, 1974.

Glatthaar, Joseph. *General Lee's Army: From Victory to Collapse*. New York: Free Press, 2008.

Goodwin, Doris Kearns. *Team of Rivals: The Political Genius of Abraham Lincoln*. New York: Simon & Schuster, 2006.

Green, James L. "Civil War Balloons During the Seven Days Campaign." American Battlefield Trust. Accessed October 29, 2018. www.battlefields.org/learn/articles/civil-war-ballooning-during-seven-days-campaign.

Griffith, Lucille. *Alabama: A Documentary History to 1900*. Tuscaloosa: University of Alabama Press, 1968.

Grinstead, Marion C. *Life and Death of a Frontier Fort: Fort Craig, New Mexico, 1854–1885*. Socorro, NM: Socorro County Historical Society, 1973.

Gruber, Drew A. "The Battle of Williamsburg." *Encyclopedia Virginia*. Virginia Humanities. Accessed September 13, 2018. https://www.encyclopediavirginia.org/Williamsburg_The_Battle_of#start_entry.

Gwynne, S. C. *Rebel Yell: The Violence, Passion, and Redemption of Stonewall Jackson*. New York: Scribner, 2015.

Hardy, Michael C. *North Carolina and the Civil War*. Charleston: The History Press, 2011.

Harrison, Kimberly. *The Rhetoric of Rebel Women: Civil War Diaries and Confederate Persuasion*. Carbondale, IL: Southern Illinois Press, 2013.

Harrison, Lowell H. *The Civil War in Kentucky*. Lexington: University Press of Kentucky, 1975.

Hartje, Robert J. *Van Dorn: The Life and Times of a Confederate General*. Nashville: Vanderbilt University Press, 1967.

Harsh, Joseph L. *Taken at the Flood: Robert E. Lee and Confederate Strategy in the Maryland Campaign of 1862*. Kent, OH: Kent State University Press, 1999.

"Hatteras Inlet Batteries." CWSAC Battle Summaries. American Battlefield Protection Program. Accessed September 8, 2018. https://www.nps.gov/abpp/battles/nc001.htm.

Hearn, Chester G. *When the Devil Came Down to Dixie: Ben Butler in New Orleans*. Baton Rouge: Louisiana State University Press, 1997.

Hess, Earl J. *The Knoxville Campaign: Burnside and Longstreet in East Tennessee*. Knoxville: University of Tennessee Press, 2013.

Hewitt, Lawrence Lee. *Port Hudson: Confederate Bastion on the Mississippi*. Baton Rouge: Louisiana State University Press, 1994.

Hibbert, Christopher. *Edward VII: The Last Victorian King*. 1976. Reprint, New York: Palgrave Macmillan, 2007.

"Historic Poolesville." The Blue Hearth. Accessed September 17, 2018. https://thebluehearth.com/find-us/historic-poolesville/.

"Historical News and Notices." *Journal of Southern History* 19, no. 1 (February 1953): 117–34.

History of Jackson County, Alabama. Clanton, AL: Heritage Publishing Consultants, Inc., 1998.

"History of the Town of Paint Rock, Alabama." *Paint Rock News*. Accessed September 13, 2018. https://paintrockal.webs.com/historyofpaintrock.htm.

Holt, Michael F. *The Election of 1860: "A Campaign Fraught with Consequences."* Lawrence: University of Kansas Press, 2017.

Horn, Stanley F. *The Army of Tennessee: A Military History*. New York: The Bobbs-Merrill Co., 1941.

Horwitz, Tony. *Midnight Rising: John Brown and the Raid that Sparked the Civil War*. 2011. Reprint, New York: Picador, 2012.

Hughes, John S., ed. *The Letters of a Victorian Madwoman*. Columbia: University of South Carolina Press, 1993.

Hughes Jr., Nathaniel C. *General William J. Hardee: Old Reliable*. 1965. Reprint, Baton Rouge: Louisiana State University Press, 1992.

Hurff, Carmen. *Within the Great Bend: Our Families of Alabama's Tennessee River Valley: The Fennells of Marshall County, the Esslingers of Madison, the Russells & Austins of Jackson County*. Guntersville, AL: Carmen Hurff, 2000.

Hyde, Sarah L. *Schooling in the Antebellum South: The Rise of Public and Private Education in Louisiana, Mississippi, and Alabama*. Baton Rouge: Louisiana State University Press, 2016.

Iobst, Richard W. *The Bloody Sixth: The Sixth North Carolina Regiment, Confederate States of America*. Durham, NC: Christian Printing Co., 1965.

Janke, Lucinda Prout. *A Guide to Civil War Washington, D.C.: The Capital of the Union*. Charleston: The History Press, 2013.

Johannsen, Robert W. *Stephen A. Douglas*. New York: Oxford University Press, 1973. Reprint, Chicago: University of Illinois Press, 1997.

"John F. Fore, Pine Apple, Ala., writes of Forrest." *Confederate Veteran* 6, no. 1 (Jan 1898): 24–25.

Johnson, Timothy D. *Winfield Scott: The Quest for Military Glory*. Lawrence: University Press of Kansas, 1998.

Jones, Rev. J. William. *Christ in Camp or Religion in the Confederate Army*. Atlanta, GA: The Martin & Hoyt Co., 1904.

Jones, Robert C. *Alabama and the Civil War: A History & Guide*. Charleston: The History Press, 2017.

"A Journalist's Perspective on the Invasion of Huntsville." *Huntsville Historical Review* 16, no. 1 & 2 (Spring-Fall 1989): 23-38.

Justice, George. "Georgia Secession Convention of 1861." *New Georgia Encyclopedia*. Accessed September 2, 2018. https://www.georgiaencyclopedia.org/articles/government-politics/georgia-secession-convention-1861.

Keller, David L. *The Story of Camp Douglas: Chicago's Forgotten Civil War Prison*. Charleston: The History Press, 2015.

Kennamer, John Robert. *History of Jackson County*. Winchester, TN: Press of Southern Printing and Publishing Co., 1935.

Klunder, Willard Carl. *Lewis Cass and the Politics of Moderation*. Kent, OH: Kent State University Press, 1996.

Krolick, Marshall D. "Brig. Gen. Abraham H. Buford." In *Kentuckians in Gray: Confederate Generals and Field Officers of the Bluegrass State*, edited by Bruce S. Allardice and Lawrence Lee Hewitt, 49–55. Lexington: University Press of Kentucky, 2008.

Lankford, Nelson D. *Cry Havoc: The Crooked Road to the Civil War, 1861*. New York: Penguin, 2007.

———. "Virginia Convention of 1861." *Encyclopedia Virginia*. Virginia Humanities. Accessed September 2, 2018. https://www.encyclopediavirginia.org/Virginia_Constitutional_Convention_of_1861.

"Laurel Hill and the First Land Battles of the Civil War." The Battle of Laurel Hill. Accessed September 4, 2018. http://www.battleoflaurelhill.org/history.html.

Leonard, Elizabeth. *All the Daring of the Soldier: Women of the Civil War Armies*. New York: W.W. Norton & Co., 1999.

Lesser, W. Hunter. *Rebels at the Gate: Lee and McClellan on the Front Line of a Nation Divided*. Naperville, IL: Sourcebooks, Inc., 2004.

Levine, Bruce. *The Fall of the House of Dixie: The Civil War and the Social Revolution that Transformed the South*. New York: Random House, 2014.

Levy, George. *To Die in Chicago: Confederate Prisoners at Camp Douglas, 1862–1865*. 2nd ed. Evanston, IL: Evanston Publishing, Inc., 1994. Reprint, Gretna, LA: Pelican Publishing, 1999.

Lewis, Herbert J. "Jim." "Selma Ordnance and Naval Foundry." *Encyclopedia of Alabama*. Accessed September 23, 2018. http://www.encyclopediaofalabama.org/article/h-2331.

Long, E. B., with Barbara Long. *The Civil War Day by Day: An Almanac, 1861–1865*. 1971. Reprint, New York: Da Capo, 1985.

Lowry, Terry. *September Blood: The Battle of Carnifex Ferry*. Charleston, WV: Quarrier Press, 2011.

Luvaas, Jay, Leonard Fullenkamp, and Stephen Bowman, eds. *Guide to the Battle of Shiloh*. Lawrence: University Press of Kansas, 1996.

"Mallory, Stephen Russell." Biographical Directory of the United States Congress, 1774–present. Accessed September 8, 2018. http://bioguide.congress.gov/scripts/biodisplay.pl?index=M000084.

Maroney, Mickey, ed. "The Civil War Journal of Octavia Wyche Otey." *Huntsville Historical Review* 18, no. 1 (Winter-Spring 1991): 1-30.

Marshall, Anne E. *Creating a Confederate Kentucky: The Lost Cause and Civil War Memory in a Border State*. Chapel Hill: University of North Carolina Press, 2010.

Marszalek, John F. *Commander of All Lincoln's Armies: A Life of General Henry W. Halleck*. Cambridge, MA: Belknap Press, 2004.

Marten, James. *The Children's Civil War*. Chapel Hill: University of North Carolina Press, 1998.

———. *Civil War America: Voices from the Home Front*. Santa Barbara: ABC-Clio, 2003.

Martin, Bessie. *A Rich Man's War, A Poor Man's Fight: Desertion of Alabama Troops from the Confederate Army.* Introduction by Mark A. Weitz. Tuscaloosa: University of Alabama Press, 2003.

McClintock, Russell. *Lincoln and the Decision for War: The Northern Response to Secession*. Chapel Hill: University of North Carolina Press, 2008.

McClinton, Oliver Wood. "The Career of the Confederate States Ram Arkansas." *Arkansas Historical Quarterly* 7 (Winter 1948): 329–33.

McGlone, Robert E. *John Brown's War Against Slavery*. New York: Cambridge University Press, 2009.

McIlwain, Christopher Lyle. *Civil War Alabama*. Tuscaloosa: University of Alabama Press, 2016.

McMillan, Malcolm. *The Alabama Confederate Reader.* Tuscaloosa, AL: University of Alabama Press, 1963.

———. *The Land Called Alabama*. Austin, TX: Steck-Vaughn Co., 1968.

McPherson, James M. *Ordeal by Fire: The Civil War and Reconstruction*. New York: Alfred A. Knopf, 1982.

———. *War on the Waters: The Union and Confederate Navies, 1861–1865*. Chapel Hill: University of North Carolina Press, 2012.

"McRae, John Jones." Biographical Directory of the United States Congress, 1774–present. Accessed October 8, 2018. http://bioguide.congress.gov/scripts/biodisplay.pl?index=M000596.

Melton, Tracy Matthew. *Hanging Henry Gambrill: The Violent Career of Baltimore's Plug Uglies, 1854–1860*. Baltimore: Maryland Historical Association, 2004.

"Middle Creek." CWSAC Battle Summaries. American Battlefield Protection Program. Accessed September 9, 2018. http://www.nps.gov/abpp/battles/ky005.htm.

Mitcham, Sam. *Vicksburg: The Bloody Siege that Turned the Tide of the Civil War.* Washington, DC: Regnery History, 2018.

Molloy, Marie S. *Single, White, Slaveholding Women in the Nineteenth-Century South.* Columbia: University of South Carolina Press, 2018.

Morris Jr., Roy. *The Long Pursuit: Abraham Lincoln's Thirty-Year Struggle with Stephen Douglas for the Heart and Soul of America.* New York: HarperCollins, 2008.

"Most Hallowed Ground: Portraits and stories of those who rest at Arlington National Cemetery." Military Images. Accessed January 16, 2020. https://militaryimages.atavist.com/most-hallowed-ground-winter-2018.

"Nathan G. Evans." American Battlefield Trust. Accessed October 29, 2018. https://battlefields.org/learn/biographies/nathan-g-evans.

"Nathaniel Lyon." State Historical Society of Missouri Historic Missourians website. Accessed September 2, 2018. https://shsmo.org/historicmissourians/name/l/lyon/#reference.

Neal, Diane, and Thomas W. Kremm. *Lion of the South: General Thomas C. Hindman.* Macon, GA: Mercer University Press, 1997.

Nelson, Megan Kate. *Ruin Nation: Destruction and the American Civil War.* Athens: University of Georgia Press, 2012.

Ness Jr., George T. *Regular Army on the Eve of the Civil War.* Baltimore: Toomey Press, 1990.

Nevins, Allan. *War for the Union*, vol. 1, *The Improvised War, 1861–1862.* Reprint, New York: Konecky & Konecky, 1960.

———. *War for the Union,* vol. 2, *War Becomes Revolution, 1862–1863.* Reprint, New York: Konecky & Konecky, 1960.

Newell, Clayton. *The Regular Army before the Civil War, 1845–1860.* Washington, DC: Center of Military History, United States Army, 2014.

Newell, Clayton R., and Charles R. Shrader. *Of Duty Well and Faithfully Done: A History of the Regular Army in the Civil War.* Lincoln: University of Nebraska Press, 2011.

Noe, Kenneth W. *Reluctant Rebels: The Confederates Who Joined the Army after 1861.* Chapel Hill: University of North Carolina Press, 2010.

Oakes, James. *Freedom National: The Destruction of Slavery in the United States, 1861–1865.* New York: W. W. Norton & Co., 2013.

———. *The Scorpion's Sting: Antislavery and the Coming of the Civil War.* New York: W. W. Norton & Co., 2014.

Oates, Stephen B. *To Purge This Land with Blood: A Biography of John Brown.* Amherst: University of Massachusetts Press, 1984.

O'Brien, Sean Michael. *Mountain Partisans: Guerilla Warfare in the Southern Appalachians, 1861–1865.* Westport: Praeger, 1999.

O'Brien, Steven. *American Political Leaders from Colonial Times to the Present.* Santa Barbara, CA: ABC-Clio, 1991.

Oickle, Alvin F. *Disaster in Lawrence: The Fall of the Pemberton Mill.* Charleston: The History Press, 2008.

Oliver, Robert T., ed. *A Faithful Heart: The Journal of Emmala Reed, 1865 and 1866.* Columbia: University of South Carolina Press, 2004.

Ott, Victoria E. "Love in Battle: The Meaning of Courtships in the Civil War and Lost Cause." In *Children and Youth During the Civil War*, edited by James Marten, 125–41. New York: New York University Press, 2012.

Owen, Thomas McAdory. *History of Alabama and Dictionary of Alabama Biographies*. vol. 2. Chicago: S. J. Clarke Publishing Co., 1921.

Parks, Joseph H. *General Edmund Kirby Smith, C.S.A.* 1954. Reprint, Baton Rouge: Louisiana State University Press, 1992.

Parrish, T. Michael. *Richard Taylor: Soldier Prince of Dixie*. Chapel Hill: University of North Carolina Press, 1992.

Paysinger, Christopher B. "Sack of Athens." *Encyclopedia of Alabama*. Accessed February 1, 2020. http://www.encyclopediaofalabama.org/article/h-1819.

Pearce, George F. *Pensacola During the Civil War: A Thorn in the Side of the Confederacy*. Gainesville: University Press of Florida, 2000.

"Pearce, James Alfred." Biographical Directory of the United States Congress, 1774–present. Accessed October 8, 2018. http://bioguide.congress.gov/scripts/biodisplay.pl?index=P000161.

"The Pemberton Mill Disaster." The New England Historical Society. Accessed October 8, 2018. http://www.newenglandhistoricalsociety.com/pemberton-mill-disaster/.

Phillips, Christopher. *Damned Yankee: The Life of General Nathaniel Lyon*. Baton Rouge: Louisiana State University Press, 1996.

———. *Missouri Confederate: Claiborne Fox Jackson and the Creation of Southern Identity in the Border West*. Columbia: University of Missouri Press, 2000.

Pickenpaugh, Roger. *Johnson's Island: A Prison for Confederate Officers*. Kent, OH: Kent State University Press, 2016.

Pittman, Walter. *New Mexico and the Civil War*. Charleston: The History Press, 2011.

Poland Jr., Charles P. *The Glories of War: Small Battles and Early Heroes of 1861*. Bloomington, IN: Author House, 2004.

Pollard, E. A. *The Lost Cause: A New Southern History of the War of the Confederates*. New York: E. B. Treat Co. Publishers, 1866.

Powell, David A. *The Chickamauga Campaign—A Mad Irregular Battle: From the Crossing of the Tennessee River Through the Second Day, August 22–September 19, 1863*. El Dorado, CA: Savas Beatie, LLC, 2014.

Pruitt, Raneé, ed. *Eden of the South: A Chronology of Huntsville, Alabama, 1805–2005*. Huntsville, AL: Huntsville-Madison County Public Library, 2005.

Prushankin, Jeffery S. *A Crisis in Confederate Command: Edmund Kirby Smith, Richard Taylor, and the Army of the Trans-Mississippi*. Baton Rouge: Louisiana State University Press, 2005.

Quarstein, John V. *Big Bethel: The First Battle*. Charleston: The History Press, 2011.

———. *Yorktown's Civil War Siege: Drums Along the Warwick*. Charleston: The History Press, 2012.

Quigley, Paul. "Independence Day Dilemmas in the American South, 1848–1865." *Journal of Southern History* 75, no. 2 (2009): 235–66.

———. *Shifting Grounds: Nationalism and the American South, 1848–1865*. New York: Oxford University Press, 2012.

Quitt, Martin H. *Stephen A. Douglas and Antebellum Democracy*. New York: Cambridge University Press, 2012.

Ramage, James A. *Rebel Raider: The Life of General John Hunt Morgan*. Lexington: University Press of Kentucky, 1986.

Record, James. *A Dream Come True: The Story of Madison County and Incidentally of Alabama and the United States*. vol. 1. Huntsville, AL: John Hicklin Printing Co., 1970.

Reed, D. W. *The Battle of Shiloh and the Organizations Engaged*. Knoxville: University of Tennessee Press, 2008.

Reeves, Jacquelyn Proctor. "Thunderbolt of the Confederacy." In *North Alabama Civil War Generals: 13 Wore Gray, the Rest Blue: A Selection of Essays from the Authors of the Tennessee Valley Civil War Round Table*, 58-65. Madison, AL: Tennessee Valley Civil War Roundtable, n.d.

Resnick, Brian. "Would the Confederacy Have Celebrated the Fourth of July." *The Atlantic*, July 3, 2014. Accessed September 7, 2018. https://www.theatlantic.com/politics/archive/2014/07would-the-confederacy-have-celebrated-the-fourth-of-july/454464/.

Rice, Charles. *Hard Times: The Civil War in Huntsville and North Alabama, 1861–1865*. Boaz, AL: Boaz Printing Co., 1995.

———, ed. *The Sword of Bushwhacker Johnston by Reverend Milus Eddings Johnston*. Huntsville, AL: Flint River Press, 1998.

———. "W. R. W. Cobb—Jackson County Giant Killer." *Old Huntsville Magazine* no. 55 (1995): 46-54.

———, ed. "Youthful Innocence Shattered: The Diary of Private George T. Anderson." *Huntsville Historical Review* 18, no. 2 (Summer-Fall 1991): 7-22.

"Robert S. Garnett." American Battlefield Trust. Accessed September 4, 2018. https://www.battlefields.org/learn/biographies/robert-s-garnett.

Robertson, James. *Stonewall Jackson: The Man, the Soldier, the Legend*. New York: MacMillan Publishing, 1997.

Robertson, Mary D., ed. *Lucy Breckinridge of Grove Hill: The Journal of a Virginia Girl, 1862–1864*. Columbia: University of South Carolina Press, 1994.

Rohr, Nancy M., ed. *Free People of Color in Madison County, Alabama*. Huntsville, AL: Huntsville History Collection, 2015.

———. *Incidents of the War: The Civil War Journal of Mary Jane Chadick*. Huntsville, AL: Silver Threads Publishing, 2005.

"Rose Adele Cutts Williams." Find A Grave.com. Accessed October 8, 2018. https://www.findagrave. com/memorial/27718453.

"Rowlett's Station." CWSAC Battle Summaries. American Battlefield Protection Program. Accessed September 8, 2018. https://www.nps.gov/abpp/battles/ky004.htm.

Rubin, Anne Sarah. *A Shattered Nation: The Rise & Fall of the Confederacy, 1861–1868*. Chapel Hill: University of North Carolina Press, 2005.

Sacher, John M. "Louisiana's Secession from the Union." *Know Louisiana: The Digital Encyclopedia of Louisiana and Home of Louisiana Cultural Vistas*. Accessed September 2, 2018. https://knowlouisiana.org/entry/louisiana-secession-from-the-union.

Salling, Stuart. *Louisianians in the Western Confederacy: The Adams-Gibson Brigade in the Civil War*. Jefferson, NC: McFarland & Co., 2010.

"Santa Rosa Island." American Battlefield Trust. Accessed September 8, 2018. https://www.battlefields.org/learn/maps/santa-rosa-island-october-9–1861.

"Santa Rosa Island." CWSAC Battle Summaries. American Battlefield Protection Program. Accessed September 8, 2018. https://www.nps.gov/abpp/battles/fl001.htm.

Schott, Thomas E. *Alexander H. Stephens of Georgia: A Biography*. Baton Rouge: Louisiana State University Press, 1988.

Settles, Thomas M. *John Bankhead Magruder: A Military Reappraisal*. Baton Rouge: Louisiana State University Press, 2009.

Shaffer, John W. *Clash of Loyalties: A Border County in the Civil War*. Morgantown: West Virginia University Press, 2003.

Shawcross, Edward. *France, Mexico and Informal Empire in Latin America, 1820–1867: Equilibrium in the New World*. Cambridge: Palgrave MacMillan, 2018.

Shea, William L., and Earl J. Hess. *Pea Ridge: Civil War Campaign in the West*. Chapel Hill: University of North Carolina Press, 1992.

Sifakis, Stewart. *Compendium of the Confederate Armies: Alabama*. New York: Facts on File, 1992.

———. *Compendium of the Confederate Armies: Tennessee*. New York: Facts on File, 1992.

Silver, James W. *Confederate Morale and Church Propaganda*. Tuscaloosa: Confederate Publishing Company, Inc., 1957.

"The Skirmish at Blackburns Ford." National Park Service. Accessed September 4, 2018. http://www.nps.gov/mana/learn/historyculture/the-skirmish-at-blackburns-ford-htm.

Sledge, John S. *These Rugged Days in Alabama in the Civil War*. Tuscaloosa: University of Alabama Press, 2017.

Smith, John David and William Cooper Jr., eds. *A Union Woman in Civil War Kentucky: The Diary of Frances Peter*. Lexington: University Press of Kentucky, 2000.

Smith, Larry, ed. *Guntersville Remembered*. Albertville, AL: Creative Printers, Inc., 2001.

Smith, Sam. "Winning the West." American Battlefield Trust. Accessed September 2, 2018. https://www.battlefields.org/learn/articles/river-war.

Smith, Timothy B. *Corinth 1862: Siege, Battle, Occupation*. Lawrence: University Press of Kansas, 2012.

———. *The Mississippi Secession Convention: Delegates and Deliberation in Politics and War, 1861–1865*. Jackson: University Press of Mississippi, 2014.

———. *The Untold Story of Shiloh: The Battle and the Battlefield*. Knoxville: University of Tennessee Press, 2006.

Snead, Thomas L. *The Fight for Missouri: From the Election of Lincoln to the Death of Lyon*. New York: Scribner's Sons, 1888.

Snell, William R., ed. *Myra Inman: A Diary of the Civil War in East Tennessee*. Macon, GA: Mercer University Press, 2000.

Snow, Barbara. "Flames Along the Tennessee River." *Huntsville Historical Review* 44, no. 2 (Fall 2019): 51-61.

Snow, Richard. *Iron Dawn: The Monitor, the Merrimack, and the Civil War Sea Battle that Changed History*. New York: Scribner, 2017.

Snow, Whitney A., and Barbara J. Snow. *Wyeth City: Alabama's Model Industrial Experiment*. Birmingham, AL: Banner Digital Printing and Publishing, 2019.

Sparks, Ferrell, and Charles McClendon. *Country Grave Yards: Part Two; Cooley, Ridgeway*. Self-published, 1996.

Sparks, Ferrell, Charlies McClendon, and J. F. Sparks Jr. *Country Grave Yards, Warrenton and Bennett*, rev. ed. Birmingham, AL: Banner Digital Printing and Publishing, 2013.

Sparks, J. F. *A River Town's Fight for Life: A History of Guntersville, Alabama in the Civil War*. Self-published, 2011.

Steenburn, Donald H. *A Man Called Gurley*. Meridianville, AL: Elk River Press, 1999.

Stephens, Elise Hopkins. *Historic Huntsville: A City of New Beginnings*. Woodland Hills, CA: Windsor Publications, 1984.

Sterling, Robin. *People and Things from Marshall County, Alabama, Guntersville Democrat, 1901–1908*. Raleigh, NC: Lulu Press, 2016.

Stevens, Joseph E. *1863: The Rebirth of a Nation*. New York: Bantam Books, 1999.

"Stevenson and Ft. Harker." Historical Marker Project website. Accessed September 17, 2018. https://www.historicalmarkerproject.com/marker/.

Stocker, Jeffrey, ed. *From Huntsville to Appomattox: R. T. Cole's History of 4th Regiment, Alabama Volunteer Infantry, C.S.A., Army of Northern Virginia*. Knoxville: University of Tennessee Press, 1996.

Stoker, Donald. *The Grand Design: Strategy and the U.S. Civil War*. New York: Oxford University Press, 2010.

Storey, Margaret M. *Loyalty and Loss: Alabama's Unionists in the Civil War and Reconstruction*. Baton Rouge: Louisiana State University Press, 2004.

Stowe, Steven M. *Keep the Days: Reading the Civil War Diaries of Southern Women*. Chapel Hill: University of North Carolina Press, 2018.

Sutherland, Daniel E. *A Very Violent Rebel: The Civil War Diary of Ellen Renshaw House*. Knoxville: University of Tennessee Press, 1996.

———. "Culpeper County during the Civil War." *Encyclopedia Virginia*. Virginia Humanities. Accessed September 2, 2018. https://www.encyclopediavirginia.org/Culpeper_County_During_the_Civil_War#start_entry.

Tate, Allen. *Jefferson Davis: His Rise and Fall*. Nashville, TN; J. S. Sanders & Co., 1998.

Thomas, Edison H. *John Hunt Morgan and His Raiders*. Lexington: University Press of Kentucky, 1985.

Thornton III, J. Mills. *Politics and Power in a Slave Society: Alabama 1800–1860*. Baton Rouge: Louisiana State University Press, 1978.

Trudeau, Noah Andre. *Southern Storm: Sherman's March to the Sea*. Harper Collins e-book, 2009.

Uffelman, Minoa D., Ellen Kanervo, Phyllis Smith, and Eleanor Williams, eds. *The Diary of Nannie Haskins Williams: A Southern Woman's Story of Rebellion and Reconstruction, 1863–1890*. Knoxville: University of Tennessee Press, 2014.

Weintraub, Stanley. *Uncrowned King: The Life of Prince Albert*. New York: The Free Press, 1997.

Wharton, Mary E., and Ellen E. Williams, eds. *Peach Leather and Rebel Gray: Bluegrass Life and the War, 1860–1865: Farm and Social Life, Famous Horses, Tragedies of War: Diary and Letters of a Confederate Wife*. Lexington: University Press of Kentucky, 1986.

Wheeler, Joseph W. *Confederate Military History—Alabama*. Cartersville, GA: Eastern Digital Resources, 2003.

Wiener, Marli, ed., *A Heritage of Woe: The Civil War Diary of Grace Brown Elmore, 1861–1868*. Athens: University of Georgia Press, 1997.

Wiley, Bell Irvin. *The Life of Billy Yank: The Common Soldier of the Union*. Indianapolis: The Bobbs-Merrill Co., 1952. Reprint, Baton Rouge: Louisiana State University Press, 2008.

William, David. "Civil War Dissent." *New Georgia Encyclopedia*. Accessed September 7, 2018. https://www.georgiaencyclopedia.org/articles/history-archaeology/civil-war-dissent.

Wise, Stephen R. *Gate of Hell: Campaign for Charleston Harbor, 1863*. Columbia: University of South Carolina Press, 1994.

Wolfe, Brendan. "Centreville During the Civil War." *Encyclopedia Virginia*. Accessed October 29, 2018. www.encyclopediavirginia.org/Centreville-During-the-Civil-War.

Woodall, Eliza B. *The Stevenson Story*. Stevenson, AL: Stevenson Depot Museum, 1982.

Woodward, C. Vann, ed. *Mary Chesnut's Civil War*. New Haven, CT: Yale University Press, 1981.

Wortman, Marc. *The Bonfire: The Siege and Burning of Atlanta*. New York: Public Affairs, 2009.

Wright, Catherine M. "Staunton During the Civil War." *Encyclopedia Virginia*. Virginia Humanities. Accessed September 13, 2018. https://www.encyclopediavirginia.org/Staunton_During_the_Civil_War.

Wyatt-Brown, Bertram. *The Shaping of Southern Culture: Honor, Grace, and War, 1760s–1880s*. Chapel Hill: University of North Carolina Press, 2001.

Wyeth, John A. *History of LaGrange Military Academy and the Cadet Corps, 1857–1862*. New York: The Brewer Press, 1907.

———. *Life of General Nathan Bedford Forrest*. New York: Harper & Brothers, 1899.

———. *With Sabre and Scalpel—The Autobiography of a Soldier and Surgeon*. 1914. Reprint, Charleston, SC: Bibliolife, 2009.

Wyllie, Arthur. *The Union Navy*. Morrisville, NC: Lulu Press, 2007.

Index

Page numbers in **boldface** refer to illustrations.

www.ingramcontent.com/pod-product-compliance
Lightning Source LLC
Chambersburg PA
CBHW031935090426
42811CB00002B/195

* 9 7 8 1 6 2 1 9 0 6 0 6 3 *